**Capital and Labour in the British Columbia
Forest Industry, 1934-74**

Capital and Labour in the British Columbia Forest Industry, 1934-74

Gordon Hak

UBCPress · Vancouver · Toronto

16 15 14 13 12 11 10 09 08 07   5 4 3 2 1

Printed in Canada on ancient-forest-free paper (100 percent post-consumer recycled) that is processed chlorine- and acid-free, with vegetable-based inks.

Library and Archives Canada Cataloguing in Publication

Hak, Gordon H. (Gordon Hugh)
     Capital and labour in the British Columbia forest industry, 1934-74 / Gordon Hak.

Includes bibliographical references and index.
ISBN-13: 978-0-7748-1307-5
ISBN-10: 0-7748-1307-5

     1. Forests and forestry – British Columbia–History. 2. Forest products industry – British Columbia – History. 3. British Columbia–Economic conditions–20th century. I. Title.

HD9764.C33B75 2006   338.1'74909711   338.4'7674'09711   C2006-905377-4

Canadä

UBC Press gratefully acknowledges the financial support for our publishing program of the Government of Canada through the Book Publishing Industry Development Program (BPIDP), and of the Canada Council for the Arts, and the British Columbia Arts Council.

This book has been published with the help of a grant from the Canadian Federation for the Humanities and Social Sciences, through the Aid to Scholarly Publications Programme, using funds provided by the Social Sciences and Humanities Research Council of Canada.

Printed and bound in Canada by Friesens
Set in Minion and Helvetica Condensed by Artegraphica Design Co. Ltd.
Copy editor and proofreader: Frank Chow

UBC Press
The University of British Columbia
2029 West Mall
Vancouver, BC V6T 1Z2
604-822-5959 / Fax: 604-822-6083
www.ubcpress.ca

Contents

Illustrations

Acknowledgments

Some twenty-five years ago, Allen Seager introduced me to the wonders of political economy and this book, in many ways, began then. More recently, Lori Bessler at the Wisconsin Historical Society and David Kessler at the Bancroft Library made my American research trip a success. Librarians at the University of Victoria, the British Columbia Legislative Library, and Malaspina University-College lightened my labours appreciably, as did archivists and staff at the British Columbia Archives, Library and Archives Canada, the Campbell River Museum and Archives, the Courtenay and District Museum, the University of British Columbia Special Collections Division, and the University of Victoria Archives and Special Collections. Richard Mackie kindly shared his knowledge of Vancouver Island historical records.

George Brandak, at Special Collections, University of British Columbia, was, as always, extremely helpful, and deserves a paragraph to himself.

Malaspina University-College supplied needed research and writing time, as well as financial assistance in the form of a Malaspina University-College Research Award. Two Malaspina deans, Steve Lane and John Lepage, were very supportive.

Randy Schmidt, Holly Keller, and the staff at UBC Press guided me through the publication process; Mark Leier and anonymous reviewers offered numerous thoughtful, helpful suggestions on the text. Stuart Daniel produced the maps. I am grateful to them all.

I would finally like to recognize the people who donate papers to archives, for without corporate, union, and personal records, this study would not exist.

Abbreviations

AFL	American Federation of Labor
BCFP	British Columbia Forest Products
CCF	Co-operative Commonwealth Federation
CCL	Canadian Congress of Labour
CIO	Congress of Industrial Organizations
CLC	Canadian Labour Congress
COFI	Council of Forest Industries
CPC	Communist Party of Canada
E&N	Esquimalt and Nanaimo Railway
FIR	Forest Industrial Relations
FML	Forest Management Licence
IBEW	International Brotherhood of Electrical Workers
IBPM	International Brotherhood of Paper Makers
IBPSPMW	International Brotherhood of Pulp, Sulphite and Paper Mill Workers
ICA Act	Industrial Disputes Conciliation and Arbitration Act
ITCCA	Independent Timber Converters Co-operative Association
IWA	International Woodworkers of America
LPP	Labour Progressive Party
LRB	Labour Relations Board
LWIU	Lumber Workers Industrial Union
NDP	New Democratic Party
PHA	Pulp Harvesting Agreement
PPWC	Pulp and Paper Workers of Canada
PWC	Public Working Circle
RFMDA	Rank and File Movement for Democratic Action
SPEC	Society for Pollution and Environmental Control
TFL	Tree Farm Licence
TLA	Truck Loggers Association
TLC	Trades and Labour Congress of Canada
UPP	United Papermakers and Paperworkers
WIUC	Woodworkers Industrial Union of Canada
WUL	Workers Unity League

**Capital and Labour in the British Columbia
Forest Industry, 1934-74**

Introduction

Sometimes the work was physically hard. A problem with the cutters would send thousands of sheets of pulp onto the machine room floor. The labourer, the worker with the least seniority on a crew of five, picked up the sheets and manually deposited them in the repulper, a deep, concrete casing the size of a small swimming pool that contained swirling, white liquid. The repulper broke down the sheets into a porridge-like consistency. This now watery pulp was piped back to another part of the mill, an earlier stage in the production process. If the problem had been bad, the labourer could spend a whole shift toiling in this steamy, sweat-inducing environment. But on the whole, the work was tedious rather than difficult, and often there was little to do. Workers were there largely to ensure that there were no glitches in the operation of the machinery. When the crew was doing nothing – reading or playing crib in the lunchroom – the owners of the operation were getting the best results. Worker inactivity meant that the mill was running smoothly.

The machine room was the second-last stage in the production process. Seven-metre-wide sheets of pulp came out of a series of dryers at a very rapid speed and went into the cutter. The cutter chopped the sheets into metre squares and stacked the sheets into seven piles, each about 120 centimetres high. The machine decided when the stacks were high enough and sent them along on a conveyor to a scale. At this station, a worker adjusted the pile to ensure that the weight was appropriate, and then pushed a button, sending the pile along to a massive press. The hydraulic press came down on the pile, condensing it to about one-third of its original size. After being squeezed, the bale of pulp went to a machine which automatically put a wrapper around it and snapped on four wires to secure both the wrap and the bale. The bale was then transported along the conveyor through a hole in the wall into the warehouse, a vast hall containing bales of pulp stacked to the ceiling and two rows of railway cars. The warehouse, the last phase in the production process, and the machine room were in close proximity and the two crews often intermingled during working hours. Inside the warehouse, a machine, again without human intervention, stacked the bales either four high or six high, depending on the requirements of the customer. The warehouse labourer used a stencil to manually stamp the final market destination on each bale. This was the end of the chain. Now fork lifts, operated by workers, transported the stacked bales to nearby railway boxcars. Once every day the full boxcars were pulled out of the warehouse and replaced by ones that were empty.

Workers in the machine room and the warehouse concentrated on the tasks at hand, having little interest in earlier phases of the process that began in logging camps hundreds of miles away and eventually produced the sheets of pulp that flowed out of the dryers. Nor was the final purpose or destination of the product of concern, though, judging by the ink names stenciled on the bales, most was headed to Asia. The ownership of the mill was vaguely known – British and German money was involved – but hardly seemed important. The machinery, too, was from far away, imported from the United States, central Canada, and, drawing a conclusion from corporate names emblazoned on the equipment, perhaps Europe.

When things were running smoothly, management rarely disturbed the crew. On these good days, the shift supervisor, with his blue hard hat, just showed up to chat and collect the time sheets. But when machinery problems shut down production, senior management officials, distinguished by their white hard hats, appeared. The breakdown also attracted the normally slow-moving tradesmen, who now scurried about with worried looks on their faces, rushing to solve the problem and get the mill running again. For workers and management, down time was stress time.

Workers turned to the union when they had problems with management regarding schedules, safety procedures, and job assignments. Occasionally, rumours of an impromptu strike swept through the mill. This, more often than not, was a threat delivered in response to a management decision to discipline a worker, usually by imposing a one or two day suspension. The rumours animated workers and reminded them of their importance in the operation: they could shut the whole damn thing down! But the threat was usually sufficient, forcing union and management officials to find an acceptable solution. Union politics were of little interest on the shop floor, even though a bitter, public battle between competing unions had rocked the plant less than a decade earlier. The union ensured high wages and secure jobs, it was recognized, but in day-to-day operations, union officials were more distant than management officials.[1]

Across British Columbia in the 1970s, workers lived variations on this work experience every day. Owners, workers, and managers were located in impressive systems that linked the forests and towns of the province to markets and consumers around the globe. Complex institutions – corporations, unions, and markets – situated people in relationships with each other and with machines. From the perspective of the shop floor, these arrangements, which produced boring, unsatisfying days as well as a comparatively high standard of living, seemed appropriate, obvious, inevitable, necessary, and even natural. How this work routine, this regimen that consumed so many hours, days, months, and years in the lives of thousands and thousands of workers, had come to be was rarely considered. Investigating this historical process is the subject of this book.

The British Columbia forest industry was the heart of the twentieth-century provincial economy, and its glory days were from the 1930s to the 1970s. The

British Columbia coastal lumber industry began to recover from the depths of the Great Depression in 1934. Existing companies expanded production facilities, new companies entered the field, and for the next four decades the coastal forest industry prospered. Initially lumber led the way, but in the 1940s pulp and paper emerged as the driver of economic expansion on the Coast. In the Interior, the smaller, less developed lumber industry, which had been completely devastated during the 1930s, finally began to rebuild and expand in the 1940s. In the 1960s, the Interior also made the transition to a pulp and paper economy. Unions took advantage of changing circumstances after 1934, launching organizational drives, and in the 1940s their efforts bore fruit. Unions became entrenched in the camps and mills of the province.

In 1970 the forest sector directly employed 9.1 percent of the British Columbia workforce, and at least two indirect jobs were associated with each job in the forest industry. Thus, the industry supported some 30 percent of full-time employees in the province, 225,000 workers.[2] The good times began to unravel in the 1970s. While there had been dips in the economy before, 1974 and 1975 were particularly difficult. The American lumber market collapsed, sawmills laid off workers, and logging camps closed. In 1975 prices in the international pulp market dropped precipitously. Responding to the distress, the provincial government lowered stumpage charges, the rate that companies paid to log Crown-owned timber, in order to prop up economic activity in the province.[3] A depression and a recession, then, were bookends for the period from 1934 to 1974.

The downturn of the 1970s was not just another fluctuation in the business cycle. It marked a more serious transition, presaging new circumstances that ultimately challenged relations and institutions established in earlier years. While pulp and lumber markets recovered at times after 1974-75, the forest economy was unstable, and in the first half of the 1980s the industry suffered a particularly devastating string of bad years.[4] The province had entered a new era, a new reality. Management personnel were laid off, and worker benefits and unions were attacked, part of a new corporate agenda.[5] More broadly, the forest industry played a proportionally smaller role in the provincial economy. In the 1990s the forest sector accounted for only about 5 percent of provincial employment, and its contribution to the provincial gross domestic product had shrunk to about half of its 15 percent of the 1960s.[6]

Existing histories probe distinct aspects of the industry. There are celebrations of business magnates, union leaders, and unions;[7] detailed accounts of the machinery and techniques used in logging;[8] critiques of government forest policy;[9] and defences of particular historical agents, including communist union activists and small-time loggers.[10] This study casts a wider net, incorporating these themes and actors while looking at both the coastal region and the often-neglected Interior between 1934 and 1974. The narrative primarily examines two institutions:

companies, which were organized to further capitalist accumulation, and unions, which represented the interests of workers. The history of the forest industry was worked out in the context of the ongoing interaction between capital and labour, which created and sustained a web of economic, social, and ideological relationships in the years after 1934. Embedded in this larger whole were the personal histories of lumber magnates, such as H.R. MacMillan, and anonymous Port Alberni paper mill workers; the organizational histories of corporate giants Canadian Forest Products and Crown Zellerbach Canada and unions such as the International Woodworkers of America and the Pulp and Paper Workers of Canada; and even the technological histories of the new machines continually introduced into the production process. Worker/employer institutional relations, of course, were not self-contained. Most importantly, there was interaction with the state, which had a role in industrial relations and the allocation of timber, and, in the early 1970s, with the environmental movement. Both of these warrant special treatment, but they too operated in a context determined in many ways by labour and capital.

The scope is wide-ranging but it is not comprehensive. Corporate marketing strategies, product development, links between forest industry owners and the larger business community, and ancillary enterprises such as consulting firms and provincial equipment manufacturers, for example, are given short shrift. Similarly, the leisure activities of workers, gender, injury at the workplace, camp life, and the social dynamics of the shop floor are not fully developed themes. The study still covers much, however, teasing out a rather shadowy economic, political, social, and ideological structure while simultaneously paying heed to concrete historical events. Three bodies of literature locate the discussion that follows. First, the Fordist approach offers a broad interpretation of the political economy of the era and serves as a good starting point for a study of the BC forest industry. Fordist theorists also highlight the importance of studying institutions in order to understand social realities. Second, labour process studies draw out the importance of production at the heart of capitalist societies. Finally, recent, postmodernist discourse theory situates production processes, institutions, and individuals in relation to each other. Each of these will be discussed in turn.

Fordism

The history of the British Columbia forest economy between 1934 and 1974 reflected a pattern evident across the western world. The political economy after the early 1970s is now often referred to as the Post-Fordist era, and the characteristics of this period as Post-Fordism. Post-Fordism is studied in relation to Fordism, which describes the period from roughly 1940 to the early 1970s. Social scientists – sociologists, geographers, and economists, especially – generated Fordist ideas to divine the future direction of society, and in some cases to suggest strategies to divert the march of history along a more congenial route. Studies abounded to capture the essence of Post-Fordism, but the Fordist era was mostly reduced to a list of key points, a paragraph or two in studies eager to get on with discovering and mapping the Post-Fordist landscape.

Post-Fordist/Fordist theorists constructed a big tent, housing a variety of perspectives and political postures.[11] There are, however, some widely agreed upon points. Fordism draws out the relationship between productive forces and consumers in a regulated or organized society during a particular historical time. Mass production of standardized products in long runs was the economic cornerstone of the age, and large corporations, with bureaucratic management structures, controlled production. At the point of production in the factories, there was advanced mechanization and close control of labour; the archetypal workers were unskilled or semi-skilled, performing repetitive, simple tasks, tending machines and ensuring that there were no mechanical breakdowns. Massive industrial unions represented workers, reaching accords with corporations and ensuring general stability in industrial relations. The goods produced in the Fordist age were commodities geared towards consumers: automobiles, household appliances, and houses. Ordinary consumers were important in this economy, and social and economic stability depended on regulating equilibrium between supply and demand. Unions, by maintaining high wages and a disciplined workforce, contributed to this stability, and governments, too, took on a major role. Using fiscal measures recommended by Keynesianism, governments worked to manage the economy. And by providing social supports, sickness insurance systems, and unemployment insurance – the "welfare state" – governments sought to ensure a society of healthy, contented, productive people, people who contributed to the production system both as workers and as consumers.

Beginning in the 1970s, this regime came undone. Unstable oil prices, inflation in the United States generated by the demands of the Vietnam War, increased economic competition due to the successes of Asian and European economies, falling profit margins, eroding productivity, and a disenchanted workforce protesting tedious jobs ended Fordism. The new era, Post-Fordism, was rooted in new productive and institutional arrangements. Flexibility and specialization, rather than mass production, were stressed, and companies restructured to enable them to move quickly in response to rapidly changing circumstances in the global marketplace. The lethargy of the Fordist firm would not do: companies had to be leaner and less bureaucratic, while workers had to be more flexible and better educated, willing and capable of taking on a wider variety of tasks in the workday. In the new times, sclerotic management systems and rigid worker rights enshrined in long-term collective agreements protected by powerful unions were deemed no longer appropriate. Moreover, for companies to successfully adapt to the new environment, governments were forced to curtail their own influence in the marketplace. Expensive social programs, legislation propping up unions, and government regulation were burdens. Overall, the institutions and relations of Fordism no longer applied, having become economic liabilities. While the change was hardly abrupt – mass production continued and unions and government programs, though battered, persisted – the trend was clear.[12]

The Fordist model offers historians two things: a coherent account of the events of the years from 1940 to the 1970s, and an approach to the past, a way to study history. In British Columbia, the Fordist interpretation makes much sense. During the 1930s and 1940s, corporate consolidation was evident, and a few large companies assumed an increasingly prominent role in the forest industry. In 1951 two of the largest, the H.R. MacMillan Export Company and Bloedel, Stewart & Welch, merged to form the industry giant MacMillan & Bloedel. The addition of the Powell River Company in 1960 made the firm even larger. In the 1940s, industrial unions established themselves. The International Woodworkers of America (IWA) became the dominant union in the province's logging camps and saw, shingle, and planer mills. The International Brotherhood of Pulp, Sulphite and Paper Mill Workers was the biggest organization in the pulp and paper mills. At the same time, provincial and federal governments were active. Federal and provincial legislation in the 1940s created a legal framework for managing relations between workers and employers, giving collective bargaining legitimacy and legal protection. Social programs such as unemployment insurance and hospital insurance were brought in during the 1940s. In the 1950s and 1960s, richer pension and welfare schemes, as well as medical insurance, were added to the mix. Painted with broad strokes, Fordism was alive and well in BC.

Geographer Roger Hayter recently applied Post-Fordist language to the provincial forest industry: from his technoeconomic perspective, Fordism came into being with new government forestry legislation in the 1940s, when "the large international corporation, employing unionized labour in big factories manufacturing vast quantities of relatively standardized outputs, became the organizational model of development," and came undone in the 1970s, when "the technological, geographical, and institutional conditions underlying the Fordist model of BC's forest economy in the 1950s and 1960s began to change."[13] There were distinctive features in British Columbia, a peripheral resource region that "featured continuous-flow processes, rather than the assembly-type operations of classic Fordism," but the general characterization still held.[14]

Yet, while the Fordist interpretation summarizes features of the period, it does not show how this history happened or the dynamics of change within the period. In these particulars lies the history of British Columbia. Fordist accounts, in their rush to generalize, brush out the nuances of development. Large capital was extremely important in British Columbia, to be sure, but capitalist development was not all of one cloth. There were two notable divisions. One was between the Interior and the coastal region. The pace and pattern of industrial development in the Interior was different from that of the Lower Mainland and Vancouver Island. Interior firms were smaller, less technologically sophisticated, and slower to become absorbed by the pulp and paper economy. The other division was between small and large operators. The emphasis on large companies is not peculiar to Fordism. A classic interpretation of BC's history also foregrounds the role of dominant corporations. Martin Robin, in an analysis developed in a number of books and articles in the 1960s and early 1970s, argues that British Columbia, unlike central Canada or the Prairie Provinces, lacked a substantial middle class made up of farmers and small-scale producers. In BC, big companies such as the Hudson's Bay Company and the Canadian Pacific Railway, as well as a small number of major mining, fish-processing, and forestry companies, set the tone for development.[15] As we shall see, however, in the forest industry smaller firms were influential, especially in coastal logging and in the Interior generally. Not only did the owners of small firms produce commodities but their needs and desires shaped cultural and political discourse in the province.

Fordist generalizations about unions also need qualification when applied to British Columbia. Labour, in the Fordist vision, is largely passive, bureaucratic, and conservative. In this view, after the achievement of unionism in the mass-production industries during the 1940s, which involved much struggle, conservative union bosses subdued political opponents within their organizations, stymied internal democracy, and established top-heavy bureaucracies. Collective bargaining became routine. Labour historians largely concur in this assessment. Kim Moody, in a critical study of American labour, makes the point succinctly in referring to Congress of Industrial Organizations (CIO) unions, the most dynamic labour associations in the 1930s and 1940s: the unions "that grew during the 1950s were very different organizations from those that fought through the stormy 1940s. In virtually every major CIO union the bureaucratic ascendancy accomplished gradually in the 1940s was rapidly converted into one-party or one-man rule. The last vestiges of opposition were expelled, crushed or co-opted in a period of two or three years."[16] The terms "social compact," "social contract," and "labour-capital accord" were increasingly used in the 1980s to describe labour relations from 1945 to the 1970s.[17] In Canada, Peter S. McInnis, in a recent book explaining the rise of a postwar settlement, talks about a "labour-capital accord," and a "postwar social contract": "There was an implicit *quid pro quo* between opposing forces. Business conceded unions a measure of legitimacy and citizen rights, while unions accepted managerial prerogatives and labour's place within a capitalist order."[18]

Again, while the generalization contains truth, it needs qualification. There were major strikes in the forest industry, and these confrontations over wages, though hardly revolutionary, challenged the rights and power of capital.[19] Throughout the period, too, business/labour harmony was fragile; companies tolerated unions only out of necessity. There was, to use Nelson Lichtenstein's phrase, "a limited and unstable truce."[20] Nor did union politics end in the late 1940s. Despite the exclusion of avowed communists from the IWA after 1948, the left was not without resources. By 1958 there was an identifiable leftist constituency in the IWA that was significant enough to challenge the leadership a decade later. Political dissension also wracked the provincial pulp and paper unions in the late 1950s and early 1960s. Socialists, waving the flags of nationalism and democracy, created a breakaway Canadian union. Politics was also alive and well in inter-union activities, as unions fought for turf and jurisdictional control. Arguably, provincial forest industry unions suffered from a surfeit of politics in the 1960s.

Overall, accounts of labour in the Fordist era emphasize what unions did not do, especially their failure to create a serious challenge to capitalism. They tend not to look at what unions actually did on a daily basis. Here union leaders, radicals and moderates alike, sustained organizations in a hostile environment, dealt with the individual workplace concerns of members, and supported social democratic political parties. BC union leaders did not prepare the groundwork for revolution, but it does not follow that they were completely swallowed up by business, against all change, undemocratic, and weighed down with the curse of bureaucracy. That argument depends on a host of notions: that workers in the 1940s were notably radical; that communist leaders offered a more radical program than labour leaders of other political stripes; that there was a missed opportunity for a decisively different direction in the postwar era, and that chaotic expressions of worker frustration in illegal job action and protests served the goal of social justice better than organized unions and political parties.[21] All are questionable when viewed from the perspective of the west coast. Still, the limitations of unions, in action and in ideas, were evident at the beginning of the Post-Fordist era.

The Fordist conceptualization goes beyond merely offering an interpretation of the postwar era, for, like its parent "political economy," it suggests a historical methodology. There is a holistic understanding of social relations, a notion that there are connections and patterns that can be articulated, using articulation in the sense of meaningfully joining elements in systems. Monographs in business history often ignore workers and, in turn, labour histories pass over the business context in a page or two. Political histories happily ignore both business and labour. However, drawing back and focusing on a larger frame captures these historical subjects in meaningful relationships and illuminates articulations. The Fordist approach is also noteworthy in seeing institutions as important. Governments, political parties, corporations, unions, and production systems play prominent roles. Recent generations of historians have been cynical about institutions, preferring to study workers rather than unions, for example, and largely ignoring the histories of companies and political parties.[22]

While Fordist historical analysis articulates ensembles of institutions, there is debate about what connects institutions and about the relative importance of particular institutions in larger systems. Here the Marxist tradition, which situates productive relations at the core, is helpful. At the point of production, the basic work of capitalism takes place, the creation of commodities and value by labour and the expropriation of surplus value by capital. In the abstract, the production process is the site where capital and labour engage, each with its own agenda: capital to maximize output and profit, labour to sustain itself and maximize wages. The potential tension between capital and labour is at the heart of the system, a pivotal relationship defining and shaping individuals, institutions, and classes in society. Corporations are institutions put together to facilitate production, unions are institutions organized to look after the interests of workers engaged in production, and governments provide services to manage relations between workers and owners to further the goal of capital accumulation.

This focus on capital and labour at the point of production deflects attention from foreign ownership and the provincial state, two key elements in the "staples thesis," a historical interpretation that has been applied to the provincial forest economy. Sociologist Patricia Marchak developed the staples perspective most forcefully. According to her, the twentieth-century British Columbia economy was plagued by externally owned corporations that owned the means of production, scooped up the profits, and took them back to corporate headquarters, often in the United States. As such, the British Columbia economy did not develop beyond its resource base to become a balanced, stable, diversified, self-sufficient economy. The province merely produced raw or semi-finished products, such as logs, pulp, lumber, and paper, to the detriment of the workforce, which needed few skills, and the economic future. The solution, according to Marchak, was to use an aggressive provincial state to tame externally owned corporations and manage the economy for the benefit of British Columbians.

The Marchak case is developed most fully in her 1983 book *Green Gold*.[23] However, despite the elegance of the case, empirical evidence to show the negative role of outside capital is lacking. Moreover, a British Columbia-based company, MacMillan Bloedel, was the dominant firm of the era. The staples account also overestimates the independent power of the state, portrays labour as largely inert, and pays little heed to historically variable class relations. The state can indeed limit the actions of capital, but this is contingent on historical circumstances. The prominence of the state in the Fordist era reflected power relations between labour and capital and an ideological configuration at a particular time, a time when labour was assertive and a leftist discourse had some currency. During the early Post-Fordist era, when capitalist distress forced contraction of the activities of government, the impotence of the state was exposed.[24] At this time, too, as Marchak notes, workers seemed interested in little beyond wage issues: "It would be difficult to sustain a claim that there is genuine and sustained opposition to the system."[25] A history of the forest industry highlighting companies, unions, and class relations helps us better understand this predicament.

The Labour Process

A Fordist orientation, with special reference to the dynamics of capital accumulation, informs this study, but we can begin at the other end, the labour process, to elaborate the same context. In 1974 a book by Harry Braverman rediscovered the production process, putting work back at the centre of class relations.[26] The book's subtitle, *The Degradation of Work in the Twentieth Century,* states the argument. Working in the Marxist tradition, Braverman shows that the labour process had a specific history, arguing that this history was driven by the imperative of capital to control labour. From the techniques of Frederick Winslow Taylor to the introduction of assembly lines and automation, capital increasingly planned the work, giving workers very specific orders, and set the pace of production. The result was the deskilling of the workforce, more and more unskilled jobs, less and less room for initiative or creativity, tedium at the workplace, and, considering the amount of time spent at work and its role in human satisfaction, stunted lives.

The labour process in the British Columbia forest industry was constantly modernizing: new machines and techniques were brought online, some occupations disappeared while others were created, and the speed of production was intensified. Richard Rajala, following Braverman, offers an account of the changing production process in coastal British Columbia logging from 1880 to 1965. Loggers, he argues, suffered a loss of autonomy and were increasingly subject to the discipline of machine pacing. Even though some highly skilled occupations emerged, they "invariably enhanced capital's control over the collective labour process."[27]

The Braverman thesis occasioned much debate and criticism after it came out. In this study, Braverman is celebrated for reinstalling production and productive relations at the centre of social order, but the criticisms are taken seriously. Braverman focused too much on skilled workers, failed to appreciate that automation most easily replaced unskilled labour, and underestimated the creation of new skills.[28] He also wrapped up changing management techniques, the introduction of machinery, and deskilled occupations into a tight, self-contained universe, paying little heed to broader ideological and class configurations. As Bill Schwarz notes: "Ideologies of management are rarely *just* technical formulas devised to extract ever more surplus value out of the workers. More often, labour discipline is part of a much broader cultural and political strategy developed by a class to secure dominance in every aspect of social life."[29] Even the introduction of new techniques and machines was, in part, a response to the success of workers in organizing unions and raising wages. Capital intensified the labour process to extract more value from the labour of workers to meet union demands. The labour process, then, was constructed in a larger social formation and reflected institutional and class relations.

Braverman is also faulted for ignoring the role of class struggle in the transformation of the workplace, portraying workers as passive recipients of managerial initiatives. In his study of BC coastal logging, Rajala mentions that loggers largely accepted changes that supposedly worsened their working conditions.[30] He is right in that loggers did not launch direct protests against new machines and techniques. But the transformation of the workplace concerned forest industry unions, which represented mill workers and loggers, and they were involved in the automation debate that swept North America in the decade after 1955. New techniques and equipment were seen as a threat to the economic survival of workers, and unions sought broad-based political and contractual responses, where the benefits of the new technology would be shared by workers as well as owners. These initiatives achieved meagre results, but this raises the question of why workers, who identified problems with the changing labour process, did not mount a more serious challenge. This takes us into the realm of politics and ideologies. The labour process was indeed important, but must be set in the larger Fordist constellation, just as Fordism analysis is most revealing when incorporating the dynamics of the production process and capital accumulation.

Discourses and Subjects[31]

Individuals in the political economy not only sustained institutions and kept the production system operating, but were themselves, as subjects, structured by being located in these systems. Cultural and political representations, as well as physical realities, were crucial. Business practices were shot through with assumptions about progress, human nature, social relations, and the makeup of the good society. Workers did not take up militant unionism as an unmediated, knee-jerk response to high rates of injury and death, terrible working conditions, and low wages. Nor were union activism and leftist politics just simple responses to boom-and-bust business cycles or socially polarized, isolated camps and communities.[32] Rather, the achievements of unions and the political left came about because safety, workplace, and wage considerations were successfully represented as unjust, inappropriate, and susceptible to remedies. Culture shaped and informed the historical development of productive and social relations. The realm of culture and representation, where meaning in social, political, and economic life is sorted out, was defining and instrumental. Patterns or constellations of ideas and practices – ensembles articulated in systems – can conveniently be called discourses.

In the labyrinth of discourse, not all are equal. In twentieth-century western political economy, the discourse of liberal capitalism reigned supreme. Liberal capitalist ideas and interpretations persuasively explained the world and were instantiated in institutions and practices. This fixed set of meanings, albeit unstably and in relation to alternate readings, created hegemony, a dominant discourse. The term "hegemony," used in this sense, emphasizes the operation of power in everyday relations, its role in forming commonsense understandings, its ability to elicit consent from subjects, and its capability to reproduce social and discursive relations: "Power is not stable or static, but is made and remade at various junctures within everyday life; it constitutes our tenuous sense of common sense, and is ensconced as the prevailing epistemes of a culture."[33]

Nor was liberal capitalist discourse – a framework of ideas and practices built around core commitments to individualism, private property, and liberty – stable or static. Unionism, environmentalism, socialism, nationalism, and conservatism offered critiques and alternatives, forcing responses. Two provocative discourses framed the Fordist era in the British Columbia forest industry. A version of industrial unionism, itself an amalgam of competing discourses, holding different meanings for different participants, was incorporated into the dominant discourse in the 1930s and 1940s, and in the late 1960s and 1970s, the environmental discourse, with its own institutions and understandings, emerged. Alternate discourses, though, often assumed or reformulated aspects of liberalism, such as the ideals of personal fulfillment, progress, or democracy, and gains, as Ian McKay notes, came, "but only at the cost of 'editing' out their unacceptably aliberal elements."[34]

Individuals exist in relation to discourse. Indeed, individual identities are decentred and unstable, given shape and coherence by participating in discourse. To use the language of postmodernism, the "self is internally fragmented, incomplete, multiple and is produced and positioned – that is subjected to and determined – within discourse."[35] Ian McKay encapsulates the relationship between history, discourse, and identity in a comment on Canadian history, which, he argues, can be imagined "simultaneously as an *extensive* projection of liberal rule across a large territory and an *intensive* process of subjectification, whereby liberal assumptions are internalized and normalized within the dominion's subjects."[36]

We can now consider an articulation, a history of the British Columbia forest industry from 1934 to 1974 that links the building of a pulp and paper mill in Port Alberni in the 1940s, the ethos of the environmental movement, developments in power saw technology in the late 1930s, union rebellion in the Kootenays in the 1950s, the worldview of truck loggers, investment decisions by a Vancouver businessman in the mid-1930s, and the working life of a forklift operator in a Prince George pulp mill in 1972.[37] Chapter 1 tells the story of the major lumber companies and pulp and paper firms that set in motion the organizations, processes, and machinery for profitable resource exploitation. The regional division within the province is emphasized. Chapter 2 discusses the forest policy of the provincial government, which was driven by the rhetoric of sustained-yield forestry. This debate brought together smaller operators in protest, creating an identity as well as division within the business community. The establishment of the unions, which

Weighing, pressing, and baling sheets of pulp in a machine room, 1950s.
MacMillan Bloedel Collection (UBC), BC 1930/353/23

involved companies, workers, and the state, is the subject of Chapter 3. The hostility of corporations and the ability of union organizers to overcome geographic, industrial, and social differences were notable features in these years. Chapter 4 examines political relations between unions and within unions. Jurisdictional disputes, communism, socialism, and Canadian nationalism were issues that buffeted unions.

Chapter 5 looks at the everyday world of business and labour, especially during the years after the unions had become entrenched, when the new industrial relations system was in operation. Union officials cultivated relationships with rank-and-file members and provided important services to workers to sustain their loyalty. Beyond the minutiae of quotidian union life, the period was also defined by an ongoing struggle of narratives. Elements on the left critiqued existing social arrangements, while business apologists, recognizing the potential challenge of a coherent socialist, unionist radicalism, expended energy and money to stem alternative views. Chapter 6 examines the changing labour process. For capital, technological change was extolled in the language of progress, creativity, and reducing drudgery. Moreover, technological innovation and conservation goals were tightly intertwined. Unions were ambiguous in their response, and in the 1950s and 1960s, when automation was a major issue, sought to play a guiding role. They did not derail the dominant discourse, however. The final chapter examines the arrival of the new environmental movement in the late 1960s, a discourse that challenged key elements of the Fordist era, including corporations, unions, conservation goals, and even the imperatives of economic growth.

1
Companies, Markets, and Production Facilities

The business side of the British Columbia forest industry has been blessed with attention from popular historians. In the 1970s, G.W. Taylor, miffed that provincial histories focused on the political realm at the expense of industry and businessmen, wrote a book extolling the pluck of entrepreneurs who created companies and jobs in the forest sector.[1] More recently, Ken Drushka, in a series of books, has also celebrated the entrepreneurial spirit evident throughout the forest industry. Others have focused on particular companies.[2] This chapter builds on these works, emphasizing regional variations, fluctuating markets, the inherent competition in the economy, and the structure of an industry made up of a wide variety of firms that differed in size and function. By the 1930s, the coastal lumber industry was beyond small-scale, entrepreneurial capitalism, but in the Fordist era the size of major firms and the scope of their activity increased even further. Large business organizations, incorporating a range of production divisions, were created. Buoyant markets, healthy profits, and entrepreneurial ambition fuelled expansion, but so did fear – fear of competitors and fear of insecure sources of raw materials. There was also an underlying anxiety about market instability, especially in the fickle, politically structured American market.

There were three main phases in the production process: logging, converting, and marketing. Logging involved felling trees, and then cutting them into lengths and taking off their branches, that is, making them into logs. Logging also involved moving these logs from where the trees were felled to manufacturing facilities. This was the most difficult and costly aspect of logging. The manufacturing facilities, or conversion plants, came in many guises. There were shingle mills and plywood plants, but the sawmills and pulp and paper mills drove the forest industry. Sawmills converted logs into smooth, planed lumber of various dimensions. The lumber was dried, in kilns or outside in the air, to make it stronger and lighter. Pulp operations produced raw pulp, which was sometimes exported to be refined into high-grade papers, cardboard, and a myriad other products, but British Columbia mills, too, used pulp to make newsprint, and even, though to a lesser degree, higher-grade papers and specialty items such as tissues and wrapping paper. The last stage was selling the products. Some of the products were consumed in British Columbia but most were sold in export markets all over the world, although the United States and Britain were the most important.

The corporate organization of the production process varied. Some companies just engaged in logging, selling their product to conversion plants owned by others. Owners of conversion plants, however, tended to have their own timber and logging operations. Because of the substantial financial investment in a sawmill or, more significantly, a pulp and paper facility, owners were keen to have a secure source of raw material, logs. Usually big companies relied on both their own log production and that produced by independent contractors. For example, in 1950 at Ocean Falls, Pacific Mills operated its own logging camps on the Queen Charlotte Islands, on Vancouver Island, and near the mill at Ocean Falls. These camps supplied 45 percent of the company's needs; the rest came from logging contractors who worked for them, as well as from outside purchases.[3] At times, companies entered marriages of convenience. For example, a partnership between a British Columbia logging and sawmill company and a large, foreign-owned pulp and paper company, such as that which occurred between Crown Zellerbach and Canadian Western Lumber Company in the creation of Elk Falls Company, led to the construction of a pulp mill near Campbell River in the early 1950s. The logging company brought timber to the partnership, while the pulp and paper firm provided conversion plant expertise and connections to established international markets.

Marketing was done in various ways. In the 1930s lumber firms banded together to market their products globally. Pulp and paper firms relied on brokers or, if associated with a large parent company, were integrated into established sales agencies. In the early 1930s, the Powell River Company and Pacific Mills cooperated in marketing their products, but by the end of the decade, the production of Pacific Mills went overwhelmingly to its parent company, Crown Zellerbach, which had worldwide connections.[4] In the 1960s, there were many partnerships between British Columbia companies with experience in logging and sawmilling, and pulp and paper companies based in Europe, Asia, and the United States that had growing markets.

When we look beyond the Coast, the secondary literature is sparser. Drushka and Taylor write about the Interior, but it has not received the attention that the coastal industry has.[5] Drawing out the distinct Interior pattern of development is a major theme of this chapter. The pulp and paper economy did not arrive in the Interior until the 1960s, when the first mills were built away from tidewater. The Interior pulp and paper economy was imposed on a much different lumber economy from that found on the Coast; the Interior industry was made up of smaller operators who were less financially secure and less well capitalized. Capital for Interior pulp and paper operations was for the most part not generated internally, and outside interests, based in Europe, Asia, and the United States, controlled development.

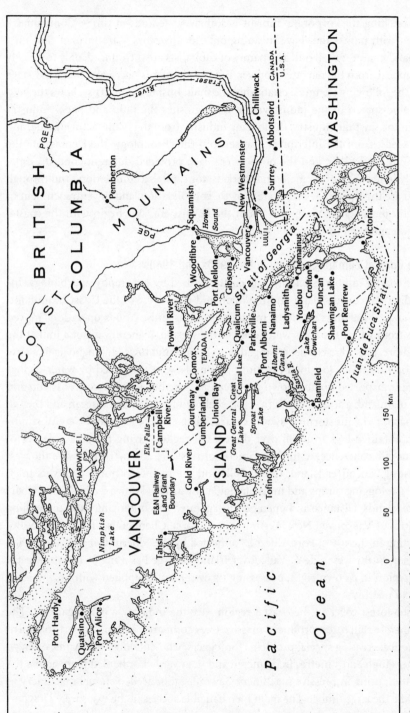

The South Coast of British Columbia

Sketching the corporate imprint is somewhat tedious at times. Companies – often with names that have meaning only for investors – are formed, and then expand, merge, or sell out. The names of capitalists are introduced, only to quickly disappear from the narrative forever. But the chapter is necessary. It sets the stage for the following chapters; establishes the main business concerns; shows the geographic spread of the industry; and distinguishes the pulp and paper industry from the sawmill industry, the logging industry from the manufacturing side, and the Coast from the Interior. It also sets out the chronology: the Depression, the Second World War, and the postwar era each provided different contexts, especially in terms of investment and markets, for capital accumulation. And through it all are the themes of corporate growth, consolidation, and the entrenchment of big business – fundamental traits of the Fordist era.[6] We begin with the coastal region and then turn to the Interior.

The Coastal Lumber Economy in the 1930s and 1940s

The coastal lumber economy was partly defined by geography and biology. Including Vancouver Island and the mainland coast west of the Coast Mountains, the coastal region is a land of mountains and islands. Woods operations moved logs from where the trees were felled to the seaside. If there was not a mill at the seashore, logs were connected together in booms and towed by tugboats to a sawmill centre. Thus logging operations and mills were connected by water, as logs were transported up and down the ocean passage between Vancouver Island and the mainland, a stretch of sea that was sheltered from the open ocean and the full impact of vicious storms. Sawmill centres, such as Vancouver and New Westminster, obtained logs from all over the coastal region, giving the area a degree of economic coherence.[7] On the perimeter of this core coastal region were the west coast of Vancouver Island; Ocean Falls and the mainland north of Rivers Inlet; and the logging camps and mills on Haida Gwaii, also known as the Queen Charlotte Islands. Distance and open ocean separated this outer ring from the milling centres of Vancouver, New Westminster, Victoria, Chemainus, and Nanaimo. Beginning in the 1930s, Port Alberni, connected by the Alberni Canal to the Pacific Ocean on the west side of Vancouver Island, emerged as a major forest industry subregion in its own right, possessing its own plants, supplied with raw material found nearby.[8]

The forest cover in the coastal region gave the industry a particular cast. The temperate rain forest produced massive trees compared with other parts of North America, creating special problems for loggers, who cut down the giants, often 70 metres high and 3 metres in diameter, and then yarded or hauled them across the ground, using impressive machinery. Sawmills, too, needed special machinery to handle the large timber. The main merchantable species in the 1930s were Douglas-fir, which constituted 60 percent of the cut, and cedar, which made up 20 percent.[9]

Coastal logging camp foreman and fir log, 1942.
MacMillan Bloedel Collection (UBC), BC 1930/19/35

In the 1940s and 1950s, hemlock and balsam became more prominent; while they were not suitable for the production of lumber, they were extremely useful in the production of pulp.[10]

Commercial logging began in the coastal region in the middle of the nineteenth century, and continued to expand despite economic ups and downs.[11] In 1929 the industry took out more logs than in any previous year. Most logs were converted to lumber. A large proportion of the lumber was shipped to the United States, some was consumed locally or went by rail to the prairies, and some was destined for a variety of international ports. Then the 1930s set in. The economic contraction devastated markets for BC lumber, but the general economic malaise was not the only factor affecting the fortunes of the BC industry. The US government brought in a new tariff policy: the Smoot-Hawley Tariff was signed in 1930 and it posted a duty of $1 per thousand board feet against Canadian lumber. This was followed in 1932 by an additional excise tax of $3 per thousand, making a prohibitive impost of $4 per thousand against BC lumber.[12] Considering that lumber prices in 1932 were about $12 per thousand, BC producers faced a bleak future in this very important market. In 1929, 55 percent of BC's lumber shipments went to the United States; in 1933, only 6 percent travelled that route. The tariff barrier was reduced by half in 1936, when the Canada–United States Trade Agreement came into effect, but sales in the American market did not immediately return to previous levels. Only 16 percent of BC's forest production was sold in the US in 1939.[13] Canadian producers continued to worry about operators in Washington and Oregon who wanted to return to a tough tariff policy against Canadian lumber.[14]

A new international trade agreement saved the BC coastal lumber industry. Prime Minister R.B. Bennett, eager to gain preferential treatment for Canadian products in the British market in order to ease the dismal economic conditions at home, convened the Imperial Economic Conference at Ottawa in the summer of 1932. While the conference has been portrayed as a failure, it was extremely important for British Columbia. Bennett negotiated an agreement that granted Canadian lumber free access into the United Kingdom market, while non-Empire producers faced a 10 percent tariff. If the agreement seemed straightforward on paper, it was not in practice. In the late 1920s the Soviet Union sold increasing amounts of lumber in the United Kingdom, and by 1931 supplied fully one-quarter of Britain's needs. The British government was reluctant to sever this Soviet trade link, and despite specific reference to non-Empire lumber producers in the Ottawa Trade Agreement, Britain refused to act decisively to curtail Soviet imports.

Finally, the British government made an informal arrangement with the Soviets that resulted in a reduction of Soviet lumber imports in return for higher prices for Russian timber.[15] This gave Canadian producers access to a sizable share of the British market, and BC lumbermen pursued this advantage with vigour. In 1931 the province shipped less than 100 million feet of lumber to the UK. By 1933 this figure had risen to over 271 million and in 1936 it reached 666 million. The percentage of BC lumber shipped to Britain increased from 7 percent in 1929 to 40 percent in 1933 to 63 percent in 1939, a mirror image of the pattern in shipments to the US.[16] Despite the steadily growing importance of the UK, however, the spectre of increased Russian penetration into British Columbia's most important market continued to haunt provincial lumber producers in the 1930s.[17]

British Columbia also increased its share in other foreign markets. The amount of lumber shipped to Australia quadrupled between 1928 and 1938, and shipments to South Africa doubled.[18] Sales in China, South America, Mexico, and Central America also increased in the 1930s. By the late 1930s the coastal lumber industry was on solid footing and log production levels in 1937 were already higher than those in 1929. In the summer of 1936, H.R. MacMillan stated bluntly: "Business in British Columbia is very good."[19] But MacMillan felt that the fortunes of the provincial economy, as well as political stability, were dependent on the Empire trade deal: "So long as we retain the British Preference markets for our forest, fishery and apple producers, we shall have fair to good conditions here, but if these preferences are reduced, there will be discontent."[20]

With the revival of trade after 1932, two themes emerged. First, the focus of the industry shifted from the coastal mainland to Vancouver Island, as more and more companies began to operate there, and, second, a corporate war accelerated exploitation of the forests and the growth of larger companies. Port Alberni, blessed with a deep sea port and surrounded by much quality timber, was at the centre of both developments. In 1933 the impact of the Ottawa Trade Agreement was already evident. Companies began to invest in new production facilities, optimistic about future returns. The Alberni Pacific Lumber Company opened a second sawmill in Port Alberni in October 1933, producing 100,000 board feet per day and employing 70 men.[21] The Bloedel, Stewart & Welch operation at Great Central Lake, near Port Alberni, was running full bore by the fall of 1933. A new logging site with five miles of logging railroad track began production and the mill employed two shifts.[22] The company also built a new sawmill in Port Alberni. This large mill began production in February 1935, had a capacity of 200,000 feet per eight-hour shift, and employed over 500 men in the milling and logging operation.[23] The mills catered to the waterborne export trade: in 1936, 92 percent of the Port Alberni mill production and 70 percent of the Great Central production were sent out by ship, largely to the United Kingdom. Port Alberni was now the second largest lumber export port in British Columbia, behind Vancouver and ahead of New Westminster.[24]

The Bloedel, Stewart & Welch mills marketed their lumber as part of a cooperative called Associated Timber Exporters of British Columbia (Astexo), originally formed in 1919. In 1936 twenty-six sawmill companies participated in the firm, including the Victoria Lumber and Manufacturing Company, Canadian Western Lumber Company, and Bloedel, Stewart & Welch. These big firms controlled 44 percent of the shares.[25]

Until the mid-1930s, the middleman between the BC producers and the buyers in Britain was H.R. MacMillan. MacMillan had first come to BC in 1907 to cruise timber near Powell River, but after a short stay returned to the United States to complete a forestry degree at Yale. In 1908 he joined the forestry branch of the Department of the Interior in Ottawa, and in 1912 he became British Columbia's first chief forester. Always aware of the importance of building an export market, MacMillan was an excellent choice to go to Britain in 1915 as a special trade commissioner, under the auspices of the federal government, to secure lumber orders. In 1916 MacMillan resigned as chief forester, and after a short stint with Victoria Lumber and Manufacturing, joined the Imperial Munitions Board to procure wood for military use. In 1919 he started his own firm, and with Montague Meyer, a leading British timber importer and wholesaler, as a partner, established the H.R. MacMillan Export Company. During the 1920s the lumber brokerage company made contacts throughout the world selling BC lumber. The firm opened offices in New York, Portland, and Seattle, and in 1924 it formed the Canadian Transport Company to charter ships and thus ensure tonnage for lumber shipments. The H.R. MacMillan Export Company also bought sawmills and invested in logging operations, most notably the Canadian White Pine Company in 1926. Montague Meyer sold his interest in the firm in 1927, leaving MacMillan as the sole owner.[26]

Throughout most of the 1920s, Astexo and H.R. MacMillan worked together harmoniously. The Astexo sawmills were content to sell the largest volume of their output to MacMillan, who had no real interest in the milling end of the industry. But tensions developed. Astexo millmen grumbled that they were shortchanged by MacMillan, while MacMillan was perturbed because some of the larger Astexo mills dealt directly with overseas customers without going through him. The first overt sign of rebellion came in 1928, when the Astexo mills set up their own sales agency to cater to the American eastern seaboard. The new company, Seaboard Lumber Sales, had thirteen member mills. Seaboard lured some of MacMillan's staff to the new operation. Markets beyond the eastern seaboard were still serviced by MacMillan, and when the American market collapsed in the early years of the 1930s, MacMillan once again controlled most lumber exports from British Columbia. He blamed Seaboard, however, for the prohibitive tariff against Canadian lumber. According to MacMillan, as the economic downturn set in, Seaboard management continually forced Canadian lumber into the American market, "incurring the growing enmity of the American lumber producers." Seaboard also increasingly bypassed American wholesalers to deal directly with retailers and flouted the conventions of the US shipping industry, thus earning the hostility of American wholesalers and the American Shipowners' Association. These strong, aggressive enemies were influential in setting US tariff policy.[27]

With the recovery of the mid-1930s, Astexo was reinvigorated, creating a new Seaboard Lumber Sales Company in 1935, modernizing its shipping methods, and setting its sights on the British market. MacMillan was invited to join Astexo in 1934, but declined.[28] By 1935 Astexo was pushing MacMillan from the British market, but he remained confident that he would prevail. He estimated that Seaboard members provided considerably less than 90 percent of British lumber, and that he would be able to procure sufficient lumber to maintain a "satisfactory independent position." A telegram to a British correspondent concluded: "This fight far from finished[.] fully expect [to] survive[.]"[29]

To ensure his survival in the British market, MacMillan acquired more production facilities in British Columbia. The Alberni Pacific Lumber Company was for sale. The operation had been owned by a British timber-trading firm, Denny, Mott and Dickson, since 1925, using the output of the Port Alberni mill to supply British customers. It operated independently of Seaboard and MacMillan, and was accused of flooding the British market with cheap lumber to the detriment of the trade as a whole.[30] Denny, Mott and Dickson contracted out the management of its mill, and was somewhat uncomfortable in the sawmill business. In the late 1920s it almost sold its interest in the Alberni Pacific Lumber Company to J.H. Bloedel, and as its timber supply diminished in the 1930s, it once again discussed a sale.[31] In 1936 a deal was cut: H.R. MacMillan bought Alberni Pacific Lumber Company for $1.7 million.[32] To supply the mill, MacMillan acquired a

H.R. MacMillan Export Company, Board of Directors, 1944. H.R. MacMillan
is second from left.

MacMillan Bloedel Collection (UBC), BC 1930/44/1

large private timber reserve that had been staked by the Rockefeller interests in
the early years of the century. The timber, located in the Ash Valley, assured the
mill a log supply for twenty-five years and cost the H.R. MacMillan Export Company $2.6 million.[33]

With MacMillan as an active player, there was now increased competition in the
British market as well as for timber in British Columbia. The two competing export companies, according to BC foresters, were "responsible for an unnecessarily
low selling price in the United Kingdom market due to cut-throat competition."
BC, they said, "was selling at five dollars [per thousand board feet] below the poorest
European region."[34] To keep his market share, MacMillan remembered in 1976, his
company high-graded: "he explained that the company's mill at Alberni from 1935
to 1939 logged only the choicest trees from the company's limits and yet had to sell
its entire output for the period on the world market at less than $12 per 1000 board
feet. This was below the company's cost of production."[35] In 1938 Seaboard, with
thirty-eight member mills, controlled some 70 to 80 percent of the province's
lumber exports. Seaboard's member mills dealt exclusively with the agency, and

British timber agents were contractually tied to doing business with Seaboard. It was an all-out effort to squeeze out MacMillan.[36]

In coastal British Columbia, MacMillan expanded his holdings, purchasing more mills and more timber, including the Shawnigan Lake Lumber Company and the Thomsen and Clark Timber Company. In 1944, in a celebrated deal, MacMillan acquired the Victoria Lumber and Manufacturing Company. The company did not want to sell to MacMillan for personal reasons – it hated MacMillan. To get around this, MacMillan enlisted the help of central Canadian capitalists, notably E.P. Taylor, who secretly purchased the holding on MacMillan's behalf. Once the deal was done, MacMillan took control of the renamed Victoria Lumber Company.[37] The acquisition of standing timber was a major reason for the purchase. Of the estimated $16 million paid, $10 million was for timber holdings and $6 million covered the mills, equipment, logging camps, and logging railway.[38] Similarly, after MacMillan purchased the Shawnigan Lake Lumber Company in 1943, he let the sawmill operation on Vancouver Island run down, eventually closing it in 1943. The logs taken from timber limits held by the Shawnigan Lake Lumber Company were transported across Georgia Strait and processed in MacMillan's Vancouver sawmill.[39]

MacMillan was not the only company expanding. The stronger markets, as well as the concern that if they did not get control of timber then someone else would, leading to the closure of conversion plants due to lack of logs, stimulated investment.[40] Until 1941, Canadian Forest Products, a subsidiary of the American company International Harvester, merely held timber in the Nimpkish Valley on northern Vancouver Island. In 1941 it took over an operation from Wood and English and began logging, shipping the logs to Vancouver conversion plants. In 1942 Canadian Forest Products purchased some 500 to 600 million more feet of timber in the Nimpkish area to add to its holdings.[41] Two Vancouver-based businessmen acquired the Nimpkish holdings in 1944. John G. Prentice and L.L.G. "Poldi" Bentley arrived in BC from Austria in the late 1930s and went into the furniture, veneer, and milling industry. In 1940 they purchased Eburne sawmills in Vancouver, and the Nimpkish holdings added timber to their growing concern. In 1947 they adopted the name Canadian Forest Products for all their holdings.

Another major company was formed in 1946, when central Canadian capitalists, including E.P. Taylor, Hugh MacKay, and Austin C. Taylor, put together British Columbia Forest Products. With shares raised in a public sale and bond sales, the company bought the Cameron Lumber Company in Victoria, the Hammond Cedar Company on the Fraser River, and the Industrial Timber mill at Youbou on Lake Cowichan. With these operations came timber holdings, which were supplemented by the purchase of other companies that merely held timber.[42]

Corporate consolidation continued. In 1951, the MacMillan companies joined with Bloedel, Stewart & Welch to form MacMillan & Bloedel. The new giant company operated six sawmills and two shingle mills. It controlled 747,000 acres of

Cut-off saws in a Vancouver shingle mill, 1942.
MacMillan Bloedel Collection (UBC), BC 1930/19/5

timberland and operated a dozen logging camps with over 175 miles of logging railway and 386 miles of logging roads. It managed the Canadian Transport Company and BC Forest Products. The company "produced 25 percent of the 2.5 billion feet of lumber manufactured yearly on the B.C. coast. Including [BC Forest Products] input, M&B marketed 32 percent."[43] MacMillan & Bloedel moved beyond the lumber economy. In 1951 it owned two plywood plants and two pulp mills, and in 1960 it also absorbed the Powell River Company. The new company was called MacMillan, Bloedel and Powell River Limited until 1966, when the firm became MacMillan Bloedel Limited.

Lumber was still very important to the coastal region and production levels continued to rise. In 1951 the coastal region produced 2,520,000,000 board feet of lumber; in 1972 the amount was 4,027,000,000.[44] The American market was once again the main destination for coastal lumber. In 1956, 37 percent of coastal lumber production was shipped to the US, while Britain absorbed only 13 percent. This trend continued over the next decades. In 1972, 54 percent of coastal lumber shipments went to the continental US and only 8 percent to Britain.[45]

Still, the American market was always vulnerable. During an economic downturn, the export of British Columbia lumber to the US was again threatened in the early 1960s, when American lumber producers fought to keep Canadian products out. In 1961 rumours began circulating that congressmen from west coast lumber-producing states, concerned about the rise in imports from Canada, were preparing to impose stiff duties against all Canadian lumber. BC supplied about 15 percent of the US market. By 1962 the matter was public, and Canadian and American officials began meeting. The American government appointed a commission to investigate the grievances, and hearings were held in October. BC sent a delegation to represent the lumber industry. Several BC representatives also attended the convention of the National Association of Home Builders in Chicago to argue against the proposed tariff and to enlist support. In February 1963, the US Tariff Commission released a report that favoured the Canadian position.[46] In May the manager of the BC Lumber Manufacturers Association commented that the protectionist drive in the US "does appear to be losing momentum" but that there is still "no room for complacency."[47]

Lobbying by both sides continued throughout 1964. The Americans wanted removal of any tariff up to a point that one country supplies 10 percent of the domestic consumption of the other, at which level a 10 percent tariff would apply; measures to counter perceived currency manipulation by the Canadian government; and the expansion of the "Buy American" principle. BC's timber allocation procedures and its stumpage rates were used to justify the demands of the American producers.[48] When the increasingly protectionist Congress adjourned on 3 October, though, no measures aimed specifically at lumber had become law.[49] American efforts to curb Canadian imports continued, but now the focus was on the Kennedy Round of the General Agreement on Tariffs and Trade. BC lumber producers were pleased with the results of the negotiations in 1967, however.[50] In 1980, 53 percent of BC lumber shipments went to the US.[51]

The Pulp and Paper Industry in the Coastal Region

The early history of the British Columbia pulp and paper industry has been much less studied than the early history of lumbering. Fewer people were involved in the pulp and paper sector, and the early pulp and paper industry was controlled by Ontario, Oregon, and San Francisco capitalists, not British Columbians. There was little interconnection between the business worlds of the pulp and paper and sawmill sectors. Moreover, pulp and paper mills were situated on the sea, and from their wharves commodities were shipped directly to Asian and American markets, not through Vancouver. The mill towns were self-contained, situated in isolated areas away from Vancouver and Victoria.

In 1930 there were five mills in the coastal region.[52] At Powell River, an American interest, Brooks-Scanlon, which had logging operations in the area, founded the Powell River Company in 1911. The first two paper machines started up in 1912 and two more went into production in 1915.[53] Up the mainland coast at Ocean Falls, the Ocean Falls Company, financed by English and French capital, established a mill around 1909, but it soon ran into financial difficulties. An American company, based in Portland, Oregon, the Crown Willamette Paper Company, took over the bankrupt operation in 1915. The Canadian subsidiary was called Pacific Mills.[54] It acquired more timber from the provincial government and began constructing a chemical pulp and paper facility in 1916. Production began the next year. In 1924 Crown Willamette became part of Crown Zellerbach, headquartered in San Francisco.[55]

The early histories of the other three mills are murky, but by 1920 two were part of Whalen Pulp and Paper Mills. The Whalen family, from Ontario, had been active in British Columbia since at least 1909 as part of the British Columbia Sulphite Fibre Company.[56] They were involved in a number of pulp and paper ventures in the second decade of the century, a time of much turmoil and litigation in the industry.[57] In 1920 they owned three operating mills: the 80-ton capacity Woodfibre mill on Howe Sound; the 60-ton Port Alice operation at the northern tip of Vancouver Island; and a 40-ton capacity mill at Swanson Bay, north of Ocean Falls on the mainland. The Reliance Mill and Trading Company, a US concern, served as the operating management.[58] In 1920 the Whalen operations in BC produced 47,962 tons of pulp, 12.7 million feet of lumber, 1.5 million feet of boxes, and 61,198 shingles.[59] The directors included James Whalen and W.D. Ross from Toronto, I.W. Killam from Montreal, Lawrence Killam from Cape Breton, Nova Scotia, and M.R. Higgins of Zellerbach Paper in San Francisco.[60] The owners and managers were optimistic about the future and expanded all three facilities, but in the depression of the early 1920s the company went bankrupt. It was in receivership in 1923.[61] In 1925 BC Pulp and Paper, dominated by the Killam family, was created to take over the assets of Whalen Pulp and Paper Mills.[62] Production at Port Alice and Woodfibre was revived, but the Swanson Bay mill never reopened.

The corporate history of the mill at Port Mellon, near Gibsons on the Sunshine Coast, was equally convoluted. It began in 1908 or 1909 as British Canadian Wood Pulp and Paper, owned by Captain H.A. Mellon. Over the next decade, it was operated by British Columbia Wood Pulp and Paper Company, Colonial Lumber and Paper Mills, Rainy River Pulp and Paper Company, and Western Canada Pulp and Paper Company. Vancouver Kraft Company owned the operation in 1928.[63] Extensive renovations were undertaken and were practically completed when markets collapsed in 1929. The mill remained largely unused during the 1930s.

The Depression years, especially the late 1930s, were difficult for the pulp and paper industry. In 1929, a record year, the province produced 305,000 tons of wood pulp. This rose to 335,000 tons in 1930, dropped to 260,000 in 1932, rose to 426,000 in 1937, and then plummeted to 242,000 in 1938. In 1941 the industry produced a record 508,000 tons. Paper production showed a similar pattern: 1930 was an excellent year and 1932 and 1938 were particularly weak.[64] In the 1930s about 20 to 25 percent of the pulp produced was exported; the rest was used locally to make paper. In export markets, the US absorbed over 50 percent of the paper, and Asia and the Antipodes about 25 percent; the Canadian domestic market accounted for about 12 percent. South America and the West Indies accounted for 6 percent and a small margin went to the UK. Japan and the US consumed most of the exported baled pulp.[65] In 1937 the Powell River operation sold 11 percent of its newsprint in Canada, 67 percent in the United States, 6 percent in Australia, 11 percent in the Orient, and 3 percent to other overseas markets.[66] The mills at Woodfibre, Port Alice, and Port Mellon were more reliant on Japan, but this market collapsed in the late 1930s, when Japan invaded China. With Japan at war, the BC companies faced serious problems. New management took over the Port Mellon mill in 1937, headed by F.W. Leadbetter of Portland, Oregon, who had mills in the American Pacific Northwest. He again upgraded facilities, but Japanese entry into war with China led to the collapse of the Japanese market and the closure of the mill after only a few months of operation.[67] Vancouver Kraft Company was broke in 1939, and its assets were purchased by Columbia River Paper Mills.[68]

With the outbreak of war, provincial mills were ordered to produce items for the war effort: pulp was used in special chemical papers and paper for food wrapping, shells, small arms ammunition, gas masks, ration books and operational forms, documents, high explosives, parachute rayons, and surgical dressings. Moreover, 60 percent of the spruce used in the construction of Mosquito airplanes was cut in sawmills affiliated with the pulp and paper industry.[69]

Pulp and paper production levels did not rise dramatically during the war years, but companies were active. In 1941 the Port Mellon operation was acquired by an American paper company, Sorg Paper, to supply its plant at Middleton, Ohio. Prior to the war, the Sorg operation was supplied from Scandinavia, but shipping problems due to blockades and loss of tonnage led to the acquisition of the BC mill.[70] Another company, Pacific Mills, owned by Crown Zellerbach, expanded its timber holdings during the war years. In 1941 it purchased forty timber licences from the Cargill Company of Canada, an American company with headquarters in Minneapolis, Minnesota. This timber was in the Nimpkish area on Vancouver Island. The next year the company purchased nineteen timber licences from Canadian Forest Products, also in the Nimpkish area, and in 1946 it purchased forty-one timber licences from the Rat Portage Lumber Company that were located on the mainland north of Ocean Falls.[71] In December 1946 it purchased a logging company, J.R. Morgan, Ltd. 1946.[72]

Postwar economies demanded cellulose products, and provincial production increased. In 1948 production levels in pulp were 35 percent higher than the previous record year of 1941, and paper production was 21 percent higher.[73] The Powell River Company continued to be mainly a newsprint operation, bringing its eighth

Harmac Operation, ca. 1960.
MacMillan Bloedel Collection (UBC), BC 1930/65/15

paper machine online in 1948. A number of subsidiary logging companies, including Kelley Logging, which had five camps in the Queen Charlotte Islands; Alice Lake logging at Port Hardy on Vancouver Island; and O'Brien Logging with a camp at Stillwater, fifteen miles south of Powell River, took logs from the company's forests. The firm also controlled a log brokerage company, a timber holding company, a towing company, and a department store in Powell River. Capacity of the operation was over 750 tons per day. The Port Mellon mill continued to supply pulp for the manufacture of paper in Ohio. In 1948 the company was in the process of increasing its pulp production from 125 to 165 tons per day. The company also owned a sawmill on its site, a barging company, which took its pulp to a railhead in Vancouver, and a hotel and summer resort adjacent to its townsite. Pulpwood and sawlogs were obtained from the company's holdings throughout the coastal region.[74]

While primarily pulp and paper companies expanded and diversified, coastal lumber companies moved into pulp and paper. Bloedel, Stewart & Welch announced in 1940 that they were going to build a sulphite pulp mill at Port Alberni, but the war curtailed construction. In 1945 construction resumed, and a 165-ton daily capacity mill was completed in 1947. Two new logging camps were opened in the Alberni Valley area, one at Sproat Lake in 1944 and another at Sarita River in 1947. While Bloedel, Stewart & Welch handled the sales of its logs, lumber, and shingles through its headquarters in Vancouver, the Mead Sales Company was its exclusive agent for sales in the US and Price and Pierce for the UK.[75] The H.R. MacMillan Export Company joined Bloedel, Stewart & Welch as a BC company in the pulp industry. Construction began on the $19 million sulphate facility at Harmac, near Nanaimo, in 1948, and it was formally opened in August 1950.[76]

Other companies consolidated, too. A new company, formed by an established pulp and paper firm and an established lumber company, built a mill on Duncan Bay, at Elk Falls, near Campbell River. The new company, Elk Falls Company, was equally owned by the Crown Zellerbach subsidiary Pacific Mills and the big lumber and logging company Canadian Western Lumber. Each partner subscribed $4,550,000. Canadian Western Lumber initiated the plan in 1948 when it applied for a Forest Management Licence. Besides timber, the Duncan Bay site was chosen because of available electrical power. Crown Zellerbach offered a secure market. From the time the mill opened in 1952, Crown Zellerbach in the US guaranteed that it would buy a minimum of 60,000 tons of newsprint per year for the next ten years.[77] In 1953 Crown Zellerbach bought the common shares of Canadian Western Lumber by exchanging one share of Crown Zellerbach stock for each three shares of Canadian Western Lumber. Shortly thereafter, Pacific Mills, Canadian Western Lumber, and Elk Falls were consolidated into one company, Crown Zellerbach Canada.[78] In 1955 Crown Zellerbach Canada, a subsidiary of Crown Zellerbach, owned timber holding companies (Canadian Western Timber and Baydun Holdings), logging companies (Comox Logging and Railway, and Northern Pulpwood), towing companies (Canadian Tugboat and Badwater Towing), sawmills (Canadian Western Lumber Company), pulp and paper mills (Pacific Mills and Elk Falls), fine paper and box factories (Canadian Boxes, Bartram Paper, and Hudson Paper), and retail lumber yards in the Canadian prairies (Crown Lumber [Calgary], Security Lumber [Moose Jaw], and Coast Lumber [Winnipeg]).[79]

Prince Rupert finally got a pulp and paper operation after years of hope and promises.[80] Columbia Cellulose, a Canadian subsidiary of Celanese Corporation of America, was formed in 1946. Celanese Corporation began the manufacture of acetate yarn at Cumberland, Maryland, in 1925, and by 1951 produced over half the acetate yarn in the US. The company at mid-century had yarn plants in Virginia, South Carolina, and Georgia; weaving mills in Pennsylvania and Virginia; a petrochemical plant in Texas; two plastic plants in New Jersey; and two research laboratories, one in New Jersey and the other in Texas. Company subsidiaries also operated facilities in Mexico and South America. Another affiliate, Canadian Chemical Company, was set to erect a petrochemical plant near Edmonton.[81] The Prince Rupert facility was located on Watson Island, just outside Prince Rupert, and logging operations were at Terrace, ninety-seven miles east of Prince Rupert.[82]

Mergers, consolidations, and expansions continued. In early January 1951, Canadian Forest Products purchased the Port Mellon operation from Sorg, using the new name Howe Sound Pulp Company. The mill had been idle for about two years due to low kraft prices and high operating costs.[83] Four months later, in May, ownership of the Port Alice and Woodfibre mills also changed. A merger between British Columbia Pulp and Paper and Alaska Pine created Alaska Pine and Cellulose. The Koerner family built Alaska Pine and a central Canadian company, Abitibi Power and Paper Company, owned BC Pulp and Paper. Besides Woodfibre and Port Alice, the new company controlled lumber subsidiaries that ran logging camps, sawmills, and sales agencies, including Alaska Pine, Universal Lumber and Box, Alaska Pine Sales, Alaska Pine Trading, Northern Timber, Pioneer Timber, Jones Lake Logging, Empire Machinery, Alaska Pine Purchasing, Canadian Puget Sound Lumber and Timber, and Western Forest Industries.[84] As the 1950s progressed, the large American firm Rayonier came to control the company. Rayonier began as a pulp producer in Washington state in the 1920s and was engaged in producing rayon. In BC, Rayonier began by taking control of 80 percent of Alaska Pine in 1954; in 1959 the name of the corporation was changed from Alaska Pine and Cellulose to Rayonier Canada.[85]

The growth of pulp and paper markets outpaced even the high expectations of company officials. As the president of the Canadian Pulp and Paper Association noted in 1959, in a letter to the Canadian Minister of Northern Affairs and National Resources: "You may have heard that we had a world pulp conference in 1949 in Montreal when an attempt was made to forecast supply and demand through 1955. At the time most of us felt that ... estimates were too optimistic, but in the event they proved to be too conservative, to a substantial degree."[86] In the late 1950s and 1960s, the final three pulp and paper operations came onstream in the coastal region. In 1955 BC Forest Products (BCFP) secured major timber licences from the provincial government. To raise capital and secure markets, the company entered into an arrangement with US giant Scott Paper. By 1954 Scott Paper had acquired a 50 percent interest in the Westminster Paper Company, a conversion plant in New Westminster. It used slabwood from two Lulu Island sawmills to manufacture toilet and facial tissues, napkin and towel papers, and other specialty paper grades. The president of Westminster Paper acknowledged that the sale was made because of the anticipated competition from Scott in the Canadian field, and rationalized the sale by noting that now Westminster Paper would have access to Scott advertising, more secure access to chemical pulp, and access to

Scott patents for new products.[87] Scott furthered its presence in BC by buying up a 29 percent interest in BCFP (Argus Corporation remained the other major shareholder). Moreover, Scott agreed to purchase a minimum tonnage of pulp produced at the new mill.[88] In July 1955 Mead Pulp agreed to sell the pulp in export markets. Construction of the Crofton mill began in 1956, and the first ton of unbleached pulp rolled off the line in December 1957. In 1960 Scott Paper sold its one million shares in BCFP to Brunswick Pulp and Paper, a company jointly owned by Scott and the Mead Corporation. Newsprint production at Crofton began in 1964. In 1969 Noranda Mines, one of Canada's largest resource companies, took controlling interest of BCFP. The major shareholders were now Noranda (28.9 percent), Brunswick Pulp and Paper (26.9 percent), the Mead Corporation (15.5 percent), and Argus Corporation (13.5 percent).[89]

In the late 1960s, the industry was still expanding. A second pulp mill was built at Prince Rupert; it began production in 1967 and produced 290,000 tons per year. The builder was Skeena Kraft Company, a joint venture between Columbia Cellulose (60 percent) and Svenska Cellulosa Aktiebolaget of Sweden (40 percent). In mid-1968 the Swedish company exchanged its interest in Skeena Kraft for Columbia Cellulose shares, giving Columbia Cellulose total ownership. The final coastal mill was at Gold River on the western side of Vancouver Island, and it too involved European and American investment. A Dutch firm, the East Asiatic Company, in partnership with Canadian International Paper, a subsidiary of International Paper of New York, worked out an arrangement in 1965 forming the Tahsis Company, and the kraft pulp mill began production in 1967.[90]

The integrated nature of large coastal forest industry companies, which controlled a wide variety of production facilities, often including both pulp and paper operations and sawmills, was reflected in the creation of the Council of Forest Industries (COFI) in the spring of 1960. Whereas the different sectors in the industry had previously had their own trade associations, COFI amalgamated them into one body to better represent the interests of the industry. Two of the organizations, the British Columbia Lumber Manufacturers Association and the BC Loggers' Association, traced their origins back to the first decade of the century. The other three, the Consolidated Red Cedar Shingle Association, the Canadian Pulp and Paper Association (BC Division), and the Plywood Manufacturers' Association of BC, had been formed between 1936 and 1950. In the new corporate era, coastal interests were best represented by one body.

The Interior

The Interior did not have the geographic and economic cohesion of the coastal region, where the sea linked logging and milling centres.[91] The Interior was divided into a number of subregions, each dominated by a few milling centres. In the Kamloops/Okanagan region, Kamloops, Kelowna, and Lumby were notable

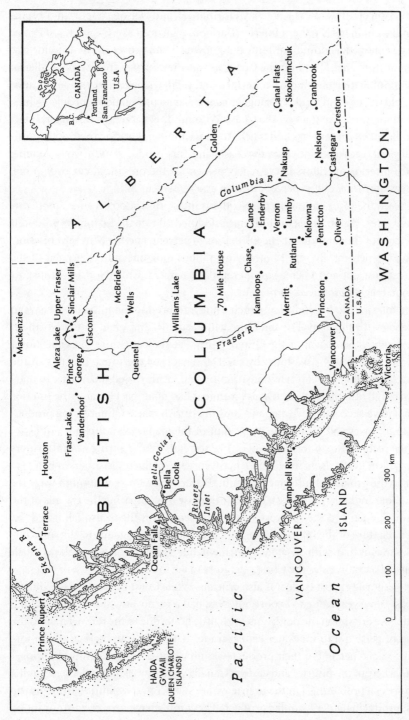

The Interior and North Coast

ALBERTA

BRITISH COLUMBIA

WASHINGTON

CANADA
U.S.A.

Pacific

Ocean

VANCOUVER ISLAND

HAIDA G'WAII (QUEEN CHARLOTTE ISLANDS)

Mackenzie

Aleza Lake   Upper Fraser

Sinclair Mills

McBride

Wells

Prince George

Giscome

Quesnel

Williams Lake

70 Mile House

Golden

Columbia R

Canal Flats

Skookumchuk

Cranbrook

Creston

Castlegar

Nelson

Nakusp

Canoe

Enderby

Vernon

Lumby

Kelowna

Penticton

Oliver

Rutland

Chase

Kamloops

Merritt

Princeton

Vancouver

Victoria

Fraser R

Fraser Lake

Vanderhoof

Houston

Terrace

Prince Rupert

Skeena R

Bella Coola R

Bella Coola

Ocean Falls

Rivers Inlet

Campbell River

0   100   200   300 km

CANADA
B.C.

Portland

San Francisco

U.S.A.

production centres; in the Kootenays, Cranbrook and Nelson supported substantial mills; and in the Northern Interior/Cariboo, Williams Lake, Quesnel, and Prince George emerged as dominant lumbering towns. Forest cover in the Interior was different from that found on the Coast, as was the climate. Trees were smaller in the Interior, with less volume per hectare, and yielded smaller dimensions of lumber. Cold winters and muddy springs and falls shaped production schedules, which were more restrictive than on the Coast. Without direct access to tidewater, Interior mills relied on railways and trucks to move lumber, limiting their opportunities in global markets. Until 1972, the coastal industry produced more wood volume: in 1929 Interior operators harvested 17 percent of the provincial cut by volume, whereas they took out 41 percent in 1960 and 53 percent in 1973.[92]

Between the 1930s and 1970s, the Northern Interior/Cariboo became a more important forest region, while the Kootenays declined. In 1936 the Kootenays produced 44 percent of the Interior cut, the Okanagan 39 percent, and the Northern Interior/Cariboo 17 percent. By 1973 Kootenay operations took out only 19 percent of the total Interior cut and Okanagan operators 22 percent, while Northern Interior/Cariboo loggers produced 44 percent.

The Interior lumber industry, which came into production in the Kootenays in the 1880s with the arrival of the Canadian Pacific Railway, and in the Northern Interior with the arrival of the Grand Trunk Pacific just before the First World War, was completely devastated by the Depression of the 1930s. Farmers in the prairies had no money for new construction and tariffs closed the American market. Significantly, the Ottawa Trade Agreement had no impact because the Interior did not have access to tidewater and thus the British market. Interior log production in 1937 was still only about 75 percent of the 1929 level; it was not until 1943 that the record of 1929 was surpassed. The secretary of the Spruce Manufacturers Association, J.O. Wilson, based in Prince George, explained the situation in a 1934 letter to the provincial minister of labour. Requesting a lower minimum wage for the lumber industry in his area, he made the case by comparing the travails of the Interior industry to the recovery being experienced on the Coast. He noted the seasonal nature of the Interior industry: "Seasonal operation, due to climatic conditions means that, with an equal investment, our operators have to make as much money in six months as the Coast operators make in a year." The lack of access to the waterborne export trade was also crucial: "While Coast operators have, during the past three years, due to export business, had a turnover which is approaching normal, we are still in the doldrums, with little hope, due to the railway haul to the Coast, of getting into the water export trade." The American market, which formerly took 80 percent of their product, was now closed due to tariff prohibitions. The markets in the prairies and eastern Canada were dismal, but BC Interior mills faced special problems: "On the prairie we are subject to competition from prairie mills, producing a very similar product. These mills have no minimum wage or hours of work regulation, pay wages as low as fifteen dollars per month and board, and enjoy a freight rates advantage of rarely less than one hundred percent." On lumber going to central Canada, coastal mills enjoyed a special freight rate from Vancouver to meet competition from the Panama Canal, again disadvantaging the mills Wilson represented. The quality of Interior lumber was also noted: "Our timber product is of a far lower standard than Coast lumber. We get none of the select grades. Coast operators, having sold select grades at high prices for export, can cut the ground from under our feet on the prairies, being able to dispose of their inferior product, which is equal to our best, at low prices."[93]

The war economy finally led to recovery for the Interior forest industry. As a Nelson correspondent noted in the spring of 1941, Interior mills had been very busy in the past year, "cutting for the Prairie market, where, in addition to military works, war industries, and housing, there is a strong demand for lumber for auxiliary grain storage. Many temporary structures are required, both on the farms and at the elevators, to house the nation's surplus grain stocks."[94] The rail trade to the US became increasingly lucrative. This turnaround set the stage for a forest boom in the Interior. There was increased production and a plethora of new operations. In 1939, 237 sawmills operated in the Interior, with a daily cutting capacity of 2,590,000 board feet. In 1945 there were 543 operating mills with a daily capacity of 5,122,000 board feet.[95] The trend continued, and the years from 1940 to 1960 were buoyant for the Interior lumber economy.

Operations varied in size. A 1945 survey of the Interior industry gives a sense of the structure of the industry.[96] In the Kootenays, there were 155 active sawmills. Twelve had a daily capacity of 30,000 board feet or more. The largest were the Columbia Contracting operation at Canal Flats (60,000), Cranbrook Sawmills at Cranbrook (50,000), the Wm. Waldie and Sons mill at Castlegar (60,000), Burns Lumber and Coal Company at Aery Creek (40,000), Rogers Lumber at Rogers (40,000), and Cranbrook Sash and Door at Lamb Creek (41,000). In the rest of the Southern Interior, the Kamloops and Okanagan regions, there were 150 active mills, 10 of which had a daily capacity over 30,000 board feet. The S.M. Simpson mill in Kelowna was the largest, capable of producing 50,000 board feet per day. It was the only Southern Interior operation capable of producing more than 35,000 board feet per day. Operations that produced between 30,000 and 35,000 board feet per day included the Shuswap Lumber Company at Canoe, the H. Sigalet and Company mills at and around Lumby, Penticton Sawmills, Oliver Sawmills, Long Brothers at Merritt, and the Co-operative Lumber Association mill at Kamloops.

The Fort George Forest District covered a massive geographic area, but the focal point of the lumber operations was Prince George. The largest operations were on the East Line, the string of communities and mill towns that stretched east from Prince George along the Canadian National Railway (CNR) line, which followed

Interior bush mill, 1951.
BC Archives, NA-12422

the Upper Fraser River, to McBride. There were two very large operations, Eagle Lake Sawmills at Giscome and the Sinclair Spruce Lumber Company at Sinclair Mills. These mills had daily capacities of 100,000 board feet. Mills with capacities between 50,000 and 65,000 feet included Shelley Sawmills, Penny Sawmills, the S.B. Trick operation at Aleza Lake, and Upper Fraser Spruce Mills. There were a total of forty-three of these stationary mills, some capable of producing only 5,000 board feet per day.

Besides the stationary mills, there were eighty-nine portable sawmills, also known as bush mills, in the northern region. This was a new phenomenon, spawned by the rapid market growth during the war. These were small operations capable of being readily moved around the woods. A few large portable mills produced up to 20,000 board feet per day, but in 1945 two-thirds (fifty-nine) were capable of producing only between 2,000 and 3,000 board feet per day. These small operations moved a mill into the bush, logged and cut planks until the nearby timber was gone, and then moved on to a new site.

The bush mills turned out green, unfinished lumber. To finish the lumber, planer mills were constructed. Lumber from the small portable mills scattered around Prince George was trucked into city planer mills, where the lumber was run through the planers, which smoothed their sides. The lumber was then dried, either in kilns or outdoors, before being loaded on railway cars for transport to points west and south. The planing and drying improved the quality of the lumber and made it lighter, significantly lowering transportation costs. The first planer mill was built on River Road, along the CNR line at the edge of Prince George, in 1928, and by 1945 there were three at the same site. In 1958 there were 17 planing plants on what was known as "Planer Row."[97]

Some of the larger Interior facilities had external ownership. A coalition of prairie cooperatives, with headquarters in Saskatoon, Federated Co-operatives, purchased the Shuswap Lumber operation at Canoe on Shuswap Lake in 1947. In 1956, after a fire, a $500,000 expansion increased mill capacity to 85,000 board feet per day. It now employed 150 sawmill workers and 100 loggers. The mill provided lumber for co-op members across Saskatchewan, Manitoba, and northern Ontario.[98] The opening of a plant at Quesnel by Western Plywood Company in late 1950 marked the introduction of plywood manufacture in the Interior. Western Plywood was formed by John Bene, a Hungarian immigrant based in Vancouver, who had been associated with the Bentley family and the creation of Canadian Forest Products. This was a major operation, capitalized at $250,000 and needing over 100 employees.[99] In 1961 a merger with three other firms led to the creation of Weldwood of Canada.[100] Local people also controlled larger operations. H. Sigalet and Company based in Lumby, the ever-expanding Simpson family operations headquartered in Kelowna, and Cranbrook Sawmills all were local concerns. Smaller operations were overwhelmingly local. Owners had to be on the job, not just to supervise but to do actual labour. Individuals with little capital entered the field with a portable bush mill, and often family members banded together to provide capital and labour for fledgling concerns. One commentator noted in 1951 that "small mill owners, particularly those who have enough members in the family so that they do not have to employ outside help, are cleaning up."[101]

Fathers, sons, and brothers were the core of these operations. George Melville Geddes was born in Owen Sound, Ontario, and began lumbering in British Columbia in the Columbia Valley in 1927. From 1933 to 1941, he operated a lumber business at Wells. With his son Clinton, he set up the Geddes Lumber Company and went into the sawmill business in the Prince George area. In 1944 the Geddes Lumber Company on Chief Lake Road had a capacity of 9,000 board feet per day and a second mill at Wright Creek had a capacity of 6,000 board feet.[102] Brothers Engel and Rex Ganzeveld came to Canada from Holland as infants and grew up on a farm in Alberta. During the Second World War, Engel went overseas as a mechanic while his brother worked as a machinist in a munitions plant. In 1947 they purchased a small, rough sawmill at Vernon and, using their mechanical skills, upgraded the operation.[103] In 1947 Mel and Carl Rustad, with partner James Adams, started a planer mill in Prince George. They added a sawmill to their operation the next year, and employed 40 people in 1954.[104] Four brothers created Lloyd Brothers Lumber in the Prince George area in 1951, operating a sawmill with a capacity of 10,000 board feet per day. By 1960 three of the brothers ran the mill, which had increased its capacity fourfold and employed fifteen men and a further twenty in a logging camp, while the fourth brother had gone out on his own, operating a logging camp with seven employees.[105] In 1957 four Hanford brothers banded together in Hanford Sawmills to run a 15,000 feet per day operation near Prince George.[106] A.L. Patchett and Sons began when A.L. Patchett entered the logging business in Merritt during the 1930s. His wife was also part of the operation; she obtained her log scaling licence in the early 1930s and apparently was BC's first licensed woman scaler. During the Second World War, the family moved to Quesnel to log birch, used in the construction of the Mosquito bombers. The company later expanded into sawmilling and planing, and in 1958 employed fifty men. A.L. Patchett supervised timber cruising and road location, while his sons served as managers: Don was the general manager, Roy the superintendent of field operations, Cyril the superintendent of Mill No. 1, and Lee the equipment supervisor.[107]

Not all operations were built on family connections, of course. In 1951 Fred Harrison was dreaming of a fuel delivery business in Vernon, and working as a home products salesman. He decided to go into the lumber business, and began logging and sawing on contract near Williams Lake. In the spring of 1951, he put together the financing to set up a sawmill on Sharpe's Lake, near 70 Mile House in the Cariboo. In 1953 he ran a mixed logging, sawmill, and planing operation employing nineteen workers.[108]

The Interior lumber economy of the 1950s and 1960s, then, was at an early stage of development. Despite the existence of a few larger companies, there was still room for the small operator to become involved and expand. No company or group of companies dominated or controlled production, and companies were often family operations. The scale of operations in the Interior, in comparison to the Coast, reflected lower levels of capitalization, greater ease of entry, and the prominence of smaller firms. In the Interior in 1955, only 1 operation had a daily capacity over 75,000 board feet per eight-hour shift. On the Coast there were 29 such operations and 5 could produce over 300,000 feet per shift. On the other hand, on the Coast there were only 69 small mills that had a shift capacity between 6,000 and 25,000 board feet per shift; in the Interior, some 874 operations had this capacity.[109]

The logic of Fordist capitalism was playing out, however, and in the 1950s there were signs of internally generated concentration and consolidation in the Interior.

The S.M. Simpson Company of Kelowna purchased a number of smaller operations in the Okanagan region; Crestbrook Timber was formed in the Kootenays in 1956, bringing together a number of milling and sawmill operations; and Eagle Lake Sawmills of Prince George continued to press for permission to build a pulp mill, a course of action it had been investigating since 1943, when W.B. Milner became the major shareholder.[110] In 1960 Midway Terminals Ltd., of Vancouver, merged ten interior sawmill and holding companies in the Okanagan and Prince George regions into one operation, National Forest Products.[111]

External capital associated with the pulp and paper industry brought the instruments of mature capitalist exploitation to the BC Interior, however. The first pulp and paper operation there began production at Castlegar in 1961. This facility had been on the books since the early 1950s. The company, Celgar Development, was created in 1951 as a subsidiary of Columbia Cellulose, which in turn was owned by the American giant, the Celanese Corporation of America.[112]

In 1962 plans for a pulp operation in Prince George were announced, and construction proceeded quickly. Prince George Pulp and Paper was a joint venture involving Canadian Forest Products and the Reed Paper Group. Reed Paper was a British firm with net assets exceeding £100 million, with manufacturing interests in eastern Canada, Norway, Italy, Australia, and New Zealand, as well as in the UK. The firm thus both consumed and marketed products from the Prince George facility.[113] Production at the $84 million facility began in May 1966. With a German partner, Feldmuhle, A.G., Reed Paper and Canadian Forest Products established Intercontinental Pulp Company, which built a second facility at the site to produce only pulp, starting in 1968. A third pulp operation at Prince George, Northwood Pulp, a joint venture between Noranda Mines of Central Canada and the American multinational Mead Corporation, also began production in 1966. The value of the mill was estimated at $54 million.[114]

Other pulp and paper operations sprang up in the Interior in the 1960s and 1970s. At Kamloops, local entrepreneurs pushed for a pulp operation in the late 1950s, in conjunction with Crown Zellerbach,[115] but only when the American giant Weyerhaeuser became involved did the project succeed. Kamloops Pulp and Paper began production in December 1965. American and Japanese interests constructed the pulp and paper facility at Quesnel. Cariboo Pulp and Paper involved Weldwood of Canada, a subsidiary of United States Plywood, and two Japanese companies, Daishowa Paper and Marubeni-Iida. A second Kootenay operation, Crestbrook Forest Industries, began production at Skookumchuk in 1969. It involved local interests as well as two other Japanese companies, Mitsubishi Shoji Kiasha and Honshu Paper Manufacturing. North of Prince George, at the newly created "instant-town" of Mackenzie, two pulp operations commenced during the 1970s. BC Forest Products, owned by Noranda Mines and Mead Corporation in 1969, and Finlay Forest Industries, a joint venture started by Cattermole Timber and two Japanese firms, Jujo Paper and Sumitomo Forestry, built the mill. In 1980 BC Forest Products took control of the Finlay Forest Industries operations.[116]

The Interior lumber industry did not disappear with the coming of the large pulp and paper operations. Sawmills continued to exist, using the most valuable trees to turn out lumber that fetched better prices per tree than pulp and paper. Pulp and paper companies operated their own sawmills, sometimes taking over and operating existing facilities. Celgar Development, anticipating construction of its pulp mill at Castlegar, took over the William Waldie and Sons mill at Castlegar, the Big Bend Lumber Company at Nakusp, and the Columbia River Timbers operation near Revelstoke in late 1952. Northwood Pulp bought Eagle Lake Sawmills near Prince George in 1966.[117]

The geographic reach of the pulp and paper operations was immense. The corporations needed guarantees that sufficient fibre, in the form of wood chips, was available before making the major investments necessary to establish a pulp and paper operation. In the 1950s, 1960s, and 1970s, Interior forests were carved up into vast tracts and the pulp rights were allotted to pulp and paper operations. The facilities in Prince George or Castlegar drew from a resource base that stretched hundreds of miles from the conversion plants themselves.

By the 1970s, the Interior forest industry had become much more extensive, more capital-intensive, and more technologically sophisticated with the addition of the pulp and paper industry. Communities such as Quesnel, Kamloops, and Castlegar were nodes in the global capitalist economy, and links with international capital were clear and direct. External firms were key in making decisions about production and marketing, and about the fates of the forest communities. Economic development in the Interior had catapulted to a new stage.

In 1972, reflecting the greater importance of the Interior industry and the greater number of companies that operated in both the Interior and coastal regions, the Northern Interior Lumberman's Association, a trade organization representing Interior lumbermen, was amalgamated into COFI. Regional divisions seemed less important.

IN 1975, IN ANTICIPATION OF THE END of a number of long-term timber contracts with major forest companies, the provincial government established a Royal Commission to investigate the industry. The commissioner, Peter Pearse, considered the character of capital in the industry. The presence of large corporations was notable. MacMillan Bloedel was the largest operator in British Columbia: "In 1969, the Company had 22,282 shareholders, 18,632 employees, a total income of $644.5 million and capital expenditure of $105 million."[118] Its sawmills at Vancouver, New Westminster, Nanaimo, Port Alberni, Powell River, and Chemainus were capable of producing almost 1.7 million board feet of lumber per shift; its plywood plants at Vancouver and Port Alberni could produce 469 million square feet of ⅜ inch plywood per year; its pulp capacity at the Nanaimo, Powell River, and Port Alberni mills was almost 2 million short tons per year; and its paper capacity at the Port Alberni, Powell River, and New Westminster plants was 1.2 million short tons per year. In terms of the company's income, 52 percent came from lumber, plywood, and shingles; 38 percent came from pulp and paper; and 10 percent came from other sources. The main market was the United States, which absorbed 42.6 percent of its products in 1969, followed by Canada (24.4 percent), Japan and other Asian countries (9.6 percent), and the United Kingdom (7.2 percent). The two largest lumber-producing firms, MacMillan Bloedel and BC Forest Products, controlled 13.6 percent of provincial lumber manufacturing capacity in 1975. The five largest firms controlled 25 percent of the total; the eighteen largest, 50 percent.

In pulp, fourteen companies operated twenty-two mills; the four largest controlled 84 percent of the capacity. In paper production there were seven companies, and the three largest controlled 84 percent of the capacity. Of sixteen companies that produced plywood and veneer, four controlled 55 percent of capacity.[119] Large, integrated corporations mass-producing a limited range of raw and semi-processed commodities accounted for the bulk of production.

2
The State, Sustained Yield, and Small Operators

In British Columbia, the Crown owned over 90 percent of provincial forestland, and timber was allocated to private companies through leases and licences. As demand for standing timber rose in the twentieth century, private interests competed to secure access to the valuable resource. There was also growing concern about the longevity of the industry. Government timber policies evolved in the context of the North American conservation movement that developed after the 1880s, and, as Richard Rajala notes, the provincial debate on conservation took on a sense of urgency in the 1930s when it became evident that the industry was overcutting in coastal forests.[1] With increasing public awareness, officials within government mobilized for change. The result was a Royal Commission, followed by legislation in 1947 establishing a new relationship between the state and the private forest companies. Forest Management Licences (FMLs), later called Tree Farm Licences (TFLs), gave large companies access to vast amounts of standing timber in return for following government direction in its management.

In the historiography of the provincial forest industry, the growth of large companies, conservation ideals, and the government timber policies of the 1940s are intertwined. Roger Hayter locates the emergence of Fordist big companies in the context of the 1947 legislation, and Patricia Marchak argues that the large corporations orchestrated these changes to further their interests.[2] Ken Drushka condemns the government, provincial Chief Forester C.D. Orchard, and a contingent of large companies for this misguided timber policy that led to the dominance of large corporations.[3] Rajala, focusing on large companies in the coastal logging industry, tweaks the connections among conservation science, forest policy, and larger firms, arguing that new production technologies, devised to enhance labour exploitation, dictated a government timber allocation policy that supported corporations that adhered to a debatable conservation science sustaining clearcut logging.[4]

Timber holdings did largely fall into the hands of large corporations, of course, but new timber holding procedures do not fully explain corporate growth. As Chapter 1 argued, capitalist competition fuelled the drive to corporate concentration and this process was well underway before the 1940s.[5] Nor did large corporations write government policy in the 1940s. They wanted more timber, to be sure, but they were very much against the government's particular policy. Most notably, they wanted private ownership of timber. They adapted, however, to take advantage of the change, largely to pre-empt corporate rivals. Nor was the provincial state engaged in a plot against small business. C.D. Orchard and others believed that their timber and conservation policy was best administered by large forest companies, but they expected, perhaps naively, that the policy would also satisfy small operators.

This preoccupation with integrated forest companies has overshadowed one particularly significant consequence of government timber policy – the creation of a province-wide fraternity of small operators. The small operators' material circumstances and their sense of grievance led to the creation of a number of organizations that were part of a discourse celebrating free enterprise, private property, and equal opportunity, while damning the role of government and monopolies. The history of the small-operator fraction of the forest business community is a major focus of this chapter.

In the end, big businesses achieved a measure of stability and predictability. Discussing logging practices, Rajala concludes that the provincial government was a mere client of corporate forest interests, "incapable of achieving more than an endorsement of forest practice standards already observed by leading firms."[6] This chapter suggests a more autonomous role for the state in setting timber-allocation policy, however. Political and community pressure emboldened civil servants and government members, while at the same time the sense of crisis, in part manufactured by government foresters, allowed provincial officials to shape public support and give the government the opportunity to pursue its own course. Overall, the provincial state managed the larger exigencies of capitalist expansion, working to adjudicate between different interests in the industry, preserve the forest economy's long-term future, rationalize the industry along Fordist lines, and satisfy big and small operators.[7]

Timber Policies of the Provincial Government to 1930

The beginning of commercial forestry in mid-nineteenth-century British Columbia did not lead to wholesale alienation of timberland. Following British precedent and concerned about timber speculators, the Crown retained ownership of timber. It then distributed cutting rights to private firms. Companies and the state entered into various licensing and leasing arrangements that stipulated the obligations of logging companies, usually the construction and operation of a sawmill, and established fees such as land rental taxes, stumpage, and royalty payments. A boom in the provincial lumber industry in the first decade of the twentieth century, as well as a new form of timber licence that could be bought and sold by holders, giving it value as a commodity, dramatically increased revenues from the forest industry. Revenue from the forests, especially stumpage and royalty fees that were paid based on the quantity of trees logged, became increasingly important in the provincial budget.

The Crown also had the power to regulate cutting methods and set procedures to ensure the successful growth of a new forest on cutover land, giving the government an important role in reforestation. Indeed, after an area was cut, the land reverted to the Crown, making the government's role particularly significant in the long-term viability of the forest industry. In the nineteenth century, fire prevention and control were the main interests of the government. Logged-over areas were left to naturally reforest themselves, and logging companies continually moved from one area to the next. With the vast supply of timber, careful stewardship seemed unnecessary.

For forest companies the arrangement was largely satisfactory in the early years. They did not press for private ownership of the forest land because there was plenty of forest to go around and the cost of buying land outright was too expensive. Cutting fees were not onerous and governments were malleable, often catering to the needs of companies in times of weak markets. Regulations governing reforestation were largely nonexistent, and governments agreed with the companies that proper and potentially expensive conservation practices were not appropriate until the old-growth forests had been logged off. The posturing of government officials around the time of the first Royal Commission on Forestry, the Fulton Commission of 1910, about the need to act now to protect the resource and ensure revenue and community stability for future generations was largely rhetoric. Only in the late 1930s did a focused consensus for change emerge.

Some timberland fell into private hands. Most notable was the 2 million-acre block of land on Vancouver Island, known as the Esquimalt and Nanaimo Railway Belt, the E&N Belt, which contained some of the best timberland in the world. The E&N Belt was transferred to private hands in the 1880s as part of a deal that rewarded railway capitalists for building a short railway line on Vancouver Island. As the lumber industry expanded in the early twentieth century, the value of the timber increased, and now the advantages of the private ownership of timber were clearer. Private timber gave owners security of tenure, a wonderful piece of collateral when approaching a bank for a business loan. Banks were skeptical about timber licences because they were short-term and believed to be too readily open to change by government officials. Private timber was also beyond many government fees, log export restrictions, and regulatory, conservation measures. As timber became more valuable, private timber, beyond the purview of the state, became more attractive to forest companies. Tradition, public opinion, and political opposition, however, countered the call for private ownership of the province's primary resource made by the logging companies.

By the first decade of the twentieth century, there were calls for closer management of the resource. People were aware that without positive policies the resource would be depleted and the economy would suffer. "Sustained yield" was the rallying cry, implying a perpetual yield of trees to sustain companies, jobs, communities, and government spending. Sustained-yield thinking was part of the broader conservation movement that swept North America after the 1880s. It was based on the belief that scientifically based, rational forestry was possible, that the power of science applied to the forest resource would generate higher yields, perpetual growth, and increased company profits. The conservation movement was not anti-business; activists were adamant that their goal was to facilitate profitable exploitation of the resource, unlike the other high-profile naturalist group of the era, the preservationists, who wanted to preserve forest areas in a pristine state.

Conservationists wanted efficient use of the forests to serve economic and social ends, and, as such, prominent lumbermen in the United States and central Canada supported conservation. A key aspect of conservation thinking was that only after the old-growth forest had been logged off could a new crop of trees of a preordained species and of the same age be managed effectively using scientific measures. Scarcity and value were necessary backdrops for the inauguration of intensive management: in an era when loggers could easily keep moving to new stands of virgin timber to satisfy the market for logs, conservation techniques and ideals were seen as uneconomic and superfluous, and so economic conditions and the financial health of companies restricted government options. The industry largely dictated forest policy until the 1930s, when, due to changed circumstances, the call for sustained yield forced government to act.[8]

Forest Policy in the 1930s and 1940s

The revival of the coastal industry after 1934, and the corresponding accelerated cut, brought to the fore the rapid depletion of the resource. The push for sustained yield and the creation of a persuasive discourse came from civil servants within the government: professional foresters generated the data, created the knowledge, and offered a persuasive account of the province's situation. Part of the appeal of sustained yield was that it was a very nebulous term, offering much to a variety of interests. Just exactly what was to be sustained? For scientific foresters, sustained yield meant ensuring that on average the yearly cut would not exceed the yearly growth in the forests. There would be a sustained yield of merchantable timber. This would provide the industry with a guaranteed source of logs and wood fibre, and so for companies and investors, profits and economic growth would be sustained. The government, for its part, sought stable, growing revenues in perpetuity. Workers envisioned secure employment and a higher standard of living, while small businessmen hoped for growing, prosperous communities. Sustained yield, then, was much more than a technique to maintain the biological forest.

A 1937 government study by F.D. Mulholland, known as the Mulholland Report, set the stage for serious discussion. The report, based on years of work by the Forest Branch, provided a scientific account, based on statistical evidence, of the state of the forests in coastal British Columbia, arguing that the future was bleak unless sustained-yield forestry was introduced. There was a crisis looming: it "will be impossible to avoid a conflict between the desire of private interests to utilize all the mature stands as quickly as markets can be found for timber, and the public interests which requires that great basic industries dependent upon natural resources should be regulated on a permanent basis."[9]

Professional foresters in the government concluded that the time for sustained-yield management had arrived. In the 1920s Chief Forester P.Z. Caverhill ridiculed the idea of sustained yield in British Columbia, arguing that "as long as we had more old growth timber than the mills could use there was no excuse, or function, for sustained yield forest management."[10] By 1935 Caverhill recognized problems in coastal forests, notably that Douglas-fir, the most valuable species, was being overcut. It was impossible to reduce the cut, however, because of the Depression: logging operators needed to produce logs as cheaply as possible in order to survive the tough economic times.[11] In 1937 the Forest Branch went on the offensive. The improved economic climate, the evidence of the Mulholland Report, and a new aggressive chief forester, Ernest C. Manning, put the forestry issue front and centre. In a speech to the Forestry Committee of the provincial legislature in November 1937, Manning encapsulated the problem in a quotable phrase: "At the present rate of cutting, our Douglas fir lumber industry will definitely be on the downhill grade within 15 years."[12] Fifteen years was not very long, and the implications in terms of jobs and community stability were dire indeed.

On Vancouver Island, the focus of the coastal forest industry in the 1930s, the concerns were taken seriously. Roderick Haig-Brown, the Campbell River conservationist and writer, was impressed by Manning's speech to the Forestry Committee and concluded that it was time for action: "My own opinion is that future work should concentrate on a realistic acceptance of the fact that 12 or 15 years will see the end of major logging operations on Vancouver Island as we know them."[13] Haig-Brown, who was a member of the Forestry Committee of the Associated Boards of Trade of Vancouver Island, wanted to see a slowing down of logging, more reforestation, and a government inquiry into the state of the forests. Residents of Vancouver Island pressured the provincial government to bring in positive forest policies.[14]

Over the next four years, foresters from the Forest Branch and from the University of British Columbia spoke to public organizations such as the Vancouver Kiwanis Club, the Vancouver Natural History Society, and the Vancouver Institute. Speakers offered a historical perspective, based on studies of countries that had already experienced what BC was going through. It was a four-stage model of history. The first stage was the era of exploitation, where resources seemed inexhaustible and humans vigorously and wastefully exploited the natural accumulation of growth over many centuries. The second stage was the era of protection, where there was recognition that virgin timber was limited and forest products were valuable. Protection largely took the form of fire prevention and control. In the third stage, there was a realization that cutover lands must be reforested and that forest management was necessary for reforestation, waste elimination, and cutting timber on a sustained-yield basis. The final stage occurred when forest land was managed according to the best social and economic interests of the majority, and each use was managed permanently for the highest value. In the late 1930s, BC was at the close of the second or the beginning of the third stage.[15]

Expert speakers drew attention to the fate of regions that did not carefully look after their resources. The history of the lumber industry in East Kootenay was a lesson for the rest of the province. As Manning remembered in his 1939 speech to the Forestry Committee of the BC legislature, when he began work in East Kootenay in 1912 there were "logging camps and mills almost everywhere." Due to excessive logging and the resulting lack of timber, however, more than 30 sizable mills had been forced to close, two in the last year.[16] All accounts of the state of the coastal forest industry drew on the Mulholland Report. Industry, too, accepted the data of the report, thus acknowledging that new policies were necessary.[17]

If forestry professionals, especially those in the Forest Branch, defined the problem, outlined its historical context, provided the data for the discussion, and spread the message, they also provided the solution. Sustained yield was to be managed in working circles, units of land where sustained yield would be practised. In late August 1942, Chief Forester C.D. Orchard, who attained the post after Manning's death in a plane crash on 6 February 1941, wrote a thirty-one-page memorandum on working circles that set out the essential application of sustained-yield forestry in BC for the Minister of Lands.[18] Major questions remained unanswered, however. How big would working circles be? If the whole province was designated a working circle, then it would be possible to log off the coastal region totally, and then move all logging operations to the Interior, where the same level of cut could be maintained, thus preserving the principle of sustained yield. Coastal lumber communities would be devastated, of course. On the other hand, if working circles were too small, they would contain insufficient timber to maintain lumbering operations through a growth cycle of some 100 years.

There were other questions. How would logging rights in the working circle be allocated – would small operators get some timber or would all the cutting rights fall into the hands of large corporations, where they would remain for generations? Would there be more private timber holdings? How much authority would the state have in telling operators where to log and how much to log? How much influence would market factors have on setting the yearly cut? Would bureaucrats manage by fiat? The public had concerns about the people's timber falling into the hands of large corporations. So, too, did the small operators in the logging community. Big forestry companies worried about the influence of the government in their businesses, the fate of their current cutting rights contained in existing licences and leases, and the threat to private property. Thus, while the idea of sustained yield was greeted favourably in all quarters, there were serious hurdles.

J.H. Hodgins, an assistant forester with the BC Forest Service, commented in 1941 that the public and the industry had to be prepared for sustained-yield forestry: "The importance of 'public relations' cannot be over-emphasized when considering the introduction of a sustained yield policy. Support not only of the public but of the timber industry for a reasonable forest practice directed along lines of continuous forest production is essential."[19] The Forest Service played an important role. A speech written by Chief Forester Manning and delivered by his successor, C.D. Orchard, to the Canadian Society of Forest Engineers in February 1941 touted the role of his department: "Progressive forestry policies involved in the 'introduction of sustained yield' will not exist ... until facts and remedies are established and made public property and until the need of forest policies is explained, advocated and popularized. This is the first responsibility of a Forest Service which ... should be the most competent authority to perform the work."[20]

By 1942 other issues regarding forestry were also festering. Representatives of the fishing industry complained about the negative effects of logging on spawning streams. Communities and individuals questioned the practice of high-lead logging, whereby cut logs were dragged to a central source, a spar tree, using donkey engines and cables. Dragging the logs, with one end in the air and the other on the ground, destroyed the small trees and scraped the forest floor. The technique of selective logging, taking out merchantable trees while leaving small growth for a later cut, was offered as an alternative. In 1933 the Associated Boards of Trade of Vancouver Island met in Saanichton, and high-lead logging was a topic of discussion. The convention sent a resolution to the premier calling for a commission to investigate the long-term implications of high-lead logging. The Island boards of trade felt that high-lead logging was wasteful because it destroyed immature timber, thus threatening the future of forestry in the province. They were also of the opinion that high-lead logging created a more serious fire hazard than selective logging. For industry the costs of selective logging were too high, and the Forest Branch agreed. Beyond economics, the science of selective logging, sustained-yield forestry was predicated on removing all old-growth forest cover and beginning again with a human-made, manageable crop of trees.[21]

The increased rate and extent of logging after 1934 brought logging closer to urban areas: Cumberland on Vancouver Island and North Vancouver on the mainland were worried about the fate of their watersheds.[22] Some sawmill communities worried about jobs. In the rush to acquire timber holdings in the late 1930s and 1940s, companies at times bought up sawmill operations just to gain access to their timber holdings. In a celebrated case, as we have seen, the H.R. MacMillan Export Company purchased the Shawnigan Lake Lumber Company in 1941, and let the eastern Vancouver Island sawmill operation run down, eventually closing it in 1943. Logs that were once processed at the Shawnigan Lake mill were now transported by raft across Georgia Strait to a sawmill in Vancouver. For the company it made good economic sense.[23]

The provincial government was concerned about revenue and jobs. Especially vexing was the timber in the E&N Belt. Timber on this land was not subject to taxation, and it was estimated that this was costing the province some $800,000 a year in revenue. Nor was E&N land subject to provincial restrictions on log exports. Holders of privately owned E&N timber could export raw, unprocessed logs as they saw fit, and because the logs were not converted into lumber in BC sawmills, the chief forester estimated in 1939 that the province was "probably losing annually in the neighbourhood of $750,000 in wages."[24] The government was also critical of logging, forestry, and reforestation practices on E&N land.[25]

The provincial government faced political pressure. A new political party, the Co-operative Commonwealth Federation (CCF), emerged from the 1932 provincial election as the Official Opposition, having elected seven Members of the Legislative Assembly (MLAs). Effective management of the province's resources was a significant aspect of the socialist CCF's program. From 1934 to 1937, Ernest Bakewell, CCF MLA from the Mackenzie riding and the forestry critic in the legislature, predicted an imminent timber shortage, attacked logging methods, and castigated the government for allowing loggers to destroy salmon spawning grounds.[26] After 1937 Colin Cameron, CCF MLA for Comox, took over the role of forestry critic, and he was even more outspoken. His 1941 pamphlet *Forestry ... BC's Devastated Industry: A Frank Discussion* was a stinging critique of the behaviour of government and industry. By this time, the CCF critique had more authority. Dr. Max Paulik, a trained forester who had worked in the forests of Europe and the Soviet Union, headed the CCF Economic Planning Commission from the mid-1930s. Steeped in the principles of scientific approaches to forestry, Paulik had the expertise to confront government and industry foresters, emboldening the CCF critique. Paulik subscribed to the conservationist ethos: "One fact to be kept in mind in connection with Forestry is that it is not based primarily on sentiment nor upon the desire to preserve the trees for their beauty, but that the entire forestry business is conducted on sound economic principles."[27] An advocate of sustained-yield forestry, Paulik offered an alternative to government policies of the 1930s.[28] The political influence of the CCF rose in the 1941 provincial election, when the party got more votes than either the Liberal or Conservative parties. The success of the CCF led to the formation of a free enterprise Liberal-Conservative coalition government, dominated by the Liberals.

In 1943 the government began moving towards a new forest policy based on the principles of sustained yield. To prepare for new legislation, it set up a Royal Commission. The premier believed that a commission was necessary because "he couldn't hope to get such a radical change of policy through the legislature if it were introduced 'cold.'"[29] Beyond political pressure and encouragement from the Forest Service, the immediate prompt for the commission came from the Truck Loggers Association and the BC Natural Resources League, both of which made representations to the government in early 1943. The major operators were rather surprised that the call for the commission came when it did.[30] It was recognized, however, that the commission would "constitute a blue print for a forest-wide 'tree farm' from which successive generations may harvest a paying crop in perpetuity."[31] Gordon McGregor Sloan, a judge and former Liberal member of the legislature, was the commissioner. The Sloan Commission formally opened in Victoria in February 1944, and over the next months held hearings throughout the province, producing over 10,000 pages of testimony from witnesses interested in the forest industry. Sloan's visits raised the hopes of professional foresters, as one district forester noted after the commission visited Prince George in 1944: "This gave us renewed faith that forestry will become a reality in British Columbia; that the Forest Service will develop from a half starved revenue collecting agency into the kind of an organization all foresters feel it should be."[32]

In 1945 Sloan submitted his report to the legislature, and his recommendations, while not followed fully, guided the writing of a new Forestry Act in 1947, the first major revision of forestry legislation since the original Forest Act of 1912. There were a number of aspects to the act, but most important and controversial was the establishment of a new system of forest management. Working circles were now called Forest Management Licences. Companies that received long-term FMLs would practise scientific, sustained-yield forestry under the supervision of the Forest Service. Owners of private timber would be given more government timber if they agreed to follow government regulations. Minister of Lands and Forests E.T. Kenney said in a March 1948 radio address that "the Forest Management Licence [was] a compromise between rigid government regulation and outright exploitation of the forest resource."[33]

The industry had a number of qualms. For one thing, the new legislation did not set up a forestry commission, as Sloan had recommended, that would manage the forests supposedly beyond political interference. Kenney was adamant already in the spring of 1946 that there would be no administration of the forests by a commission.[34] Forest industry companies also wanted a guarantee that a greater portion of forest revenue would be reinvested in forest management and protection, and hoped for a greater role for private ownership of provincial forests. Many foresters, in both government and private companies, believed that the private ownership of forest land would lead to proper forestry policies. Forester John D. Gilmour, hired by MacMillan to develop company forestry policy, wrote an analysis of the Sloan Report in an eight-page pamphlet in 1946: "The best results will be obtained by a system of sustained yield management resting on the broadest possible base. This should include as many private owners, both large and small, as can be got into the scheme."[35] Overall, companies were wary of the new arrangements. If it had been left up to them, they would not have invented the Forest Management Licence system.[36] Oscar Lundell, a lawyer for BC Forest Products between 1944 and 1948, remembered the forest companies' attitude towards the 1947 act: "Companies were a little leery of it at first and they still are. The Crown is landlord and can fix stumpage."[37]

An internal study of the MacMillan Company by A.P. McBean shows that the firm considered all options in late 1947. It estimated that the company controlled sufficient timber to operate for twenty to thirty years. Beyond that, new timber would have to be secured. They could participate in the new government scheme or they could liquidate timberlands, logging units, manufacturing plants, and selling facilities when their current timber supply was gone. While acknowledging "certain moral obligations to the public and its employees," McBean emphasized that the decision between long-term management and liquidation must be based ultimately on the profit to shareholders.[38] MacMillan chose to remain in business and adapted to the new regime. The big companies began acquiring FMLs, but it was out of self-preservation rather than enthusiasm. If they did not take up an FML, another company would, and they would be shut out of the industry for lack of timber.

Columbia Cellulose was awarded the first FML, to support a pulp and paper operation at Prince Rupert, in 1948. By 1955 there were twenty-three FMLs. Major operators such as MacMillan & Bloedel and Canadian Forest Products secured licences on the coast, and in the Kootenays the Celgar Development Company received rights to a massive area to feed a pulp and paper complex. Besides these licences awarded to single companies, there were thirty-two Public Working Circles (PWCs). The Forest Service managed the PWCs according to sustained-yield principles, and cutting rights within the circles were allocated to private companies. The belief was that this would provide opportunities for smaller operators to remain in the industry. They would have access to timber without assuming the costs and responsibilities of forest management themselves. By the mid-1950s, almost all cutting rights in the coastal region south of Rivers Inlet had been allocated.

Truck Loggers

If the big operators and professional foresters had concerns, the small operators had fears. FMLs raised the spectre of monopoly: a few well-capitalized corporations would gobble up all the FMLs, leaving no timber for the little guys. By the early 1940s, there was already concern on the coast about the direction that the government was taking. The Truck Loggers Association (TLA), formed to represent the interests of the small operators in the coastal region, generated a sustained, biting critique of the FML system. In the Interior, concerns of small operators were evident by the late 1940s. There, too, the main issue was the FML system that was turning over forest land to large companies. In the following years, neither the concern nor the criticism ebbed, and from the 1930s to the 1970s, across the province, there was the constant question of whether the small operator could survive in an environment dominated by big corporations supported by big government.

The TLA was born in 1939 when H.J. Welch sent out invitations to some twenty-five to thirty operators in the logging industry on Vancouver Island. The meeting's purpose was to address a particular problem, the slash burning policy of the provincial government. Slash was the wood waste – branches, stumps, and smaller trees – left in the woods after logging. It was considered a fire hazard and an impediment to the growth of a new healthy forest. The provincial forestry department was keen to have operators gather and burn the slash in a controlled manner. Operators perceived the new regulations as too inflexible and too costly.[39] Welch's appeal was answered by only two people, but the early organizers did not give up and in the next few years there were more meetings.[40] Thirty truck loggers, all from Vancouver Island, attended the 1941 meeting. The president was Welch, the vice president was T.J. Brown of Brown Logging, Campbell River, and the secretary-treasurer was G.H. Van Dusen of Errington Logging, based in Parksville. The directors headed logging companies headquartered in Victoria, Parksville, Campbell River, and Nanaimo.[41] The first regular meeting took place at the Malaspina Hotel in Nanaimo in November 1942, with triple the membership of the previous year.[42] The TLA incorporated and continued to grow. In 1943 members of the organization produced 36 million board feet of logs, and in 1944 the eighty-five members produced 300 million board feet.[43] The organization expanded to include members from the Lower Mainland and Fraser Valley, and Earl Brett and Harold Clark, from Chilliwack, were elected as directors. The 1944 convention was held at the Hotel Vancouver, reflecting the broader base of the organization. In 1947 the head offices of the organization were moved from Nanaimo to Vancouver.[44]

The annual January meetings grew in importance and size. In 1946, 500 members and representatives of associated industries attended the three-day meeting. Members of the government, representatives from the Forest Service, university experts, and visitors from large firms attended. Papers were presented on issues of concern to logging operators, and the meetings provided an opportunity to discuss new machines, logging techniques, trends in other regions, market prognostications, government policies, and labour issues. The committees appointed in 1950 – Log Prices, Legislative, Forestry, Public Relations, Finance, Membership, and Safety – give a sense of the range of interests of the organization.[45] The association hired its own forester in 1945 to help deal with government policy and scientific issues.[46] In 1946 the TLA consisted of 114 coastal operators, producing 28 percent of coastal logs; in 1958 it represented 169 logging operators in coastal British Columbia, and its members produced 45 percent of the total annual cut in the Coast Forest Region.[47]

Who were the truck loggers? As the name suggests, at one level they were defined by technology. After the 1930s, trucks became more common in coastal logging operations. Up to this time, railways were used to transport logs from the woods to mills or tidewater, but after the First World War, the availability of trucks with sufficient power to carry the heavy logs up and down the steep grades and over primitive roads made truck logging feasible. Trucks enabled companies with little capital to enter logging. Railway logging was an expensive proposition: it was costly to construct the lines, and to justify the railway grades, extensive timber holdings were needed, another cost.[48] Yet the term "truck logger" does not accurately describe who belonged to the TLA. Beginning in the mid-1930s, the large operators also began to convert from railway logging to truck logging. In the 1940s and 1950s, large companies continued to run both railway and truck shows, but trucks were clearly becoming dominant. Perhaps the simplest way to describe the members of the TLA is negatively: they were not the major forestry companies. If we remove the big sawmill and pulp and paper companies from the logging industry, we are left with the members of the TLA. For the most part, truck loggers did not own sawmills (if they did, the mills were small), and they certainly had no ownership interests in pulp and paper facilities. Moreover, while the large firms had corporate offices in Vancouver, the truck loggers were based in smaller Vancouver Island and Fraser Valley communities. Truck logging companies varied in size, but rarely had more than 30 employees. Companies were owned by one man or perhaps a few partners who were close to their operations and their workers and involved in the day-to-day physical activities of producing logs.

Profiles of the owners of a few prominent truck logging companies gives a sense of these operations.

Herbert J. "Bert" Welch, the founder of the TLA, was born in New Westminster in 1893 and the family moved to Nanaimo four years later. At the outbreak of the Great War, he was studying medicine and immediately joined the Army Medical Corps. He later transferred to the Royal Navy and then to the Fleet Arm of the Navy. He graduated from the Royal Navy College at Greenwich and spent considerable time flying with the North Sea Patrol. After a "crack-up" in 1917, he was invalided home. He worked as a salesman in a number of businesses, first selling roofing products, then refrigeration, and then equipment for General Motors. In the early 1930s, he went into the refrigeration business on his own, but it did not work out. In 1932 he entered the logging business with his father and brother-in-law, forming the W.F. Clarke Logging Company. They also acquired a sawmill capable of cutting 50,000 board feet per day. After the mill was destroyed by fire in 1936, Welch bought out his partners and created the Olympic Logging Company.

In 1942 the company was running three logging operations, using a gas donkey engine and a truck at each site. The company also owned road-building equipment and had about forty-five employees. It remained the same size over the next decades. In 1945 Welch, although "never particularly impressive in his public speaking efforts," was elected to the provincial legislature as a Coalitionist, representing the Vancouver Island riding of Comox.[49]

Ole Buck was born in Norway and came to British Columbia as a child. At the age of fifteen, after three years at the Pacific Lutheran Academy in Tacoma, Washington, he went to work in the woods. He worked as a supervisor for a number of large logging operations before forming his own firm, B. & T. Logging (Ole Buck and W.B. Turner). After the company dissolved in 1939, he formed a partnership with A.E. Simpson in BATCO Development, a company that controlled some 300 million feet of timber in the Campbell River area. Severe illness curtailed his activities but he re-entered the logging business in 1943 and became president of the TLA in 1945. He died in 1950.[50]

The three Baikie brothers came from a logging family. Their father logged in British Columbia at the turn of the century. In 1920, at the age of eighteen, W.W. "Wallace" Baikie, the eldest, started working full time in the woods, including seven years for Comox Logging. In 1934 he went into logging on his own in partnership with his brothers Harper and Jack at Union Bay on Vancouver Island. At times they had their own timber to log, but they often contracted to large firms such as Comox Logging, Timberland Lumber, Canadian Collieries, and MacMillan Bloedel. Baikie Brothers employed twenty workers in 1950 and twenty-five in 1960. Both Jack and Wallace Baikie served as presidents of the TLA.[51]

Some TLA members ran logging shows that were considerably larger. A.P. Allison, a native of London, England, came to Canada in 1892. In 1900 he entered the lumber industry, getting a job with the massive Victoria Lumber and Manufacturing Company's mill at Chemainus. Soon, however, he began running his own logging operation. In the 1930s he logged spruce in the Queen Charlotte Islands. In 1942 his camp at Cumshewa Inlet on the Queen Charlottes, a railway operation, employed 250 men. The operation was taken over by Aero Timber Products, a government corporation set up to produce spruce for wartime airplane construction. Allison then set up a sawmill operation called Lions Gate Lumber in North Vancouver, and began truck logging on Vancouver Island. He died in 1947, shortly after being elected president of the TLA.[52]

Truck logging developed in two ways in the 1930s and 1940s. Some truck loggers worked as *contractors*, taking out logs from timber limits controlled by the large sawmill and pulp and paper companies. The truck loggers cut the trees and transported them by truck either to the conversion plants or to ocean side, from where they were moved on the water to manufacturing plants. Other truck loggers, the *independents*, secured their own timber and sold the logs to the company that offered the highest price. In the late 1930s and 1940s, this open log market began to shrink. Large companies, such as MacMillan, BC Forest Products, and Bloedel, Stewart & Welch, scrambled to control more coastal timber limits. In 1956 it was estimated that only 10 to 15 percent of coastal logs were bought and sold in the coastal log market.[53] Moreover, the large firms ran their own logging operations. Even by the early 1940s, the number of small, independent operators with their own supply of timber was on the decline, and small loggers more and more operated as contractors, working on the timber limits of large corporations. Hale H. Hetherington, of H. & R. Timber, commented in 1944 that "before the war there were nine independent loggers in my district [Dewdney]. These are now all controlled by the mills. The independent or open market logger is on his way out. Whether or nor he will retrieve his position, I do not know."[54] The economic environment was increasingly inhospitable to the smaller operators.

Small Operators and Timber Policy

Concentration of ownership and control of the timber resource was well underway before 1947, but from the perspective of the small operators, the new forestry legislation exacerbated the situation. The government went out of its way to reassure the small operators that timber would be available for them in the new regime. Not all land would be under FML tenure, and the government, said Minister of Lands and Forests E.T. Kenney, is "determined to keep ample areas in reserve to supply local needs and small operations."[55] H.R. MacMillan, who would increase his vast holdings of timber after 1947, also felt that the future looked good for small operators. He thought that once the old-growth forests were removed, the need for large companies would disappear. Large logging operations were still necessary because costly machinery was needed to take out the massive trees. Second-growth trees, which would mature in about sixty years, would not need the elaborate equipment. He concluded: "Therefore I do not feel that the sustained-yield policy will result in the timber industry being carried on by a small number of firms; rather the exact reverse will happen as is already the case in the Interior where the trees are small."[56] Such thinking, however, did not reassure small operators, as the following plea to the government in 1948 makes clear. Small operators sought a competitive economic environment that would enable individuals to improve both themselves and the society around them. The concentration of timber in the hands of a few major operators was bad not only for the small operators but for the province as a whole:

Another reason of the utmost importance for the Minister of Lands and Forests not establishing Forest Management Licences throughout the Coast District is that he will be establishing forest monopolies. The size of such monopolies is of no moment. Monopolies may be considered advisable in such things as public services where competition would mean duplication. Competition, however, is the essence of success-ful industrial progress. We have in the Coast District the ideal geography for free competition. What is to be gained by putting up arbitrary walls? Is it desirable to protect or subsidize one company, or one group of companies? Is it advisable to em-bark on a program that will ultimately stifle individual initiative? There can be only one answer to these questions. The one thing the Government of the Province of British Columbia must maintain "in perpetuity" is the opportunity for individual initiative.[57]

The truck loggers did not quietly accept the new regime once it was in place. They protested the granting of every new FML in the coastal region. H.T. Kenney, the government minister responsible for the legislation, was a noted presence at the TLA convention in January 1950: he "deserves a bouquet for attending the conference at all. The Association has opposed much of the forestry legislation he has sponsored, and some of the members have been very bitter."[58] In the summer of 1952, the secretary-manager of the TLA made a plea for change to the premier: "There is ... a fear on the part of many small operators that continued granting of Forest Management Licences as presently constituted will ultimately eliminate them from the industry or reduce them to the status of sub-contractors."[59] The 1953 TLA convention also discussed the contentious forestry legislation. It was seen as a danger that would soon eliminate the small operators and place the bulk of the province's forest resource in the hands of a few. A reporter noted that "this is a hardy peren-nial and has been since the forest management licence legislation first came into effect."[60]

There were coastal organizations besides the TLA. In the summer of 1948, a delegation representing small loggers in the Powell River District waited upon government officials in Victoria and protested the granting of an FML in their district to Evans Products of Vancouver. They wanted a new system, challenging the whole policy.[61] In October 1949 the Independent Loggers Association was formed, representing small logging operators from the Minstrel Island area. Its purpose was to combat the government's forest tenure policy.[62] In early 1952 Kel Robinson led the challenge in Port Alberni against a MacMillan & Bloedel FML. This group soon coalesced into the West Coast Small Operators Association, rep-resenting some twenty-two small operators in the district. These firms together employed some 200 to 225 workers.[63]

Criticism of the FML system was province-wide. In November 1948, a small mill owner in Chase, R. McKay, opined that the FML system would concentrate the province's timber resources in a few hands, arguing that small companies, even when formed into a syndicate with other small operators, could not meet the terms of the licence in bad economic times.[64] In the Cariboo, a forest licence application stirred up much unrest. Western Plywood was keen to secure an FML to supply its plant being projected for Quesnel. Small sawmill and logging operators perceived the proposed forest licence as a threat. Indeed, even when the licence was at a tentative, rumour stage, thirty-five Quesnel-area millmen organized the North Cariboo Lumbermen's Association to fight the application. When the proposal was announced, the protest increased. A newspaper editorial commented in January 1948: "Small operators have become alarmed fearing that they would be crowded out by big business under the new forest management set-up."[65] In February mill operators met the minister of lands and forests to state their case and retained a Vancouver lawyer to represent their interests. Public meetings in Quesnel followed, and speakers defending the government's plan included the local MLA, the chief forester, and even the premier of the province, "Boss" Johnson. In late July 1948, it was announced that Western Plywood would get its FML, the fifth allotted in the province.[66] The bitterness lingered and Western Plywood purposefully moved to mend relations with the Cariboo community. As many local contractors as possible were used in construction of the facility, local people were chosen for key positions in the mill, often sent to Vancouver to be trained, and as much material as possible was purchased from Quesnel stores.[67] Still, sawmill operators worried about the next licence application in their region and its implications for their survival.

The Celgar application for a massive FML in the Kootenays occasioned much protest in 1952. Celgar proposed a pulp and paper complex for Castlegar, and its FML application was made public by the government on 8 January 1952. Letters to the editor, protest petitions, and public meetings followed, articulating a concern that most small logging and sawmill operators had about their future.[68] The Nakusp newspaper editor commented on public opinion: "The blows of the woodsman's axe on the giants of the Arrow Lakes Forests, never resounded through the woods with louder echoes than the differences of opinion between [the] Forest Service [and the] Independent Loggers Association, in their battle over disposal of the timber of this district. Celgar's application takes in the whole timber stand, pushing the present operator, away back on the fringes."[69] Celgar got the licence.

In the Okanagan area, the BC Sawmill and Logging Operators' Association was formed in Lumby in the fall of 1954 to "protect the rights of small operators."[70] By the mid-1950s, Kamloops and Okanagan-area lumbermen were split down the middle with regard to FMLs: "Larger mills favored the present land allotment system. Generally, smaller mills were opposed."[71] To the north, the Vanderhoof Lumbermen's Association was formed in 1955, and the twenty local mill operators voiced their opposition to the issuing of more FMLs.[72] Based in Golden, the Columbia Valley Loggers Association was formed in 1958 to represent the interests of small-scale logging and sawmill operators.[73]

The small operators were not without resources; they could not be completely ignored by the government. With much public support in their communities, they could make themselves heard politically. Even members of governments criticized the forest policy at times. The Liberal-Coalitionist H.J. Welch, founder of the Truck Loggers Association, spoke out, as did Liberal-Coalitionist B.M. MacIntyre. In 1952 the Alberni Liberal Association went on record against the FMLs.[74] In the Social Credit government that came to power in 1952, Cyril Shelford, a Social Credit MLA, was a prominent critic of FMLs. In newspapers and from the legislature's opposition benches, the persistent Gordon Gibson harangued the government over its timber tenure policies throughout the 1950s.[75]

The provincial government responded in 1953 with the "contractor clause," also referred to as the "30 percent clause." In all FMLs granted after No. 13, a new clause was added. It stipulated that at least 30 percent of the allowable cut in the licensed area had to be harvested by contractors other than the licencee's own employees or shareholders who held more than 1 percent interest in the timber holding company. In difficult circumstances, when such a policy was not feasible, the government minister could waive the requirements, but the intent was clear. The regulation was also effective, ensuring a role for small companies in logging, but the Truck Loggers Association found much to criticize. The 30 percent clause was a mere sop to the independents, dramatically emphasizing that the commitment not to crowd out the small operator that had been made in the late 1940s when the FML system had been introduced had been a lie. The reason was that even with the contractor clause, the timber rights would go to the majors and the independents would be mere contractors, working on someone else's timberland. The ability of major companies to manipulate circumstances to squeeze out the independents and the discretionary power given to the minister to relieve companies of any obligation to contractors were viewed with alarm. In 1957, when some twenty new FMLs were being considered, the Truck Loggers Association was pessimistic: "FMLs granted to date have done enough damage to the independent – further FML licences will do still more." Moreover, "the 30 percent clause is impractical of application and still leaves [the] independent logging contractor at the mercy of FML holders."[76]

The 1945 Sloan Report called for a review of forest management in ten years, but by 1952 there were already calls for an immediate full-scale inquiry into the FML system, and some wanted it abolished. The government opposition parties, the Liberals and the CCF, were clamouring for action as well. Social Credit Minister of Forests R.E. Sommers was adamant, however, that there would be no early commission.[77] Questions also arose about the allocation of FMLs. This was an important issue as the FMLs were awarded by the government and thus the decision was conceivably open to influence. Critics asked who were getting the licences and why. Was the process open? Was the government favouring particular companies? Forest Management Licence No. 22, finally approved in May 1955, showed the weakness of the system. BC Forest Products had been lobbying for a timber licence on Vancouver Island but the Forest Service rejected its proposal. Then in 1954, while the chief forester was away, Minister Sommers awarded the licence to the company without Forest Service approval. Opposition protest, an inquiry, and an eventual court case tied Sommers to a number of financial bribes. On 5 November 1958, a jury found Sommers guilty of five charges of taking bribes for awarding the contract. He was sentenced to five years in jail.[78] Sommers went to jail but, strangely, neither the company, which was the apparent briber, nor the government, Sommers's overseers, suffered any serious consequences.

During the public and political turmoil of the Sommers affair, Gordon McGregor Sloan again headed a commission to investigate the state of the forest industry. His 1957 report offered a few minor recommendations for change, including some aid to small operators, but largely endorsed the system he had helped create a decade earlier.[79] Again Sloan served the state well. The inquiry and the apparent serious consideration of the complex forestry issues convinced the public that the government's sustained-yield policy was in the general interest of the province and further legitimated the authority of the state in forestry issues. Cosmetic changes recommended by Sloan in 1957 were also reassuring: "Forest Management Licences" became "Tree Farm Licences" and "Public Working Circles" became "Public Sustained Yield Units." The skepticism of small operators was palpable, however. Jack Gibson captured the sense of futility, noting the considerable competition among small operators who made presentations to the commission, all vying to "tell Mr. Sloan how extremely sorry and concerned they are about the plight of the small logger. I now have an idea as to how the carrier pigeon must have felt just before he became extinct."[80]

Events of the 1960s did little to appease small operators. The coming of the pulp and paper economy to the Interior set off alarms. Before investing in pulp and paper facilities, companies needed assurance that there would be sufficient resources available to them to pay for their investment and profit. A new form of tenure, the Pulp Harvesting Agreement (PHA), was introduced in 1961 to jumpstart the pulp and paper industry in the Interior. This was a formula to impose a pulp and paper economy on a sawmill economy. Investors who agreed to build a mill were guaranteed the right to use wood not normally used by sawmills (the smaller-dimension timber that could be transformed into wood chips) at a lower stumpage rate than wood used for dimension lumber. The plan was to use the existing sawmills to produce wood chips, which had previously been waste, so that the sawmill and pulp and paper sectors could coexist symbiotically. With this security of supply, mills were built in the Interior. The forest industry was now big business on the Coast and in the Interior. The response of the Truck Loggers Association to the new PHAs was pointed: "In the opinion of this association, the granting of Pulpwood Harvesting Licences would have a worse effect on logging operators than Tree Farm Licences have had."[81]

Small operators across the province continued to feel vulnerable in the 1960s. In the Vancouver Forest District, a group of twenty-two smaller lumber manufacturers banded together to create the Independent Timber Converters Co-operative Association (ITCCA). They argued that the BC forest policy threatened their survival because about two-thirds of the annual allowable cut was controlled by TFL holders and the remaining third, upon which the association members relied, was open to all comers, including TFL holders, resulting in a "terrific scramble" for the scarce resource. They hoped that cooperation might give them some influence and stability. They proposed to the government that 50 percent of the log production from new timber sales be allotted to members of the ITCCA at market prices or that the production of three Public Working Circles up the mainland coast be set aside for their members.[82]

In 1961 Larry S. Eckardt, a past-president of the Truck Loggers Association, offered a response to a positive assessment of the government's forest management system. From the perspective of the independent logging and sawmill operator, he said, the TFL "is a monster that is putting me out of business." He argued that the "concept of the TFL *may* be sound, but the basis of ownership is *odious.*" Some thirty-eight or thirty-nine TFLs were in existence by 1960, and the favoured few – large corporations – controlled the provincial forest industry. "Thus we find a 'battle-line' drawn between the 'haves' and the 'have-nots' i.e. those who possess Tree Farm Licences and those who do not."[83] Despite the concerns of the small operators, the large firms continued to win, as large chunks of the Interior forest were turned over to pulp and paper companies in the 1960s and 1970s. In the province as a whole, lumber production increased by 49 percent between 1962 and 1971, but the number of sawmills decreased by 61 percent. The small operations were disappearing.[84]

Even small operators with TFLs felt pressure. In 1971 the TFL held by Bendickson Logging on Hardwicke Island and the adjacent mainland in the coastal region was acquired by Crown Zellerbach. Bendickson Logging employed about thirty men and the family had been active in logging in the area for over sixty years. A.B. Bendickson said that the company faced the choice of either expanding by adding needed specialists and obtaining additional capital, or associating with a company that already had those assets. Bendickson Logging continued as a contractor on the land, taking out logs for the new owner.[85]

The vagueness of the contractor clause remained controversial. In 1963, when there were thirty-nine TFLs in the province, a Forest Service report concluded that most major operators on the Coast were meeting the requirements. The minister, however, had allowed three companies to ignore the contractor clause. Moore-Whittington Lumber, with TFL 27, claimed that isolation and a small annual cut made using contractors unfeasible. F&R Logging said that its annual cut was too small to need outsiders. More controversially, Canadian Forest Products, with a TFL at Nimpkish, was granted an exemption because the company had always conducted its own operations and had no applications from contractors. In the Interior, three companies were found contracting out less than their commitment.[86]

Coastal truck loggers had other concerns with what was now known as the "30-50 percent clause." They believed that the clause implied that the contractor should be a "stump to dump" operator, meaning that the contractor would be responsible for the whole logging process, including felling trees at the stump, bucking logs, road building, yarding, and hauling the logs and dumping them at the conversion plant. What was often happening was that the various stages of the logging process were contracted out independently, with one company hired to do the hauling, another to do the bucking and felling, and another to build the roads. The truck loggers saw themselves as complete loggers; they wanted to control and operate the entire process. The piecemeal contracting, opined a TLA spokesperson in 1963, was "working to the serious detriment of the independent logging operator, reducing him from the category of a skilled integrated unit to that of a mere 'sharecropper.'"[87] The grievances concerning the contractor clause persisted. In 1969 some TFL holders argued that there were insufficient independents to do the whole job as one package, and truck loggers responded quickly that this was the fault of the major companies, who had let out their logging in a piecemeal fashion.[88]

The companies that performed particular duties in the production process were known as phase contractors. Some companies specialized in log hauling only. In 1949 W.E. "Bill" Schnare was the largest independent log hauler in the province. Based in Abbotsford, Bill Schnare and his son Stan began in the 1930s, and by 1950 their firm, S. & S. Trucking, operated a fleet of sixteen trucks and sixteen trailers. They contracted for the MacMillan company and Bloedel, Stewart & Welch on Vancouver Island, hauling logs from camps at Iron River, Great Central Lake, and Sarita.[89] In 1966 Greenwood Contractors, owned by Don MacMillan and Tommy Hamilton, had a crew of about fifteen men and operated on two sites on Vancouver Island. They contracted for the Pacific Logging Company, and in turn felling was done by S&B Logging and some of the truck hauling was done by another contractor, Nixon and Sons. Greenwood did the yarding and hoisting, and operated one truck.[90]

Relations between big and small companies were testy at times. Some major companies disliked the contractor clause. L.L.G. Bentley, vice president of Canadian Forest Products, felt that it was unnecessary and unfair, a result of political

Coastal loggers felling a tree, 1957.
MacMillan Bloedel Collection (UBC), BC 1930/440/9511

pressure. A 1963 report listed a string of contentious comments by Bentley: "The timber became available through our own efforts and our own money. I don't see why I should let anybody in when I have opened it up and developed it ... If there is any profit to be made in logging I think I'm entitled to it ... The fate of the independent operators if it were not for the TFL system, would be a hell of a lot worse than today ... If anyone can show us that they can operate more efficiently than we can, we will be glad to turn logging over to them."[91]

The report cited John Hemmingsen, vice president of logging for the MacMillan, Bloedel and Powell River Company, as being much more sympathetic to the contractor clause. In private, too, MacMillan, Bloedel and Powell River Company executives defended the independent logger, arguing that they were an asset to the large companies. The small logger served as a continuing reliable source of logs from timber not controlled by the company; a source of extra production in a hot market; and a source of equipment and men for contracting MacMillan, Bloedel and Powell River timber if required. The independent logger was also "valuable to us as a buffer against unrealistic *Union* demands that would break a small operation (wages and fringe benefits)."[92]

Interior winter logging, 1951.
BC Archives, NA-12482

In the Interior the use of logging contractors was extensive. In 1953 both Western Plywood in Quesnel and the S.M. Simpson Company of Kelowna used contractors for logging. Over fifty contractors worked for Western Plywood. Horace Simpson noted that "his group found the use of contractors perfectly satisfactory, and that they eliminated many of the headaches."[93] The contractors had an important role in the pulp and paper economy of the 1960s and 1970s, but they felt pressure. In the summer of 1966, thirty-six trucking and logging contractors quit working to protest the money paid by Crestbrook Timber in Cranbrook. The men returned when the company agreed to review the financial terms of each contract on an individual basis.[94]

In 1967 Peter Dyck, president of the Interior Logging Association, an association of small loggers formed in 1959, decried the disappearance of the contractors, blaming, in part, the big sawmill and pulp and paper companies. The low contract prices offered by the manufacturers, as well as higher taxes and stumpage costs, were threatening the survival of the small operators:

> In the process of development the major lumber producers saw fit to request the government to give them some assurance of further timber supply. By diligent lobbying they achieved this through fully committed SYU's, TFL's, PHL's, etc.
>
> We, the loggers and truckers kept mostly silent because the extent of our ambition was to contract for the lumber processors. After all they were our friends from the days of the early sixties when we worked together for more liberal legal load regulations. However, we soon found big business does not recognize the word "friend" and having lost our defense – the right to buy standing timber – many contractors were being forced into a price squeeze they could not live with. Some have gone broke and lost all. Others – like myself – realized we were getting nowhere, got out and salvaged what we could by a quick auction sale.
>
> In the long run this policy of merciless elimination of the legitimate logger can only do much harm. The mills need us just as bad as we need them and I do hope they will come to their senses before there are no independents left.[95]

In the early 1960s, the small Interior sawmills had been forced out of business or bought out, and now it seemed the turn of the small loggers.

The Perspective of the State

The small operators blamed the provincial government for their plight. This was not completely unwarranted. From the perspective of Forest Service officials and the government, large companies brought capital investment and had the financial wherewithal to weather the boom-and-bust economy better than small, poorly capitalized firms.[96] Experience had also shown that in tough economic times, desperate small operators were more likely to cut corners and run roughshod over the basic principles of scientific forestry. As a Prince George government forester had already noted in 1921, during an economic downturn and when outside interests were contemplating constructing a pulp mill in the area, "I certainly believe conditions in this Northern Interior, which are very bad and will always be bad until a permanent industry is established, justifies the Government in making pretty heavy concessions to get these men interested in immediate development. This skinning of timber lands by shoe string sawmills is a crime."[97] From a management perspective, the Forest Service recognized that the government was not willing to fund fully a forest department capable of managing the province on a sustained-yield basis. Large firms, however, could afford to hire professional foresters to look after the reforestation side of their companies.

While the government and Forest Service were very attentive to the needs of big companies and were luring outside capital investment, it does not follow that they expected the FML system to undermine small operators. Indeed, considering the large firms' initial wariness of the scheme, it was a surprise when these corporations rushed to take up as much timber as possible. The government's defence of the small operators, however, was not helped by C.D. Orchard, the province's chief forester from 1941 to 1956, who blamed small operators for their own misfortune. Speaking to the annual meeting of the Truck Loggers Association in January 1952, Orchard claimed that the small man was doomed. Just like oxen logging of the past, the small operator was fated to disappear. The problem was not the large companies but the small operator, who was "frustrated and bewildered," unable to keep up with rapid changes. And without the ability to engage in global marketing, like the big operations, the small firm had little chance to grow.

Accounts of the "small man doomed" speech were reprinted in newspapers across the province.[98] As public griping about the plight of small operators continued through the 1950s, Orchard had little sympathy. As he noted in his 1960 memoirs, despite the whining, small operators used the system to their advantage. According to him, small operators operating on slim margins wanted to be sheltered from competition and were capable of abusing the system. In one case, a disgruntled operator used a loud voice and political pressure to get cutting rights. He then appealed to the minister for the right to sell his licence, claiming falsely that he now had a heart condition and was unable to log. The request was granted on humanitarian grounds, but shortly thereafter, with the profit from the sale in his pocket, he was logging again elsewhere. The second owner sold the licence making a similar plea, but when the third licencee sought the same privilege, he was refused. "There was too much to be made by capital gain to keep small licences, which we very much favoured, in the hands of small operators," said Orchard. "Cupidity, lack of initiative, and their reluctance to accept attendant responsibilities, ruined the chances of small operators in the management licence system ... They, their misguided sympathizers, and professional agitators, spent their energies fighting the whole system."[99]

As Orchard's comments suggest, although small operators worried, they often did well financially. In 1964 two companies, Canadian Forest Products and Northwood Pulp, were committed to building pulp mills in Prince George. Both needed wood chips from local sawmills. The mill owners were in a good bargaining position, and pitted the two pulp companies against each other for chip contracts. The two companies offered high prices, guaranteed loans, and purchase of sawmill operations at high prices. Their employees were seeking out wood chip supplies long before the mills were ready to operate. As one frustrated Northwood official responsible for securing wood chip contracts noted in September 1964, the pulp and paper companies were "received by the lumbermen with courtesy," but always in "anticipation of obtaining from us more in the way of price or additional concessions."[100] On one occasion, the Northwood representative was trying to make an appointment with a mill owner, unaware that the Canadian Forest Products representative was sitting in the mill owner's office while his meeting was being scheduled.[101] In another instance, Fraser Lake Sawmills offered to provide chips to Northwood if Northwood backed a substantial loan; otherwise, Fraser Lake Sawmills was willing to sell its operation to Northwood.[102] In October 1966 the Leboe Lumber Company offered to sell out, but Northwood president A.H. Zimmerman felt that the asking price was "far too rich to consider."[103] An industry analyst from the Kamloops Forest District commented in 1970 that the number of sawmills in the region had shrunk by 25 percent in the past five years, and he began his magazine article with a question: "Is the day of the small mill over?"[104] Small operators were indeed anxious, but when many of them left the industry, especially if they held timber rights, they did so with a big bank account.

SMALL OPERATORS HAD AN IDENTITY that was given particular resonance by an accepted enemy, the government's timber policy. Pro-capitalist and anti-state, they were wary of monopoly and saw monopoly as a creation of government policies, not a result of the dynamics of capitalism, even though corporate concentration in timber rights was underway before the passage of sustained-yield legislation. Small operators did not disappear, and neither did the clamour to make more timber available to them and to allow more privately owned timber.[105]

   If competition, fear, and dissension defined the Fordist forest industry in BC, so too did unity: big and small companies in all sectors and all regions agreed that unions were not good for the industry. That is the subject of the next chapter.

3
Establishing Unions

On 3 September 1953, a Prince George newspaper editorial celebrated Labour Day, citing a new spirit of cooperation between workers and employers in Canada: "Trade unions themselves would be the first to acknowledge that the day of outright hostility between labor and management has ended, that narrow-mindedness on both sides has no place in the building of a greater Canada."[1] Just over three weeks later, lumber workers in the Northern Interior went on strike. Within a month, camps and mills in the Southern Interior were also shut down. It was a long, hard strike, punctuated by violence, which lasted into 1954: employers wanted to crush the union, and the union, the International Woodworkers of America (IWA), was fighting for its life in the region. The story of the building of the IWA in coastal British Columbia has been told before, but less well known is the history of its establishment in the Interior.[2] Almost unknown is the history of unionization in the pulp and paper industry. All three groups developed a new institutionalized relationship with employers, a hallmark of the Fordist era, in the years after 1940. So, in one sense the Prince George newspaper editorial was right: a new industrial relations system emerged in the 1940s.[3] As the Interior strike made clear, however, it was not yet established province-wide. Moreover, employer antagonism towards unions in all sectors and regions was never far below the surface. This chapter begins with the Coast and then discusses the Interior.

The Coastal Region in the 1930s
Besides hostile employers, union activists faced formidable difficulties organizing coastal camps and mills. Loggers were geographically dispersed in isolated camps up and down the coast, while mill workers were separated in various urban settings and small mill towns. Loggers and mill workers shared little history and geography. Operating in different work spaces, they also performed different jobs. The skills needed in the logging camps were largely irrelevant in the mills. This meant that besides being unfamiliar with each other's workplaces and immediate concerns, there was little personal interaction among people moving back and forth between the sectors. There was diversity within sectors too. Logging camps included highly paid fallers, buckers, hooktenders, and train engineers, as well as lesser skilled and lesser paid chokermen, whistle punks, and labourers. Similarly in the sawmills, highly paid sawyers, saw filers, tallymen, edgermen, and steam engineers worked in the same facilities as lumber pilers and clean-up men. In the

mills especially, there were also racial divisions; a significant minority of sawmill and shingle workers were of Asian descent. Worker transiency also made organization difficult; loggers were renowned for moving from camp to camp and for quitting jobs on short notice when conditions were unappealing, and sawmill workers, especially the less skilled, were notorious for enduring only short periods of work before moving on. The increased concentration of capital, which meant that more workers, both loggers and mill workers, were employed by the same company, helped create a greater degree of solidarity, but organizers still faced great difficulty in persuading all workers in the camps and mills to come together.

There had been previous attempts to organize workers. After the First World War, sawmill workers launched a series of strikes, with no lasting success. In 1919 loggers built a province-wide union for themselves, launching a series of strikes that won improved camp conditions on the Coast, but the union was short-lived. The recession of the early 1920s, internal disputes within the union, and a coordinated response by employers killed the organization.[4] In the late 1920s, a new Lumber Workers Industrial Union (LWIU), with roots in Ontario, began to organize in British Columbia. In 1931 the LWIU led a strike against the massive Canadian Western Lumber Company at Fraser Mills, near New Westminster, in the Lower Mainland. After a series of wage cuts, some 653 sawmill workers engaged in a two-and-a-half-month strike. Building on a strong community base, they stemmed the wage cuts, even if they did not gain union recognition.[5]

The LWIU launched its biggest strikes in the woods during the 1930s. Organizers focused on Vancouver Island, near Campbell River. Companies were moving further north on the mainland and west across Vancouver Island in their search for high-quality, accessible timber. Bloedel, Stewart & Welch closed its mainland logging camps, transferring equipment and crews to Campbell River to join other large operations, such as Elk River Timber, the Lamb Lumber Company, and Campbell River Timber. The district forester estimated that one-sixth of the total provincial cut in the early 1930s came from this small area.[6] In December 1931, 36 fallers and buckers near Campbell River went on strike over wages. The employer responded by closing the camp. In early February 1932, 50 loggers struck, again unsuccessfully. These initiatives alerted the provincial police, the government, and the logging companies to the existence of the union. In the fall of 1933, the LWIU was involved in a dispute at the Sproat Lake Lumber Company near Port Alberni, when 70 loggers went out. By this time, the union felt more confident and was represented in most Vancouver Island camps. With improving economic conditions due to the opening of the new British market, workers were keen to win back the losses of the previous four years. The men in the Vancouver Island camps had sufficient organizational strength in January 1934 to challenge employers, and a new wage proposal was presented to the companies. The BC Loggers' Association, representing the owners, rejected the proposal. On 27 January, loggers at Bloedel, Stewart & Welch camps near Campbell River went on strike. Over the next weeks, most of the larger operations on Vancouver Island were shut down. Campbell River and Port Alberni were the focal points of the strike.[7]

Wages were a major issue. In the early years of the Depression, there were a series of wage cuts as log markets weakened. The first came in the larger camps in December 1929, when a 10 percent reduction was imposed. There were further cuts through to 1933. By this time, hooktenders and high riggers averaged $4.80 to $5.00 per day; rigging slingers, $3.20 to $3.50; and chokermen, $2.50 to $3.00. Fallers and buckers, who were paid a piece rate, faced a similar decline in pay. In some smaller operations, loggers worked for only board and tobacco money. In January 1934, loggers wanted their wages to reflect the turnaround in the coastal lumber economy. Fallers and buckers demanded a 10 percent increase per thousand board feet and a guaranteed minimum daily wage of $4.00; high riggers wanted $6.50; hooktenders, $6.00; rigging slingers, $4.25; and chokermen, $3.50. The men demanded no Sunday work, time-and-a-half for overtime, and the sale of camp commissary goods at cost plus freight charges.

The strikers also wanted the abolition of the ruthless blacklist system that governed the lives of loggers. After 1920 the BC Loggers' Association, which represented the overwhelming majority of coastal logging companies, set up its own employment office, the Loggers' Agency, to monitor the workforce. This agency, with headquarters in Vancouver, sent men out to the coastal camps. All coastal camps submitted reports on their workers, and the agency collected this information on the work habits and union proclivities of the men. The intent was to keep poor workers and, more importantly, union activists out of coastal camps. Moreover, workers employed through the employment agency signed a contract that included a clause forbidding workers to "to invite or allow any person ... in the camp without the owner's permission."[8]

The intertwined issues of safety and speed-up also concerned loggers. Logging had always been dangerous work, but the rate of death in the woods rose in the 1930s. As a member of the Workmen's Compensation Board noted in 1932: "At one time the average used to be one [man] killed for every 50 million feet of logs hauled, now this has increased to one killed for every 47 million feet."[9] Workers blamed unsafe equipment and speed-up for the rising death toll. They argued that employers and foremen pushed men to work faster and thus less safely. If workers complained, they were fired and blacklisted. A Vancouver Island member of the provincial legislature noted in 1928: "There are altogether too many casualties in the logging industry and juries invariably return a verdict of accidental death ... When a man goes before a coroner's jury and tells the truth about deficient equipment, he is blacklisted in every logging camp in the country."[10]

This statement shows the importance of having a permanent organization to protect the men and to represent their long-term interests. The strikers in 1934 wanted the companies to recognize the elected camp committees as their legitimate representatives. Union recognition would eliminate the blacklist, allow workers to work safely without fearing the loss of their livelihood, and ensure that employers lived up to agreements. At one point during the strike, the employers agreed to recognize the camp committees as part of a broader settlement, but whether due to shortsightedness or an exaggerated sense of power, loggers voted to reject the package because they considered the proposed wage rates too low. Companies later accepted a richer wage schedule proposed by the provincial government, but withdrew the offer of union recognition. They began reopening camps using strikebreakers in the middle of April, and in early May the loggers, realizing that union recognition was not to be achieved, voted to return to work. The blacklist prevailed: camp committees were banned in all but a few operations and organizers were barred from the vast majority of coastal camps. There were no recorded logging strikes in British Columbia in 1935.[11]

The LWIU did not disappear. In 1934 it had established itself as the legitimate representative of the loggers, and through the twists and turns of the next years, it maintained a consistent leadership, largely communist, that retained the support of pro-union workers. Due to international political and union shifts, the British Columbia LWIU briefly merged with the Lumber and Sawmill Workers Union, which was affiliated with the United Brotherhood of Carpenters and Joiners. In 1937 there was another change. The BC lumber workers withdrew from the Carpenters and Joiners and joined with loggers and mill workers in the United States to form the International Woodworkers of America, affiliated with the fledgling Congress of Industrial Organizations (CIO). BC was District 1 in the new international union. Through these changes, the men from the LWIU days remained in charge. Harold Pritchett, the first president of District 1 in 1937, had been the chairman of the strike committee at Fraser Mills in 1931.

The last half of the 1930s was a difficult period for the union. Following the 1934 strike, the LWIU leaders noted five failings. Not involving sawmill workers had allowed mills to keep operating during the strike using stockpiled logs or imports from the US; larger funds of money and foodstuffs would have helped sustain the strike; better coordination would have enabled the union to mobilize workers more quickly to defeat the running of scabs; greater involvement of women would have increased solidarity; and more attention to educational work during the strike would have helped boost morale.[12] Yet to outline the problems was not to solve them, and the union struggled in the years after 1934. Women's auxiliaries of the lumber workers' union were formed in a number of places.[13] Greater attention was paid to organizing workers in sawmills, where speed-up was increasingly a pressing issue. In 1936 a sawmill worker, who with a partner was responsible for taking lumber off the pony edger, stated that the lumber was coming so fast that he could not keep up with the chain. The boss came around and chewed them out, "in no nice manner either," for being unable to pull sufficient lumber off the moving chain before it passed them.[14] Despite a few mill and camp strikes, however, largely on Vancouver Island, the union floundered.

In the last years of the 1930s, a strike at Blubber Bay on Texada Island, off the coast near Powell River, consumed the IWA's energy and money. It was an odd struggle for the union. At Blubber Bay, the Pacific Lime Company operated an open face mine that produced lime for BC and the American Pacific Northwest. Near the lime quarry, a small sawmill cut lumber for local markets and fuel for the lime kilns. The company employed 150 workers, 76 of whom were Chinese, and operated Blubber Bay as a company town. In 1937 the lumber workers' union became involved in a six-week strike at Blubber Bay against wage reductions. After a favourable settlement for the union, however, the company refused to live up to the agreement and engaged in questionable hiring practices to keep out union men. A major strike ensued, beginning in June 1938. It lasted eleven months and included violence, evictions from company houses, and arrests. Ultimately the company won. For the IWA, the loss was very costly in terms of both money and energy, leaving it a spent force at the onset of the Second World War.[15]

There was more to the Blubber Bay strike, however. Up to 1937, union activists concentrated on organizing workers in the camps and mills. This was not successful. The union was weak and the power of employers appeared unassailable. Then, in December 1937, the provincial government brought in Bill 94, the Industrial Disputes Conciliation and Arbitration Act (ICA Act). It seemed that the government was supporting workers, and that British Columbia was getting its equivalent of the American Wagner Act, which had stimulated union organization in the US after it was passed in 1935. In Port Alberni, the new provincial legislation prompted an aggressive organizing drive in area sawmills. The two main companies responded by dismissing seventy-five men. The companies argued that it was due to an economic downturn, but the union claimed anti-union discrimination. The workers appealed to the provincial government, but the government refused to take the workers' perspective and the union was defeated.[16] Blubber Bay became a larger test of the new legislation.

The ICA Act was drafted by BC Minister of Labour George Pearson. Pearson felt that as soon as labour conditions "stabilized" in the United States, American unions would make strenuous efforts to organize BC workers. "During this attempt," he argued, "industry will suffer tremendously in this Province, through strikes, unless we are prepared to meet it."[17] Bill 94 was designed to provide a bureaucratic framework to manage industrial disputes with the least possible impact on the economy. Compulsory conciliation and arbitration before any strikes or lockouts could occur were the main features of the bill. The measure sanctioned unions that registered with the government and followed specific regulations. The actual role of the government in the organization of an industrial facility, though, was unclear, as Port Alberni mill workers found. Blubber Bay also exposed the weaknesses of the act and the position of the government. One Blubber Bay company official commented: "It was quite apparent ... that the Minister was in considerable doubt and confusion as to the exact meaning of many parts of the Bill."[18] At the request of the union, the conciliation and arbitration procedures of the new ICA Act were invoked. In the end, the board set up under the act supported the company, and despite the overwhelming support of the Blubber Bay workers for the union, refused to recognize the IWA as the legitimate, legal representative of the workers. The provincial government was willing to support employee representatives in the plants and even some unions, but not those linked to American-based unions led by radicals. The union and the employees challenged the decision but the weight of the united forces of the company and the state were too much.

Although the IWA leaders railed against the government's actions and the ICA Act, they were not against state involvement in labour relations per se. The ICA Act was inadequate, but a better, improved piece of legislation, similar to the Wagner Act in the US, would give the union legitimacy and legal protection, and it would force companies to negotiate with unions supported by a majority of workers in a plant or industry. For union activists this offered an opportunity. The traditional method of organizing, building up a democratic, grassroots organization with support in all the camps and mills of the province, stalled in the late 1930s, and so the IWA complemented on-the-ground organization with a political strategy. As Stephen Gray notes: "The ICA Act, if far short of the dreamed-of Canadian Wagner Act, was an opening through which the union hoped eventually to find a legislative solution to its organizational problems."[19] The engagement at Blubber Bay was the beginning of a new strategy by the IWA that would continue in the 1940s.

The situation was similar in the pulp and paper industry at the end of the 1930s; the union had made breakthroughs in two operations but other employers remained adamantly anti-union. There had been unions in the North American pulp and paper industry even before there were pulp mills in British Columbia. In July 1909, the International Brotherhood of Pulp, Sulphite and Paper Mill Workers (IBPSPMW) was granted a charter by the American Federation of Labor (AFL). A second AFL union with headquarters in the US, the International Brotherhood of Paper Makers (IBPM), was also active in the industry, and in 1909 the two worked out a truce. The IBPM represented the more skilled workers, especially on the paper machines, while the IBPSPMW represented the less skilled. The IBPM was stable, but its exclusivity meant that it had less room to grow, and so the IBPSPMW expanded much more rapidly, taking in workers in paper preparation and handling as well as workers in the converting operations. The IBPSPMW grew steadily from 1,500 members in 1910 to over 15,000 in the early 1920s. A disastrous strike against wage cuts in a New York mill, lasting from 1922 to 1926, devastated the union, however. North American membership in 1926 was only 6,000.[20]

Powell River was the site of union organization in this early period. In 1914 the IBPM established Local 142 in the mill, representing a small number of skilled workers. In the labour upsurge after 1916, the general mill workers became more militant. At a meeting on 7 May 1917, they decided to quit if they did not get a 15-cent per hour raise and the eight-hour workday. Around noon the next day, the company acceded to their demands. The workers then sent a letter, complete with the signatures of 250 mill workers, to the headquarters of the IBPSPMW requesting to join the international. A local charter was granted and by the end of June there were 450 paid-up members in the new Local 76. Over the next years, there were strikes, coordinated with the IBPM, and successes, including the achievement of the union shop. The success was short-lived, however. In July 1921, as economic conditions deteriorated, the company announced a 10-cent per hour wage cut, which the local accepted, effective 1 September. The company was not finished. Workers were dismissed in August, and an announcement followed that the Powell River Company was going to discontinue recognition of the union at the end of September. On 1 October 1921, a new wage schedule was imposed, and the company reserved the right to bring in the ten-hour day. Further dismissals, on the charge of disloyalty to the company, followed. The local was dead, unable to maintain the requisite 7 regular dues-paying members in the plant.[21]

Unionism revived in the 1930s. The Powell River Company thwarted a union drive in 1934 by firing union activists. The dismissals occurred in the wake of a provincial election that saw the chief chemist from the Ocean Falls pulp mill, Ernest Bakewell, elected as a representative of the socialist Co-operative Commonwealth Federation (CCF) to represent the Mackenzie riding, a constituency that included Powell River. There was much speculation that the mill workers were fired because of their connection to the CCF, but the mill's general manager was adamant that they were fired because of their union activism. He recognized that at least 60 percent of the mill's 1,250 employees had voted CCF in the election, but the company had "never interfered in any way with the political leanings of ... employees and we have as happy a community as any company I have known." Union agitators, however, were different. They were dismissed and "some of these men were not C.C.F. supporters."[22] Democracy in the political arena was accepted but not in the industrial sphere.

In the spring of 1937, union agitation in Powell River returned, despite a 5 percent wage increase on 1 March. An IBPSPMW organizer came from Everett, Washington, in the middle of May, meeting secretly with workers in the woods and on beaches, away from company premises and beyond the surveillance of the company and provincial police. By 15 May, the Powell River local had 160 paid-up members. A vote on 27 May endorsed the union: 1,132 voted in favour and 106 voted against. IBPM Local 142, representing about 350 workers, and IBPSPMW Local 76, representing over 1,000 workers, were once again in operation.[23] Negotiations with the company ensued and an agreement was finally signed covering the period from 1 August 1937 to 30 April 1939.[24]

In the heady days of 1937, British Columbia pulp and paper workers, with the support of the internationals, organized beyond Powell River. At Ocean Falls, IBPSPMW Local 312 and IBPM Local 360 were established, and by July an international organizer claimed that the plant was 100 percent organized. In August IBPM Local 367 was set up at Sidney Roofing and Paper, a converting operation in Victoria.[25] Other operations were more intractable. The Port Mellon mill reopened on 23 August 1937, after a shutdown, but workers with union sympathies, who had been meeting in Vancouver in anticipation of the start-up, were not hired back. The mill manager stated that "rather than recognize the union he would shut the plant down."[26]

The two operations of BC Pulp and Paper were even more difficult. The facilities at the company towns of Port Alice, on northern Vancouver Island, and Woodfibre, on Howe Sound, were very isolated and the towns were controlled by the company. Led by president Laurence Killam, the company made it difficult for organizers. To get into these towns, all outsiders, including "doctors, lawyers, and reputable salesmen," had to acquire a pass from company offices in Vancouver. Public transportation went only within ten miles of Port Alice, enabling the company to keep out people that they did not like. According to a provincial police officer, the firm investigated all workers' histories and hired no union men.[27] In the fall of 1937, an international organizer spent two weeks trying to organize Port Alice workers but was able to sign up only one man, and this man lived at Quatsino, the town ten miles from the mill.[28]

In late 1937 the international pulp and paper market entered a period of distress, spelling the end of the organizational drive. The Port Mellon mill shut down indefinitely, and the IBPSPMW local was officially defunct in February 1939.[29] In Powell River, despite the downturn and operating on average only sixteen days per month in 1938, the locals survived, signing a new agreement with the company in April 1939.[30] The Ocean Falls locals also survived despite difficulties, and continued to sign agreements with the employer, Pacific Mills.[31]

The 1930s saw union breakthroughs in the forest industry, but the IWA, the IBPSPMW, and the IBPM were fragile entities. Employers remained vigilant against union incursions. In 1940 organization in the pulp and paper industry was at low ebb, and the IWA was unsuccessful it its attempt to organize three logging camps that year. The outgoing chairman of the BC Loggers' Association, C.D. Anderson, captured the sentiments of employers in the early years of the Second World War in his January 1941 address: "And so another year has ended with our members running their own business without Union regulation or Union permission."[32]

Employers remained confident that despite breakthroughs in the forest industry in the US, British Columbia, with its different labour legislation, designed to prevent strikes and not to support collective bargaining, would continue to be union-free. The industry was also willing to expend money and energy to ensure this result.[33]

The Workforce during the Second World War

The war years brought full employment, more women in production facilities, and an even more transient work force. Longstanding racial and ethnic tension remained challenges for organizers. Unions pursued two tactics. First, both the IWA and the pulp and paper unions stepped up organizational activities, attempting to bring more workers into the fold. Second, unions, especially the IWA, sought an improved industrial relations act. The two strategies were intertwined. A more militant, united membership could pressure the state for legislative changes, while favourable legislation would help organize workers in the camps and the mills.

The presence of workers of Asian descent was a longstanding feature of the coastal forest industry in BC. Industry data from the late 1920s and early 1930s give a good picture of the racial makeup of the workforce (Table 1).

The trend, however, was toward fewer workers of Asian descent, with these workers making up a smaller proportion of the workforce. Estimates based on government census data, which differ somewhat from 1931 industry figures, show that in 1951, about 1 percent of provincial loggers were of Asian descent, down from 10 percent in 1931. In the saw and shingle mills, workers of Asian descent constituted about 7 percent of the labour force in 1951, down from around 23 percent in 1931. In the pulp and paper industry, Asians made up less than 4 percent in 1951, whereas they had constituted some 16 percent in 1931.[34] The declining Asian presence in the pulp and paper industry, as well as the lower percentage in sawmills, is explained in part by restrictive immigration policies and the evacuation of the Japanese from the Coast during the Second World War. In the spring of 1942, some 700 Japanese employees of provincial pulp and paper mills were evacuated, mostly from Ocean Falls but also from Port Alice and Woodfibre. Some of the men had been in the mills for twenty years.[35] As we shall see, the pulp and paper unions also played a role in keeping out Asian workers.

Great Central Sawmills, some twelve miles from Port Alberni on Vancouver Island, operated from 1925 to 1952, and surviving employee records, which are especially rich for the period from 1934 to 1942, expose some of the dynamics of race in provincial mills.[36] The sawmill, the fourth largest on Vancouver Island, employed between 273 and 285 men from 1936 to 1942. Workers of Asian descent made up 61 percent of the workforce in July 1932, 54 percent in April 1936, 42 percent in June 1940, and 38 percent in April 1942. In terms of ethnic background, there were Chinese, Japanese, and Sikh workers (see Table 2). The most striking feature of the

Table 1

Numbers of forest industry workers of Asian descent and their percentages of the total workforce, 1929-35

Workers		1929	1931	1933	1935
Logging	Chinese	700 (4.0%)	142 (2.0%)	280 (3.8%)	301 (3.1%)
	Japanese	422 (2.5%)	211 (3.0%)	301 (4.1%)	217 (2.2%)
	Sikh/East Indian	84 (0.5%)	31 (0.4%)	34 (0.5%)	47 (0.4%)
	Total Asian	1,206 (7.0%)	384 (5.4%)	615 (8.4%)	565 (5.7%)
	Total	17,196	7,186	7,286	9,846
Sawmills	Chinese	1,644 (12.0%)	601 (7.8%)	717 (9.3%)	567 (6.7%)
	Japanese	1,411 (10.3%)	903 (11.8%)	850 (11.0%)	733 (8.6%)
	Sikh/East Indian	784 (5.7%)	380 (5.0%)	448 (5.8%)	428 (5.0%)
	Total Asian	3,839 (28.0%)	1,884 (24.6%)	2,015 (26.1%)	1,728 (20.3%)
	Total	13,754	7,658	7,701	8,497
Shingle	Chinese	753 (31.2%)	304 (25.3%)	395 (23.7%)	643 (25.6%)
mills	Japanese	129 (5.4%)	47 (3.9%)	62 (3.7%)	122 (4.9%)
	Sikh/East Indian	15 (0.6%)	0 (0.0%)	5 (0.3%)	1 (0.04%)
	Total Asian	897 (37.2%)	351 (29.2%)	462 (27.7%)	766 (30.5%)
	Total	2,413	1,204	1,670	2,509
Pulp and	Chinese	64 (1.9%)	55 (1.7%)	34 (1.4%)	201 (6.5%)
paper	Japanese	598 (17.9%)	443 (13.6%)	382 (15.3%)	475 (15.5%)
	Sikh/East Indian	0 (0.0%)	0 (0.0%)	0 (0.0%)	0 (0.0%)
	Total Asian	662 (19.8%)	498 (15.3%)	416 (16.7%)	676 (22.0%)
	Total	3,337	3,254	2,493	3,072

Source: University of British Columbia, COFI Papers, Box 66, File 9.

table is the disappearance of the Japanese from the workplace. There were 29 Japanese employees at Great Central on 8 December 1941, the day after the attack on Pearl Harbor. Sixteen were Japanese nationals, 5 were naturalized Canadians, and 8 had been born in Canada. Eleven of the workers had wives and families living in the community at Great Central Lake. Shigezo Fukasaka had a wife and five children, and C. Shotaro Kitamura had a wife and three children. The other married men had one or two children. All told, the Japanese community at Great Central Lake consisted of 58 people; by the spring of 1942, they were all gone.

At work in the 1930s, the sheds were the preserve of the Japanese. In 1934 and 1936, in fact, only Japanese worked in the sheds. The shed foreman, S. Fukasaka,

Table 2

Asian workers at Great Central Sawmills

	July 1932	April 1936	June 1940	April 1942
Chinese	28 (27.5%)	54 (36%)	50 (43.5%)	71 (66.4%)
Japanese	42 (41.2%)	47 (31.3%)	34 (29.6%)	00 (0%)
Sikh/East Indian	32 (31.3%)	49 (32.7%)	31 (26.9%)	36 (33.6%)
Total Asian	102	150	115	107
Total Workforce	166	276	274	285

Source: Tabulated from BC Archives, MacMillan Bloedel, Alberni Pacific Division, Schedule of Wages, 1930-1979, Add MSS-1641, Reel A1237.

was Japanese, as were the rest of the crew of twelve. By 1940 the ethnic mix had changed. The foreman was white and the crew consisted of three Japanese, seven whites, and one Chinese. By April 1942, after the evacuation of the Japanese, the ethnic mix had changed again. The foreman was white, but the whole crew of eight was Chinese. The Japanese were also very prominent in the dry kilns. The kiln operator was always white but Japanese made up most of the workers. The Japanese in the dry kilns constituted a contract crew; the company sublet the loading and unloading of the kilns to a Japanese contractor. The contract crew consisted of a foreman and a number of workers called, in a straightforward manner, loaders and unloaders. In 1941 the Japanese contract crew consisted of twelve men and the foreman, S. Fukasaka, who had formerly been the Japanese foreman in the sheds. Besides the twelve Japanese in the kiln division, there were seven Chinese workers and one white; the latter was the kiln operator, A.C. Raikes. After the evacuation of the Japanese, the Chinese took over the dry kilns. In April 1942 the dry kiln consisted of fourteen Chinese workers and three white workers.

Japanese were prominent in the sheds and dry kilns but they also worked in other parts of the mill. In 1936, when there were forty-seven Japanese workers at Great Central, three were in the shipping and yard crew, five were in the day shift mill crew, five worked in the night shift mill, and ten worked in the planer mill. Although the Chinese came to dominate the dry kiln division, they were also distributed throughout the mill. In 1936 there were fifty-four Chinese workers in the mill. Four worked in the power and maintenance division, sixteen were on the shipping and yard crew, eight worked in the day mill, four in the night mill, twelve in the day planer, and eight in the kilns. The East Indian workforce was much more concentrated. There were no Sikhs in the kilns, the sheds, the planer mill, or power and maintenance. They worked either in the sawmill or in the yard crew. In 1936 fourteen of the Sikhs worked in the day mill, eleven in the night mill, and twenty-three on the yard crew.

Throughout the mill, particular jobs were associated with particular ethnic groups. The power and maintenance division was a white preserve, employing skilled tradesmen such as machinists, millwrights, and carpenters, as well as steam engineers. If a job involved lifting, manipulating, or piling heavy, green lumber, then the worker was likely of East Indian descent. Feeding the resaw; manoeuvring the lumber through the edger, resaw, and kiln jump rolls; and pulling lumber off the green chain were almost exclusively East Indian occupations. East Indians rarely operated machines, but Japanese and Chinese workers did.

Asians were concentrated at the bottom of the wage ladder. This was partly because they worked at less skilled jobs, but ethnicity was also an independent variable. When white and Asian workers did the same job, Asians were often paid less. In the spring of 1936, the white firemen were paid 45 cents per hour while the one Chinese fireman received 40 cents. White carloaders were paid 40 cents per hour, but Japanese carloaders got only 35 cents. White doggers received 45 cents, while the Japanese and Chinese doggers got only 40 cents. There was also a pecking order within the Asian workforce. In 1941 the company calculated the average daily wage of mill workers: white workers averaged $5.36 per day, East Indians $4.37, Japanese $4.25, and Chinese $4.04. Statistics from 1942 show that when doing the same job, East Indian workers earned more than workers of Chinese descent.

Mills, camps, and their environs were complex social environments. Workers were spatially and ethnically separated as they performed their duties, building on patterns that had been formed in the nineteenth century. Owners manipulated the workforce to maintain internal divisions, divisions reinforced by white workers, whose pay was augmented by the presence of lower-paid workers with limited opportunity for advancement and who shared the prejudices of the broader white community. Within ethnic segments, too, hierarchies based on constructions of skill also differentiated workers. Beyond the mill gate, the community was divided into ethnically defined areas. In Great Central Lake, distinct areas housed workers of Japanese, Chinese, Indian, and European descent.

A labour shortage was another feature of the war years. There was an abundance of workers in the early and mid-1930s, but as the coastal industry recovered, workers were in demand. By the summer of 1939, William Black, head of the Loggers' Agency, an organization operated by the BC Loggers' Association to hire workers for coastal camps, claimed that "there were now between 800 to 1000 more men working in the woods than at this time last year, and substantially more than the previous high year of production namely 1929, thus accounting for shortage of men for skilled occupations in the woods."[37] The Second World War created a labour crisis in the British Columbia forest industry, especially in the woods. Men left to serve in the armed forces and to work in other industries in the cities, which also needed labour. Japanese workers were uprooted and there was little immigration. There was also a surge in demand for wood products. In the spring of 1942, Black said that they had "unfilled orders of 377 men, including 139 fallers and 160 rigging men."[38] They expected to lose more men to the shipyards in Vancouver and to the fishing industry as summer approached. Sawmills also experienced a labour shortage, and it was estimated that because of it production had been "reduced by from 10 to 15 percent per shift."[39] According to employers, sloppy management and control of labour by the federal government worsened the problem. The chairman of the BC Loggers' Association noted in his 1944 annual report: "The importance of [our Loggers'] Agency and the incompetence of the Government Employment Service are too well known to all of you to dwell upon."[40] In late 1944, the government estimated that the BC sawmill and logging industries could easily absorb another 1,500 men if they were available.[41] By 1946 the situation had eased, but there was still a shortage.[42] The forest industries had tried to cope with the problem by recruiting workers from elsewhere in Canada. In 1942 Black made a special trip to Edmonton and Calgary to recruit workers, and thereafter there was a concerted effort to attract farmworkers to BC forests after the prairie harvest.[43]

The pulp and paper mills also had difficulties recruiting sufficient labour. Turnover was high. At Powell River, where the mill's complement was roughly 1,250 workers, some 800 local men entered the armed forces between 1939 and late 1943; 650 of these were employees, while the rest were potential employees. In the first ten months of 1943 at Ocean Falls, which employed some 850 workers, the mill hired 983 men, but during the same period 1,108 left their employ.[44] Workers from Vancouver were choosy and reluctant to go to the isolated mill towns, and workers brought in from central and eastern Canada did not always work out satisfactorily.[45]

One solution was to take on more female workers. Census data give a glimpse into the makeup of the workforce in 1941 and 1951. In logging in 1941, there were only 162 women in a total provincial workforce of 18,296, and they were all in traditional female occupations, such as cook, stenographer, or waitress. Ten years later, the pattern was the same, and census data provide similar pictures in pulp and paper mills and sawmills. The census, which records populations every ten years, does not capture the surge of women into the production end during the Second World War. Logging remained traditional, but sawmills, shingle mills, and pulp and paper facilities hired women to replace workers who had gone overseas or who had gone to different jobs elsewhere in the province.

At Ocean Falls, where Pacific Mills had a pulp and paper mill and a sawmill, women began to be hired in October 1942. The company constructed three new restrooms and set up a female dormitory, with a matron in charge, to house some 120 women. By the summer of 1943, there were 146 female employees out of a total of 1,200, including 56 in the sawmill. With low seniority and in line with gender stereotypes, women worked largely in secondary roles. One exception was Eleanor Stade, who worked as a sawyer, one of the most skilled and important jobs in a mill. Stade came to Ocean Falls from Chilliwack in the fall of 1942, and began working as a sorter. She next worked as a planer's helper, and then as a dogger on the pony carriage. One day the sawyer fell ill and Stade volunteered to take over. She had been watching the sawyer's duties for some time and was given a chance. She worked out well and soon the company was bragging that it had the "only female sawyer on the continent engaged in cutting aeroplane spruce."[46]

At the Powell River newsprint plant, there were sixty "girls" in production jobs in early 1943. Before the war, the company had not hired women for work outside the office. The women took over jobs "in the beater room, finishing room, screen room wet machines, pulp and paper testing departments and in other sections." The company hired local women. Margaret Moriarty, who supervised and assisted female employees, was a trained nurse, "well qualified to advise and assist women in special problems arising from industrial employment."[47] In September 1943, there were thirty-four single and fifty-two married women between the ages of eighteen and forty employed at the plant. Sixteen had husbands and four had sons in active service. Twenty of the women had children under sixteen years of age.[48]

Except for plywood mills, women largely left the plants after the war.[49] The experience of women in the plywood sector was different for a number of reasons. First, although there had been plywood plants for a number of years, production expanded dramatically during the war. At a time of labour shortage, women were recruited to new jobs. Since they were not replacing men, and thus were not expected to leave at the end of hostilities, many continued in what were now women's jobs after the war.[50] Second, the manufacture of plywood involved gluing and pressing together thin sheets of veneer. These light sheets could be readily manipulated by women, overcoming concerns about the need for male brawn. Canadian Western Lumber Company, at Fraser Mills, employed 100 women, working three shifts, in 1942. Another plywood plant employed about 400 women and 200 men during the war. BC Plywoods employed about 160 "girls" out of a workforce of 560 in 1942.[51] The Alberni Plywood plant also hired more women during the war. Census data show that women remained prominent in the plywood sector after the war.[52]

The trade journals portrayed women as more punctual, more safety conscious, more reliable, more responsible, and more patient, and thus suitable for detail work. Women also apparently elevated the level of morality, dress, cleanliness, and conversation on the job. However, one exasperated and overexuberant company official at the Thomsen and Clark plywood mill in Vancouver suggested that at least some of this was cant. He captured another side in a 1942 directive to matrons regarding the women's living quarters:

As from this date no women employees shall throw paper or cigarette butts on the
floor, put hair or any other articles in the wash basins, mark the walls with rouge, or
in any other manner mark or misuse company property.

Failure to comply with this order will result in dismissal for any party or parties
accused, whether or not the accused be guilty.[53]

Paternalism and self-interest informed attitudes toward women workers. In late
1940, the IBPSPMW locals negotiated an agreement that covered women working
at the mills in Ocean Falls and Powell River. Where women could do the established
job, they received the going job rate, but if it required two women to replace one
man, they would be paid 7 cents an hour below the base rate.[54] They also agreed that
no man would be replaced against his will, and that no new women would be hired
until men on the seniority list had been taken care of.[55] It was further determined
"that no married women would be employed with children unless they could as-
sure officials of the Company that these children would be adequately taken care of,
since they could not contribute to child delinquency. At the same time preference
would be given to single girls in the community."[56] War labour shortages led to
relaxation of the terms, but at the war's end, married women were laid off first and
the union secured a policy that no married women would be employed whose husbands were gainfully employed. The international president-secretary of the
IBPSPMW, John P. Burke, disagreed with the action of the BC locals, making the
case that the union frowned on discrimination "against women just because they
have obeyed natural law and have married."[57] But H.L. Hansen, who had negotiated
the policies of the 1940s, held his ground: "We feel that a married woman's place is
in the home, not in the plant or working in other industries, because this invariably
happens, particularly in isolated communities. The husband works in a mill; the
wife goes out and takes a job in the store or laundry or other such work and because
she has her husband's income in addition to her own, she works for sub-standard
wages, which isn't conducive to good Trade Union principles."[58] Hansen's perspective prevailed. Women were not noticeably active in the union.[59]

More attention was paid to bringing workers of Asian descent into the unions.
At Pacific Mills, the 200 Japanese pulp and paper workers were solid members of
Local 312 from its inception in 1937. A special Japanese Section of the local was
established, with its own officers, and Japanese unionists helped organize other
mills. Since many Japanese could not read English, they translated the constitution and bylaws of the union into their language. By 1941 all Japanese employees at
Ocean Falls belonged to the union, whereas 19 whites did not. At the beginning of
the organizing drive at Ocean Falls, the union moved to reduce the difference in
wages between Japanese and other workers, and by 1942 the wage differential was
gone.[60] This pleased the company's competitor at Powell River as well, as that
operation hired no Asian workers.

The Woodfibre and Port Alice operations were difficult to organize, but Chinese workers posed a particular problem. During an organizational drive at Woodfibre in 1944, 90 percent of the white workers joined Local 494, but only 45 of the 150 Chinese workers, despite the activities of Thomas Wong, a Chinese organizer, and the translation of union literature into Chinese.[61] The IWA, too, was conscious of the necessity of enrolling Asian workers, and hired organizers of Asian descent. In 1942 Darshan Singh was the recording secretary of the Victoria local and Fred Lowe was the union's Chinese interpreter.[62] In 1944 Roy Mah became the first Chinese-Canadian to have a full-time position with the union, and Darshan Singh was on the district executive. The union published a Chinese version of its newspaper.[63] IWA leaders also spoke up in favour of rights for minorities. In 1943 the president of the IWA, Harold Pritchett, accompanied the leader of the CCF, Harold Winch, and nine Sikhs when they met with the provincial cabinet, demanding "British justice and employment of democratic rights for the East Indian community of British Columbia."[64]

Despite the seeming reconciliation between workers of Asian descent and other workers, the story was complicated. At the same time that the pulp and paper unions were enrolling Japanese workers and fighting for pay equity at Ocean Falls, they secured agreements with the company to hire no more Japanese workers. The company stood by the agreement, but in 1941 began hiring more Chinese employees. The union was furious, as this undermined their goal of removing all workers of Asian descent from the mill over time.[65] The goal of white workers was to bring Japanese workers into the union in order to get it established, and this meant protecting the rights of existing Japanese workers and reducing the wage differential between whites and Asians. At the same time, white workers wanted to prevent any further employment of Asian workers. Through attrition, there would be no more workers of Asian descent in the mill. The IBPSPMW organizer noted in 1937: "This makes the problem a very complex one."[66]

The IWA was more accepting. A September 1945 resolution proposed by the IWA's BC executive demanded full rights of citizenship, freedom of movement, and full restoration of property to all citizens of Japanese origin whose lives had been disrupted during the war. Still, this caused some controversy within the union. At the October meeting of the district council, one delegate noted that while he supported the resolution, he knew that the members of his sublocal at Chemainus had no desire to see the Japanese returned to the Coast, and he had been instructed to vote against the resolution. The delegate from Local 1-71 agreed, but he did note that the union rights of the Japanese workers had to be respected. In the end, the resolution was endorsed.[67]

Another problem for union organizers during the war was the fluctuation in the workforce. Often full employment and the great demand for workers in the forest industry are interpreted as a great boon to union organizers, but this state of affairs also led to increased worker mobility. Workers were leaving jobs to join the armed forces; disenchanted workers quit, knowing that they could easily be hired elsewhere; and workers followed rumours of higher wages in other camps or other sectors, leaving one logging camp for another or for another industry, such as shipbuilding. In the fall of 1940, loggers at a Vancouver Island camp demanded a wage increase and circulated a petition. By the time they got to a second meeting over the issue, most of those who had initially signed the petition had left in search of better wages. By 1942 the problem was so pressing that the IWA launched an educational campaign to stop it.[68] The pulp and paper unions faced the same problem, a problem that undercut the stability of established locals as well as organizing drives. In 1943 the Ocean Falls local suggested that a booklet on the successes and history of the union might help give transient workers a better understanding of its importance.[69]

Victories on the Coast

Overall, though, the buoyant economy, the labour shortage, the increasing public acceptance of unionism, and the examples of other workers across North America in areas such as the steel and automobile industries aided organization, and the ensuing pressure pushed recalcitrant companies to accept unionization. During the Second World War, the three non-union pulp and paper mills were organized. At Port Mellon, a new IBPSPMW local was established in July 1941, but despite some initial optimism, the union still struggled to win recognition from the company. In May 1942, a provincial board recommended recognition of Local 297, and in the next months an agreement was signed between the local and the Sorg Paper Company.[70]

Woodfibre and Port Alice remained non-union, and in 1943 the international hired Powell River Company employee and union activist Henry L. "Stubby" Hansen as international representative. His job was to organize the two outlying operations, although he was also expected to make headway in the Vancouver converting plants, which were being organized under the auspices of IBPSPMW Local 433, which had been established in 1941. Woodfibre was chosen as the breakthrough plant but progress was slow. A local was chartered and Hansen used fifteen former IBPSPMW members now working at Woodfibre to spearhead the drive. He held meetings off company premises at nearby Squamish, fourteen miles from Woodfibre. By April there were 25 paid-up members. In mid-April Hansen challenged the company, which had responded to the union drive by establishing a company-run council. He crashed a meeting of the company union after sneaking onto company property on a fishing boat, forcing the workers to vote on whether or not he should be expelled. Much to the surprise of management, the men voted to allow the union representative to remain in the hall.[71] The Woodfibre local was certified by the end of the year, and Port Alice was organized in 1945.

The pulp and paper plants were now organized and recognized. The Powell River Company had about 1,400 mill employees, Pacific Mills 1,200, Sorg Paper 300, and Woodfibre and Port Alice a combined total of about 1,130.[72] In Vancouver, the Vancouver Converters Local 433 had a number of box, bag, and envelope companies organized and had negotiated contracts.[73] After the war, when new pulp and paper mills came online, the union began negotiating with the company even before any workers were hired. In 1953 the IBPSPMW and the IBPM represented some 4,800 workers in nine coastal pulp and paper mills, as well as workers in a number of Vancouver converter plants.[74]

The IWA also established itself in the 1940s. Loggers on Vancouver Island were at the forefront of the struggle. In the summer of 1941, some 330 loggers employed by the Lake Logging Company at Cowichan Lake struck, mainly over the issues of seniority, leaves of absence, and union recognition. The workers rejected an employer offer on 30 July by a vote of 231 to 18, and the dispute went to arbitration; the workers won a favourable decision in October.[75] At a nearby Ladysmith camp of the Comox Logging Company, loggers reached an agreement with the company in March 1942. There were 250 loggers in the camp, and 225 were union men.[76] The IWA was also making headway in the mills. At the MacMillan Plywood Plant in Vancouver on 4 May 1942, workers, in a government-supervised vote, chose an IWA slate over a non-aligned employee committee to be their bargaining agent by a vote of 352 to 138.[77] Workers in this plant had been trying to overturn a company union for a number of years, and many activists had lost their jobs because of their support for the union.[78]

At a conference of delegates in Nanaimo on 1 November 1942, the IWA district council articulated its strategy. The union executive was committed to full production and total efficiency in support of the war effort. To attain this, the executive counselled cooperation between union and management, and the establishment of joint committees to deal with eliminating wasted time and materials, rates of absenteeism, and worker incentives. Separate committees, though, were necessary to handle collective bargaining, which would deal with wages, hours, working conditions, and job security. As Nigel Morgan, Canadian international executive board member, noted: "Indeed, unless proper consideration is given to the establishment of decent working conditions, adequate wages, the regulation of hours, so as to prevent undermining of productive health and energies, the work of our Production Committees will be seriously curtailed in evidence."[79] The final aspect of the IWA's strategy was to secure favourable labour legislation, labour law similar to the Wagner Act in the United States.[80] Pressure from unions, including the IWA; the growing popularity of the CCF; and the provincial government's desire to stabilize war production led to a new Industrial Conciliation Act in 1943. The major breakthrough for the IWA, however, came in a dispute that took place under the jurisdiction of federal labour law.

By the summer of 1941, IWA organizers had established a union presence in eight camps on the Queen Charlotte Islands that employed some 650 loggers. Camp delegates drew up a list of demands, which was endorsed by the men in the camps, and a union negotiating committee began meeting with the companies in October. Union recognition was the key union demand. Talks with the four main companies proceeded through 1941 and 1942, and the federal Department of Labour became involved. Logging operations had been designated a vital war industry, and as such, labour relations in the Queen Charlotte Islands camps came under federal jurisdiction. Like the provincial government, Mackenzie King's federal Liberal government sought to reduce work stoppages as more and more workers joined unions and engaged in job action in the early 1940s. Federal legislation encouraged, but did not force, companies to bargain with representatives of their workers. Results were disappointing. In the BC logging industry, reflecting the national pattern, companies stalled; despite protracted negotiations, they had no intention of recognizing the IWA in their camps.

Two things raised the stakes in the evolving conflict. First, the Queen Charlotte Islands camps produced Sitka spruce, which was being used in the construction of fighter airplanes, notably the Mosquito. Its lightness and strength, as well as its ease of repair, created a demand for this commodity. The federal government set up an agency, Aero Timber Products, which absorbed one of the Queen Charlotte Islands logging companies, Allison Logging. Also important was the significance of the Queen Charlotte Islands logging camps for the pulp and paper mills at Ocean Falls and Powell River. One of the companies, Pacific Mills, operated a camp on the Queen Charlottes. A shutdown in the woods would have major repercussions for the war effort and profit margins.[81] The situation was exacerbated by the overall shortage of logs during the war years. In March 1943, the Powell River Company was curtailing production because of an insufficient log supply. The company owned timber but operated no camps of its own; it had contracts with four logging companies to supply it with logs. War controls were diverting logs to other uses, and the company was short 3 million feet of logs if it wanted to maintain even a curtailed production of newsprint for the last nine months of the year.[82]

The companies refused to recognize the IWA and negotiate a contract. Despite wariness by the IWA district leadership, who did not want production curtailed by a strike, Local 1-71 initiated a strike vote on 1 October 1943, and loggers voted in favour of action. After negotiations broke off, the loggers struck the Queen Charlotte Islands camps on 9 October. With pressure from governments and the pulp industry, the strike was settled on 23 October. In the settlement, the IWA was recognized as the representative of the workers in the camps on the Queen Charlotte Islands, seniority provisions were established, and arbitration machinery was put in place.[83] The settlement, which included union recognition and a signed contract, was a breakthrough and opened the door for industry-wide bargaining. In

March of IWA strikers, Victoria, 1946.
BC Archives, I-01404

December that year, the IWA signed a coastal agreement covering twenty-three camps and 8,000 workers.[84]

With recognition won, the IWA consolidated its presence in the coastal region. Organizational drives in Vancouver shingle mills and Alberni Valley sawmills, among other places, brought results.[85] Workers came to see the IWA as a positive force, as the legitimate representative of forest industry employees. Employers followed new provincial and federal labour law. They were legally bound to recognize certified unions that represented a majority of the workers and they had to bargain with them in good faith. In 1946 a province-wide strike solidified the hold of the IWA in the coastal region. The thirty-seven-day strike, involving some 37,000 employees, began on 15 May. The union leadership won a 93 percent strike vote and there was remarkable solidarity at the outset. Although the IWA did not get a union shop, there was a wage increase, a shorter work week, and provision for pay for overtime work.[86]

The IWA was now a solid presence on the Coast. Remarkably, it survived a bitter internal struggle between two factions for control of the union in 1948 (which will be discussed later), and was able to mount a major strike in 1952. At this time the

IWA represented some 26,000 workers in eight coastal locals.[87] Union security remained a concern, as companies and government arbitrators refused to grant full checkoff and the union shop. Checkoff is a bookkeeping measure. The employer agrees to deduct union dues from employees' paycheques and pass along the funds to the union. In voluntary checkoff, the company agrees to collect dues from workers who request it. So instead of union people going around every month to collect dues, a dicey situation depending on workers' personal situations or inclinations and perhaps the vagaries of the economy, there was an automatic procedure. Sometimes checkoff was linked to a negotiated maintenance-of-membership provision. In this case, after the signing of a contract, workers would have a time period, such as a month, to declare whether they were union members and thus wanted checkoff, and then they would be bound by this decision for the duration of the labour agreement.

In the 1940s, checkoff was bolstered by the "Rand formula." During a 1945 strike at Ford Windsor in Ontario, arbitrator Justice Ivan C. Rand ruled that all workers covered by a collective agreement should pay union dues, even if they were not union members. The argument was that all workers benefited from the work of the union and so should share the costs. For unions, it meant even more security, with a guaranteed, steady flow of cash into union coffers.

The security was even greater when coupled with the union shop. In the early 1950s, the IWA had won only checkoff and maintenance of membership. Gordon McGregor Sloan, the government arbitrator in the 1952 strike, ruled against the Rand formula, which was at the forefront of the dispute. The employers were firmly against the formula, arguing that the union was too irresponsible and prone to flout the law. The Rand formula would force even non-union employees to support questionable leadership. Sloan sided with the employers, ruling against a mandatory checkoff clause in the new contract.[88] The 1954 IWA convention opened with a warning that the union was still in an immense fight for its existence.[89] The coastal IWA had largely organized the mills and camps of the region, however, and in 1955 the union represented the vast majority of coastal woodworkers – 27,302 workers in certified operations – of whom 25,302, or 92 percent, were union members.[90] In 1957, without a strike, the coastal IWA signed an agreement with employers that included provision for the union shop. Persistence had paid off.

The IWA in the Interior

Workers in the Interior participated in the 1946 strike, but the IWA hold in this region remained tenuous. Employers did not yet accept the inevitability of the IWA in their operations. In the mid-1940s, the lumber workers of the Interior were an afterthought to IWA organizers, who were located in Vancouver and in the camps and mills of the coastal region. This made sense. The greatest concentration of workers was in the coastal region and resources had to be focused on

victories there. The British Columbia IWA envisioned a province-wide, even national union, but that was for the future.

There were particular circumstances in the Interior that retarded organizational
drives. Unlike the coastal region, the Interior forest industry did not experience an
economic recovery in the 1930s. Coastal producers taking out high-quality timber
and having access to the waterborne export trade tapped into the British market
while the Interior industry wallowed. Working-class activists organized the unemployed in many Interior areas, but the lumber industry was too weak to even be
considered for unionization.[91] The industry was revived by the war, but its nature
posed extreme difficulties for organizers. Operations were small and poorly capitalized. Many employers were operating on a very tight margin. Considering a
wage increase for 1946, Mike Sekora of Local 1-417 commented during an IWA
negotiations conference on the state of affairs in the Kamloops region: "There are
a large number of operations that can't stand a 25¢ increase. It would drive a lot of
operators broke. The membership is scared of that. It would mean that the Union,
instead of improving working conditions, would cause the shut down of operations and increase unemployment."[92] Delegates from Princeton and Nelson agreed
that this assessment also applied to their regions. The situation was somewhat
better in the Prince George area, where union officials concluded that "the Prince
George operations are able to pay a 25 cents per hour increase in wages, after reducing the working week to 40 hours, and without any further increase in prices."[93]

Interior operations were more seasonal than coastal operations. Logging occurred in the winter and summer, and in the fall and spring between the productive seasons, "operations [were] brought to a virtual standstill, because of the deep
mud and gumbo on the roads."[94] The seasonal nature of the industry led to higher
rates of transiency, as Al Parkin of Local 1-405 noted in October 1946: "Transiency
is the big problem, with the boys moving on an average of once a week. Right now
we are experiencing an influx of prairie workers who want to get in a week's work
and then head for the coast for the winter. In a few weeks we will be getting the
better class of worker who will stay five months."[95] The employer at the new Quesnel
plywood plant also lamented the transiency in June 1952: "During the period January 1st to April 30th, 75 employees left and had to be replaced. This is particularly
hard during the initial operation of the plant when the 'steady' personnel is not
yet fully skilled."[96] In August 1949, IWA organizer J.C. Mueller commented in his
report on the Prince George area, after visiting an area sawmill: "Out of 40 men
seven attended the meeting, which is none too good. Signed up 1 new member.
The conditions in this particular camp are deplorable and the type of men employed here are strictly drifters, here today and gone tomorrow. It is indeed a state
of affairs how little interest these men take in their own welfare and self protection."[97] Some of the smaller operations relied on family labour, as Mueller noted
with some exasperation when he visited another mill in the Prince George region:

"We have an agreement with this company, but due to it being a family affair and a few farmers working there, it is nearly impossible to make any headway. We have 5 members which consist all the outside help, the rest being 52nd cousins, grand-fathers and other relatives one may desire."[98] Union organizers also complained about workers from the prairies and farmers who were willing to work for lower wages.[99]

Distance and transportation were problems. Mills and logging camps were strung out along the Canadian National Railway line for 200 kilometres to the east of Prince George. There was no road to these camps and communities, and in 1946 the train went each way only three days per week. For a worker attending a re-gional meeting in Prince George, this would mean the loss of two days of work.[100] In 1951 the IWA had one certified plant in McBride, east of Prince George, but there were about six other operations with about a hundred potential IWA mem-bers. The costs of either shipping in an automobile by train or constantly using a taxi were dear, and even if McBride area mills were unionized, it would be very expensive to service the membership.[101]

Ethnic divisions were also notable in the Interior. There were Japanese workers in the Okanagan. To the west of Prince George and on to Prince Rupert, many loggers were Aboriginal. In 1952 the IWA recruited Frank Calder, an Aboriginal ac-tivist and CCF politician, to help organize the area.[102] In the Kootenays, Doukhobor workers were a concern for organizers, who were convinced that employers were trying to divide the workforce along ethnic lines, but many Doukhobors joined the IWA. In 1945 G. Argatoff, a Doukhobor delegate to an IWA conference, said that most Doukhobors were willing to join the union. They realized that their position in industry was weakened by division. There were, he said, two groups among the Doukhobors themselves, and the younger group was more anxious for union or-ganization than the older group.[103] Still, the Doukhobor workers needed special at-tention, and organizers had to deal with prejudice against them. The Nelson district forester was reprimanded in 1933 for his comments on the Kootenay Doukhobor community: "In the Interior there is no Oriental menace, but there is a Doukhobor menace that is just as serious ... Public opinion up here is that the Doukhobor be-longs on the land, and once he gets in the bush he is a public nuisance."[104]

Despite the difficulties, there were issues that facilitated unionization. Wages and hours of work were a major consideration. Logging camp conditions in the Interior were abysmal, much worse than on the Coast. Stan Simpson, president of Local 1-417, Kamloops, commented in 1946: "The camps in this area are deplor-able. They are not fit to live in. They should be made sanitary, because after all, what is money without health, and that is what our boys want most."[105] A com-ment on camps in the Terrace area was even blunter: "Conditions in the Terrace camps are a disgrace to the twentieth century, with men still packing their own bindles in 1946. There are no showers, no dry rooms, no sanitary facilities, and many men cook and eat in the same hovels."[106] In 1954 the provincial medical health officer threatened to close a number of Interior operations because health standards were unacceptable, holding off only because of poor economic conditions.[107]

Wage rates were lower in the Interior, and the call for parity with the Coast was an ongoing issue for the union, as were wide discrepancies in wages across the vast Interior. Common labour rates varied from 58.8 cents per hour in the Kootenays to 65.4 cents in the South Okanagan; head sawyers were paid 95 cents in the South Okanagan and $1.17 per hour in the Prince George area; and planerman rates ranged from 70 cents in the South Okanagan to 91.1 cents in the East Kootenay area. Overall, sawmill workers in the Prince George area were the highest paid, while those in the Kamloops area were the lowest. In logging, East Kootenay was the highest paid region and North Okanagan the lowest paid.[108]

In the spring of 1945, the IWA, using three paid organizers, launched a drive in the Interior, beginning in Cranbrook, where Local 1-405 was established. In July 1945, an IWA local was chartered in Prince George (1-424) after organization of the major sawmill in the region, and it soon had over 350 members.[109] By the spring of 1946, there were also locals in Kamloops (1-417), Kelowna (1-423), Nelson (1-425), and Princeton (1-418). Although incompletely organized, workers in the Interior participated in the 1946 strike, but even employers that ran union operations barely tolerated the union, and often abused the terms of the contract. In 1944 Penticton Sawmills tried to thwart a union drive by setting up a company union, and a Lumby firm intimidated employees by saying that wages would be cut if they did not drop out of the union.[110] In Kelowna, at the notorious anti-IWA Simpson operation, the company shut down the mill in 1947 for repairs, and when it reopened, a large number of anti-union workers were hired. Overtures were also made to the United Brotherhood of Carpenters and Joiners in an effort to forestall IWA efforts.[111]

Despite pleas from Interior activists, the union could not afford to send in needed organizers,[112] and some organizers were not effective. The union representative in Terrace, who left Youbou on Vancouver Island to become an international organizer for the Interior in 1944, was up for dismissal in 1948 because he was not showing results: "Bill has been up there for nearly eight months now and the average membership is only about ninety, which is less than Local 1-71 turned over to Local 1-469."[113] An assessment by Local 1-424 in Prince George in 1949 showed the tenuous hold of the union in Interior mills that were certified. At the larger mills, the union was strong: at Eagle Lake Sawmills, 130 out of 140 men were union members, as were 65 of 75 workers at Sinclair Spruce. Standard Tie and Timber, however, employed 70 workers but only 12 belonged to the union; Shelley Sawmills had 10 union men out of a workforce of 60; and Prince George Planing Mills employed 27 IWA workers out of a total of 50. Some seventeen certified operations, employing from 15 to 25 men, had no IWA presence at all.[114] In early 1951, some nine firms were refusing to adhere to the terms of the negotiated agreement, and Upper Fraser Spruce Mills and Standard Tie and Timber were "on a rampage trying to get rid of the union." Standard Tie and Timber stopped allowing the union to hold meetings in the bunkhouse and posted notices announcing that workers did not have to belong to the IWA to work for the company.[115] In the early 1950s, then, the union, which was building slowly, had little respect from employers and was seen as vulnerable. Employers believed that there was still an opportunity to drive the IWA from the field. They were well organized and determined. L.J.A. Rees, secretary-manager of the Interior Lumber Manufacturers' Association, told his members in October 1953 that victory for the employers would come by keeping the mills operating despite action by the IWA: "If we are to win this battle with the Union – and let us recognize that today it is a battle – it is essential that every operator in the Association be firm and aggressive in his attitude towards the Union."[116]

A showdown came in 1953. Negotiations between the IWA and Southern Interior operators began in Kelowna on 6 July, and negotiations with Northern Interior operators opened in Vancouver on the same day. Talks broke down, a conciliator was called in, and strike votes were taken in late September in the north and in the middle of October in the south. In both regions, workers endorsed strike action. In Prince George, workers began shutting down plants on 26 September, and the action became regional two days later. Southern Interior workers walked out on 23 October.[117] Although a majority of workers in IWA plants, as well as a majority of the operations, voted in favour of the strike, there were pockets of resistance. In the Prince George region, the large facilities supported the strike: Eagle Lake workers voted 145-31 in favour; Standard Tie and Timber, 64-18; Sinclair Spruce, 97-16; and Prince George Planing Mill, 70-20. At Fort Lumber, though, the vote was 41-4 against the strike; at the Geddes sawmill, 55-13; at Northern Planing Mills, 48-19; and at Shelley Sawmill, 31-13.[118] This caused problems for the union and enabled employers to try to divide employee ranks.

The strike was bitter, involving much intimidation and violence. At Creston on 29 October, a foreman drove his car off the road into a group of union men, narrowly missing several; one of the men escaped by jumping on the bumper. The foreman then got out and struck one of the men. At Nakusp on 30 October, the mill manager went out to the picket line and hacked down a tent that had been erected by the pickets.[119] In Vernon the owners of the Ganzeveld Bros. sawmill sent a letter directly to the wives of the workers just before the strike vote, setting out the economic problems faced by the firm and questioning the size of the IWA strike fund. At the Ganzeveld plant, workers voted 18-8 against striking.[120] Seven weeks into the strike, District Third Vice-President F. Fieber described the situation in Prince George, suggesting that discipline and violence were concerns on both sides:

Crews full of fight. Injunctions are a problem as crew are prepared to ignore them. Peaceful picketing is allowed and crews have to be kept peaceful ... Back to work move stopped but injunctions are next round. Feeling in Prince George is high. Employers making test here and something will have to give ... Rustad [local mill owner] has a "goon" squad but that has   been taken care of. Sausage, balogny [sic] and wieners is steady diet and must be improved ... More help needed.[121]

From the employers' perspective, "the Union had adopted rough tactics in the Prince George area and ... there is a goon squad of some 35 men doing their best to keep all plants closed."[122]

In December 1953, Justice Arthur Lord was appointed as conciliator. His recommendations reflected the offer of the employers. He called the IWA irresponsible and lawless, undeserving of the union shop or compulsory checkoff. He also noted that the IWA did not yet have a sufficient hold on the minds of employees in the Interior.[123] The IWA District Policy Committee recommended rejecting the report, and in a vote in late December, Lord's recommendations were rejected by 92 percent. The strike had taken its toll, however, and negotiations proceeded between the IWA and employers in the Northern Interior. A deal, which included maintenance of membership and voluntary checkoff, was signed between Local 1-424 and the Northern Interior Lumbermen's Association on 5 January 1954.[124] Southern Interior woodworkers settled shortly thereafter. For the union, victory was in its survival, but the weaknesses of the organization had to be recognized. Many workers were unhappy with both the settlement and the union. Unlike on the Coast, Interior logging camps – small, often family-run and worked – remained non-union. The union had not been driven from the mills. In the Cranbrook area in 1955, of some thirty-three operating mills, twenty, employing some 535 workers, were certified. The uncertified plants employed some 597 workers. Even in the union plants, only 85 percent were union members, and no operation had total compulsory checkoff.[125] Unionists persisted, however, and finally, after a strike in the Southern Interior in 1959, both the Northern and Southern Interior got the union shop.[126]

THE ESTABLISHMENT OF UNIONS in the BC forest industry signified both the beginning of a new era and an extension of an earlier era. The achievement of unionization in the camps and mills paralleled the struggle for unions in other North American industries, such as steel, rubber, and auto, and employers were now forced to deal with workers in the burgeoning mass production industries of the Fordist era. Besides forging a new relationship, the unionization of these industries was also the culmination of an expanding notion of industrial citizenship. In the nineteenth century, skilled workers were at the forefront in successfully organizing unions. Skill was associated with craft workers, such as carpenters,

White-collar workers, new MacMillan Bloedel head office, Vancouver, 1968.
MacMillan Bloedel Collection (UBC), BC 1930/216/6

machinists, and stone masons, and their possession of exclusive knowledge and special abilities ostensibly enabled them to gain union status and achieve a higher standard of living. As has been oft-noted, however, skill is not a simple objective category. The skilled also tended to be overwhelmingly white, male, and of British descent. Ethnic, racial, and gender considerations, then, were also at the core of the social construction of the skilled worker. The union drives of the 1930s and 1940s expanded the definition of who should have union rights. While the historical conditions of the 1940s, as well as the material concerns of workers – wages, camp conditions, and benefit packages – were important in the history of unionization in the BC forest industry, so too was the growing sense that workers from minority groups and races, often so-called unskilled workers who just tended machines or piled lumber, deserved the rights that skilled workers had won generations earlier. This discourse brought together union organizers from diverse political and philosophical positions and underpinned increased public sympathy and new government legislation. It also sustained workers during the difficult struggles in the camps and mill towns.

In the context of this larger discourse, forest industry employers, who were overwhelmingly anti-union, were forced to cede ground. They did so grudgingly. Unions were an irritating disease, and there was always the fear of a further outbreak. Companies were ever alert to stem its spread and stamp it out. In late April 1967, for example, management at MacMillan Bloedel learned that a technician in the company's Central Research Laboratory, a non-union division, had suggested to another worker that a union should be organized. MacMillan Bloedel responded quickly. The employee, a former IBPSPMW official and known New Democratic Party activist from Powell River, was permanently transferred back to Powell River: "in the light of his background, he should never have been transferred to Central Research in Vancouver."[127] The company also devised new policies: all newly hired technicians were to be screened for previous union affiliations before hiring, and all technicians transferred into the Central Research Laboratory would be investigated to determine whether they should be transferred back to where they came from. The company was also going to address areas of discontent in the department and counter an impression that their counterparts at another mill were making more money. Finally, at training sessions for the approximately thirty supervisors at Central Research, experts from the Industrial Relations Department "counseled them on what causes union organization, what conditions are favourable for union activity, how Supervisors can identify these conditions, [and] what Supervisors can do to help correct the conditions, if identified, and prevent them from arising in the first place."[128]

4
Union Politics

There were constant struggles between unions and within unions in the British Columbia forest industry. Best known is the battle to wrench control of the International Woodworkers of America (IWA) from its communist leadership in the late 1940s, but the resolution of this dispute did not end political dissension in the IWA. Pulp and paper unions also experienced internal turmoil in the postwar years. Moreover, unions also struggled with each other. Raids induced workers to leave one union to join another, and jurisdictional disputes, often bitter, sorted out which competing unions would represent a particular group of workers. In the heady days of the Second World War, when Canadians as a whole favoured unions and even the federal Conservative party came out in support of free collective bargaining,[1] a union discourse drew together people of diverse dispositions and orientations, but there was still plenty of room for disagreement. Communist, socialist, and nationalist discourses mobilized activists and, at times, the rank and file during the Fordist era. Division remained pronounced in the 1970s.

Craft Unions and the Lumber and Sawmill Workers Union

The craft unions were an irritant to the industrial unions. Craft unions organized skilled workers into organizations that represented just one trade – painters in a painters' union, electricians in an electricians' union, and carpenters in a carpenters' union – while industrial unions organized all workers in one industry, including the skilled from all crafts and the unskilled, in one body. Just after the formation of the International Brotherhood of Pulp, Sulphite and Paper Mill Workers (IBPSPMW) local in Powell River in 1919 (an industrial union), the skilled workers – machinists and engineers – split from the fledgling local to join their respective craft unions.[2] Some three decades later, in 1947, the International Brotherhood of Electrical Workers (IBEW), much to the consternation of the IBPSPMW, was able to get representation of the five or six electricians and their helpers at the Port Alberni pulp and paper mill. The IBPSPMW international representative in BC commented: "It appears to me we have again been placed in a defensive position, whereby we have to defend our rights as an Industrial Organization, over that of an over zealous Craft organization attempting to claim and gain jurisdiction over craftsmen employed as maintenance employees in the Pulp and Paper industry."[3] He anticipated that this was the beginning of an IBEW campaign to raid other locals.

Besides reducing the membership of the IBPSPMW locals, the incursion of the craft union could set a precedent for other skilled trades in the industrial union and sow dissension. It also raised the possibility that less than ten electricians could go on strike and shut down a whole mill because union workers would respect the picket line, putting IBPSPMW members on the street with no income. In 1949, when the hiring began for the new Harmac mill at Nanaimo, the IBPSPMW worried about the IBEW. To forestall the joining of a different union by electricians, the IBPSPMW international representative expedited the certification process by getting a special blank charter, signed by the international president, on which he filled in the names of local charter members as soon as they had been hired, and quickly sending it off to the Labour Relations Board (LRB) before the IBEW had time to organize.[4]

The International Union of Operating Engineers was a serious antagonist. This union claimed jurisdiction over engineers and firemen in steam plants, as well as their assistants and the repairmen. The IWA, an industrial union, fought off raids by the Operating Engineers at three Port Alberni mills in 1944 and 1945, and the IBPSPMW, with the help of the company, fought off a raid at Port Mellon in 1947, winning the support of the Labour Relations Board. Some engineers at the Port Mellon mill were very unhappy with this turn of events and remained disgruntled within the IBPSPMW.[5] Ocean Falls also experienced raids by the Operating Engineers in the 1940s and 1950s. The secretary of IBPSPMW Local 312 vented his anger in 1955: "And now we witness the sorry spectacle of attempted infiltration by an organization whose hallmark has been a cynical disregard for pioneer organizing activity by the great industrial unions in an effort to attach it's [sic] parasitic growth on the established tree."[6] In November 1955, the Operating Engineers, representing the steam plant engineers, struck sixteen BC saw and shingle mills, promising to get the engineers higher wage rates than those paid to engineers in the IWA contract. The IWA was against the strike and members crossed picket lines in a number of cases, but with the steam plants down, power to the mills was shut off and the facilities had to close, forcing IWA workers to lose pay. At Youbou sixteen engineers and firemen caused 439 mill workers to lose work, and at Port Alberni seventeen strikers sent 2,000 IWA members home.[7] In the summer of 1951, British Columbia's four largest industrial unions – the IWA, the IBPSPMW, the Allied Fishermen's Union, and Mine-Mill – entered into a pact "whereby any one of the organizations mentioned would protect the other in the event of an attempted raid by any craft union."[8] When the Operating Engineers requested readmittance to the Canadian Labour Congress (CLC) in 1964, a number of unions, including the IWA, protested vociferously.[9]

The IWA's main annoyance was the Lumber and Sawmill Workers Union, a subsidiary of the United Brotherhood of Carpenters and Joiners. A member of the Vancouver local noted during the 1946 IWA strike that "the biggest problem today

Skilled workers constructing and equipping a pulp bleach plant, 1957.
MacMillan Bloedel Collection (UBC), BC 1930/61/1

is the AF of L Carpenters and Joiners Union ... who are attempting to drive a wedge in our union by signing up scabs and obtaining closed shop agreements with struck operations."[10] In the Okanagan, at Vernon, Rutland, and Summerland, the Lumber and Sawmill Workers organized a number of mills in 1947 after bitter, even violent, confrontations with IWA supporters. In the same year, sawmill workers at the S.M. Simpson Company mill in Kelowna voted 111-42 to leave the IWA and join the Lumber and Sawmill Workers Union. Part of the latter's appeal was their offer of full union membership for $1 per month, compared with IWA dues of $2 per month.[11] In the 1950s, there was conflict in the Kootenays. In 1953 and 1954, Creston Sawmills was the focal point of a raid by the Lumber and Sawmill Workers, leading to the decertification of the IWA, and in 1958 it won the Crestbrook Timber workforce in Cranbrook away from the IWA.[12] The IWA, of course, responded in kind. In 1957 it tried to win back control of a Rutland sawmill from the Lumber and Sawmill Workers, but failed to win a government-supervised vote. A week later, it lost another vote at Swan Lake Lumber near Vernon.[13] Even after a truce in 1964, the Lumber and Sawmill Workers and the IWA still tried in the 1970s to take advantage of each other's weaknesses.[14]

Despite cool relations, unions often worked together. The IBPSPMW was continually refining arrangements with the building trade unions regarding construction work in the pulp and paper mills. When outside firms whose workers belonged to craft unions came into the mills to do construction, the IBPSPMW maintenance crews did not interfere. Periodically, if there was a disagreement, the unions held meetings to sort out differences.[15] In 1970 the demarcation lines were still being refined and there was a joint committee at the international level, made up of three representatives of the IBPSPMW and three representatives of the Building Trades Councils, to settle disagreements.[16]

Strikes posed particular problems. In 1952, for example, British Columbia carpenters, members of the United Brotherhood of Carpenters and Joiners, went on strike. At the time of the strike, union carpenters were working on a construction job inside the Powell River pulp and paper mill, and so the carpenters established a picket line. This could have shut down the operations of the mill had the IBPSPMW or the IBPM honoured the picket line, and before the picket line was set up, representatives of the unions negotiated an agreement whereby the production workers would be allowed to cross the line and keep the operation running. There was still potential for conflict between the unions, however, as tension would increase as the strike dragged on – in order to put pressure on employers, the carpenters might want to completely shut down all operations in the province, including production of newsprint. Moreover, if carpenters on the picket lines started calling the pulp and paper workers scabs, it could lead to the latter honouring the picket line to save face, and a full walkout of all mill employees could ensue. The potential was great, noted an observer, because the "pickets build up courage when frequenting beverage rooms which are directly across the street from where the picket line is assembled."[17]

The sanctity of the picket line usually prevailed, however. In late 1967, when IWA members threw up a picket line around the new pulp mill that was being built at Skookumchuk, the trades respected the IWA lines, despite the fact that the trades got no strike pay and were ineligible for unemployment insurance and welfare, and the labour market was poor. Even members of the United Brotherhood of Carpenters and Joiners, which often raided IWA work sites, honoured the line.[18] During the difficult 1953 IWA strike in the Interior, an official from the carpenters' union counselled the Lumber and Sawmill Workers local in Creston to honour the IWA pickets, although the advice was not followed to the letter: "We may disagree with the I.W.A. ... but to the best of my knowledge we have never joined with the employer at a time when their backs were to the wall in a fight, and tried to influence them in any way. Never before to the best of my knowledge have we crossed their picket lines."[19]

The Pulp and Paper Unions and the IWA

The IBPSPMW and the International Brotherhood of Paper Makers (IBPM) generally coexisted peacefully. The two unions organized new locals and negotiated with employers together, and they cooperated at the local level, often sharing the same offices. The much larger IBPSPMW set the pattern and led in bargaining. Still, both unions guarded their jurisdictions. In early 1955, the executive board of the IBPSPMW in the United States made a decision to transfer two employees at the Powell River Company's pulp mill from IBPSPMW Local 76 to'IBPM Local 142. The question revolved around which union had jurisdiction over an oiler, a man who oiled and greased machinery in the mill, and a machinist. Job responsibilities had changed, and now the IBPM claimed the membership of the two men. The question was submitted to the IBPSPMW executive board in the United States, which ruled in favour of the Paper Makers. It was a very unpopular decision in Powell River and spawned protest by members of Local 76. The two union brothers also disliked the decision.[20] In explaining the decision of the international executive, IBPSMW president-secretary John P. Burke began with the 1909 agreement between the IBPM and the IBPSPMW that gave the former jurisdiction over all the workers in the paper machine room with few exceptions. "We recognize," he went on, "that the Paper Makers have a limited jurisdiction in newsprint mills and we want them to have enough jurisdiction so that they can maintain effective local unions." Responding to the arguments of the local, Burke expanded on the difficulties of discussions with the Paper Makers at the international level, noting that the Paper Makers also had a long list of grievances against the IBPSPMW over jurisdiction. In the interests of North American harmony between the two unions, the decision regarding the two Powell River workers could not be changed.[21] In the 1940s and 1950s, there were ongoing discussions about amalgamating the two internationals. Both unions had concerns. The Paper Makers worried about their small membership within the IBPSPMW and their loss of skilled status by becoming part of an industrial union. The IBPSPMW was concerned that joining the two organizations would exacerbate problems with other skilled workers, the tradesmen, in the industrial union.[22]

Relations between the IWA and the IBPSPMW/IBPM were largely amicable, despite the constant refrain from the IWA that they wanted all workers in the forest industry to belong to their union. The IWA slogan was "One Union in Wood." Jurisdictional divisions between the unions were established early, however. In May 1937, when the better-established IBPSPMW began an organizing drive in BC, an agreement was worked out with the BC district council of the Lumber, Sawmill Workers and Shingle Weavers Union, soon to become the IWA. Most satisfying to the pulp unions was that they got jurisdiction over all breakdown plants, where logs were transformed into wood chips, and chippers in BC, as well as the pulp and paper mills themselves.[23] As the IWA became established, expansionist

goals were still expressed. In 1946 the IWA recognized the IBPSPMW/IBPM jurisdiction at a pulp and paper mill being constructed at Port Alberni, but it discussed
whether this arrangement should be permanent. Hjalmer Bergren, an IWA activist, commented: "If we intend to extend out activities into that field, this is not a
decision that can be made by the local union but must be discussed with the International, as it would entail an out and out fight."[24]

There were merger discussions at the international level. The IBPSPMW was
affiliated with the American Federation of Labor (AFL), while the IWA was a member of the Congress of Industrial Organizations (CIO). After the merger of the
AFL and the CIO in 1955, creating the AFL-CIO, high-level talks began in Chicago
in the summer of 1956. Joe Morris, president of BC District No. 1, was a member of
the IWA committee involved in the discussion. An interim agreement of mutual
aid was agreed to, which, importantly, included a clause recognizing the continuation of the No-Raid Pact.[25] Meetings of the Merger Committee continued into
the 1960s, but a deal could not be struck. This pleased the smaller BC IBPSPMW
locals and dismayed BC IWA leaders.[26]

Strikes increased pressure on both unions. On 29 May 1946, during an IWA
strike, the IWA put up pickets around the Powell River pulp and paper mill, and
IBPSPMW refused to cross the line, thereby shutting down the operation. The
IWA argued that they could legitimately picket because the logs in boom storage
were under their jurisdiction. The IBPSPMW international representative was
angry over this turn of events, because he felt that the IWA was wrong and that the
shutdown jeopardized his union's collective agreement and thus could harm relations with the mill company. Meetings were quickly held and the IWA agreed to
withdraw the picket line.[27] The next year, Local 76 passed a resolution condemn-
ing the IWA action and declaring that all logs cut and boomed were fair logs.[28] In
the lead-up to the 1952 IWA strike, it was "agreed that Logs in transit to Pulp or
Paper Mills or in Pulp and Paper Mill booming grounds be declared fair. Under no
circumstances may Logs previously assigned to or in transit to Sawmills, or in
Sawmill or Logging Camp booming grounds, be diverted to Pulp or Paper Mills."[29]
IWA picket action did not stop the operation of the province's pulp and paper
operations, although a shortage of wood chips due to the strike in the logging
camps did.[30] Despite the 1952 agreement, there continued to be debates about what
constituted fair and unfair logs, and in 1959, in preparation for a strike, the IWA
offered a new interpretation of fair logs, much to the consternation of the
IBPSPMW.[31] During the strike, however, the IBPSPMW gave $10,000 to the IWA
to help with the struggle.[32]

Both unions were aware of the competition. If IWA mechanics won a wage increase, then IBPSPMW mechanics wanted the same, and it was incumbent on the
leadership to deliver. If they did not, the workers would look elsewhere. H.L. Hansen

noted in 1953 that there would always be the danger of a takeover of his BC IBPSPMW locals by the IWA, "more especially should we fail to maintain our rights and continue to keep working conditions better than anything the I.W.A. has to offer."[33] The IBPSPMW/IBPM presented their workers as more skilled, positioning them above the IWA and making them out to be more deserving of higher wages.[34]

Communists and the IWA

The communist presence in the IWA has prompted much historical debate, especially with regard to the split in 1948, when communist leaders withdrew from the IWA and, hoping to take the membership with them, created a new union, the Woodworkers Industrial Union of Canada (WIUC). They failed and thus lost control of BC lumber workers. Partisan views are blunt in interpreting these events, one side portraying the communists as irredeemable troublemakers who betrayed the workers, and the other side praising the union skills of communists and blaming their loss on a wider conspiracy that included governments, other trade unions, and the IWA leadership in the United States.[35] Some historians and participants also argue that the communist leaders made tactical mistakes, both in leaving the IWA – unnecessarily giving up control of a union that they might have held, even during the Cold War – and in failing to manage votes effectively in meetings of the British Columbia Federation of Labour.[36] In the most extensive analysis of IWA politics in the 1940s, Stephen Gray persuasively argues, in an unpublished doctoral dissertation, that while the communists had legitimate claim to leadership of the union through the Second World War, their increasing interest in national and international politics in the immediate postwar period sapped their effectiveness as trade unionists and gave opposition forces an advantage to exploit.[37]

Communists and communist sympathizers were crucial in organizing the IWA in the 1930s. The Communist Party of Canada (CPC), which had links to the Soviet Union, was established in 1921. The Lumber Workers Industrial Union (LWIU), formed in Ontario in 1928, was a communist organization, and it soon had a presence in British Columbia. In the first half of the 1930s, there were communist-led unions in a number of sectors, united in the communist-dominated Workers Unity League (WUL), a labour central established in late 1929. The communist-led unions were aggressive and militant, often antagonizing workers and leaders in the more staid Trades and Labour Congress of Canada (TLC) and in the AFL in the US. Driven by belief in a new world order, communist organizers were dedicated and talented, organizing many workers during the Depression years. They were prominent in the Fraser Mills strike of 1931 and in the loggers' strikes of 1934 and 1936.[38]

Besides going head to head with the craft unions, communists antagonized Canadian socialists in the new Co-operative Commonwealth Federation (CCF), which was formed in 1933. CCFers were labelled allies of the bourgeoisie, and accused of stifling the revolutionary spirit of workers. Much of the non-communist Canadian left had come together in the CCF, which was dedicated to replacing capitalism in a Canadian, democratic manner. In British Columbia, the party was immediately successful, winning seven seats in the 1933 provincial election, enough to form the Official Opposition, and an astounding 32 percent of the popular vote. The victorious Liberals won 42 percent of the popular vote. The CCF supported unions and aided loggers during the 1934 strike, despite the fact that communists were in leadership positions. In the first half of the 1930s, then, two organizations competed for the support and leadership of the British Columbia working class. The conflict between the CCF and the CPC was bitter: CPC rhetoric against CCF leaders was biting and at times personal, and CPC activists physically tried to break up CCF meetings. For example, on 25 August 1933, a contingent of communists attended a CCF meeting in the Princess theatre in Prince George. There was a capacity crowd, with Dr. J. Lyle Telford, a prominent British Columbia CCFer, as the guest speaker. The communists in the audience disrupted the meeting by booing Telford, singing "The Red Flag," a labour anthem, and making disparaging remarks about J.S. Woodsworth, the national CCF leader: "The outstanding feature of the evening was the demonstration that there is no immediate connection between this phase of communism and the CCF."[39] The animosity of these years between members of the two parties of the left did not disappear.

International events redirected the tactics of the Canadian communists in 1935, when the Comintern gave priority to the struggle against world fascism. As part of this policy, the previous emphasis on building communist-led organizations, such as the WUL unions, was replaced by a strategy to create a broad anti-fascist alliance with social democrats, moderate union leaders, and even the Liberal party, against perceived fascist and reactionary elements in Canadian society. As a result, some of the communist-led organizations, including the WUL, were disbanded and militants became involved in a wide range of non-communist groups. In line with this change, on 29 December 1935, LWIU delegates from coastal sawmills and logging camps met in Vancouver and endorsed a resolution favouring merger of the LWIU with the Lumber and Sawmill Workers Union, which was affiliated with the United Brotherhood of Carpenters and Joiners, an international, American-based AFL union with jurisdiction over woodworkers.[40] In March 1936, the membership voted by an overwhelming margin in favour of the proposal. At first glance, the formation of the Lumber and Sawmill Workers Union of British Columbia seemed like a positive step. The lumber workers' union was weak in 1936 and the added support of the AFL, with which the union was now affiliated, would strengthen the bargaining position of the forest industry workers. Further, membership in the AFL would enhance the legitimacy of the lumber workers' union and help deflect the virulent anti-communist rhetoric that was hurled at the LWIU. It soon became evident, however, that the new affiliation would not last long. The Vancouver Trades and Labour Council fought to restrict the representation of the Lumber and Sawmill Workers Union in their assembly; they feared the spread of the Red influence.[41] At the United Brotherhood of Carpenters and Joiners convention in Lakeland, Florida, in late 1936, the attitude of the traditionalist unionists was exposed. The carpenters wanted to maintain the craft nature of their organization and refused to grant voting rights to the ostensibly unskilled and semi-skilled lumber workers. The Lumber and Sawmill Workers Union was relegated to second-class status in the carpenters' brotherhood.[42] In the spring of 1937, the vice-president of the United Brotherhood dismissed the lumber and sawmill workers as "a bunch of communists," and the large craft union ordered several Lumber and Sawmill Workers Union locals to turn over members such as painters, truck drivers, and engineers to the appropriate craft union.[43]

The lumber workers recognized that their presence within the carpenters' brotherhood and the AFL was untenable and so joined the recently formed CIO, a new American-based union congress dedicated to supporting industrial unions. In July 1937, lumber worker union delegates from British Columbia and the American Pacific Northwest voted to affiliate with the CIO, a decision later ratified by the membership. The new CIO union was called the International Woodworkers of America (IWA), and British Columbia was District 1.[44]

Going into the Second World War, the leadership of District 1 was closely aligned with the CPC, which was tied to the Comintern. In the first years of the war, this caused problems as the Soviet Union and Germany were allied, and Canadian communists attacked the government's war effort. After Germany invaded the Soviet Union in June 1941, however, Canadian communists exhorted their fellow Canadians to do everything possible to win the war and save the homeland of the international communist experiment, the USSR. Leaders of the IWA became super-patriots. In 1943 communist leaders in BC, such as Harold Pritchett and Nigel Morgan, were against strikes because they undermined the war effort, and in January 1944, District 1 endorsed the international IWA and CIO no-strike pledges for the duration of the war.

The communists were effective, dedicated unionists, legitimate leaders of the IWA who were endorsed by the membership in union elections. The leadership, was also involved in the political activities of the Labour Progressive Party (LPP), a Canadian communist party created in 1944 to give the communists legal standing. The IWA and LPP leaders in British Columbia saw themselves as soldiers in a worldwide struggle for socialism, and this included support for the Soviet Union and its foreign policy. As the IWA became larger and more influential in the mid-1940s, the leaders came to see themselves as leading a communist crusade for workers across Canada.

While they saw their trade union duties and political duties as cut from the same cloth, others saw things differently. CCFers were critical, of course, remembering their stormy history with the CPC. This was exacerbated in 1945 when the CPC recommended electoral support for the Liberal Party, not the CCF, as part of the world strategy to try and create a partnership between the Soviet Union and progressive governments elsewhere in the world. In addition, there were other anti-communist voices in the international IWA and in the larger Canadian union movement. As the Cold War unfolded after 1945, there was pressure to rid North American unions of their communist influence. This led to a pitched battle over who would direct the BC district of the IWA.

The political activities of the IWA leaders became more controversial. In 1947 the BC IWA leadership condemned the anti-communist Taft-Hartley Act passed in the United States, which required union officers to sign affidavits swearing that they were not associated with communist organizations. The leadership also criticized the American Marshall Plan, which involved sending money to European countries to help them rebuild their economies in order to prevent the spread of communism. In line with the international communist line, the United States was declared an expansionist, imperialist nation, and a threat to Canada's economic and national sovereignty. Further, the LPP now called for support of the federal CCF, rather than the Liberals, to further the leftist goals.[45] By 1948, then, continental and international political issues were at the forefront. The membership, which had confirmed by a healthy margin the communist slate in the 1946 IWA district officer elections, was much more divided in 1948, and support for the leadership was slipping.[46]

There had always been anti-Red groups and people active in the woodworkers' union, but the leadership delivered the goods and so rank-and-file members continued to support them. As the union grew in the 1940s, however, so too did opposition. Within the union, the New Westminster local, 1-357, spearheaded the opposition, known as the White Bloc. This local was chartered in 1942 and was initially controlled by individuals supportive of the Red Bloc. In 1946 the oppositionists in the New Westminster local challenged the financial management of the local's monies, claiming irregularities. An investigating committee found no egregious or illegal acts, but recommended the resignation of the president and financial secretary for being poor administrators. Using the issue of administration, the White Bloc took control in ensuing elections, and Stewart Alsbury became president of the local in early 1947.[47] From this beachhead, the White Bloc attacked the political proclivities of the district leadership and called into question their management of union funds.

On 4 February 1948, White Bloc activists, trying to oust the Red district officers in an upcoming vote, outlined their grievances on a radio program. The three speakers had long been active unionists in the provincial forest industry. Stewart Alsbury explained that he had run for the presidency of Local 1-357 because he, "like hundreds of others [was] under the iron heel of the executive board controlled by the Labor Progressive Party," and that the main problem was "lack of administrative efficiency, particularly with regard to bookkeeping, finances and general office routine, a natural result of choosing people, not for their ability but for their political views." Now he was running for president of the district council. On the same program, George Mitchell, vice president of the New Westminster local, took aim at the officers on the district council

who have consistently placed their own political ambitions ahead of the interests of the men they are supposed to represent. This was amply demonstrated at the last District Convention, where one full day was spent discussing the Marshall Plan and another debating Greenall's suspension [from the IWA for refusing to sign an affidavit stating that he was not a communist under the terms of the Taft-Hartley Act], leaving no time at all for the discussion of wages, hours and working conditions. Three whole days which should have been devoted to union business were used instead to [discuss] the foreign policy of the Labour Progressive Party.

Another White Bloc speaker, Lloyd Whalen, belittled the trade union achievements of the Red Bloc and condemned their political activities on behalf of the LPP. Whalen felt that the IWA, like the Canadian Congress of Labour (CCL), should endorse the CCF as the legislative arm of labour.[48] In the spring of 1948, the White Bloc voiced its support for the Marshall Plan.[49]

The American executive of the IWA was also keen to oust the Red leadership in BC. The international had more money and was able to hire paid organizers. Much to the chagrin of the provincial Red Bloc, they hired people who were anti-Red. In 1945 the district launched a campaign to organize the Interior of the province. They transferred three coastal organizers – Hjalmer Bergren, Mike Freylinger, and Tom MacDonald – to do the work, but the international's director of organization, George Brown, cancelled the appointments, sending instead pro–White Bloc organizers Mike Sekora, Ralph New, and Nick Kaptey. The BC leadership protested, saying that the three brothers were "green and incompetent" and that seniority was ignored, but to no avail.[50]

The Canadian trade union establishment and the provincial media also wanted to see the Reds removed. Already in 1945, the president of the CCL and the president of the IWA in the United States were corresponding, anticipating getting rid of the Red influence in BC.[51] In the summer of 1948, Local 1-357, bastion of the White Bloc, questioned the management of funds by the district leadership, and requested an audit by the international. On 19 July 1948, the international began investigating the finances of District 1. Questionable practices were uncovered, insufficient to force criminal charges but sufficient "to build up a record of lack of administrative ability, which will carry with it, by inuendo [sic], the impression that something could have happened to their funds, and likely did, even though it cannot be proven in Court."[52] The White Bloc was also making inroads into the local at Mission and the large Vancouver local.

Feeling cornered, the Red Bloc decided on a drastic course of action. On 3 October 1948, they disaffiliated from the IWA and set up a new Canadian organization, the Woodworkers Industrial Union of Canada.[53] The Red Bloc hoped that the membership would follow into the new organization. Thus began the open battle between the White Bloc and the Red Bloc. It was fought in all locals across the province, on shop floors and in the camps. It was extremely bitter. Name calling, threats, and violence were part of the battle. To destabilize the IWA financially, the WIUC called on its supporters to revoke their checkoff to the IWA. This became the test of WIUC supporters: if you revoked your checkoff, you were a Red. A White Bloc supporter from Prince George reported on Red activities in late November: "They are getting one hundred percent of some of the small mills and owing to the number of them the majority of the workers are in them. In one mill all but one check off has been rescinded and in another all but three and so on. The large mills are holding their own."[54] The Kootenays were particularly fertile ground for the Red Bloc. The Cranbrook local had disaffiliated on 6 October and aggressively moved to hold members and certify operations in their new name. By early December 1948, the WIUC had applied for certification in thirteen Kootenay operations, and these were granted by the Labour Relations Board.[55]

A nasty confrontation took place at Iron River, near Campbell River on Vancouver Island. On 10 November 1948, the Iron River Logging Company, a subsidiary of the H.R. MacMillan Export Company, discharged three loggers on the grounds that they were incompetent. WIUC supporters, the majority in the camp, called a meeting, demanded reinstatement of the workers, and established a picket line. IWA officials, on the other hand, took the issue to arbitration, following the process laid out in the collective agreement. Contrary to the collective agreement, the WIUC, with supporters from the surrounding area, maintained the picket line. The camp was shut down for three weeks. On 6 December, the IWA held a vote at the camp and the majority decided to return to work and await the decision of the Arbitration Board. The WIUC, however, refused to take down the pickets, and, respecting trade union principles, loggers were reluctant to cross the line. To break the impasse, three IWA leaders, including district president Stewart Alsbury, went to Iron River and told the pickets that the strike was illegal and that IWA members were going to cross the line. Violence followed. According to an IWA account, "The WIU men immediately attacked these brothers. The final result was that Stu

Alsbury had four ribs broken from kickings – also several minor bruises from beatings. Brother Tom Bradley was knocked down and kicked in the face – a deep cut being made in his eye (this required six stitches) and several other minor cuts from caulk boots. Brother Wessburg received many bruises about his face and body."[56]

Charges were laid against the attackers. During the rest of the day, there were reprisals and threats throughout the Courtenay–Campbell River region, and some 30 IWA members arrived from Port Alberni and Ladysmith to shore up their union's ranks. The next day, about IWA members and officials went to the camp at 7:00 a.m., where they found some seventeen WIUC supporters and twenty-five provincial police. That afternoon, the IWA put on a show of strength, with some 150 members marching through the streets of Campbell River. They then proceeded to the Iron River camp, but there were no WIUC members there.[57]

By 1950 the IWA had prevailed in most camps and mills across the province. Using the courts and legal avenues, the union had an air of authority, while the WIUC was forced to engage in illegal activities. In the Cold War era, this behaviour fit the stereotype of the lawless communists. Moreover, the Red Bloc had alienated itself from the rank and file after 1945 by increasingly engaging in international political affairs and not spending enough energy servicing the basic material interests of the workers. The Red leadership misread support for the IWA as support for the LPP political agenda. The White Bloc, importantly, kept the IWA name and thus seemed the legitimate guardian of the union: workers had joined the IWA, not the IWA-LPP. Had the Red Bloc chosen to fight it out within the IWA, its chances of retaining control would have been greater. Nor was the WIUC appeal to Canadian nationalism particularly effective. The CPC adopted the slogan "Keep Canada Independent" in January 1948, meaning independent from the "imperialist United States,"[58] but while Canadian control of the economy and the unions may have been the policy of the CPC, it had not yet made an impact on workers. CPC national leader Tim Buck remembered that when he visited BC during the winter of 1948-49, workers gave little thought to Canadian "independence": "Their attitude was: What difference does it make to me if the company that exploits me is a Canadian company or an American company? If I've got to be exploited, I don't care who it is. I just want to get the most I can for my labour."[59] Indeed, the WIUC position sounded opportunistic and the IWA had a strong counterargument, as noted by IWA director of research Virgil Burtz when he visited Vancouver Island logging camps in May 1949: "Even if the W.U.I.C. leaders have suddenly become nationalists the Logging and Mill owners have not – they have holdings on both sides of the international boundary. It is very difficult for a union to bring up wages in one section of the country if wages are much lower in another."[60]

In 1949 the IWA endorsed the political program of the CCF, but for Canadian labour officials, the BC CCF also posed problems. Canadian Congress of Labour leaders were furious at the behaviour of the more radical party members from BC in the spring of 1949. When moderates were out of the convention hall, the radicals passed a resolution repudiating the Atlantic Pact (NATO), thereby rejecting the position of the national CCF and the CCL. CCL secretary-treasurer Pat Conroy, emboldened by the successful purge of the Reds from the IWA, opined that it was "now time to clean out the Provincial C.C.F. organization," and that if nothing changed there would be no money forthcoming to help the BC CCF at election time.[61] Relations grew closer in subsequent years. In 1952 three IWA members were elected to the provincial legislature for the CCF.[62] In March 1961 the IWA was the second-highest union contributor, following the Steelworkers, funding the "New Party," an interim organization that in the summer of 1961 became the New Democratic Party.[63]

In the Kootenays, the WIUC persisted longer than in other parts of the province, and in the early 1950s, the WIUC represented about one-half of unionized woods and mill workers in the region. The WIUC and the IWA competed, trying to get the richest contracts they could in order to solidify their hold and perhaps even expand. In the 1953 IWA strike in the Interior, WIUC members in the Kootenays crossed IWA picket lines. Over the decade, however, the influence of the WIUC waned: in 1955 the IWA had contracts with some twenty-seven companies in the Cranbrook area and the WIUC with only eight. In 1957 the remaining Kootenay WIUC locals, rather than become part of the IWA, merged with the Lumber and Sawmill Workers Union.[64]

Under the IWA constitution, those associated with the Communist Party or the WIUC could not be active in union affairs. Harold Pritchett went back to work as a shingle weaver, Hjalmer Bergren as a faller, and Ernie Dalskog as a logger.[65] Former WIUC leaders had to apply to be accepted into the IWA, and this was not a straightforward affair. In 1950 Arne Johnson, a union activist since the 1930s, applied for membership in Local 1-71, but Fred Fieber, the local's financial secretary, was not convinced of his intentions and put his application on hold.[66] In 1955 Gordon W. Elder was expelled from the IWA. Elder was the secretary of the IWA Plant Committee at the Vancouver Plywood Division of MacMillan & Bloedel, and was found guilty by a union panel of taking directions from persons outside Local 1-217, of which he was a member – namely, the LPP.[67] In 1957 two Vancouver men who had been barred from the IWA forever because of their political activities applied for readmission. One was recommended to the international convention for readmission, the other was not.[68] In 1960 the Duncan IWA local rooted out a member who had run as a Communist Party candidate in the previous provincial election.[69]

Oppositionists in the IWA: The 1950s to the 1970s

The disappearance of the communists did not lead to harmony in the IWA. An opposition sprang up, staking out a position to the left of the established leadership.

The large Vancouver local was its bailiwick and Syd Thompson its leader. Thompson had been a communist organizer in the 1930s, and as a member of the Relief Camp Workers Union had participated in the On-to-Ottawa Trek in 1935. He served in the army during the Second World War and then worked as an LPP organizer in Alberta until 1948, when he left the party. He worked in Lumby in 1952 before going to Vancouver, where he got a job in a plywood plant in 1954. He was soon elected plant chairman and became third vice president of Local 1-217 in 1955. In 1958 he became president of the local and his supporters controlled the execu-tive.[70] The Thompson slate lambasted the local and district leadership for its weak performance over the previous decade. While lumber company profits soared, they argued, IWA members had not even kept up with pulp and paper workers, ship-yard workers, or civic employees in their wage increases. They accused the district leadership of being too close to the bosses. One associate of Thompson, Al Pol-lard, accused the district IWA leaders – Joe Morris, Lloyd Whalen, and Stuart Hodgson – of accepting bribes from the companies' negotiator during the 1958 wage discussions, a serious accusation indeed. These and other statements prompted a committee appointed by the international president to investigate Local 1-217. The committee found no evidence of bribery, deplored the malicious accu-sations, and noted the influence of communists in the 1958 Local 1-217 elections.[71] There was again open division in the IWA, and the press speculated on the close-ness of the relationship between the Thompson slate and BC communists.[72]

The Thompson group was not content to control just Local 1-217; they were preparing to take over the district. Their two main tactics were to question the militancy of the incumbents in terms of achieving material gains for the mem-bers, and to question the lack of democracy in the union. In the summer of 1961, the IWA negotiated a contract with BC coastal employers. Locals overwhelmingly ratified the settlement, except Local 1-217, whose members felt that the IWA nego-tiating committee had not pushed hard enough for more.[73] At the international convention in Miami, Florida, in October 1961, Local 1-217 moved a resolution that each local had to have two general membership meetings each year. This infu-riated the executive of Local 1-71, the loggers' local, whose membership was spread throughout the coastal region in distant isolated camps, making it logistically im-possible and too costly for members to gather in Vancouver for full-scale meet-ings. Local 1-71 saw the proposal as an attempt by the Thompson group to undermine its legitimacy and give more power to loggers in Vancouver, who would more easily come under the sway of the Local 1-217 leaders.[74] IWA district leaders complained about growing communist influence in the union: "The Communist Party seeks to discredit officers who obey membership instructions, and establish 'cells' as a preliminary to Communist domination of the Union. We will fight this as we did in 1948."[75] In 1964 Local 1-217 oppositionist leaders once again criticized the contract negotiated by the regional IWA negotiating committee: "Regional leadership over the years has shown considerable ability in grabbing the first offer made. Determination and a willingness to fight on the part of the Regional leadership could have brought much better results."[76]

By 1967, noted one union paper, the Communist Party had switched from a policy of "causing trouble by division to making another bid to take over labour bodies and work from the top."[77] In 1968 the IWA negotiating committee reached an agreement with coastal operators and it was put to the membership for ratification. While the membership endorsed the contract, only 68 percent of those who voted supported the settlement, meaning that a significant minority were unhappy with the behaviour of the leadership.[78] In August the oppositionist forces announced that they were going to challenge Jack Moore and the IWA district leadership, and Syd Thompson ran for the presidency against Moore. The Moore slate had solid support from east and north of the Fraser Canyon – the Interior – and had made sure to consolidate that strength by paying special attention to Interior negotiations in 1967.[79] They also had support on the Coast, but the oppositionists had particular strength in Vancouver, Duncan, New Westminster, and the loggers' local. The oppositionists were defeated, losing races for the presidency and the three vice presidencies. The presidential vote gives a good sense of the support for the two groups: Jack Moore won 15,928 votes, compared with Syd Thompson's 9,044 votes.[80]

Although the oppositionists did not win control of the regional district, they continued to be a force, constantly challenging the leadership. Jack Munro, who succeeded Jack Moore as IWA district president in 1973, remembered: "I think the membership was afraid of where Syd would take them. He was militant. I don't know if I was really opposed to that group as much as I was afraid of them. We'd been indoctrinated against the left wing ever since we were young business agents."[81]

In the late 1960s and early 1970s, the Communist Party continued to be involved in the IWA, and Reds from the 1940s, such as Harold Pritchett and especially Nigel Morgan, were notables. Pritchett counselled fallers who were challenging the IWA leadership in the 1970s, criticizing the party for causing division in the IWA, blaming "leading Trotskyists" for fomenting trouble, and chastising activists for focusing on the fight against Jack Moore rather than against the companies and monopoly capitalism: "Our Party must fight to unite the membership of the I.W.A. around a program directed in the main against the monopolies and in this process of developing struggle, elect progressives to any and all union positions."[82] In the spring of 1973, the Communist Party hosted a conference in Nanaimo to set out policy goals for their activists in the forest unions. Thirteen woodworkers who were party members participated.[83]

The exact role of the CPC and other leftist elements is unclear. Indeed, the murky place of left-wing organizations in IWA politics, as well as the ill-defined political position of Syd Thompson and the oppositionists, tells us much about the political manoeuvring of this era. No principles or political positions were articulated in a straightforward manner. Material benefits and questions about rank-and-file democracy were the issues out in the open. Workers were not mobilized for clearly defined political causes but rather to install new leadership, which would provide better jobs for leftists. It is doubtful whether life on the shop floor or in the camps would have changed. The communists and CCF differed in foreign policy, but their domestic programs for workers and unions were extremely similar. Had the oppositionists been elected in the late 1960s, the outs would have pressured for more militancy, richer contracts, and greater democracy.

In Local 1-217, home of Syd Thompson and the oppositionists, there was a challenge from a militant faction in 1971. The challengers used the same language that dissidents in the IWA had long used: the executive was too distant from the membership, there needed to be more control of the union by the members in the camps and on the shop floor, and the bureaucracy was too entrenched – leaders should return to the camps and shop floor on a regular basis. The Local 1-217 executive responded to the charges by defending their actions and their role in improving the security and material well-being of their members. Revolution was not part of the immediate agenda: "The trade union movement ... is not an instrument for revolutionaries to play around with. Working people belong to the Union of their choice because they recognize that without an organization an employer will trample all over them. Increased wages, fringe benefits and improved working conditions are the main issues that they expect their Union to fight for and bring about. Among industrial workers, the IWA is second to none in this field of endeavour."[84] Leaders in the IWA had progressive, even revolutionary ideas, but doctrinal differences between the various leftist factions were unclear except to those on the inside. Trade union executive positions were jobs for activists, and were kept by delivering material gains, protecting the union, and speaking a generic leftist language.

Democracy, Nationalism, and Socialism in the IBPSPMW

The IBPSPMW was not wracked with battles between communists and anti-communists in the 1940s and 1950s, although activists with questionable political affiliations were closely monitored. Orville Braaten, the business agent from the Vancouver Converters, Local 433, was close to the Communist Party, but there was no hard evidence. At the 1950 TLC convention in Montreal, H.L. "Stubby" Hansen, an international organizer from BC, tested Braaten's allegiance. He nominated Braaten for an executive position, knowing that he would lose but also knowing that in order to run he would have to swear that he was not a member of the CPC or a communist sympathizer. Braaten took the non-communist pledge and was

Sheet of pulp coming out of the dryer and being cut to bale size, 1957.
MacMillan Bloedel Collection (UBC), BC 1930/440/9506

easily defeated on the first ballot.[85] Hansen also felt that there was communist activity at Ocean Falls, Woodfibre, and Watson Island (Prince Rupert) in the early 1950s. International president-secretary Burke counselled patience: "I am very sorry that the members of Local 312 have elected a president and vice-president who are either Communists or have Communist leanings ... A local union and an International Union must stand or fall upon the decisions made by the members. The only thing you can do in this situation is to take it easy, not worry too much about it, and see how it works out."[86]

Another issue grabbed Burke's attention more forcefully. In 1955 a number of British Columbia unionists began to clamour for more Canadian autonomy within the international. In the late 1950s, just over 20 percent of the 171,037 members of the IBPSPMW were in Canada. Of these, 28,926 (16.9 percent) were in eastern Canada and 6,517 (3.8 percent) in western Canada, essentially British Columbia.[87] Canadians, then, were significant in the union, and independence threats were serious. Burke responded strongly to a Woodfibre correspondent, leftist Cy Harding, who claimed that there was "a strong undercurrent of feeling for a national, Canadian labour movement" and who was going to raise the question of Canadian autonomy at the Western Canadian Council of Pulp and Paper Workers in 1955.

Burke told Harding that he was on the wrong track because Canadian and American workers were essentially the same, due to their shared British heritage, and because international unionism was positive, contributing to peace, harmony, and goodwill between countries.[88] It was more than coincidence that the CPC was advocating an "Independent Canada" policy at the same time.

In 1957 British Columbia pulp and paper workers waited until the IWA had reached an agreement, planning to use the IWA settlement as a pattern. In the fall, however, a downturn in the pulp and paper market made employers intransigent. On 14 November, some 6,000 workers went on strike, and the job action dragged on until 4 February.[89] This first-ever shutdown of coastal BC operations was a local strike; there was no strike in the US in 1957.

Some BC members were unhappy about the role of the international in the strike. Angus Macphee, president of the Watson Island local at Prince Rupert, expressed his sentiments in early 1958: "The strike may last some time yet and it is felt here that more can be done by the International in raising funds and winning support for us from other bodies." He added, "It would be folly to ignore the fact that among union members there is doubt as to the value of International unions."[90] Three years later, international president-secretary Burke was still defending his actions during the BC strike: "You again bring up the matter of support given by the International Union to our local unions in British Columbia when they were on strike. The record shows that the International Union expended from its Defense Fund eight hundred thirty-three thousand, five hundred fifty-nine dollars and sixty-seven cents ($833,559.67) in support of our local unions in British Columbia when they were on strike."[91] The international representative, "Stubby" Hansen from the Powell River local, was criticized for the behaviour of the negotiating committee: "The boys feel that the committee have a job to do but it does not involve meetings with management in the Board room. The job is to tie a strike together and speak to unionists."[92]

Grumblings were typical in a protracted, difficult job action, but in the late 1950s, these issues became relevant in a larger debate about the conduct of the international. Feeling that the international was controlled at the top by closely linked bureaucrats in the eastern United States, rebels in the western United States and British Columbia fought for increased democracy, regional recognition, and more autonomy at the local level. The hiring practices of the executive, hints of corruption, and constitutional questions were fiercely discussed. The IBPSPMW locals in the western US had had a degree of cohesion and autonomy since the 1930s, and in response the hierarchy tried to tighten its control and centralize power in the national office. In 1957 a New York newspaper linked New York Local 679 to corruption, and the local was discussed before the very public McClellan Senate Committee on labour racketeering that found corruption in a number of American unions. Western rebels wondered whether the IBPSPMW executive was connected and whether their union was also corrupt. In 1960 reformers were dismayed when it appeared that the executive had manipulated procedures to ensure that their people dominated the executive, and they were outraged in January 1961 when the popular, reform-minded George Brooks, director of research and education, resigned because of pressure.

The Brooks issue was the catalyst for a meeting of the reformers in Denver in March 1961, when the Rank and File Movement for Democratic Action (RFMDA) was formed. Besides the reinstitution of Brooks, the RFMDA sought the regional election of the eleven vice presidents, secret election of all officers, an international convention every two years, mandatory retirement of officers at age sixty-five, and more stringent, transparent audits. At the 1962 Detroit convention, reformers tried to win seats on the executive and pass reform measures, but they were consistently defeated. The eastern locals, especially the large New York locals, supported the hierarchy. The revolt appeared over, but in 1964, after a confrontation between western locals and the international executive over contract negotiating procedures, anger flared, and in May the western locals formed a rival union, the Association of Western Pulp and Paper Workers, made up of over 11,000 workers in twenty-nine locals. Despite legal challenges, the new union survived.[93]

British Columbians were prominent in the reform movement, corresponding with reformers throughout the United States and criticizing the international executive. A 1960 RFMDA manifesto, "A Program for Militant Democratic Unionism," was drafted by R.B. McCormick, president of Local 312 in Ocean Falls. The program called for democratic reforms, more militant collective bargaining, more attention to organizing the unorganized, stamping out corruption within the union, and unity within the wood industry.[94] John P. Burke was especially angry at the suggestion of corruption and quickly responded to McCormick: "I resent very much anyone referring to this union as corrupt, as a corrupt organization. It is an idealistic union, it is a union interested in the cause of labor and humanity."[95] But there was skepticism about the union and the international president-secretary. Orville Braaten of Local 433 wrote to Angus Macphee of Local 708 in 1961: "The more I look at this thing Angus, the more I am convinced that Burke is in this thing up to his ears and that he may have been pulling quite a sham for a good many years."[96]

In early 1961, ten BC locals representing 6,200 workers established a Committee of Inquiry to investigate recent events in the international.[97] At the March meeting in Denver that created the RFMDA, Angus Macphee of Prince Rupert was named temporary secretary. Orville Braaten and Murray Mouat, from the Powell River local, also attended.[98] Four BC locals affiliated with the RFMDA.[99] Twenty-four BC members representing eight IBPSPMW locals attended a joint meeting of the BC Board of Inquiry and the Northwest Committee for Union Justice in Bellingham, Washington, on 15 April.[100]

If British Columbians were active in the RFMDA, sympathy for socialism and the Castro revolution in Cuba, as well as overt participation in electoral politics, differentiated them from their American reform allies. In the Cold War years, activists did not wear their Marxist credentials on their sleeves, but Robert McCormick from Ocean Falls, Angus Macphee from Prince Rupert, and Orville Braaten from Vancouver all espoused socialist views. In 1955 a Vancouver newspaper labelled the Ocean Falls local a "left-wing local," noting that since 1953 the local had been against suspending members because of their communist beliefs.[101] Macphee was proudly socialist. His father, a machinist, had been active in the labour movement of the Clyde in Scotland before moving to Prince Rupert, where he worked as a steam engineer, in 1927. Angus was born in 1917 and went to work in the Prince Rupert pulp and paper mill when it opened in 1951. In the 1970s, he commented on his Marxist beliefs, "having," as he said, "accepted the theory of permanent revolution in my youth."[102] Another major player, Orville Braaten was likely, as IBPSPMW international representative H.L. Hansen suspected, close to the Communist Party in the 1950s. In 1952 he ran in the provincial election under the banner of the Labour Representation Committee, a group supported by the communist LPP and hostile to the CCF.[103]

In the summer of 1961, Macphee and McCormick were part of a BC delegation of unionists that travelled to Cuba to celebrate Castro's victory. Upon his return, Macphee spoke to Prince Rupert Rotarians, gave an account of his trip in the local newspaper, and published a sympathetic three-page account of his perspective on Cuba in the *Pulp, Sulphite and Paper Mill Workers' Journal*. In the late 1950s, Macphee, Braaten, and other IBPSPMW members were active in the CCF and the creation of the New Democratic Party, the CCF's successor. Braaten was at the founding convention of the new party in Ottawa in the summer of 1961.[104] As the NDP was being formed, there was a provincial election in British Columbia, and both Macphee and Braaten ran as CCF candidates in the 1960 campaign. Braaten was easily defeated but Macphee won almost 37 percent of the vote in the Prince Rupert riding and came in second, only 228 votes behind the leader.[105]

These socialist activities did not go down well in the United States. Macphee's favourable account of Cuba was dismissed by the former president of an Arkansas IBPSPMW local as "another left winger's attempt to apologize for the communist criminals who control Cuba."[106] BC activists defended their involvement in labour politics and often had to explain Canadian political culture to American colleagues. In 1961 Macphee elaborated on the Canadian situation to an Alaskan correspondent:

> You must know that a political party in Canada is not the loosely knit parliamentary apparatus it is in the U.S. Our parties vote in a bloc; members are subject to discipline. But the really important fact is that here most active trade unionists believe in

political action *independent* of the bosses' parties. Our counterparts of your Democrats and Republicans, (i.e.: Liberals and Conservatives and in B.C. Social Crediters), are shunned by all thinking trade unionists.[107]

In a letter to Henry Rogers, president of Philadelphia Local 375, Braaten explained the virtues of the Canadian political system, noting: "Yes, Henry, I believe we have a healthier climate for free discussion and freer avenue of expression than what you people now have in your country."[108] In 1962, Braaten and Macphee, delegates to the IBPSPMW convention in Detroit, were refused entry into the US, apparently because of their political affiliations.[109]

Canadian nationalism became more pronounced. Macphee offered an analysis of the Canadian situation in a 1961 letter to Rogers:

> The Canadians have their identity and it has to be served regardless of American tradition or opinion. Did you ever stop to realize that Canada to a lesser degree is comparable to Cuba? That American capital dominates our economy? That few secondary industries exist? [T]hat our unemployment figures are higher than yours, and in similar industries (excluding the South, where freedom is restricted to a large section of your citizens and in some congested areas) our wages are substantially lower? These facts are related. Think about them. And realize, too, that a great many Canadians resent the Yankee (to a large extent misguidedly), and that in many local unions this feeling could be exploited to withdrawal from International Unions.[110]

At the 1962 convention, the Prince Rupert local submitted a resolution critical of the Columbia River Treaty, but "the predominantly American Resolutions Committee decided that such matters were not the concern of trade unions." John West, from the Prince Rupert local, lambasted this position:

> Here in B.C. we have some of the finest if not finest, stands of timber in the world. We also have the greatest untapped source of Hydro power on the North American continent. Coupled together, this means that we have a great potential in the pulp manufacturing world. All of this, of course, means jobs for Canadians – and our American brothers tell us that this is not the concern of trade unions. It most certainly is, particularly to B.C. trade unions: it's our water, our resources and our jobs that are being given away and it's our province that is to be flooded and spoiled.[111]

The Creation of the Pulp and Paper Workers of Canada

American dissidents were left deflated and numb after the defeat of the RFMDA initiatives at the Detroit convention, but in British Columbia, the socialist activists pursued another route. Canadian nationalism, coupled with concerns about the international and demands for local control, led to meetings in Vancouver in early December 1962. The result was a new, independent Canadian union, officially founded in January 1963, that waved the Canadian flag and embodied the principles of grassroots, rank-and-file control.[112] Initially only four coastal locals joined the breakaway union – Crofton, Woodfibre, Prince Rupert, and the Vancouver Converters. Notably, the 950-member Ocean Falls local, home of activists Peter Marshall and Robert McCormick, decided to remain in the IBPSPMW. Loyalty to the IBPSPMW was not irrational. The international had a tradition and represented BC workers well. Moreover, the union president was not a "trade union hoodlum," and rumours and allegations of rampant corruption had no substance: "The membership was not denied its rights under the constitution, funds were not embezzled or misappropriated, nor was there suppression of members' right to speak against their officers."[113]

Initially the international executive accepted the secession of the BC locals with regret but without acrimony.[114] Soon, however, this harmony dissipated. Over the course of the 1960s, six pulp and paper facilities were constructed in the Interior of the province, five after 1965, and there was a nasty battle over which union would represent the workers. To staff the new mills, companies poached experienced workers from coastal mills and central Canadian operations to take on the skilled jobs especially, and these workers brought their union loyalties with them.

Unionizing the Castlegar mill in the first years of the 1960s was an extremely messy affair. Even before the mill was running, the United Papermakers and Paperworkers (UPP) gained certification in the plant. This was challenged by the IBPSPMW, setting off months of Labour Relations Board rulings, charges of raiding, and interventions by both the Canadian Labour Congress and the AFL-CIO.[115] In the end, the workers established an independent Canadian local; delegates from this local were present at the Vancouver meeting in January 1963 that created what was then called the Canadian Pulp and Paper Union, which later became the Pulp and Paper Workers of Canada (PPWC). Castlegar became Local 1.

Conflict was bitter at the Prince George Pulp and Paper operation. The IBPSPMW was recognized, and a PPWC application for certification was rejected by the Labour Relations Board in May 1966, even though there was majority support for the Canadian union. In the fall of 1966, PPWC supporters successfully ran for the executive offices in the IBPSPMW local. The executive then began a PPWC organizing campaign, agreeing among themselves that the same executive would stay in place if they were successful. The international responded in late October 1967 by expelling eight members who they believed were affiliated with the raiding PPWC. The Prince George and District Council fully supported the international: the expelled members had been deceitful, violating their IBPSPMW oath to serve the union. In early November, under the supervision of two local newspapers and the local radio station, a vote was held. There was an 80 percent turnout (252 out of 313 employees); 228 endorsed the PPWC and only 24 the IBPSPMW. In early 1968, the company refused to recognize the PPWC local, arguing, correctly, that it still had a contract with the international. The latter demanded that the company dismiss 144 activists. Finally, the LRB certified PPWC Local 9 at the Prince George mill in the summer of 1968.[116]

Besides establishing itself in new facilities in the Interior, the PPWC actively raided on the Coast. At the Harmac plant, just outside Nanaimo, workers had long been represented by Local 695 of the IBPSPMW. In union elections in May 1966, PPWC supporters secured control of the executive, creating Local 8 of the PPWC and signing up more workers. To get control of the finances, the PPWC supporters created the Nanaimo Hourly Paid Pulp Workers Benevolent Society, and money, bonds, and certificates were transferred to the new entity.[117] Workers, perhaps as many as 95 percent, signed cards showing that they supported the PPWC, but on 2 August, the LRB denied certification.[118] IBPSPMW vice president Pat O'Neal, who was from BC, argued on an open-line Nanaimo radio show that, contrary to what the PPWC was saying, it was not because of a technicality that the LRB acted as it did – rather it was PPWC members' cheating, lying, bribery, and violations of the Labour Relations Act that prompted the decision.[119] The PPWC then applied to have Local 695 decertified, but the IBPSPMW lawyer argued successfully that the international was fulfilling its mandate in the collective agreement and serving the workers effectively.[120]

The struggle shifted to the streets. On the morning of 13 August 1966, a protest cavalcade involving some 800 people began in Nanaimo. Workers and their families drove to the provincial capital, Victoria, picking up supporters along the way. They marched from Victoria City Hall to the legislature, where they presented a petition to the government demanding representation by the PPWC and promising that they would abide by the existing contract negotiated by the IBPSPMW. The PPWC argued that this was a basic fight for democracy. The forces arrayed against the union included the LRB, the government, the IBPSPMW, and the trade union establishment in the province. MacMillan Bloedel, the owner of the Harmac mill, favoured the IBPSPMW. MacMillan Bloedel president J.V. Clyne chatted with LRB chairman Bill Sands during an airplane trip in late August, and then gave his assessment of the Harmac situation to an official in the company's Industrial Relations Department:

> Macphee and Braaten are following the usual communistic tactics. They are being reasonable and democratic in their attitudes, but will undoubtedly cause trouble in the future. It would be best to avoid the Canadian union, but it does not look possible. Sands thinks that it will take over a year for [international representatives] O'Neal and Green to persuade the men to go back to the International. In the meantime, we are faced with a very awkward situation in that the great majority of the men have elected to become members of the Canadian union.[121]

In early 1967, the IBPSPMW expelled a number of Local 8 activists, then demanded that the company meet the terms of the collective agreement and dismiss them from their jobs because they were no longer union members. The situation was becoming absurd, as an IWA leader pointed out, when the BC Federation of Labour considered the suspension of the 823 PPWC supporters out of a total of 950 mill employees: "To now request the suspension of these 823 workers can only be interpreted as the doings of a mad man or someone deliberately desiring to damage the entire labour movement."[122] In the end, the PPWC prevailed; the IBPSPMW local was decertified and Local 8 was certified as the legal representative of the workers on 20 June.

The IBPSPMW had its successes. At Campbell River, charges against twenty-one IBPSPMW members for participating in PPWC activities in 1966 had a "demoralizing effect," and the international was sustained.[123] The Port Mellon IBPSPMW local thwarted a PPWC raid in the late 1960s. In Prince George, two operations went PPWC, but Northwood Pulp, a few miles away, remained in the international,[124] as did the big Powell River and Port Alberni operations on the Coast.

The IBPSPMW was not oblivious to the rising nationalist tide. In 1963 central Canadian IBPSPMW leaders were at the forefront of an initiative, accepted by the AFL, that recognized the CLC as the final arbiter in all jurisdictional disputes in Canada.[125] A Canadian Identity Committee was established at the first Canadian conference of IBPSPMW locals in 1967. The committee recommended that four members of the executive board be Canadians selected by the Canadian caucus, that the Canadian director should report directly to the president-secretary, that Canadian per capita payments should go to the office of the Canadian director, and that "the Canadian membership of the I.B.P.S. and P.M.W. shall be affiliated to the International World Federation of Labour as a separate entity in keeping with its status as a nation and in order that Canadian delegates may participate on a National level with all countries."[126] Negotiations followed, and the international, recognizing that the game was up, facilitated the breakaway of the Canadian locals. In June 1974, at a convention in Toronto, the Canadian Paper Workers Union was founded. The new union had 220 locals and some 54,000 members; the western region had 33 locals and 11,500 members. Although the two big unions in the BC pulp and paper industry were independent Canadian unions, their swords remained unsheathed, as they organized raids and attacked each other.

The IWA was drawn into these battles. All three unions fought to gain certification at the Tahsis Company's new integrated pulp mill and sawmill at Gold River, on the west side of Vancouver Island, in 1967. Syd Thompson, president of the large Vancouver IWA local, who had long desired to organize all woodworkers into one union, declared that the IBPSPMW was unfit to represent the workers and that the PPWC was even worse: "Wrapping itself up in the Maple Leaf flag and shouting Canadian slogans is a poor substitute for a proper trade union job."[127] To the dismay of Thompson and three other local presidents in the IWA opposition group, the IWA district council decided to work with the IBPSPMW in a joint application. In the end, the IWA proposal was thrown out by the LRB, and there was a runoff vote between the IBPSPMW and the PPWC, which the latter won by twenty-three votes.[128] PPWC raids on IWA locals at Chemainus, Houston, and Mackenzie sawmills prompted an IWA response: "These people [the PPWC] have declared war on the IWA and it still holds true that the best defence is an offence."[129] At the IWA regional convention in October 1971, the union declared "all-out war" against the PPWC.[130]

In 1973 the PPWC launched a raid on the Port Alberni local of the IWA, trying to organize the 1,100 employees at the Somass sawmill. The maintenance workers, who had much mobility within the mill and thus could talk to many workers, led the charge. The PPWC also had pockets of support among carrier drivers and in the planer mill. The IWA responded by putting six Somass workers on the IWA payroll; their job was to keep workers in the IWA and woo PPWC supporters back. The six, according to the IWA, persuaded over 80 percent of the defectors to revoke their PPWC memberships, but, to the IWA's dismay, the LRB decided to hold a vote to find out which union the workers supported. An IWA steering committee managed the campaign. They decided that instead of attacking the PPWC, their printed leaflets would emphasize the virtues of the IWA. The anti-PPWC campaign would be carried out by word-of-mouth attacks. The IWA recognized the appeal of Canadian nationalism in the early 1970s, "that all things being equal the members would prefer to belong to an all-Canadian Union," and "therefore they had to be shown that they couldn't afford to leave the I.W.A." No international officers were involved in the campaign, and the union literature often stated that "the Canadian section of the I.W.A. had *always* had full autonomy." Activists were carefully coached:

> The I.W.A. supporters were asked to challenge the P.P.W.C. every time they opened their mouths, given embarrassing questions to ask the P.P.W.C. (such as asking them in front of other members "explain to Joe here why you are trying to do him out of his pension", or "what's going to happen to the four boommen who will have to come back into the plant", or "how come you want us to pay 2% of our wages to support the pulp strike this summer") and it was suggested that whenever a P.P.W.C. supporter got up to speak in a lunchroom he be told to "sit down and shut up."

IWA machine operators were asked to keep the millwrights, who tended to be PPWC, busy by continually getting them to do small repairs, and thus not allow them to speak to other workers. IWA loggers and members of the IBPSPMW telephoned friends who worked at the Somass mill to reinforce the positive aspects of belonging to the IWA, as did respected members of the East Indian community in Port Alberni. In the end, the IWA won. Of the members who voted, 670 supported the IWA and 300 the PPWC.[131]

The situation did not improve. In 1975, during a total shutdown of the pulp and paper industry, Syd Thompson mused about inter-union cooperation but concluded that "the unions are so far apart on what is possible to achieve that it is hopeless to even think about working out a common approach."[132]

The Public Face of Unionism

By the mid-1960s, unions in the forest industry presented a rather sorry spectacle. Nasty internal squabbles, based more on confrontations between the ins and the outs than on principles, and inter-union battles made a joke of the supposed goal of solidarity. For outsiders, and even many union members, unionism was no longer the standard bearer of a great crusade for justice but merely a locale for battles that were incomprehensible to those not directly involved. In the mid-1960s, two unsavoury issues, one involving the IWA and the other the pulp unions, made provincial newspaper headlines.

In 1967 the presidents of four IWA locals, including Syd Thompson, publicly attacked Joe Morris, the executive vice president of the CLC and former district president of the IWA, claiming that Morris had interfered in the internal affairs of IWA Local 1-85 and its attempt to organize workers at Gold River. The BC Federation of Labour, to which the IWA locals belonged, demanded a public apology, claiming that the "statement constituted a vicious and personal attack on a respected trade unionist."[133] The four locals were then suspended on 9 June for not publicly retracting the statement.[134] Other IWA locals came out in support of the four suspended locals, plunging the BC labour movement into crisis. The dispute continued through the summer, and a CLC committee attempted to mediate. The CLC felt it necessary to remind the BC labour community of its history, linking the current situation to the Red Bloc/White Bloc split in the province in 1948, when "scandalous attacks were made on Congress officers."[135] In the end, the BC Federation of Labour blinked; the IWA was too big to antagonize. The suspension was lifted even though there had been no apology.[136]

In the other case, an overexuberant international pulp and paper union representative pushed the boundaries of legality. E.P. "Pat" O'Neal was hired by the IBPSPMW as regional director of organization, specifically to meet the challenge posed by the PPWC. O'Neal was well known in BC labour circles. He had been secretary of the BC Federation of Labour for eight years, prior to which he had been president of the Prince Rupert IBPSPMW Local 708. He was also an executive member of the federal New Democratic Party. O'Neal was responsible for saving Harmac for the international, and as the Harmac situation deteriorated and confrontations became uglier, he decided to resort to extraordinary measures. He hired a private detective, a former member of the Security and Intelligence

Branch of the Royal Canadian Mounted Police, recommended by a police officer whom he knew from Prince Rupert, and paid the private detective $250 with a union cheque. The possibility of planting an informer in the PPWC was discussed, but O'Neal suggested using electronic listening devices to eavesdrop on meetings at the upcoming PPWC convention. On Saturday, 5 November 1966, PPWC executive officer Angus Macphee found a wireless microphone "on top of a portable cupboard in the corridor meeting room that separates Room 206 and Room 207 of the Ritz Hotel" in Vancouver. The PPWC hired Ace Agencies to debug its rooms, and on Monday a second microphone was found. Authorities were notified[137] and the anti-union Social Credit provincial government appointed a commission to investigate the incident and the issue of invasion of privacy more generally. The Sargent Commission held hearings in late 1966 and early 1967. Orville Braaten spent one week in Oakalla Prison in late February 1967 because he refused to discuss internal union business before the commission. When the commission's report came out that summer, it exonerated O'Neal, claiming that the PPWC was so despicable that extraordinary measures were justified.[138]

Strong industrial unions were established in the forest sector early in the Fordist era. The crusade for justice and dignity that animated the organizational drives of the 1930s and 1940s brought together activists from a broad political spectrum, but this fragile unity was not maintained. Social democrats, communists, nationalists, and internationalists fought for union leadership positions, and institutional rivalries were rarely far below the surface. Unions from 1945 to 1974 could not transcend these divisions.

In 1959 Angus Macphee, an activist in the Prince Rupert IBPSPMW Local 708, and international president-secretary John Burke, exchanged comments on the history and future of the labour movement. Macphee felt that harmony and unity were crucial for the labour movement, and he could not understand why his international, an AFL union, did not merge with the United Papermakers and Paperworkers, a CIO union. This seemed very logical after the union of the AFL and CIO in 1955. Burke, who had been active in the IBPSPMW since the first decade of the century, patiently outlined the history of their union and the testy relations with the CIO papermakers. He noted that CIO unions had been organized in the 1930s expressly to displace the two AFL unions in the pulp and paper industry, and that for ten years, the UPP, CIO, had made war upon the IBPSPMW, raiding many locals. He also reminded Macphee that just before the merger of the AFL and CIO, which officers of the UPP knew was pending, the CIO union led a raid in New Hampshire and launched "a most vicious campaign" against the IBPSPMW and its officers. It cost the IBPSPMW $13,000 to defend the local. Burke also went back to the early years of the century in discussing the foundations of the union.

He noted: "Of course you may say that this is all ancient history. This may all be true, but we cannot separate ourselves altogether from history even though some of it may be ancient."[139] Within months Macphee came to the conclusion that labour unity could be sacrificed at times and he became a leader in the breakaway PPWC, writing another chapter in the history of division and discord in the provincial labour movement.

5
The Daily Grind

Dramatic strikes and lockouts too often represent the point of contact between capital and labour, obscuring the ongoing relations that bind them together in the production system. In the Fordist era, collective agreements formalized and structured relations, but tension remained. In large companies, special industrial relations and personnel departments dealt with employee concerns, while smaller firms relied on persuasion and goodwill to maintain productive work sites. For most union officials, radicals and moderates alike, daily life involved representing workers who had disputes with management and ensuring that the terms of the collective agreement were followed faithfully by employers. Labour relations were just one activity among many for corporations, but for unions, defending the workplace interests of members was a primary responsibility. Indeed, they could do little else. Unions established themselves in the forest industry in the 1940s and won the right to negotiate collective agreements, but companies maintained control of operations. Unions were permitted to negotiate only a narrow range of issues that pertained to the workplace, wages, and benefits, and the limited government support unions obtained was predicated on their acceptance of the legalistic, bureaucratic industrial relations system and the prerogatives of capital. Unions, which were much poorer financially than companies, spent the bulk of their resources monitoring employer activities at the job site and speaking for their members.

Successful union officials maintained both the support of the membership and a working relationship with companies. This was not always easy. Workers at times disagreed with the leadership, and participation in routine union affairs was spotty. Even in the heady days of the 1930s and 1940s, workers often showed little interest in the day-to-day activities of their union, much to the chagrin of activists, although in times of personal need or during contract negotiations, workers recognized the importance of the union in their lives. If relations between union leaders and the membership could be testy, as could relations between unions and companies, there were also instances where union officials, workers, and company representatives worked together, instituting safety programs on the shop floor and participating in committees to enhance productivity. The everyday world of work was thus governed by conflict and accommodation.

Day-to-day production at the job site was enmeshed in a more general struggle about the meaning of social and economic relations. Leftists offered critical readings of Fordist society; employers, in turn, defended their worldview, presenting it to workers as plausible and appropriate. Employers saw the union movement, if infused with socialist interpretations, as a threat. They forcefully countered even moderate proposals that hinted at restricting the prerogatives of capital, enhancing the role of the state, or highlighting class conflict. This chapter looks at the particular and the general in relations between capital and labour: the day-to-day interaction at the workplace and the larger struggle over meaning that kept capital in control and labour circumscribed.

Union Officials and the Rank and File

Union officials of the Fordist era have been slammed as a conservative, staid lot, concerned merely with their jobs, perpetuating an ossified, stagnant union structure, a bureaucratic leadership stifling spontaneous worker radicalism. Forest industry union leaders saw it differently, however. They were involved activists, taking a long-term view of the union, while members were more concerned with immediate material interests. Workers had insufficient union consciousness, they often argued, were concerned only with money, and did not appreciate the efforts of union officials. Moreover, the membership failed to understand the broader principles that informed trade union positions on issues such as overtime, incentive schemes, and piecework.

Attendance at union meetings was a concern from an early date. In 1940, three years after the International Brotherhood of Pulp, Sulphite and Paper Mill Workers (IBPSPMW) Powell River local was revived, a union officer proposed a $4 fine on members who did not attend one out of four meetings, an idea that was approved by the international president.[1] Fifteen years later, the IBPSPMW local at Port Mellon instituted a similar policy. Dues were raised to $4 per month, but there would be a refund for attendance at two meetings out of six. The membership endorsed the idea despite some grumblings, and the results satisfied the executive: "Members who did not make a practice of attending meetings are now taking an active interest, and also an active part on committees. With larger attendance meetings are more constructive and interesting."[2] A year later, the Harmac local also considered imposing fines on members who did not attend monthly union meetings.[3] John P. Burke had been coping with member apathy since becoming international president in 1916. While he was reluctant to endorse compulsion, preferring persuasion, he did exhibit frustration in 1955, stating that a large proportion of the membership of most unions neglected their organization: "Some union members never attend their union meetings. Just think of it! After all this union of ours has done to better the conditions of its members we would logically assume that all meetings would be packed to the doors."[4] In the International Woodworkers of America (IWA), too, member commitment to the union was seen as a problem. In 1954 union leaders at the district annual convention criticized rank-and-file members for "a lackadaisical attitude."[5]

Union officials lamented that members were too obsessed with monetary issues rather than broad trade union principles, favouring wage increases over sustaining the union as a permanent institution. Within months of the establishment of the IBPSPMW local in Powell River, workers were restless because the union was not delivering sufficient material gains, and when the contract was signed, it took much explaining by union officials to overcome the dismay of disheartened workers who had hoped for a larger wage increase.[6] Union officials saw the larger goal of union recognition as more important than short-term wage benefits. The situation had not changed by the early 1950s, as a Powell River union official noted:

> It appears to me that our so-called members are merely card-packers only interested in how much money they can put in their pockets rather than in promoting Trade Union principles to which we subscribe ... They have no respect for the International Union or the Local Officers who have worked so diligently to bring about proper working conditions, vacations with pay, superannuation and many other items too numerous to mention.[7]

Attitudes towards piecework, incentive schemes, and overtime divided officials and the membership. In trade union tradition, these were seen as methods to exploit workers, rob them of leisure time, and, in the case of overtime, sustain high levels of unemployment because companies did not need to hire more workers. Workers, however, often thought otherwise. The Pas Lumber Company logging operation near Kamloops introduced an incentive system in 1948, whereby skidder operators received an hourly rate plus $1.80 for every thousand board feet over a set daily production level. Both production levels and worker wages increased: "Union officials make it plain that they dislike the plan, but the employees at the Pas indicate that they do."[8] Piecework also existed in the coastal region. Shingle workers were often paid by the unit produced, and in the woods, fallers and buckers worked for piece rates, also known as contract rates. The IWA was officially against piece rates but loggers favoured it. The highly paid, skilled fallers, who were at a pivotal point in the production process, often had both a day rate and a piece rate. By the 1950s, they had secured such a high rate of pay that employers were concerned that it was causing discontent in the camps and raising worker expectations, as fallers earned more than double the industry average, and so employers sought a day rate.[9] The problem was to set a day or hourly rate that in the loggers' minds fairly compensated them for their efforts. This issue festered through the 1960s, and the fallers engaged in strike action in 1972 to sustain piece rates, despite opposition from both employers and their union.[10]

The IWA and the pulp and paper unions were strongly against overtime work but employers pressed for it, and, as the IBPSPMW president noted in 1953, "I don't have to tell you how difficult it is to curb overtime because so many workers want to work overtime and get the extra money."[11] He added that when the unions first negotiated premium pay for overtime work, it was intended as a disincentive, to make it too costly for employers to make employees work beyond eight hours, not as a reward for workers. At times workers refused to work overtime, claiming that they did so to create more jobs, but overtime bans were usually brought in to force the company, which relied on overtime work, to deal with other issues. In 1961 a Port Alberni sawmill was shut for two days when the men refused to work weekend overtime. Union officials publicly stated that the stoppage was an attempt to curb the use of overtime, but the shutdown was actually a strategy by the mill workers to influence a wage dispute over a particular job in the mill.[12] Similarly, at the Powell River pulp and paper mill in February 1954, maintenance workers refused to work overtime on the changeover of the number 8 paper machine. It was a way of protesting the company's failure to promote the men's favourite candidate to the job of foreman of the millwright crew.[13]

Union officials bemoaned the attitudes of workers and the lack of worker recognition for their efforts, but complaints of worker apathy need qualification. During contract negotiations and in strike votes, the membership was very involved. In the fall of 1953, 89 percent of the workers in the IBPSPMW who were employed in the nine BC pulp and paper locals cast ballots for or against a strike.[14] In 1967, with an IWA strike pending in the Interior, 3,857 out of 4,344 eligible voters (89 percent) cast a ballot.[15] Despite the lack of interest in day-to-day issues, workers prized their union, and rallied to it during confrontations with employers.

Servicing the Membership

There were reasons why workers did not participate in the daily activities of their union. Much of what union officials did applied to only one or two workers. These issues, unlike overall wage increases, did not affect the whole membership. Those not involved in the specific case knew little about the details and often had little interest in the outcome. In 1944 the Powell River Company discharged a union member for striking his superintendent. The union grievance committee investigated the case for two days and decided that the worker had been provoked into striking the superintendent. The union took the issue to the mill manager, who deliberated for a few weeks. The local union had made a procedural error, incorrectly following the process set out in the Adjustment of Complaints section of the collective agreement. The procedural aspects were cleared up and the case, which by now had been going on for almost three weeks, proceeded, with the union confident of a satisfactory result.[16] In 1954 the IWA fought the case of six employees who had been fired by Strom Lumber in the Prince George area. The affair was taken to an arbitration board and eventually five of the employees were reinstated and won compensation. The dismissal of the sixth man was upheld: he had been intoxicated on the job.[17]

The language of collective agreements was complex, and discussions over aspects of the contract could be interminable and tiresome. Elected union officials performed these important duties, relieving the membership of them. In September 1953, newly appointed IBPSPMW international representative Stanley Green, who had been a worker in the Woodfibre mill and was now based in Vancouver, travelled north to spend a week in Prince Rupert, dealing with the concerns of the Watson Island local. He met first with the local's bargaining committee to discuss the report of a conciliation board for a new contract, which he anticipated that the local's membership would reject. Along with members of the joint local-company standing committee, he also had a number of meetings with the company concerning interpretations of the contract and adjustments to it.

One meeting concerned overtime and how the rules would be applied. The Standard Labour Agreement, which covered all the BC pulp and paper mills, specified a particular overtime rate, but it had to meet the needs of scheduling, internal job transfers, and the peculiarities of each mill. It was complicated:

> It was agreed at that meeting that the hours of work in that particular plant would be averaged on an eight week basis, (previous agreement), and that the periods would commence on July 1st, 1953. The basis will be understood to be a period of 320 hours, and all work performed in excess of that time will be calculated at overtime rates. This is necessitated by their system of days off, which is a six on and two off arrangement. There have, however, been many instances where, due to promotion, a man has had his days off eliminated by transferring from one crew to another, and has received no compensation for same. Under this new method of calculation the men will receive the overtime which they should; keeping in mind, however, that any work which is paid for at overtime rates, such as working on a designated day off, or work in excess of eight hours, will be eliminated from the calculation. All work performed on Sunday will be calculated on the basis of eight hours worked, even though payment is at the time and a half rate. This was agreeable to both parties.[18]

It is little wonder that most workers were content to leave the affairs of the union to an interested few, content to see the change on their paycheque.

Another meeting pertained to job classification adjustments to the existing contract. One case involved establishing a pay rate for a new position in the mill, that of "tool clerk." The union was unhappy with the company's offer to pay the tool clerk only $1.60 per hour, arguing that the two other companies in the province that had established pay rates for tool clerks paid $1.70 per hour. After a brief discussion, the company and the union agreed that the worker, who was now being paid $1.54 per hour, would be paid $1.65 per hour in the new classification, and this rate would rise to $1.70. Another discussion involved defining a job category.

A new class of engineer – third-class engineer, maintenance – was being created. The new position was not intended to displace the second-class engineer, but would be more of an assistant to the second-class engineer. A worker, the senior fireman, had already been performing these duties, although at a lower wage rate, so a new position was created that paid more than the senior fireman rate. Another point of contention involved only millwrights and pipefitters. The result of the discussion was inconclusive, but Stanley Green argued that the millwright's job, when on shift, was to keep the plant operating, and if an emergency involved pipefitting, the millwright would effect emergency repairs only and wait for the pipefitters to come on shift to do a full repair.

Establishing job classifications and rates of pay for different jobs took up much time. New equipment or changes to the production process led to talks and often controversy. In late 1957, Canadian White Pine, a division of MacMillan & Bloedel, installed a new attachment on the Hyster, a lift truck that moved heavy cargo at its Vancouver facility. This enabled the company to eliminate one swamper, the person who assisted the driver. The IWA and workers at the plant were concerned about the lost job and the fact that the remaining workers had to do more work. The company had offered to renegotiate the rate of the Hyster operator, but the union official responsible for the matter was slow to act. Some four months later, the company eliminated the other swamper, leaving the Hyster drivers all by themselves, both driving and swamping. The company and the drivers wanted action, but the IWA was dragging its feet at the district council level. In the end, the district council decided to withdraw from the matter "and enter into negotiations with Management on a Local basis in an attempt to get the best rate possible for the [H]yster drivers."[19]

The complexity of union contracts and negotiations with companies made great demands of union officials. This led to some locals hiring business agents – paid, not elected, officials to run the local's affairs full time. Business agents have been seen as part of the problem with unions in the Fordist era, breaking the link between the membership and elected officials and creating a conservative political environment supporting the status quo. In the BC forest industry, radicalism and the hiring of business agents were not mutually exclusive. Orville Braaten, the leftist agitator in the IBPSPMW, was a business agent, and from this position he tried to move the membership leftward. Angus Macphee, another leftist IBPSPMW activist, supported the position of business agent: "There is much that only full-time men can do ... even my own small local would have a business agent were it not for the cost. In Research and Education alone the need is great."[20] Representative democracy, where workers delegated responsibilities to union officials and hired agents, was a sensible, practical option in the era of the collective agreement.

Union/Employer Cooperation and Job Evaluation

Unions and employers recognized that each relied on the other and that issues had to be resolved to keep the machinery of production going. Special committees facilitated cooperation and dispute resolution without recourse to the collective agreement. Joint committees, with both employer and union representation, dealt with safety, job evaluation, grievances, and production issues. British Columbia Plywoods established an employee committee in 1937. Nine elected members met regularly with the general manager and assistant manager of the facility. At the first meeting, a number of issues were discussed, including whether to put an extra spotter on the dry chain, time off for dry chain employees and dryers to eat, bonuses, health insurance, soap and towels at washbasins, proper connection for the sewer pipe at the lathe end, a safety cover for bull wheel and lathe, heat in the lunchrooms, and lights at the lathe and dry table.[21] The committee continued to meet after the plant was unionized and a collective agreement was in place.

Union leaders endorsed the creation of these bodies. In 1942 the IWA recommended the establishment of labour/management production committees and industrial councils to deal daily, and even hourly, with questions that concerned sustaining and increasing production levels.[22] In 1942 the Powell River Company approached the executive of IBPSPMW Local 76 and requested the establishment of a management/employee committee. Unsure of what to do and wondering whether or not this clashed with union principles, the executive asked the international president for an opinion. He supported the proposal.[23] During the Second World War, companies and unions made joint presentations to the Regional War Labour Board to secure wage increases for workers and worked together to lobby various government agencies to ensure that the mills had a sufficient timber supply.[24] These arrangements continued into the postwar era.[25]

In the mid-1950s, the issue of job evaluation illustrated cooperation and conflict as well as the mundane complexity of much union business.[26] Companies disliked the constant bargaining over categories and pay rates, arguing that they wanted to establish a more formal, scientific way of establishing occupational categories and wage rates. This initiative, called job analysis or job evaluation, came from the United States, and drew on scientific management ideas that had been around for decades.[27] Each job was evaluated and broken down into constituent parts based on the following requirements: knowledge and skill (education, experience, and complexity of duties), effort (physical, mental, and visual demands), responsibilities (supervision or safety of others and control of materials, equipment, and products), and job conditions (hazards). The groups were weighted as follows: knowledge and skill, 50 percent; effort, 15 percent; responsibilities, 25 percent; and job conditions, 10 percent.[28] A total number of points would be assigned for the particular job. Wage rates would then correspond to the number of points awarded to the jobs. Promoted as common sense because it was rational and efficient, job evaluation set out clear criteria for judging workers and the amount of work that they performed. It was a control technique that enabled companies to reward and punish workers in a seemingly impersonal manner, thus establishing the company's standard of a fair day's work. Unions, too, accepted the general idea of detailed job descriptions, which offered some protection to workers and a clear statement of their responsibilities, but it was a corporate initiative.[29]

Job evaluation began in the plywood sector in 1955, and the union anticipated that it would be instituted the following year. Because of differences in the eleven Lower Mainland plywood plants, however, jobs in all the facilities had to be evaluated. There was much heated debate, involving the union and workers on one side and the company and consultants on the other, about the detailed evaluations. Most of the workers, 85 percent of 4,541 employees, were assigned to the lower third of the wage scale, and the company wanted to drop the base rate for some of the lowest jobs. The base rate stuck, however, and job evaluation was implemented in plywood in 1959.[30] In pulp and paper, too, companies pushed for job analysis after the mid-1950s, but union concerns postponed its implementation until 1964.[31] Companies also wanted job evaluation in the larger sawmill sector. The union saw job evaluation as a way to get rid of inequities and standardize wage rates across the region, but there were serious concerns. Was the plan just an attempt by the companies to freeze or lower wages? Was it a way to intensify work? Evidence from the plywood sector also suggested that job evaluation was having the effect of shrinking the wage differential between the lowest paid, unskilled workers and the more highly paid skilled workers, much to the chagrin of the IWA leadership.[32]

Job evaluation also began in the shingle and logging sectors. The union agreed to establish a committee made up of two employer representatives and two union representatives to evaluate new jobs and jobs where there had been changes, but the issue was hardly straightforward. Each machine, each job, and each work site had its own peculiarities, and rapid technological change meant that the process was open-ended, as a union representative noted in 1960: "It appears we are going to be successful in working out proper categories and rates for logging, but the job is never done because every time you turn around, you run into a new machine, a new piece of equipment ... Throughout the whole industry the question of categories and rates is a problem."[33] In the 1970 IWA contract, job evaluation remained important and troublesome: in the sawmill sector, there was an agreement to further discuss the issue before any implementation took place, and in the plywood sector, there was provision for a third party to adjudicate the ongoing job evaluation disputes between the company and the union.[34] The job evaluation issue seemed interminable.

The War of Position

Debates between capital and labour were not only about the nitty-gritty of particular jobs or contract language. There was also a struggle for the minds and souls of workers. Liberal capitalist discourse was overwhelming, but there was room for debate. Union officials and leftist political groups offered alternatives and modifications, and employers responded with their version of liberal capitalism, defending the rights of owners of private property, celebrating their version of democracy, and justifying economic inequality. Business narratives were more focused, united by the imperatives of capitalist accumulation. Capital was very aware of the implications of this contest. Howell John Harris, in a study of American businessmen in the 1940s, notes that for employers "there could be no rigid line between attempting to influence workers as employees and shaping their attitudes as citizens. They were engaged in a complex struggle for moral authority, not just a contest for power."[35]

Companies had more money and expertise, hiring skilled agents to coordinate their activities and win advantage. In negotiating with unions, they relied on experts such as Stuart Research, operated by R.V. Stuart, who was hired in 1942 to carry on industrial relations for the lumber industry, and preparation for strikes was elaborate and sophisticated.[36] Companies also used their resources to carry on a larger campaign against the threat of unionism and leftism. Corporate public images were shined and polished. The 1934 loggers' strike was a public relations disaster.[37] By 1936 the BC Loggers' Association had set up a publicity committee to coordinate a planned policy of public relations to improve the image of the industry in the eyes of the public and their employees. Winning over newspaper editors was given special attention. The member companies recognized the importance of this campaign and did not begrudge their financial contribution to the publicity committee.[38] In the summer of 1944, Paul E. Cooper, the new chief executive officer of Pacific Mills, stressed positive public relations as a key goal of his company.[39] The BC Lumber Manufacturers Association established a public relations department in June 1950 and a public relations counsel was employed part time. As association president W.J. Van Dusen noted, because of this "an encouraging measure of mutual confidence has been established which is hoped, will curtail the frequent misleading and at times hostile press notices, based on rumour and misinformation, which have appeared in the past. The press have agreed and are checking their information with us, and we in turn, have agreed to provide a source of factual information on industry matters."[40] The BC division of the Canadian Pulp and Paper Association also paid increased attention to image and public relations in the 1950s.[41]

The industry was ever vigilant. In 1953 an exam question and answer prepared by the provincial Department of Education was found offensive because it unfavourably compared the BC lumber industry to the European industry. Commented an industry trade journal: "This Social Studies paper, going out to thousands of students, strikes a resounding blow for the cause of communism."[42] In 1963 pressure from the industry caused the provincial government to remove from circulation a film, *Highball Logger,* produced by the Department of Lands and Forests, because of its negative portrayal of the logging practices of the industry.[43] Public opinion polls were taken to gauge the attitudes of the public and employees towards companies, unions, and forest practices.[44] In 1970 Gordon L. Draeseke, the president of the Council of Forest Industries (COFI), took the time to respond in print to objectionable comments about the forest industry in the University of British Columbia student newspaper, *The Ubyssey,* and in 1974 COFI's Communications Division produced a pamphlet to help management personnel deal with the public in their communities.[45]

H.R. MacMillan was very aware of this larger war of ideas and representation. In the early 1940s, when the IWA was battling for recognition from the companies, MacMillan was in Ottawa and Montreal engaged in government work to further the war effort. He was not involved directly in the struggle against unionization. MacMillan's biographer, Ken Drushka, suggests that he was more progressive than other BC lumbermen, willing to consider a relationship with unions as long as they evinced no leftist, political agenda. MacMillan's statements at times also suggest resignation regarding a growing role for government in labour relations,[46] but he offered these musings on labour and the state from a distance, and his companies were not notably distinct in their labour policy. MacMillan pointedly attacked the Co-operative Commonwealth Federation (CCF), which he saw "as a direct threat to the future of the province."[47] During the 1949 provincial election, he addressed the annual January convention of the Truck Loggers Association. It was a strongly worded, no-holds-barred attack on socialists in British Columbia and the threat that they posed to the free enterprise system. Capital, argued MacMillan, had made the modern history of British Columbia, attracting pioneers and ingeniously establishing industries across the province in a wide variety of endeavours. The purpose of the socialists, on the other hand, was "to tear this economy to shreds, to destroy this hard-won stability, to break down the confidence that has grown up in this province, to unsettle these people, frighten them, make them dependent, and to probably expel those who have been successful." A socialist government would mean "chaos followed by destruction of values and destruction of jobs, accompanied by a cessation of migration and an expansion and continuation of emigration of the province's best people."[48] Mixing a version of history with a statement of values, MacMillan was the exponent of a persuasive liberal, capitalist discourse.

MacMillan recognized the threat of alternative views of the world and realized that individuals could be drawn into alternative discourses. In 1935, a time when leftist radicalism was prominent in both BC electoral politics and unions, MacMillan was calm. He felt that radicals were few in number and that the press was exaggerating the difficulties. But he also knew that belief systems could recruit and define new members, necessitating proper action by employers: "I think forbearance and tact exercised by employers in every direction, together with a continual non-provocative policy of education will enable us to keep the control of our affairs in the hands of the sound rank and file of the people."[49] The chances for change were perhaps small but they were real: "It is probable that only a small portion of the people would require to be shifted from the left to the right politically to cause a great turn over in sentiment."[50] In 1949 he again alluded to the fragmented, flexible nature of individuals, as well as the importance of clear discourses in locating and confronting individuals: "It is very probable that a great many unthinking people look at this party full of promises, which masquerades under a name [Co-operative Commonwealth Federation] that doesn't mean anything to anybody, and support it in error. Therefore, I think that we should isolate this enemy to our economy and name it, and that on every occasion we should call them Socialists."[51] Besides offering a worldview, it was necessary to undermine alternatives.

The rise of unionism and the influence of the CCF contributed to increased state intervention in the 1940s, much to the dismay of forest industry owners who were hostile to government generally and to government-run social programs specifically. There is no evidence of progressive forest industry executives working with government officials to usher in the welfare, interventionist state. At one level, the argument was financial – the programs would cost companies too much money – but at another level, the argument was connected to a larger worldview that celebrated individualism, the rights of private property owners, and small government, which were seen as crucial to a healthy society. In the mid-1930s, when the provincial government considered a government-run health insurance plan, MacMillan protested against it. The Liberal proposal was "opposed by the majority of employers," and MacMillan hoped "to have the government delay it until at least they have it worked out on a sound actuarial basis," predicting, wrongly as it turned out, that his view would not prevail.[52] The BC Lumber and Shingle Manufacturers Association also came out against social legislation, arguing that "if the Industry is to be saddled with increased social legislation, and this seems to be the main object of all Provincial Governments, then the time can very well arrive when the Industry can no longer meet competition in foreign fields."[53] In 1952 the BC Loggers' Association was worried about the relatively new Hospital Insurance Program: "It will have to be watched to see that there is no radical departure from the original intention of the scheme – that the individual should pay for benefits offered under the plan. There may be an attempt to shoulder a major part of the cost onto industry in one way or another."[54]

Business leaders were not necessarily against social welfare measures, just against government and union involvement. Some in the forest business community, such as MacMillan, looked back to the era of welfare capitalism, the first decades of the

End of shift, Burnaby Paperboard, 1963.
MacMillan Bloedel Collection (UBC), BC 1930/136/1

twentieth century, when large corporations provided welfare programs for their employees. Here employers, not unions or governments, were in complete control, able to adjust programs in response to market circumstances. Indeed, such programs were a response to the threat of unions, a strategy to manufacture contented loyal employees without union interference. In 1938 MacMillan considered a pension plan for his employees, and it was still being discussed in 1947.[55] BC Plywoods established an employee medical plan and hospital insurance by 1943.[56] Bloedel, Stewart & Welch instituted a hospitalization plan at its Port Alberni and Great Central Lake operations in 1941, and soon 750 men were enrolled in the plan. The company added a pension plan in 1944. Canadian Western Lumber Company also introduced a pension plan, entirely paid by the company, in 1955. Three years of employment with the company were necessary to enroll in the scheme.[57]

These programs were meant to build loyalty, stabilize the labour force, and undermine the influence of the union. Also important, however, is the fact that they were controlled by businessmen and beyond the purview of politicians and fickle public opinion. Despite "progressive" welfare measures, companies were reluctant to entertain worker initiatives. In the summer of 1939, while MacMillan was contemplating benefit packages for his workers, one of his companies, BC Plywoods, unexpectedly dismissed some 70 workers six weeks after they had signed a petition for a wage increase. After the dismissals, a third shift was put to work and about a hundred boys under the age of twenty-one were hired. More skilled workers, crucial to the operation of the plant, were given pay raises to keep them loyal.[58] In 1942 the plywood plant laid off 140 employees, mostly women. It refused to recognize seniority in the decisions regarding layoffs, as well as the proposal by workers that would see their work time cut back if they all kept their jobs. After this the plant workers went union.[59]

In MacMillan's worldview, businesspeople should be society's leaders, and they should take this responsibility seriously, even if it meant paternalistic labour policies. The growing strength of unions, the left, and government was a contamination that threatened businessmen, social leaders, and society as a whole. In 1939 he warned of a growing state attack on one minority, the wealthy, offering a rather cynical account of the state of democracy to boot: governments, he said, use "some project or policy that will appeal to the least common denominators in the voting area, consequently one sees power taken from the people and money collected from the minority with growing impunity or arrogance by governments who are strong in the belief that they will dispose of these powers and spread that money [so] that a sufficient number of people will vote to keep them in office."[60]

In this era, democracy was a much-contested notion, and it had special resonance with regard to unions and the rights of employers. Canadians were committed to democracy, but what the term meant depended on how it was inserted into larger narratives. Communists, social democrats, reformers, radicals, liberals, capitalists, and unionists all invoked democracy as a virtue, mobilizing the idea in support of their goals. Nigel Morgan, member of the BC IWA executive and communist activist, noted in 1942: "Hitler's 'New Order' has no place for unions, free speech, fair wages, the right to vote, religious or democratic freedom ... The right to continue to organize, meet, discuss and work to correct inequalities is the essence of democracy, and we know that we must win this war in order to preserve those freedoms."[61] A 1949 union bulletin from the Duncan IWA local made the same point, locating unionism at the heart of a healthy democracy: "It is a well known fact that wherever Fascism or Communism or any other form of despotism takes over, they first destroy the trade union, for in so doing they attempt to destroy the breeding of those democratic ideas which they realize would eventually destroy them."[62] The same document argued that unions provided a training ground for the practice of democracy, that "in its meetings workers learn to act in unison following mutual discussion and majority decision, to control the policies of their union."[63]

The union battle for the democratically controlled union shop was waged against a different conception of democracy propounded by employers, one that emphasized freedom, individualism, and choice. Unions wanted the union shop, arguing that only then would the union have the security to act as an independent, free, democratic institution with control over its own affairs. In a union shop, a worker had to belong to the union in order to work for the company covered by the collective agreement. This gave the union security because companies could not build up an anti-union workforce to discredit or push out the union. The union shop also gave the union control – democratic control – over its own affairs, as it then had the authority to discipline its members if they transgressed the rules set out by the majority, a cardinal principle of democratic societies. A worker who was suspended from the union also lost his or her job, however.

Employers fought long and hard to prevent the introduction of the union shop in the forest industry. It was an attempt to restrict the power of unions and thus undermine their influence in the workplace. The employer attack on the union shop was couched in the language of democracy. In 1946 H.M. Lewis, the mill manager at the Port Mellon pulp and paper mill, told new employees that they should join the union but that there were limits to his support. He would not countenance forcing workers to join the union, and as such was completely against the union shop.[64] Bert Hoffmeister of MacMillan Industries was equally blunt in the same year, sending out an open letter to employees stating that the company was adamantly opposed to compulsory union membership. He elaborated, defending the rights of workers to join a union, just as they were free to join churches or fraternal organizations, but at the same time noted that they should be free not to join in order to work: "If you belong to a union you will always be free to do so. Most people in Canada support that idea. But surely the union should be good enough to get your voluntary support, and the employer should not be asked to recruit its members by having to fire all those who may not fall in line."[65]

In a brief to Gordon McGregor Sloan, the mediator in the 1946 strike, employers detailed the reasons for their aversion to the union shop. It violated fundamental individual rights; it denied the worker freedom of association; and it restricted the ability of a worker to earn a living in a chosen occupation. The brief went on to describe other potential injuries that the union shop would inflict on workers: that it prevented them from getting a job unless they paid "tribute" to a union; that certain classes of workers, especially the young and skilled workers from another locality, would be barred from jobs where the union shop was in force; and that undue and unreasonable fees could be imposed. The employer brief concluded: "In short, union security is a device contrived by professional labor leaders to get the employer to force his employees to do things that many of them, for the very best of personal reasons, would not do on their own accord. In other words, the employee's standing and his prospects for promotion would not depend on his ability and experience as a workman, but rather on his standing with the union."[66] The anti–union shop argument mixed naked self-interest and principle, the particular and the general.

The larger debate about democracy and its application in the union context touched an exposed nerve, even within the ranks of labour. In one trade union discourse, the union shop was very much frowned on. John P. Burke, the American president-secretary of the IBPSPMW for almost five decades after 1916, called himself an old-time socialist, having run for governor of New Hampshire on the Socialist party ticket in 1914. But Burke's union philosophy was very much rooted in the voluntarist tradition of the American Federation of Labor, of which his international union was a member. Wary of politics and government, he believed that labour relations and collective bargaining should be conducted between employers and unions. The involvement of the state was not necessary, and indeed not appropriate. From union headquarters in Fort Edward, New York, Burke carefully watched the British Columbia locals, and he was against the push of BC activists for the union shop. In 1942 he commented that sometimes he felt that union shop agreements were "the worst thing that ever happened to the trade union movement."[67] The union shop smacked of compulsion and fascism:

> In our trade union movement we should not expect to have everything done for us by the signing of an agreement. At least part of the work of organizing a union and keeping it organized should be done by the members themselves. When I joined this Union there was no such thing as a Union shop agreement, there were no agreements of any kind. We organized local unions in the face of active opposition of the employers and we kept them organized too.[68]

In this trade union discourse, a vision of democracy that was shared by employers was presented to counter the union shop.

To preserve and spread their visions of democracy and society, forest companies joined other members of the business community, hiring agents and intellectuals to articulate and spread their narratives. In the 1940s, when unions and the socialist CCF were on the rise across Canada, business kept up the educational work. Despite entreaties from Arthur Meighen, Samuel Rogers, and Gladstone Murray, H.R. MacMillan did not contribute to the Toronto-based anti-socialist and anti-union institute called Responsible Enterprise, but the company did support the British Columbia Federation of Trade and Industry, which, said W.J. Van Dusen, a MacMillan company executive, in a letter to Gladstone Murray, the head of Responsible Enterprise, "is doing locally the same type of work that you are doing. It is essential, I think, to continue this type of educational work and not abandon the field to the socialists and left-wingers."[69] In the 1950s, prominent members of the forest industry community put up money to ensure the electoral defeat of the socialist CCF provincially. MacMillan & Bloedel, the Powell River Company, BC Forest Products, Canadian Forest Products, Crown Zellerbach, Alaska Pine and Cellulose, and Columbia Cellulose all made substantial contributions.[70] Forest industry executives were instrumental in the establishment of the Fraser Institute, a right-wing think tank based in Vancouver, in 1974. The role of T. Patrick Boyle, vice president of financial planning at MacMillan Bloedel, was key in the early stages; he recruited J.V. Clyne, the president of MacMillan Bloedel, who helped bring in other corporate sponsors and raise the initial funds.[71]

Small operators in the forest industry were forceful voices for competitive capitalism, the rights of individuals, and the sanctity of private property. This ideology was embedded in a narrative of independence, resourcefulness, integrity, and masculinity, a small-town, populist vision of a society of noble, hardworking people of relatively equal wealth and status. Despite feeling beleaguered, or perhaps because of it, small operators were extremely proud of their contribution to society, and this pride was at the core of their identity. Though rather schmaltzy, the president of the Truck Loggers Association's 1945 New Year's greeting exhibited this pride:

> May the quietude of the great forests (which you are accused of despoiling) and the spirit of joy and laughter emanating from the thousands of homes, churches and public buildings (which you are primarily responsible for creating) bring you piece of mind.
>
> May you glory in the fact that you are all part of an industry wherein a man's word is still as good as his bond; where a boom of logs or a train load of lumber may be bought over the telephone, and delivery made without benefit of the written word; wherein every man's hand is not at the throat of his neighbor, but a helping hand may be found in nearly every sawdust pile.
>
> May we all, when Paul Bunyan blows the last great blast on his whistle which will call us out of the woods of 1945, look back with pride and honor on the accomplishments of the year, and say with heartfelt thanks – "I AM A LUMBERMAN!"[72]

H.P. "Harper" Baikie emphasized the merits of honesty and fairness in 1964, adjuring his fellow small loggers to be honest with their accountants, their bankers, and their workers. He concluded with a ringing sense of pride: "Well, I for one, who had gone through thirty-two years of gyppo logging, and I think I speak for the majority of medium and small loggers, would not trade my lot for any job in the industry. And if I had another life to live, I would still be an independent logger."[73] Peter Dyck, who with his brother and another partner did contract logging for Merritt Diamond Mills in the Nicola Valley, was proud that he operated without a written contract with the mill: "If a man's word isn't as good as his bond, it doesn't really matter whether you have a contract or not."[74]

Resourcefulness and inventiveness were also celebrated values. A major part of their work was to keep their equipment operating, and this demanded on-the-spot creativity and cleverness. Operators also developed new machines and techniques to take out logs and produce lumber more quickly. An editorial in 1964 stressed this aspect of the small operator's makeup, among others. The small operator "who could pull up his socks and better himself," it was argued, had made this country, and society still needed small operators because they were inventive and creative: "Big firms need to look at small ones to keep up with *all* the changing production ideas. Bigness has no stranglehold on inventiveness, and inventiveness is a key to today's good logging."[75]

Ruggedness, individuality, and masculinity were also part of the constellation of values in the world of small business. A story told with relish in the Interior involved Mel Rustad, part owner of a firm that operated a planer and mill in Prince George. During the bitter strike of 1953, Rustad, described as a "scrapper," was accosted on the street by three men. While he "took care of two," the third fled. Later at home, Rustad received a phone call, challenging him to a fistfight outside a local beer parlour. He responded verbally with a torrent of abuse "that would make a fishwife envious," and the caller backed down. Rustad commented: "I feel I have something worth fighting for! It took us eight years of hard work to build up our business."[76]

Small operators saw themselves at the head of the battle to save "free enterprise," a term that embodied their aspirations for themselves and their community. The president of the Truck Loggers Association made the point directly in 1957: "We who have been active in this association for sometime feel confident this organization will continue to grow as the greatest force for the preservation of Free Enterprise in the Timber Industry of this Province, where Government holds all the aces: the trees, and the land they grow on."[77] In 1962, when a cabinet minister was quoted as saying that the "days of the independent logger and independent free enterprise [were] almost over," the Truck Loggers Association reacted with alarm, demanding clarification from the government.[78] A bit of doggerel, entitled "Private Enterprise," from a Nanaimo correspondent expressed the ideals in 1974:

The Power to choose the work we do
    To grow and have the larger view,
To know and feel that we are free,
    To stand erect, not bow the knee.

To be no chattel of the State,
    To be the master of our fate,
To dare, to risk, to lose, to win,
    To make our own career begin.

To serve the world in our own way,
  To gain in wisdom, day by day.
With hope and zest to climb, to rise,
  That is PRIVATE ENTERPRISE.[79]

The small operator identity narrative was an integral part of small-town life across British Columbia, but it contained ambiguities. While it offered a populist vision, a world of hardworking people of relatively equal status, committed to their communities, fairness, and progress, it did not close off the option of small operators becoming big operators. The small operators railed against the privileges of the majors, arguing that they had undue clout and influence, but still reserved the right to one day becoming majors themselves. A debate at the IWA convention in Vancouver in 1968 captures this. Delegates discussed a government measure to protect small operators, and ultimately decided not to support it. During the debate, one IWA delegate was sympathetic to the plight of the small operators, respecting the need to protect their place in the industry and society, while another delegate was blunter, showing little sympathy for them: "All we would be doing would be to support little sharks to enable them to become big sharks."[80] If there were inconsistencies in the small operator worldview, it still coalesced in a defence of capitalism against its misguided foes. Moderate leftism was seen as a gateway ideology, the beginning of the slide into more radical positions.

Attacks against union officials and leftist politicians were sharp, coming from both big business and small operators. Union leaders were portrayed as irresponsible, unreasonable, strike-happy, undemocratic, economically naive, and greedy, more interested in union and socialist politics than the interests of the members.[81] At times companies appealed to their workers in an attempt to circumvent the leadership, casting the union as a negative scourge. In 1973, with a sympathy strike on at his Eburne mill, P.J.G. Bentley, the executive vice president of Canadian Forest Products, released a public statement portraying the strike as a misuse of power by union officials. He even named the union official who was so irresponsible in his mind, claiming that he "appears to place a greater priority on disruption than he does on the welfare of our employees and his union members."[82] Bentley then called on his employees to take a much more active interest in union affairs, and to denounce the union leadership and support the interests of the company. In 1969, in anticipation of a provincial election, an unnamed member of the Truck Loggers Association attacked the leader of the NDP, Tom Berger, and the party's links to organized labour:

The real issue is whether or not the reins of government are to be turned over to the NDP whose official policies of socialism are but a cover for the selfish interests of the establishment of the trade union movement, who control the party and who lust for personal power.

There are honest, dedicated socialists in the NDP, but they know their policies are doomed to fail under an organization dominated by union leaders who, by and large, have a profound disrespect for the democratic principles that insure the butcher, the baker, the farmer and the housewife have a say in the policies of government ...
To our employees we say: be careful.
If you believe in socialism, do not vote NDP. Wait until the party has a leadership that can control the policies of the party.
If you are not a socialist, but have always voted for one of your union leaders because you know him, do not vote for him this time. Tell him to stay at home and look after the legitimate affairs of your union.[83]

Company public surveys showed that this view of unions was widely shared in the late 1960s: "The unions are accredited with looking after the interests of the workers but are criticized for the excessive internal and external political maneuverings of their leaders, and for being greedy and excessive in their demands."[84] Of course, unions and the CCF/NDP countered, and they, too, had successes. In the same company-sponsored survey, forest industry companies were considered to be "primarily, if not solely, motivated by profits."

Through the prism of the forest industry, we can identify two main political narratives in British Columbia, each of which can be further subdivided. On the right, two discourses celebrated liberal capitalism. Both big business and the small operators were anti-government, anti-union, and pro–private property, favouring a democratic system that supported these positions. There was disagreement, however. Small operators chafed at the perceived privileges of the big companies, suggesting that their existence and power undermined individual initiative and that links between big government and big companies sullied democracy. On the left, a discourse sympathetic to government and unions included the idea that rights regarding property needed to be restricted at times. A vision of democracy was promoted, based on these beliefs. The IWA executive, after 1948, and the CCF supported greater state and union activity, and, overall, Fordism was an acceptable accommodation.

There were more radical discourses on the left. Within the CCF, some argued for greater government control and even nationalization of the forest industry. The state, not private companies, would appropriate the surplus produced in the production process. Colin Cameron and Max Paulik advanced such views in the 1940s,[85] but the more radical leftist voices did not dominate. After the 1956 provincial CCF convention, which defeated leftist resolutions on forestry, CCF MLA Dorothy Steeves commiserated sarcastically with Colin Cameron, now a federal CCF MP: "The country ... is safe against the onslaughts of socialism. A completely rightist Ex[ecutive] is triumphantly enthroned."[86] The IWA delegates to the CCF were notably uneasy about the call for greater socialization of the industry. Steeves concluded that "the main trouble with the IWA is that it would rather deal with private companies than with government and the trouble with our people is that they are scared."[87] The Communist Party, while similar to the CCF/NDP on domestic issues, fit local circumstances and behaviour into a larger critique of global capitalism. Within the unions, there were also more conservative positions, most notably the voluntarist tradition of American craft unionism, which was wary of government and saw self-sufficient unions and collective agreements in a healthy capitalist system as the best social arrangement.

These class and discourse configurations offer insights into twentieth-century BC political culture. In 1952 the traditional liberal capitalist parties, the Liberals and Conservatives, lost control of the government to the Social Credit Party. Social Credit took advantage of the anxiety felt by small businesspeople and others who adhered to their articulation of the good society in the face of the growing influence of monopoly capital, a vision of the future endorsed by both Liberals and Conservatives. Conflict over the implementation of the new Forest Management Licence system, the apparent epitome of state-sponsored monopoly capitalism, played a crucial role in defining this political divide. Once in power, Social Credit, under the able leadership of W.A.C. Bennett, reoriented itself, uniting big business and small business in a political alliance against the perils of unionism and socialism.[88] Under Bennett, the party ruled BC from 1952 to 1972.

The left had its successes. The CCF was a significant political agent from the 1930s to the 1960s, and the 1972 election brought its successor, the NDP, to power in the province. The forest industry was terrified, but in the end the policies of the new government were hardly revolutionary.[89] The NDP had rallied the many elements of the left, but the cohesion was short-lived and by 1975 this uneasy alliance had been shattered. In the forest industry, the pulp and paper unions went on strike in 1975, during an economic downturn. Although there had been an agreement between the IWA and the two pulp and paper unions to go out together, the IWA decided, due to economic circumstances, to stay on the job, much to the anger of the pulp and paper workers. For their part, the IWA leadership chastised the pulp and paper unions for what they considered an ill-conceived strike. In the end, the NDP government passed legislation forcing the strikers to return to work, infuriating the pulp and paper workers.[90] In December, with the left openly divided and publicly fighting, the NDP lost the provincial election.

IN THE 1940S AND 1950S, forest industry unions made a place for themselves in the liberal capitalist order, which was part of a broader Fordist social initiative. Union officials increasingly became intermediaries between workers and employers on the job site, spending a large portion of their time servicing the basic needs of the membership. Although forest industry owners and executives were not happy about the rising power of unions and the state, their core rights were not jeopardized. They retained control of capital and the production system. This result was not fortuitous – companies had effectively expended money and energy to defend their position.

6
Technology

Rapid technological change in the twentieth century has been both celebrated and damned. On the one hand, it is the great, ever-changing force that lightens the workload of human beings, creates new and interesting work, improves the world's standard of living, and allows for greater leisure time. Conversely, it is condemned because it produces unemployment, deskills occupations, provides tedious jobs, and degrades the environment. These positions all echo in discussions of technology in the BC forest industry, where the development of new machines and techniques was ongoing. All phases of the production process underwent transformations in the decades after 1934.[1]

Advances in the provincial logging industry have attracted the most interest, and the fascination with forest machines has spawned a number of popular books on the history of logging operations.[2] Assessments of the impact of these changes on working loggers vary. In a critical analysis, Richard Rajala focuses on large corporations in the coastal industry of Canada and the United States and argues that capital's drive to increase exploitation of workers forced transformations at the workplace, which, in complex ways, led to a general deskilling of the logging workforce. Drawing theoretical muscle from the work of Harry Braverman, Rajala argues that the "progressive narrowing of the task range and discretionary content of occupations and outright elimination of others, confirms the essential thrust of Braverman's degradation of work thesis."[3] Ken Drushka and Hannu Konttinen, on the other hand, stress the emergence of good, new jobs and the emergence of "professional" loggers who operate sophisticated, expensive machinery in the woods.[4]

Empirically defining the skill content of jobs is difficult, as the job evaluation studies discussed in the previous chapter illustrated. So, too, is the notion of skill itself, for it is tied to questions of gender, ethnicity, and status. Moreover, in the forest industry, jobs were not particularly skilled at the outset. In the mills, jobs involved tending and operating machines, lifting and pulling, and maintaining the equipment. There were fewer physically demanding jobs at the end of the period, but jobs remained routine and controlled. In logging, changes were more dramatic, yet the machinery created new types of work and shelved others, and it is unclear to what degree jobs demanded less or more skill. While the goals of capital – fewer workers, more control, and greater productivity – are straightforward, clear measurement of deskilling is problematic.

Technological change was simultaneously many things, and its meanings are best understood in relation to other configurations. Beyond deskilling, Rajala links technological change to clearcut logging practices, the development of forest reproduction science, government policy, and the financial needs of large coastal logging companies. Technological change, driven by the need of employers to increasingly exploit labour, is the independent variable driving the other elements in the equation. Drushka also understands logging technology in relation to another context, the creativity of small operators and equipment manufacturers who maintain the free enterprise system. This chapter looks at technology in milling as well as logging, locating the history of production innovations and its meaning for capital and labour in a discourse that intertwines understandings of capitalist relations, progress, conservation, and the future of work.

The forest industry took immense pride in the progressive transformation of the production system. Innovation was linked to the basic human drives of problem solving and the taming of nature. Inventing and employing new equipment elevated the esteem and status of the people involved; innovators were improving the lot of human beings. And results of technology were measurable: more product was manufactured more quickly, and this could be represented mathematically. The performance results of new technology allowed for a clear measure of progress. Grand narratives did not totally obscure technology's fundamental role in capital accumulation. Business competition, it was recognized, also drove innovation. British Columbia was a comparatively small producer in a global market, and the United States and Scandinavia were servicing the same customers. Innovation maintained the province's place in world markets. In the late 1960s, there was a sense of desperation: "Obviously we can retain [our competitive advantage] only by a new technological breakthrough – balloons, helicopter logging or some other system not yet devised – which will give us a new edge on our competitors. And we must develop it fairly quickly, for our competitors are crowding us already."[5] The industry also recognized that technological advance made labour more productive, squeezing more value out of the labour that workers performed. New techniques and machinery sped up production: more volume in less time meant that capital could be turned over – reinvested – more quickly, thus generating more profits. Fewer employees producing more was the goal. In 1969 the MacMillan Bloedel logging manager stated: "The real objective in our changing equipment needs is to reduce manpower requirements ... There must be a trimming in overall labor costs."[6]

Technological innovation in the forest industry was intertwined with the ethos of conservation. Scientific forest management meant regulating the yearly cut to ensure a sustained yield, but it also meant utilizing as much of the wood in the forest as possible. Turning what was once considered waste – small trees – into usable, marketable products became a fixation shared by industry and government. Pulp and paper production, which used wood chips rather than logs, served the goals of industry and conservation, and loggers developed new machines and techniques to adapt to the changed circumstances. By the 1960s, greater utilization, quipped one commentator, had become "the major god of the new religion, sustained yield forestry."[7]

In the 1930s and 1940s, workers, unions, and leftist political parties accepted the ongoing modernization of the workplace, seeing higher wages and progress as the positive results of greater productivity. Change promised workers relief from drudgery, more interesting work, and more leisure time. In the mid-1950s, though, the new threat of automation and the use of equipment to replace human capabilities of observation and decision making sent waves of fear across North America. This struck BC forest workers close to home, but challenges to the anticipated disappearance of work were weak, defeated by the more dominant discourses of progress, conservation, and the rights of capital. Automation continued at an accelerating pace.

Logging: Trucks, Power Saws, and Grapple Yarders

Even in logging, where variable terrain and tree size made standardized mass production difficult, the goal was "something in the nature of Henry Ford's endless chain in production ... so there would be no stop from the time the tree was felled until the finished product was ready for the market."[8] Though the model was clear from an early date, its realization was hardly straightforward. Problems had to be solved.

From the perspective of the log, the production process in logging began with the felling of a tree by fallers. Once on the ground, the tree was cut into log lengths, or bucked, by the buckers. Then came the difficult task of getting the logs from the place where the trees were felled to a centralized collection area, where logs were loaded onto trucks or railcars for the longer haul to the mills or to the seashore, from where they would be transported to mills. The use of trucks to haul logs began in the coastal region in the early 1920s. The first big operation to use trucks was Comox Logging. Instead of building a logging railway when it put in a new camp in 1935 at Ladysmith, on Vancouver Island, the company built roads on the logging site and used trucks.[9] Thereafter, truck logging replaced railroad logging, although railway logging continued through the 1950s. It was estimated that in 1942 approximately 50 percent of the logs produced on the coast came from truck logging operations.[10] The petroleum derivatives diesel and gasoline were replacing steam as the power source in hauling. A journalist waxed poetic, contrasting the sounds of the railroad era with the sounds of the truck era, when visiting a MacMillan & Bloedel logging operation in 1953:

Not so many years ago it was the whining of Shay gears, the clattering of Climax drive shafts, the pealing of flanges on the long curves and the shrill toot of the locie whistle that set the woods' echoes bouncing and startled whiskey-jacks to jabbering as loads of logs went rattling down the rails to the dump ...

Today it's the hoarse mutter of the Diesel or the flat bark of the gasoline engine that flushes the buck from the brush, the crunch of rubber on gravel and the long snarl of the air-horn that give warning of a load on its way to market. The basic principle alone remains: "get the trees off the ground and into the millpond."[11]

Established operations converted from rail to truck. In 1950 "the costly business of changing over from rail to road was completed by yet another Vancouver Island logging company," Salmon River Logging. The company, owned by three mainland sawmill firms, already used trucks in part of its operation but was now going to use trucks to replace its long twenty-mile railway hauling run.[12] In 1957 MacMillan & Bloedel converted its Franklin River operation near Port Alberni to trucks. It was the last of the firm's thirteen logging operations to use railroads, except for the log haul to tidewater from the Nanaimo camp.[13] By 1960 railway operations were largely of historical interest,[14] and on 1 December 1969, the last steam logging railway, the run from the Nanaimo River camp to Ladysmith, ended.[15]

When MacMillan, Bloedel and Powell River opened a camp at Squamish in 1964, the first large new logging operation in years, it used trucks. Some twenty miles of logging road were constructed in the first year, and "considerable blasting was required to put the road through the tough terrain: one rock cut or face [was] 100 feet high."[16] Road construction became a key part of logging, and graders, caterpillars, mechanized shovels, and gravel trucks were now integral to logging. Heavy duty mechanics had to keep the expensive machines operating. Road building was ongoing; as one site was logged out, roads had to be ready for more logging in a new area.

Trucks were more flexible. Railways could not operate on grades over 5 percent or curves sharper than 20 degrees, which meant that they could not get close to quality timber high up steep mountains. Getting this timber to the rail line meant greater costs in yarding. According to R.J. "Bob" Filberg, who had been instrumental in bringing trucks into the Comox Logging operations in the 1930s, there was not much difference between truck logging and rail logging, and rail was even a little cheaper once the logs were on the railcar. But "trucks can operate on 25% grades and negotiate 90 degree turns and put the logging unit into the timber, eliminating long yarding, which is inefficient and expensive; cold decking, which is an added cost; and long skylines, which had never been successful."[17] Truck logging allowed access to standing timber that could not be reached economically by railroad or skyline logging.

Interior truck logging, 1951.
BC Archives, NA-12484

The move to truck logging in the Interior came later than on the Coast. Railroad logging had never been done on any large scale here because the value and volume of timber per hectare was not sufficient to cover the heavy costs of constructing logging railroads. In the Prince George area, two operations constructed a few miles of railroad track in the 1920s, but the experiment was not successful.[18] While trucks were introduced in the 1930s, horses remained the main means of hauling logs over snow from where they were felled to the mills into the 1950s. A visitor to the Northern Interior noted that the small operations still relied on horsepower in 1950: "Horse logging is the rule rather than the exception in this country, and nearly all yarding is done with a team of nice, fat horses. They get to be slickers at the job, too, and about all the teamster has to do is hang on."[19] Over the course of the 1950s, trucks replaced horses.

Truck logging, which met the goals of efficiency and profitability, created new jobs for truck drivers and maintained a need for mechanics and steam shovel and grader operators. Occupations such as railway engineer and fireman were on the decline, but the transition was slow and not traumatic. Logging railways, after all, continued into the 1960s, and this transition caused little outcry about the displacement of labour. In the expanding economy of the era, more jobs in the woods were created, facilitating the transition from rail to truck.

The introduction of power chain saws was more controversial. There had long been a search in North America for some sort of mechanical device to cut down trees, including a wire rope saw that used the heat of friction, a red-hot electrically charged wire that burned through the wood, and many types of circular saws. The shortage of labour during the First World War stimulated research, but by the 1930s portable chain saws driven by high-speed gas engines, seemingly the best solution, were still too fragile and subject to too many motor failures. In coastal British Columbia, the revival of the industry after 1934 reinvigorated the debate about power saws and prompted action. The average man-day cut of fallers was dropping, as timber to be cut became smaller and more difficult to reach. There was also a shortage of qualified fallers to produce the increased output demanded.[20]

Jack Challenger, a superintendent at Bloedel, Stewart & Welch, was given the task of developing a machine that would be effective in BC, and the BC Loggers' Association, which donated $600 to the cause in 1937, supported the efforts.[21] The experiment took place at the Franklin River camp on Vancouver Island, and involved modifying a chain saw made by Stihl, the German manufacturer. In 1939 the company was using five power chain saws. The reaction of the men on the crews, many of whom were still hand felling, "was a mixture of well-concealed interest, and of ill-conceived scorn."[22] The International Woodworkers of America (IWA) complained that the men using the experimental saws were getting the easiest timber to fell and that they were smashing too much timber when felling, but the union leadership expected the technology to improve and supported the initiative.[23] The outbreak of the Second World War snapped the fruitful interchange of ideas between the German manufacturer and the BC company, but Canadian and American producers were now interested. By the end of the war, a number of manufacturers produced power saws and they were increasingly being used in the woods. Bloedel, Stewart & Welch used British Columbia-made machines driven by English Villiers motors. Over the course of the war, this forest company alone trained over 200 power saw operators.[24]

By 1946 power saws were part of the landscape, but questions remained about the future of the machines and the implications for workers. While there were material and maintenance costs that did not exist with hand felling, the greater investment in power saws was more than compensated for by savings in payrolls. Men using power saws produced on average one-third more per day than hand fallers. This meant that one-third fewer fallers would be required. Notably, fewer fallers meant a decrease in workers' compensation premiums, a large expense in the dangerous logging industry. An analysis of accidents at Bloedel, Stewart & Welch camps in 1939 and 1940, when the firm was still using some hand fallers, showed that accidents for buckers and fallers using power saws were 40 percent lower than for hand fallers. The greater speed of fallers using chain saws also meant that there was a reduction in felled and bucked timber inventories lying on the ground ahead of the yarders, resulting "in a savings of fire insurance premiums, decreased sap-worm damage to timber, [and] savings in interest capital invested in felled and bucked timber inventories."[25]

A 1948 report endorsed power-drive chain saws because they were "labor savers, time savers and also mean a saving in operating costs."[26] It elaborated by noting

Bucking with a power saw, 1947.
MacMillan Bloedel Collection (UBC), BC 1930/188/7

that a man using a power saw accomplished more work in less time, and thus logging required less manpower. The author said that men using power saws could produce three to five times as much as men producing by hand in the same period. In saving labour, "the power saw, because mechanically operated, requires that the operator keep up with his machine. The operator is thus working as long as the motor is running." The article also noted that 50 percent of the felling and bucking on the Coast was now done by power.[27] Soon power saws did all the cutting.

Power saw technology was constantly being improved, and there were manufacturers in Europe and North America, including Vancouver. A major goal was to reduce the weight of the machines. Early saws were two-man machines, weighing between 120 and 165 pounds, depending on the length of the bar, which ran up to nine feet. By 1948 two-man saws weighed from 60 to 130 pounds, and one-man machines weighed from 35 to 50 pounds. By the late 1960s, the new one-man saws were as light as 24 pounds, and "these saws allowed many fallers to work in the woods until the age of 65."[28]

The IWA supported the introduction of power saws: "The power saw is here to stay, just as is the caterpillar tractor, the logging truck or any other piece of modern equipment. The power saw can be an asset to the logger and not a liability."[29] The union did have concerns, however. The noise of the engines made woods work more dangerous, and machine felling in the early years appeared to cause extra breakage in the timber. A major union consideration was the practice of fallers owning their own machines. The IWA worried that these fallers would become subcontractors, small capitalists who would create divisions, if not a schism, in the union. In 1947 the IWA district executive passed a resolution against power saw fallers signing individual contracts with the companies. One member summed up the union perspective: "We can't fight the power saws. We want them in the woods, but we want them company-owned."[30] There was also the question of who was responsible for repairing the machines and whether the workers would be paid when the machines were not operating due to mechanical failure.

In 1953 a union survey tried to get a handle on how the machines were owned, and the results showed diversity. In the area around Duncan, on Vancouver Island, there were instances when the power saw was owned by a private contractor, when the crew jointly owned the machine, and when the company owned and maintained the equipment.[31] Further north on Vancouver Island, around Courtenay, few companies provided saws for fallers and buckers. Here, either felling gangs owned the machines jointly, establishing a bank account to which all contributed to cover maintenance costs, or the head faller, bucker, or machine man owned all the power saws and the crew members paid a rate per thousand board feet minus a fee for the saw.[32] The union never developed a straightforward policy. Power saws became lighter and less expensive, and so more suited to individual ownership and one-man operation. For fallers, who worked for piece rates and were

Mechanized tree harvesting, 1974.
BC Archives, H-04513

keen to keep their machines running and in tip-top shape so that they could produce, maintenance and repair were an acceptable responsibility.

In the late 1960s, further advances were made in felling and bucking technology.
On the Coast, more of the trees that were harvested were second growth and thus
smaller in diameter, making it easier to use mechanized cutting machines. In the
Interior, where even first-growth trees were small, the great expansion in logging
to feed the new pulp and paper industry made it feasible for companies to consider purchasing more expensive, sophisticated machines. Tree shears, mounted
on small crawler tractors, were used to snip trees very close to the ground. In 1969
the shears were limited to a maximum tree diameter of twenty-six inches and
could operate on relatively level ground only, but they were capable of cutting on
average 450 trees per day on the Coast and it was anticipated that soon they would
be capable of felling 700 trees in an eight-hour shift.[33]

Until the 1950s, the main changes in logging were in felling and bucking (power saws) and in hauling (trucks), not in yarding and loading, but change soon became evident here too. The portable spar enabled logging companies to avoid the time-consuming job of moving the rigging from spar tree to spar tree and moving the yarder. Perfected by S. Madill Ltd. of Nanaimo and often called the Madill spar, the portable steel spar was developed in the first years of the 1950s, adapted from the portable wooden spar that was once fixed to railway flat cars.[34] By 1970 the portable spar had largely replaced high-lead logging, which was based on stationary spar trees. The main reason for the change was "the cost of additional equipment and guy lines, plus an extra crew to rig trees ahead (and strip equipment from trees behind)." Mounted on trucks or tractors and raised hydraulically, the mobile tower, 40 to 100 feet high, had rigging permanently attached to it, allowing a crew to "move to a new location, raise the spar, connect the guy lines, run out the haulback and main lines, and be logging in one to two hours."[35] Another development of the 1950s in yarding was rubber-tired tractors to yard or skid logs from where they were felled to a collection area.[36] On Vancouver Island in 1965, grapple yarders, mechanical devices operated from a distance, replaced workers who physically hooked cables onto the logs for yarding.[37] Fewer and fewer workers were needed to do the work in the woods; as a commentator noted in 1969, "the number of yarding crews is not declining, it is their size."[38]

By the late 1960s, machines were in operation that combined felling, bucking, yarding, and loading. These harvesting machines took advantage of many changes, especially in hydraulic technology, enabling one machine operator to grasp a standing tree, shear it at its base, delimb it, cut it to an appropriate log size, load it, and transport it.[39]

The rush to innovate was alive and well in the woods in the 1960s. On the Coast, balloons were tried and found wanting, but helicopters were used effectively to lift and transport logs. Night logging also arrived. MacMillan Bloedel was night logging at nine of its twenty logging operations in coastal BC in 1969. For example, at the Cameron Division, near Port Alberni, a seventy-man shift went to work at 5:30 in the afternoon. The logging site was illuminated by twelve mounted mercury vapour lamps, which created the atmosphere of a football stadium at night. Even in poor weather the lights penetrated the darkness to a distance of 700 feet. The loggers, noted one observer, "bundled up well against the night chill, look more like miners as they go about their jobs with miners' lamps attached to their hard hats."[40]

Smallwood, Barkers, and Chippers

The expansion of the pulp and paper industry in the 1940s meshed smoothly with the agenda of the conservation movement, encouraging the invention of new equipment and techniques in logging and milling. Until the 1940s, loggers left small-diameter logs in the woods because they were uneconomical to remove. With the increased demand for wood and pulp in the 1940s, however, this potential lumber and fibre had value. In 1942 Comox Logging and Railway and the Powell River Company experimented with what became known as smallwood logging. The plan was to take salvage wood from Comox Logging's Ladysmith operation on Vancouver Island and transport it to Powell River, where it would be processed into pulp and newsprint at the Powell River Company's facility. Up to this time, pulp and paper operations had used logs of sawmill dimensions. Both the logging company and the pulp and paper firm developed new machinery and techniques to make use of smaller logs. Comox Logging built yarding machines and other equipment that was smaller and lighter than those used in traditional operations. They persuaded loggers of the merits of this type of logging because at first the loggers "felt demeaned when assigned to the salvage of this 'junk.'"[41] The Powell River Company built a new sawmill to break down the smaller logs for use in pulp and paper production.[42] The experiment was a success.

The president of the Truck Loggers Association claimed in 1964 that the use of smaller-dimension logs constituted a revolution. Where the term "smallwood" was once part of the jargon of professional foresters, it was now part of daily conversation, and "all people concerned with logging are interested in finding out better and cheaper ways to handle the small log. I doubt if any changeover phase of the industry has taken place so quickly as the change in attitude from what was waste wood to what is now commercial wood."[43] Another observer commented in 1965 on the advances made by MacMillan, Bloedel and Powell River in smallwood logging since the Second World War: "Techniques have now been developed to the point where the company is using virtually everything but the branches."[44]

While coastal operators were prompted by markets to pursue smallwood logging, in the Interior the government forced the issue. Wanting to develop a pulp and paper industry, the government and major companies needed a supply of wood. Government regulations in the early 1960s encouraged operators to utilize as much of the wood in the forests as possible – close utilization – in order to feed new pulp and paper mills. Sawmill operators learned how to get lumber from smaller logs too. In the 1960s, sawmill machinery was developed specifically to convert smaller logs into lumber. These were state-of-the art operations, using "an in-line, one pass, straight through process in which logs are fed in a continuous stream through the machine. They have very little versatility or flexibility but they produce lumber with a low labour content."[45] Smallwood logging, close utilization, and conservation ideals were all part of an increasingly efficient Fordist production system.

There were other developments in the sawmills and pulp and paper plants of the province. Unlike logging, which moved from site to site and had to cope with the vagaries of geography and biology, sawmills and pulp and paper operations were more predictable and thus more amenable to flow-through, mechanized

Barking logs by hand, 1936.
MacMillan Bloedel Collection (UBC), BC 1930/48/3

production. The 1940s and 1950s witnessed the introduction of hydraulic barkers in pulp and paper mills and sawmills. In preparing the logs for processing, the bark had to be removed. Using saws or rapidly rotating knives meant that much wood fibre was lost, but using high-pressure water to blast the bark off effected a saving of 20 to 25 percent. The process was already in use in the United States in 1944, when the Powell River mill began preparing for the new device, which was installed in 1946. Canadian Sumner Iron Works of Vancouver was involved in building four hydraulic barkers for pulp and paper operations in the summer of 1946 – one each for the BC Pulp and Paper mill at Woodfibre, the new Bloedel, Stewart & Welch mill at Port Alberni, Universal Box Company at Marpole, and the Powell River plant. It also constructed one at the Bloedel, Stewart & Welch sawmill at Port Alberni.[46] In 1952 the Victoria mill of BC Forest Products installed a $350,000 barker, and it was considered important enough to warrant a story in the local newspaper. Here the clever prose and human metaphors capture the excitement of mechanical progress in the Fordist era:

> The barker is actually a giant piece of machinery designed and manufactured in British Columbia, which does as neat a strip tease act as ever performed in vaudeville.

In the space of one minute it will remove every particle of bark from a log up to 60 feet long and five feet wide.

The log goes into the barker clad in its tough, thick forest clothing and a few seconds later it starts appearing at the other end white and smooth as a baby's skin.

The bark has been removed by hydraulic blasting. Water is thrown against the log at 1,450 pounds per square inch pressure and at the rate of 1,100 gallons per minute. In this particular mill, salt water from the harbor is used.

The purpose of the barker ... is primarily elimination of waste.[47]

Conservation, technology, and profit were marching in lockstep.

In the postwar years, waste utilization was the biggest change in the mills. Chippers transformed logs, big and small, into wood chips that could be used in pulp and paper processes. By May 1964, even sawdust was being used to produce kraft pulp at Crown Zellerbach's Elk Falls operation.[48] What had been previously viewed as sawmill waste – slabs, edgings, and trim ends – was transformed into chips and utilized in pulp mills. Sawmills were able to get money for all the wood that they purchased. In the Interior, the pulp and paper industry of the 1960s was dependent on a steady supply of wood chips provided by sawmills.[49] Due to waste utilization, opined one knowledgeable observer in 1956 on progress in the sawmill industry, "the last ten years have been far more productive from the point of view of change than had the 30-year period to 1945."[50]

Beyond the new machinery to prepare and process wood, British Columbia sawmills were continually introducing new automated saws, powered live rollers to move planks from one area of the mill to another, mechanical stampers to label loads of lumber, and forklifts and cranes to move and load cut lumber. Western Plywood at Quesnel installed new machines in 1962 and, according to the mill superintendent, the expense was worthwhile: "Production is up more than 20 percent. Yet a total of seven fewer men are now required to operate three shifts."[51] In 1970 the J. Ernst Lumber Company built a new mill in Quesnel. This operation pioneered the use of the Chip-N-Saw, a machine which produced lumber and wood chips, in the Cariboo in 1964, as well as the use of computer linear programming to move logs through its mills. To take full advantage of the sophisticated mill technology, the company spent $200,000, about one-fifth of the total cost of the new mill, on a custom-built log bucker and sorter, which prepared and sorted the logs in the yard, allowing them to be used most efficiently in the mills. Two operators in a tower operated the machinery, "one operating the bucking mechanism and the other directing logs into the different sorting bins. It is hoped," noted a reporter, "that in the future an electronic device will be installed to eliminate the need for manual sorting into the bins, and that only one man in the tower will be needed."[52]

Pulp and paper mills also expanded and improved efficiency at every stage in the production process.[53] For example, improvements were effected at all provincial operations in 1964 and 1965. BC Forest Products at Crofton added a $20 million newsprint mill; Canadian Forest Products at Port Mellon spent $7 million on a pulp mill expansion; Crown Zellerbach at Elk Falls completed a $36 million expansion and spent $1 million on cleaners and screens on the pulp dryer and $400,000 in the bleach plant; and Rayonier Canada spent $21 million expanding its mill at Woodfibre and $835,000 on a small-log woodroom at Port Alice. MacMillan, Bloedel and Powell River expenditures in its five pulp and paper facilities included money spent on a new folding box plant, replacement of groundwood washers and a machine headbox; additions to recovery boilers; and millwater line replacements.[54] Computers, too, became part of production, as a MacMillan, Bloedel and Powell River report noted in 1965: "The most significant development in the computer field during the past years has been the broadening applications from ones restricted to the commercial or accounting area to those having to do with the engineering, production and research fields."[55] From small Interior mills and logging camps to massive, diversified operations on the Coast, companies, engineering firms, and manufacturers were extremely active developing new machines and processes to lower the costs and the need for labour in harvesting timber and processing logs.

The Automation Debate

Overall, workers accepted new technologies with little direct protest. There was a push, though, to ensure that some benefits from the changes found their way into workers' pockets and created more leisure time. Jack Moore, district president of the IWA, encapsulated the position in 1967: "There is no point in fighting mechanization because it will produce more wealth." He added: "But what share of additional wealth belongs to the worker, the industry, the government – this is where the real bite will come ... Every time you bring in a piece of machinery you are going to lay off somebody along the line. It's not easy, particularly to the man who's laid off ... But ... increased production is picking them up."[56] The editor of an IWA newspaper made the same point about logging in 1964: "No quarrel can be found with the new logging methods which reduce the efforts required by men. However, the question must be asked, who receives the savings in wages?"[57]

The connection between technological change and jobs was recognized early. A BC Bureau of Economics and Statistics analysis of the logging industry for the years 1922 to 1940 made the point succinctly: the average yearly cut in BC forests was rising at the rate of 1.29 per cent per year over the past twenty years, while average employment in all forest industries was declining at the rate of 1.98 per cent. Expansions in plywood and pulp and paper had not been sufficient to stem the decline in employment, and the report, which cited technological improvements in sawmilling and especially logging, worried about a severe drop in employment.[58] A Department of Labour study of coastal logging in the years between

1950 and 1968 showed that while production doubled, the labour force dropped from 18,000 to 14,300. The author anticipated that the workforce would decline by a further thousand by 1975. He also noted the areas where technological innovation was likely to have the greatest impact, anticipating a decline in the need for chokermen, boommen, log scalers, log dump engineers, and section men, and a growing demand for fallers, truck drivers, log graders, dozer boat operators, mechanics, machine operators, and tree planters.[59]

In pulp and paper, Paul E. Cooper, newly appointed president of Pacific Mills, set out the company's goals in 1944. His policy was not physical expansion of the plant or the building of new facilities, but rather "a policy of up-grading our product and increasing production by improvements in our present operating machines, to give us increased speed of production in addition to improved production efficiency."[60] For the industry as a whole, this was achieved. Drawing on data from the Dominion Bureau of Statistics, union analysis noted that while employment was growing in the BC industry, with the building of new facilities, more was being produced per worker. Between 1958 and 1963, the pulp and paper workforce increased from 7,315 workers to 9,205, and output per employee was higher by 36.9 percent in the pulp sector and by 19.5 percent in paper and paperboard over the same years. Wages of production employees increased by only 16 percent, however.[61]

In 1955 discussions about technology were suddenly heightened when forest industry workers were alerted to a new threat – automation – which remained at the forefront of public debate for the next decade. Automation was treated seriously, as a comment by the leader of the provincial New Democratic Party in 1965 illustrates: "Automation is undoubtedly the greatest revolution that has taken place in our society since the caveman stopped hunting and fishing and started to grow his own food."[62]

Forest industry union officials took the fears to heart. Joe Miyazawa, the district IWA's associate director of research and education, introduced the issue in January 1955, distributing a letter and numerous press clippings to all BC locals. The reason, he told union officials, "is to familiarize you with automation itself and also to show that even today steps are being taken by management to introduce automation in slow stages." His letter included excerpts from an IWA report, produced in December 1954 in the United States, where concerns about automation were more advanced. The report began by announcing that automation was so new that most dictionaries did not carry a definition, and so it took its definition from one given at the recent International Automation Exposition in New York: "Automation is the substitution of mechanical, hydraulic, pneumatic, electrical and electronic devices for human organs of observation, decision and effort, so as to increase productivity, control quantity and reduce costs." Whereas previous technological advances had merely mimicked human labour, lifting, pushing, and moving things with more effect, automation inserted decision-making capabilities in the machinery, creating the possibility of removing workers completely from continuous, machine-controlled production lines. The IWA report noted that this new trend, hardly realized but in the offing, "is a big mouthful that adds up to the biggest revolution in productive methods since Eli Whitney invented the cotton gin in 1798."

There was concern about widespread unemployment. The Congress of Industrial Organizations commissioned a study to find out how much manpower had already been displaced by automation, how much would be displaced in the future, what areas were most likely to be affected, and "what plans management has for making sure that the increased productivity resulting from automation will be accompanied by increased purchasing power."[63] Examples of new procedures alerted BC union officials to incipient automation in the US. Closed circuit television was being used in a Longview, Washington, sawmill. The television screen allowed one operator to control two conveyor lines, and with the flick of a switch, he could divert the flow of materials to different places in the mill. In US plywood mills, the integration of mechanical devices into one flowing process enabled a few operators to control the process, eliminating the need for much human labour. Miyazawa requested that BC union officials be on the alert for the introduction of similar devices or processes in their plants, and to inform the union so that it could prepare a case in upcoming negotiations with companies.[64]

Concern about automation spread quickly. In the summer of 1955, the provincial Co-operative Commonwealth Federation (CCF) identified the "new industrial revolution" and bemoaned a future where many workers would be replaced by machines, facing the "dismal prospect of finding other employment."[65] In the spring of 1956, the educational committee of Vancouver Local 1-217 sponsored a weekend study session on automation. Four hundred shop stewards, IWA officers, and IWA members attended the one-day March meeting. The panel consisted of Dr. Eugene Forsey, the Canadian Congress of Labour research director; an engineer and a psychiatrist from the University of British Columbia; and the president of a management consulting company. Automation was of general concern and the panel had appeared on a local television program the previous week. The union newspaper opined that "the advent of automation presents organized labor with the greatest challenge in its history."[66] In September 1956, IWA district president Joe Morris appeared on a panel on automation sponsored by the Women's School for Citizenship at the Hotel Vancouver.[67] The IWA also noted developments in other industries, such as the Sault Ste. Marie steel mill and the post office. A 1957 report about the CPR was most alarming: "The Canadian Pacific Railway has just put into operation a mammoth electronic computer and laid off almost 250 people."[68]

In 1960 advances in automation were noted in the BC Interior: "The lumbering industry in the Northern interior is rapidly changing its production methods. In fact it can be said that the industry is introducing as much automation as possible. We now have semi-automatic green chains, a new type of re-saw which has more than doubled production with less workmen required ... there are thirty-six less employees in the plywood plant at Quesnel as compared to one year ago last September."[69] By 1960 coastal loggers were also beginning to understand technological change in terms of automation: "While automation has been effecting [sic] many Industries in recent years, it was not until the last two years that logging has seen the effects of new equipment that drastically reduces the number of men required in this section of the Industry."[70]

BC pulp and paper workers, too, were well aware of the challenge of automation. In 1956 a Port Alberni pulp and paper worker voiced concern over automation, worried about the loss of union jobs: "With automation being hastened in the pulp and paper industry by the introduction of electronics into the control of machines, it is not inconceivable that managements could eliminate many hourly paid jobs with salaried supervisors taking over."[71] In November 1960, the Western Canadian Council of Pulp and Paper Mill Unions sent Orville Braaten, the business agent for the International Brotherhood of Pulp, Sulphite and Paper Mill Workers (IBPSPMW) Local 433, to a three-day university/labour seminar on automation at Harrison Hot Springs, sponsored by the BC Federation of Labour and the University of British Columbia. Discussion topics included "Problems of Automation" and "Possible Impact of Automation on Labour Unions."[72] While believing that the professors were rather too theoretical, Braaten felt that the exchange was fruitful, in part for showing the professors "that labour is not composed of just a bunch of stupid oafs, but rather that they are quite capable of defending themselves."[73]

High levels of unemployment across Canada in the late 1950s and early 1960s heightened awareness of the perils of automation. Joe Morris, now vice president of the Canadian Labour Congress, noted in Prince George in the spring of 1962 that "the ability of automated machines to perform low-grade brain work in a high-speed way is largely responsible for the present high level of unemployment."[74] A six-page spread in the *Western Canadian Lumber Worker,* organ of Regional Council No. 1 of the IWA, in 1962 highlighted the problem in the province's camps and mills. Discussing sawmills, the article noted that no provincial mill was fully automated but that "the push-button operator is a common sight. Various units are at least semi-automatic. The transfer of material between the various stages in processing is rapidly becoming more automatic, and may yet lay the basis for complete automation in a sawmill."[75] In logging, too, the author was quick to note, the changes he was discussing did not yet represent full automation but "they represent forms of mechanization that will lead to full automation eventually in some sections of the industry."[76]

By this time the word "automation" encapsulated all technological change, including mechanization. A tour by members of IWA Local 1-424 of a Prince George pulp and paper mill gave the plywood and mill worker representatives a better sense of automation. Pulp and paper mills were much more fully automated than sawmills. In the Prince George mill, "the barker-chipper operator controlled the log deck, [and] barking and chipping machines by pushing buttons. In the rest of the mill, workers watched panel boards and made adjustments when the board lights indicated they were needed. One executive board member commented – 'It is frightening to be in a plant with so few workers; they must be lonesome.'" The union delegation then travelled to Quesnel, where they visited the Weldwood company's plywood mill, a modern mechanized operation but where there was still a large amount of manual work: "control of the flow of plywood through the mill rested with the workers."[77] In the mid-1960s, automation, mechanization, and unemployment had all become part of the same whole. In 1966 the union noted fifteen recent machine changes at the Canadian White Pine sawmill in Vancouver, which cost 25 jobs. New machines in the next year, it was predicted, would lead to the loss of 100 more positions. The union plant chairman drew out the implications for the mill employees: "What does this mean to you? You have 10 or 15 years' seniority, you think your job is safe? Will you be able to stay on the job you now hold? Will you be able to get a higher paying job? Will you be able to get an easier job for your later years? Will your son be able to get a job in this industry?"[78]

Masculine fears were also associated with the bogey of automation. In 1962 the *Western Canadian Lumber Worker* reprinted an article from an American paper with the title "Automation Lures Wives to Industry." A speaker at a New York symposium "predicted that within the next eight years wives by the thousands will be quietly slipping out of the kitchen to take over care and feeding of complex machines," expecting "the technological revolution to sweep into its fold almost half the female population over 35."[79] The possible implications for wage rates, job security, and family life needed no elaboration.

By 1955 industry envisioned the possibility of the fully automated sawmill, although recognizing that this was still in the future and that change would be incremental rather than sudden. The benefit to management was obvious: "a promise of savings that will enable the sawmill to stay in business without constantly fighting the ever-tighter spiraling of costs forced on him by the human needs of a more costly standard of living."[80] But while innovation was pushed, companies were reluctant to publicize the gains for fear of alienating unions. An industry spokesperson commented in 1962 that logging managers were privately proud to talk of new machines and their ability to replace human workers, but would add, "Please don't print that. The unions wouldn't like it."[81] MacMillan, Bloedel and Powell River was extremely cautious about publicizing technological changes. In December 1964, the company had a number of "automation projects" that were near the installation stage or in the "thinking stage," and each one involved laying off significant numbers of men: "All these projects require heavy capital investment and if we can undertake them only by retaining the people who are displaced, then we are in trouble."[82] In anticipation of these projects, management requested and received a report on collective agreements in other industries, where protection was guaranteed against loss of jobs, loss of promotion, and reduction of income caused by automation.

A.C. Kennedy of the Industrial Relations Department wrote to his superior, C.A. Specht, about the issue. Company officials, he noted, were aware of the problems associated with the introduction of automated machinery, and that to date the company had effectively introduced new machinery without disruption. In the present climate, however, the introduction of labour-saving devices would receive closer scrutiny and could trigger union and government responses: "I feel it is imperative that we avoid union or government intervention and therefore I ask that my department be involved in any automation moves where an employee or employees can be affected."[83] The company devised a policy that established a clear definition of "automation," involved the firm's Industrial Relations Department in all actions and discussions, and kept the issue in the hands of upper management. If too many people knew the details, the union would apply more pressure. As one company official noted, "There is little doubt that the unions will intensify their demands, regarding automation, in labour negotiations and contracts and we should carefully plan implementation of new work procedures."[84]

Unions offered two main responses to automation: a legislative response, involving government, and a collective bargaining response, where unions negotiated regulation of technological change and put it into contract language. Already by 1955, the IWA in the United States embraced both positions, demanding an orderly, regulated change to the new world of automated production, where unionized workers would not be left out in the cold. The IWA emphasized that it was not against automation, but that it wanted "legislative and contract guarantees to make sure that it is not recklessly and irresponsibly applied." The government had a role to play in mitigating the impact of automation on the national economy by establishing higher minimum wages, a shorter statutory work week, amendments to social security laws, and a broad public works program, but collective bargaining was the most efficacious vehicle for protection in the short term. The IWA looked for the following commitments from employers: (1) automation should be introduced when the economy was expanding, not when there were many layoffs; (2) new facilities incorporating automatic production should be situated "so as not to create mass layoffs or leave ghost towns"; (3) union contracts should now be shorter, say, two years, because of the anticipated rapid transformation that was going to be wrought by automation; (4) new job categories and pay rates were necessary for people working in jobs that monitored automation; (5) displaced workers should have access to training to upgrade their skills and should be offered new jobs in different company locations if necessary, at company expense; (6) a guaranteed annual wage should be instituted to tide workers over and facilitate the regulation of automation; (7) a shorter work week should be implemented to spread the available work around and afford workers more benefits from automated production; (8) all changes in jobs should be worked out with the union and the community before proceeding; and (9) where job loss was unavoidable, there should be a meaningful severance package, as well as assistance in finding new work.[85] The concluding paragraphs of the IWA report deserve full consideration, as they show the union's support for automation, its recognition of the problems, and its solutions:

> Automation is the second industrial revolution but it can be orderly and can immeasurably improve our standard of living if properly handled, explained and introduced to our economy. The fruits of automation will tend to offset the displacement of workers. New jobs will be made possible by cost reduction, by new products, by services in industries – including but not limited to automatic products and the new automatic controls industry – and by increased productivity.
>
> When we look back on the first industrial revolution, which is known as the Machine Age, we can all agree that the replacement of handwork by machinery has aided immeasurably the standard of living of the American people. The same things can be true of automation but there will have to be legislative and contract guarantees to make sure that it is properly applied so that the transition will be orderly, clearly understood, and its benefits shared by all working people.[86]

Automation, then, could be regulated, and if done properly, all of society would benefit.

British Columbia unions followed this agenda. In 1956 IWA BC district president Joe Morris reiterated the IWA position coming from headquarters in the United States, adding that lowering the qualifying age for old-age pensions and improved training for young people were also ways of responding to rapid automation.[87] Pulp and paper union officials in Canada took a similar stance. The *Western Pulp and Paper Worker,* a journal representing western Canadian pulp and paper workers, included extensive material on automation in its second issue, which came out in May 1956. Drawing on material from the Canadian Congress of Labour, the article described what governments could provide, including a guaranteed annual wage, lengthening of the school period, reduction of retirement age to sixty or even fifty-five, enriched unemployment insurance benefits, a general wage increase, longer vacations, and stronger penalties against overtime.[88]

The CCF suggested legislative measures as the response to automation. Chronic unemployment was to be dealt with by public works projects, a guaranteed annual income, encouragement of secondary manufacturing, a stronger Unemployment Insurance Act, and complete federal control of unemployment.[89] Canadian labour recognized the need for strong government support to deal with automation, and it was more than coincidence that the Canadian Labour Congress put out a call for a new political party in 1958, at the height of the automation concern, to strengthen labour's voice in legislative chambers. The result was the New Democratic Party, formed in 1961, which brought the CCF and organized labour together more formally to contest elections. T.C. "Tommy" Douglas, the first leader of the NDP, made automation a top priority. In 1964 Douglas, who was an honourary member of New Westminster IWA Local 1-357, spoke at the IWA regional convention: "Next to the threat of nuclear war, no problem has greater national significance than that of automation."[90] Three years later, he spoke to the IWA international convention in Portland, Oregon, and once again automation was a major theme. Acknowledging that automation was here to stay and that technology had the potential to benefit society, providing a higher standard of living and more leisure time, Douglas pointed to the underbelly of unemployment, dislocation and poverty, saying that "only the legislators can pass the kind of laws that we need to make sure that the benefits of automation are enjoyed by all, and to make sure that those who suffer from dislocation by automation are adequately compensated."[91]

There were more radical voices. Within the NDP, the irrepressible Colin Cameron, keen to distinguish the NDP from the Liberal Party, argued that automation and private ownership were incompatible, and that in time automation in the hands of private capital would produce "insoluble economic problems" and "destroy democratic institutions": "we must now start devising methods of removing the industrial complex from private hands."[92] On the streets of Vancouver, the League for Socialist Action distributed a circular that focused on a shorter work week as the solution and the general strike as the vehicle.[93]

As the 1960s progressed, neither the moderate union and social democratic positions nor the more radical options had much impact. In 1965 Grant MacNeil, the IWA regional educational director, provided a lengthy account of automation. He was skeptical about reassurances given by companies and their apologists. In the long run, automation created more jobs, said management, but MacNeil worried about the immediate future for the men in the plants and camps. He argued that automation downgraded, not upgraded, workers, making jobs and skills obsolete. Nor, said MacNeil, could the free enterprise system automatically ensure normal employment for everyone. Having critiqued the employer line, however, MacNeil offered little.[94] The IWA accepted that progress overall was beneficial and that management had the right to transform the production process. On the other hand, the NDP, the strongest political voice for workers, was not winning the support of the public or even Canadian union members. The left was divided and the impact of automation was uneven in terms of place and time: some workers lost jobs, but others did not, and wages did continue to rise. Perhaps technological change would create more and better jobs in the future, as well as more leisure, a position that the union leadership never challenged.[95] Moreover, the business per-spective was blunt and persuasive:

> There is not one substantial piece of evidence supporting the thesis that automation is anything but a vast benefaction to mankind. Not one labour leader amongst those using it as a white sheet in the cemetery at night has any capability of showing how we could get along better without the great degree of automation we already have. The whole case against automation is suppositious and insubstantial.[96]

The main response of forest industry unions was to get more money for workers in the new jobs: "The generally accepted principle is that workers' earnings on new automated jobs must exceed those on their old jobs because of the increased productivity of the operation."[97]

Pressure from labour, the NDP, and concerned members of the broader public forced the federal Liberal government of the day to appoint a commission to in-vestigate automation. The commission marked the end of concerted public dis-cussion of automation. The roots of the commission involved Canadian railway workers, long subject to the impact of technological change, who faced another crisis in the 1960s when diesel-powered engines enabled trains to travel further than steam-driven trains. This disrupted traditional work schedules. Frustrated workers launched wildcat strikes, and the federal government responded by ap-pointing an Industrial Inquiry Commission, chaired by Judge Samuel Freedman, in 1965. Freedman was sympathetic to the workers and in his report recommended that workplace changes should be negotiated with the union during collective bargaining. This would have given labour a measure of control. Companies wor-ried that if this was put into legislation, management rights would be infringed and technological innovation slowed. In the end, the government did nothing and management of technological change was left in the hands of companies. Only workers with strong unions could fight for some say, and then only regarding the impact of technological change on workers.[98] The federal Liberals enhanced social programs, including richer pension and unemployment insurance benefits and medicare, but these were not seen as measures compensating for the ravages of technological dislocations; rather, they were presented as the product of prosper-ity, produced by innovation and a generous, caring federal government. The issue of automation was successfully moved to the back burner. Labour responded to the threat of automation, but neither legislative nor collective bargaining strate-gies marshalled enough support to significantly slow the "march of progress." Workers hoped that the promises of capital would be realized, but at the same time, they protested individually and in small groups on the job, challenging, ac-cording to one union commentator in 1966, "the high-handed and arrogant man-ner in which, all too often, management decides unilaterally to introduce job destroying technological changes without even bothering to discuss them with the employees whose lives and livelihoods are to be directly affected."[99]

NEW MACHINERY AND PRODUCTION SYSTEMS were testaments to human creativity, but they were also embedded in larger structures, governed by the imperatives of capitalist production. The drive to remove humans from production prompted debate and faced scattered resistance, but overall the trend continued, overdetermined by narratives of progress and the impetus to manage and regulate nature, as well as by the promise of higher standards of living, more leisure, and more satisfying work.

7
Companies and Unions Meet the Environmental Movement

Activists in the British Columbia environmental movement of the early 1970s shook up established institutions. Unlike conservationists of earlier generations, who promoted the wise use of resources in the interests of perpetual economic exploitation and who, after the 1940s, found comfortable places in the Fordist production regime, the environmentalists asserted a different relationship between human beings and nature, challenging many of the basic assumptions underlying Fordism. In the first years, BC environmentalists targeted pulp mill pollution and demanded the creation of parks. The intensity of the critique surprised the forest industry, which had been used to handling environmental issues in the familiar world of bureaucrats and officials, all of whom were committed to similar goals.[1]

The industry was proud of its achievements. After all, it was a success during the Fordist era. Trees were taken out at an increasingly rapid rate, sustained-yield policies were in place, and the war on waste and inefficiency was being won. To be sure, there were concerns that forests were being harvested too quickly without proper consideration for reforestation, but the principles of the conservation movement were enshrined. H.R. MacMillan reflected with pride on the achievement of companies and the provincial government in a personal letter to Chief Forester C.D. Orchard in 1955: "Forest management under your leadership has progressed very rapidly in the last decade. The people need not worry – but they don't seem to know it yet."[2] Companies profited and workers received high wages and benefit packages. The province's population increased, as did the standard of living. Logging and mill towns had one of the highest per capita income levels in Canada in the 1960s. New and richer federal and provincial social programs attended to unemployment, sickness, and old age, and, it seemed, would soon offer even greater support for ordinary Canadians.[3]

But this sanguine vision masked contradictions. Industrial progress brought the pollution of rivers and the ocean. Rapid harvesting of the forests meant more cutover land, and the growing, relatively prosperous population was more likely to see these visually unappealing areas, often via logging roads constructed by forest companies. Questions arose. Why were chemical wastes dumped into rivers and the ocean? Why were forests valued primarily for their industrial utility? These questions came from outside the power nexus of company executives, government officials, and labour leaders that had established the framework for exploitation in previous decades. Human health, outdoor recreation, natural habitats, and wilderness beauty increasingly trumped profits, social justice, and the conservation goals of professional foresters. The new ideas were spread by people who tended to be young, urban, and educated, often with solid grounding in the natural sciences, and who, in many cases, were involved in the counterculture and New Left of the 1960s and 1970s. To the establishment, they seemed foreign indeed.

This chapter focuses on the engagement of the emerging environmental movement with companies and unions. It outlines the early history of environmental organizations, examines company responses to pollution and park issues in both the conservation and environmental eras, and discusses the divide that separated workers and environmentalists. Companies moved quickly to counter environmentalists, and unions also came to position themselves in the anti-environmentalist camp. Confrontations in the woods between loggers protecting jobs and environmentalists protecting trees, monitored by police and recorded by television crews, are now a classic image. Political scientist Jeremy Wilson, in a rich, book-length discussion of BC's forestry debate between 1965 and 1996, notes that capital and labour were largely on the same side in these years, that unions, with minor exceptions, were part of the pro-development coalition. His focus is on the political system, especially the cabinet room of the provincial government, and the failure of unionists and environmentalists to work together effectively is a given, not a problem.[4] The inability of the labour movement and environmentalists to forge an alliance is an important feature of Post-Fordist politics, however, debilitating development of a widespread oppositional discourse.

The environmental movement is seen here as a critical discourse, one of the "new social movements." In the first half of the twentieth century, social justice was the passionate cause of reformers and radicals. Fairness, human dignity, workers' rights, and a decent standard of living for everyone underpinned activism on a wide variety of fronts, leading to government-regulated capitalism, broadened access to education, social welfare and worker insurance programs, and increased industrial democracy. Class discourse was at the centre of debate and action. The unionization of the forest industry workforce was part of this wave, which had had the support of progressive voices. In later decades, new social movements, mobilized by gender, race, and quality-of-life discourses, emerged, and class in its traditional guise was displaced as a fundamental discourse in multicultural, multidimensional, postmodern politics.[5] The feminist movement and First Nations activism were prominent in British Columbia, but in the forest sector the first significant evocation of the new progressive voice was the environmental movement. Environmental concern was elevated to new heights in the industrial world during the 1960s, and an array of new organizations challenged existing institutions and reshaped public debate.[6] By 1970 BC had two effective environmental organizations, which, like environmental groups elsewhere, challenged progress based on unfettered industrial expansion and the behaviour of Fordist institutions, unions and corporations alike.

SPEC and the Sierra Club

The Society for Pollution and Environmental Control (SPEC) and the Sierra Club were the first effective organizations in BC that spoke the language of the new environmental movement.[7] Gwen and Derrick Mallard founded SPEC. Gwen Mallard heard a radio show in December 1968 on which the guest discussed a proposal for an anti-pollution society. Meetings and discussions followed, often at the Mallard house, and the new society held its first public meeting at Simon Fraser University, near Vancouver, on 15 January 1969. The objectives of the society were "to preserve and develop a quality environment for all forms of life"; "to prevent and eliminate pollution of our water, soil and air"; to scientifically investigate ecological and pollution problems and share findings with the public at large; and to work with others devoted to environmental control in Canada.[8] Early SPEC causes included strip mining, sound noise at a Surrey planer mill, the BC fisheries, and pollution in the Port Moody area. SPEC expanded beyond its Vancouver base, and by January 1970 the association had members in Kelowna, Kamloops, West Vancouver, North Vancouver, and Surrey, and boasted a total membership of 3,500. The group continued to expand and membership reached 8,000 in short order.

SPEC's language was at times blunt. Environmental offenders were described as "irresponsible, short-sighted robber barons operating as if the limited resources of the planet were an infinite hot dog to be gobbled at a gluttenous [sic] and greed-driven rate." These corporate plunderers polluted "with gay-abandon as if the planet had an infinte [sic] capacity to absorb such violence to its critically balanced ecology."[9]

Although the interests of SPEC were wide-ranging, forestry issues were present early. At the November 1970 convention, thirty-two resolutions were passed, three of which pertained directly to the forest industry. They called for a government commission to analyze the environmental impact of building new pulp mills, increased reforestation, and an end to pulp mill construction at Houston until it was proven that the mill would not pollute. Other resolutions on water quality, noise, and wildlife habitat also had implications for the forest industry.[10]

The Sierra Club, headquartered in San Francisco, was built on a more solid base. The club had been a force in environmental issues since the nineteenth century.[11] In 1969 a Simon Fraser University geography graduate student from California, Terry Simmons, who had been in close contact with the Sierra Club's Pacific Northwest chapter, formed a group in Vancouver with a small circle of friends. The first meeting was held in September and the constitution of the Sierra Club of British Columbia was in place in November. At about the same time, Ric Careless, a graduate student at the University of Victoria, organized a chapter there. In November there were 252 Sierra Club members in British Columbia, including 119 in Vancouver, 27 in Victoria, 13 in Burnaby, 7 in Prince George, and 7 in Vernon.[12] The Sierra Club activists in BC joined the American organization, hoping to draw on its expertise, methods, and influence.[13]

Despite being small in numbers, the Sierra Club of BC was very active. In 1971 it commissioned an American, Dave Corkran, to do a wilderness survey of the area around Talchako Lodge, 40 miles east of Bella Coola on the Bella Coola River. Talchako Lodge had been donated to the San Francisco Sierra Club in December 1969, so there was a direct interest in the area. In recruiting BC support, Corkran emphasized the importance of good data:

> There is already logging in Tweedsmuir Park in the Talchako area. We need to know how much acreage has been logged, exactly when and where, and we need to know about future logging plans for the next five or ten years. What timber types are involved, and what will be involved in the future? In short, we need to know everything possible about logging or potential loggin [sic] in the park. We need a report on this logging, giving precise locations, number of board feet cut, where it is shipped, etc. In short, we need to know *everything* about the logging in the region. We need this information so that we can get a full picture of the economic and environmental values involved: until then, we cannot speak intelligently about wilderness.[14]

For the Sierra Club, as for SPEC, quality information was a primary currency. The Sierra Club focused on wilderness preservation, but although its range was narrower than SPEC's, it was willing to become involved in broader issues. Ken Farquharson commented on the club's activities from 1969 to 1972: "We have been involved in a full range of conservation issues from freeway location, air and water pollution, to recreation and development of land and wilderness areas. Our primary concerns reflect the activities of the province. The foci of our programme are forestry practice, park management, energy policy and the like."[15]

In the early 1970s, a myriad of groups in British Columbia were interested in environmental issues. Most, however, were very local. For example, the Shuswap and Thompson River Research and Development Association had a tight mandate, as indicated by its name. Older, more traditional groups, such as the BC Wildlife Federation and the BC Federation of Naturalists, were still active, but they lacked the vibrancy and militancy of SPEC and the Sierra Club. The former president of SPEC commented on the Naturalists in 1973: "Nice people – in fact, delightful people. They are not concerned with the urban scene, growth, energy, unless a dam will obliterate the lesser fan-tailed woodpecker!"[16] Still, the environmental sensibility was becoming widespread and could be marshalled in support of a variety of causes by more aggressive organizations. In 1972 the Steelhead Society of BC, the BC Federation of Naturalists, and the BC Wildlife Federation worked with the Sierra Club of BC to preserve the Tsitika-Schoen wild land on Vancouver Island.[17] An umbrella organization, the British Columbia Environmental Council, was set up and by 1973 it had affiliated a number of organizations, including SPEC, the Sierra Club of BC, various unions, the Powell River Anti-Pollution Association, and the UBC Law Students Association. The council also had the support of many BC churches, particularly the United Church.[18]

Among professional foresters, too, new attitudes were evident. In 1972 Dr. J.P. "Hamish" Kimmins, a young UBC assistant professor of forest ecology, was in great demand for speaking engagements. Professional foresters were on the defensive, as Kimmins noted in a 1973 article: "The forester of today is constantly confronted by the criticisms and demands of environmental groups."[19] He offered lectures on the ecological principles that he believed provided the foundation for forest management. He was hardly anti-business, but he believed that all forest management, including economic investment, could be based on forest ecology.[20] Kimmins's public lectures did not deal with how to take out more wood more quickly, using increasingly powerful machinery and automated production processes, the fundamental precept of Fordist conservation forestry, but rather examined issues such as how forest plants and animals reacted with their physical environment; the place of herbicides, fertilizers, and insecticides in ecology management; and the recovery of streams after logging.[21] He saw man as part of the forest environment, just like any other forest animal, and was willing to rethink sacrosanct issues such as sustained yield.[22]

Unlike the conservation crusade of the 1930s, however, professional foresters in government and academe were largely catching up with changes already underway. Spearheading the environmental crusade were the Sierra Club and SPEC. Notably, both organizations came out of the universities: non-forestry academics and graduate students were driving forces, and many other professionals became involved at an early date. As industry apologist and environmental movement critic Ian Mahood noted in 1970: "Spokesmen or advisors to these ecology cults are invariably professional academics who spend their life cloistered in university out of touch with the real world of people and production of goods and services."[23] Quality information, especially based on an understanding of the physical sciences, underpinned the critiques offered by both SPEC and the Sierra Club, and many members were formally trained in areas such as zoology, genetics, chemistry, and engineering.[24] Moreover, if expertise in a particular area was needed, the members of the executive knew whom to contact. The generation of quality scientific information by trained people enabled the environmental groups to develop a discourse that credibly countered the scientific discourse that sustained industrial conservation forestry. For industry and government managers, this was a startling turn of events. Traditionally they had dealt with disgruntled sports fishermen, weekend naturalists, recreationists, and representatives of other industries or the government who shared their attitude towards science and resource exploitation. Now they were challenged in the scientific realm; science was debatable and critics could not be so simply dismissed or accommodated. Other experts – lawyers, geographers, economists, accountants, and philosophers – also added legitimacy to the environmental cause.

Mahood captured another aspect of the early BC environmental movement in 1970: many of the spokespersons were "displaced Americans who are dissenters that were rejected in their own land because of a dedication to promoting a revolutionary change in culture and sociology."[25] Many of the founders of the BC Sierra Club were Americans.[26] Katy Madsen was born in Palo Alto, California, in 1921 and joined the Sierra Club in 1938. She graduated from San Jose State College with a major in biological science, married, and raised a family. In 1964 the family moved to Summerland, in the Okanagan, and she involved herself in local naturalist and park issues. She was a founding director of the Sierra Club of BC and remained active into the 1980s.[27] Emlen Littell was born in Maryland in 1917, graduated from Yale, served in the Second World War, and then became an editor at a number of California university presses. He came to Canada in 1967 and was active in Sierra Club circles.[28]

More broadly, the BC environmental movement was influenced by what was going on in the United States and the world. The Sierra Club had obvious American connections, and research, policies, and tactics from south of the border were used. The people in SPEC, too, were very aware that they were part of a continental and global movement. They read studies and magazines from across North America and Europe, and attended international conferences. British Columbia was a local struggle in a much larger crusade. The BC environmental movement of the late 1960s and early 1970s represented a range of interests and groups from the radical wing of SPEC through the Sierra Club to traditional fish and wildlife advocates. The cohesion, albeit uneasy, of these diverse interests made environmentalism a formidable challenge to forest companies.

Forest companies had experience in dealing with complaints regarding their activities. Nineteenth-century critics argued that forest practices were wasteful, and the conservation movement, despite its pro-business stance, challenged BC lumbermen who thought that the ideals of the movement were impractical and uneconomic.[29] It was not until the 1940s that industry embraced the goals of conservationists. In the 1930s, as the logging industry expanded on Vancouver Island, local businesses worried about forest fires and the impact on tourism. In 1933 the Associated Boards of Trade of Vancouver Island demanded that the provincial government establish a commission to investigate the implications of high-lead logging, suggesting that selective logging might be more appropriate for the environment and the economy.[30] In the late 1930s, there was a great concern that coastal forests were being harvested too rapidly, and that this would soon lead to high unemployment and the devastation of communities that depended on the lumber industry.[31] The issue had periodically arisen in the past, but once again, as we have seen, technological innovation opened up new timbered areas and smallwood logging made more efficient use of traditional logging sites. In the 1960s and early 1970s, however, the challenge was more formidable. Two issues galvanized the new environmental movement: pulp mill pollution and the creation of parks.

Chemicals and Odours

Postwar advances in applied chemistry promised solutions to many industrial problems, and enthusiasm for new chemical treatments was evident in the BC forest industry. Experiments with chemicals, including DDT, were performed in the woods. In the early 1950s, the Western Division of the Canadian Pulp and Paper Association sponsored a research project to develop a chemical capable of debarking trees in the woods. Various poison compounds and tree-killing chemicals were used at University of British Columbia laboratories and field sites. A truckload of thirty-nine twenty-foot hemlock logs was brought to Canadian Forest Products' Eburne sawmill in the winter of 1953-54, and the results were promising. Trees killed by chemicals had less bark, which lowered the weight of the logs by 15 percent, thereby also lowering transportation costs. By the time the logs reached the mill pond, about 50 percent of the bark had fallen off and the remainder could be removed with a pen knife. These logs could be run through the hydraulic barker at three times the normal speed.[32] For unknown reasons, however, the chemical killing of trees was apparently not pursued.

Chemicals were also employed to kill pests, such as the green-striped looper and the balsam woolly aphid. In the case of chemicals, environmental criticism was voiced within the bureaucracy by government fisheries officials. A project to control the devastation of the black-headed budworm in 1957 faced difficulties, and the BC Loggers' Association agreed "to study the possibility of development of a chemical capable of destroying insect life but not as dangerous to fish as D.D.T."[33] An industrial forester noted that public opinion would not support the use of DDT spraying.[34] Two years later, the industry was still searching for less lethal chemical sprays: "Studies and experiments with new chemicals, reduced dosage, and with bacterial sprays are proceeding in an effort to eliminate all hazard to wildlife and fish."[35] Experiments with benzene hexachloride, intended to control the ambrosia beetle, were stopped in 1965 because of harm to fish.[36]

Experiments with chemical debarking and pesticides were carried out far from the public eye, but pulp and paper operations, which relied on chemical production systems and released potentially hazardous effluent, could not hide so easily. Early mills were built in isolated areas, largely single-industry towns, and public concern over environmental issues was limited. The construction of the first mill in an already colonized, more populated area, the Bloedel, Stewart & Welch mill at Port Alberni, attracted more attention. The mill, which was to have been constructed in 1940 but was postponed due to the war, finally opened in 1947. To get the approval of fisheries officials, it had to show that the operation would meet the pollution requirements of the Fisheries Act.[37] In 1949 concerns from residents forced the company to defend its operation. There were two issues. The first was water pollution. The company presented evidence that even before construction, environmental concerns had been considered, citing data from a scientific study on the water currents and depth changes of the Alberni Canal and area rivers that showed that "the pollution from [the proposed sulphate] mill would be tolerable at all times." Now that the mill was in operation, "no pollution has been observed, and none is anticipated from the existing pulp mill."

Second, Bloedel, Stewart & Welch addressed the perennial concern regarding pulp mills, odour: "It must be understood that *nowhere in the world has it yet proven possible to operate a chemical pulp mill without some smell emanating from the discharge of the cooking gases.*" However, the company was involved in research, using "some of the ablest brains in the industry," in an attempt to reduce, if not eliminate, odour. The company reminded residents that they had voted in favour of the mill "so that dollars thus expended in the further processing of the forest crop, *be kept in the Alberni Valley,* and not exported to make payrolls and prosperity in a foreign port."[38] Pulp and paper companies continued to deal with the issues of chemicals and pollution in their operations, and worried that government restrictions might be costly and deleterious to their finances. Provincial legislation bringing in measures to control water pollution alarmed pulp and paper mill operators in the mid-1950s, and they lobbied the government to ensure that their interests were met.[39]

In the mid-1960s, pollution concerns moved out of the industry/government circle again, when Port Alberni became the focus of a local anti-pollution movement. Smoke, soot on cars and houses, odour, and water quality were all cited as problems detrimental to human health, homeowners' property, and the environment. A citizens' committee in the Alberni Valley collected some 6,800 names on a petition demanding legislative remedies from the provincial government. Because of the forest industry, the area had an extremely high standard of living, but the costs of prosperity had become too high, said protesters:

> Residents of the Alberni Valley have for many years suffered under the oppression of industrial, air and water pollution ... with little option other than to accept these foul conditions as part of their daily duty to tolerate such inroads upon their civilized

right to breathe unpolluted air, and the enjoyments of unpolluted water sports and livelihoods, as the "penalty" for the economic prosperity industrialization brings to such an area as the Alberni Valley.[40]

The Alberni group wanted a province-wide movement to improve anti-pollution legislation.[41] The Communist Party of Canada, though a marginal political presence, recognized that clean water and pulp pollution had become important issues, and the party was keen to extend the Alberni protest to thirteen other pulp and paper towns.[42]

The pulp industry was a constant target in the 1960s, and the industry spent millions of dollars installing and upgrading anti-pollution equipment. The building of new pulp mills throughout the Interior intensified the scrutiny, and the industry estimated in 1965 that pollution controls in a new kraft mill cost about $2.5 million. These costs could not be recouped. The Tahsis Company stated that of the $3.25 million spent on water and air pollution at its new coastal operation, only $500,000 was justified by any economic return.[43] The older coastal mills had no pollution control equipment and bringing them up to government standards was costly. In the mid-1960s, MacMillan Bloedel spent $8 million on pollution control at its established Powell River and Port Alberni mills.[44]

The industry also spent much money to boost its public image and explain the necessary processes involved in the production of pulp. In November 1966, the Council of Forest Industries (COFI) set up a Joint Industry Pollution Committee, with representatives from the logging, sawmill, and pulp and paper sectors. The goal was to lobby government, especially to secure tax breaks for installing anti-pollution devices, and to "acquaint the public with the true facts regarding the position of our industry and the ever increasing efforts made to combat pollution."[45] In 1968 COFI held an exhibit at the Pacific National Exhibition. The focus was on wildlife, showing that despite logging the public still had access to the woods, and celebrating the anti-pollution efforts of the industry.[46]

Government pollution controls became more stringent. In August 1970, W.N. Venables chaired the Public Inquiry into Pollution Control in the Forest Products Industry, which was designed to ensure that the industry was meeting the requirements of the Pollution Control Act of 1967. Many environmental groups, including the Sierra Club, and unions made presentations, but the SPEC offering was the most comprehensive and the most worrisome to industry: "As might have been predicted, [SPEC] took a leading role in attacking the forest industry's role in allegedly creating and failing to control pollution in many areas of the province."[47] The thirty-two-page SPEC document[48] began with a definition of ecology, proposed a greater role for local and regional governments ("The age of ecology will be characterized by the spread of self-government to local areas rather than the development of massive bureaucracies"[49]), cited environmental problems near BC pulp mills, and critiqued the ideals of industrial capitalism:

> It used to be said, in this Province, and there may be some hardy soul who will still declare, that the smell of the pulp mills is the smell of money. People who take that view fail to appreciate that the social costs in air and water pollution and in destruction of public resources which accompany the buccaneer saga of the BC forest industry have never been measured. SPEC ventures to suggest that when that cost is accurately computed it is possible a good deal of our idea of "industrial progress" will turn out to have been a foolish, short-sighted view, well-suited only to the exhaustion of our forest resources with maximum speed at minimum cost. It must be recalled that 90% of BC forests actually belong to the Crown and the public is, or should be, vitally concerned that they not be stripped by industrial techniques which actually destroy other uses and resources.
>
> Recently MacMillan Bloedel company began to commence night logging work at certain Vancouver Island camps. The spectacle of a logger wearing a miner's lamp is the perfect instance of precisely what is wrong with the forest industry of British Columbia.[50]

The brief then noted the difficulty of getting relevant information from the companies and the government. The second half of the presentation was more technical, focusing on particular parts of the kraft pulp-making process and making specific recommendations, including legislation to control dust, more research attention to the ecology of the fisheries near pulp mills rather than species-specific studies of economic fish such as salmon, and the installation of primary treatment lagoons at pulp mills. The brief concluded with recommendations for logging, including enforced slash burning, leaving green belts to protect streams, the abolition of clearcut logging, and the end to human-constructed, monoculture forests.

COFI, representing the companies, offered a 260-page brief that weighed over two pounds and, speaking the language of the conservation movement, emphasized measures already undertaken by industry to ensure a sustained yield from the forests, the increased utilization of smallwood, and increased chemical recovery in pulp mills. The document also recognized "the need to manage its operations in a manner which will minimize the stress to the environment and protect it within the bounds of technical and economic feasibility."[51] The brief stated that "it would not be in the best interests of the province or the people to be so vigorous in the application of pollution control as to substantially affect our competitive position."[52]

The forest companies could not contain the popular environmental movement. SPEC activists did not care about short-term profits: "It is at all times necessary

Night logging, 1960s.
MacMillan Bloedel Collection (UBC), BC 1930/196/15

that the overall quality of our lives be not tarnished by accepting solutions to problems just because they are financially expedient ... Ultimately the cost of short sightedness might be the extinction of the human race."[53] Nor did appeals to conservation rhetoric satisfy the new environmentalists, who subscribed to a new ecological perspective that did not place the business perspective at the forefront. Business and radical environmentalists inhabited different ideological landscapes. Finally, the environmental movement could not be quickly or effectively disciplined by markets or company actions. Activists were often young or working in government jobs, and unlike established workers in the forest industry, were not sensitive to market downturns or susceptible to management decisions. They did not have to toe the line and companies could not make them. By 1970 companies had to accept the existence of an aggressive, organized, province-wide environmental movement that had come together in the battle over pollution, especially in the pulp sector. In 1972 SPEC conceded that the province had some of the best standards in Canada, but that there was no timetable to force implementation.[54] The struggle between the companies and the environmentalists was just beginning.

Creating Parks

While SPEC was active in the anti-pollution campaign, the Sierra Club was most effective in forcing the creation of parks, much to the consternation of forest companies. Public parks had been created in British Columbia since early in the twentieth century, but the late 1950s saw increased pressure from recreationists. Logging activity had expanded geographically, taking up more of the landscape and spreading closer to urban centres. Population was also increasing, people were wealthier, and the great outdoors became a playground for urbanites. The pressure for wilderness preserves, as well as public access to timber areas controlled by companies and private logging roads, was building. The BC industry was very aware of what was happening south of the border. In 1957 members of the BC Loggers' Association discussed the response of Washington and Oregon logging companies to pressure from hunters and fishermen, who wanted access to company timberland, but were still unsure of what action, if any, to take.[55] In 1959 they discussed the push by recreationists in the United States to create more wilderness areas and more lands for recreational purposes only: "It was pointed out too that the possibility of adverse action by recreationists in our own province is a growing one."[56] Within weeks they set up a recreation committee, which they hoped would include high-level participants from the provincial Forest Service and the Parks and Recreation Department.[57]

Industry concerns were not misplaced. In 1960 Roderick Haig-Brown, British Columbia's internationally renowned conservationist and outdoor writer, spoke about "the crisis in outdoor recreation." Despite BC's vast wilderness of uncut forest and relatively small population, there was an impending problem. People, he argued, were in search of something and they had the time, money, and means to embark on this search; in a prosperous economy, these drives would increase. What these people, mostly city-dwellers, were searching for, he argued, was "a measure of self-realization, a period of contrast that will help to round out their regular working lives and recreate them as people." They looked for this in "some sort of self-identification with the natural world," which offered the opportunity for mountain climbing, hunting, scenic photography, nature study, camping, skiing, swimming, and sailing, among other things. Going out into nature was a way "of finding or recovering the sense of identity with natural things."[58] BC's existing four national parks and seven major provincial parks were not going to satisfy this need. Haig-Brown advocated more wilderness, recreational parks, and other areas of multiple use, areas where industry and recreationists would coexist. Forest lands, then, should be open to people seeking the outdoor experience, and this access should be encouraged and controlled by the government.

Haig-Brown used the term "multiple use" to describe his vision of resource management, but among foresters, government officials, and industry people, "integrated use" was seen as the more appropriate term, although the terms were often used interchangeably. "Multiple use" was misleading, suggesting that all uses were equal and had to be balanced. According to BC government forester F.S. McKinnon, speaking in 1961, "rightly or wrongly, the impression was left with the public that the same acre of ground could provide forest products, grazing, water and recreation simultaneously, and to the same degree." But the reality was more complex because of tension between various users, and so "integrated use," a refinement of the "multiple use" concept, came into use. "Integrated use" recognized that there must be a dominant land use on any acre of land, a use that benefited society the most, and that other uses should be developed up to the point where further use would interfere with the exigencies of the dominant use.[59] The forest industry was committed to "integrated use," which gave forestry dominant status in most cases.

In 1965 COFI president B.M. Hoffmeister raised concerns about changing priorities and too much public use of the forests in a speech to the Truck Loggers Association. He touted the economic importance of the forest industry and gave a brief account of the importance of technological innovation, including truck logging, which had led to the building of logging roads by companies, before getting to his main point: leisure and enjoyment of the outdoors must come second to the needs of industry. Indeed, the free time and the means to enjoy the free time were a result of the efforts of the forest industry. Moreover, while private companies built these roads at great cost, now the public used the roads without any cost and at times acted irresponsibly. The industry was amenable to "multiple use" in the forests, but only after its needs were satisfied. The main-haul roads, which were the widest, more heavily gravelled, costliest, and most important had to be restricted as to use: "The livelihoods of hundreds of men, and the capital of thousands more, is jeopardized when roads are improperly used."[60]

Tension between industrial and recreational interests intensified in the late 1960s and early 1970s. There were two flashpoints that pitted forest companies against environmentalists led by the Sierra Club of BC, and both incidents were on the west coast of Vancouver Island. In both instances the environmentalists won. The first issue involved halting MacMillan Bloedel logging on Mt. Arrowsmith, a site that overlooked the city of Port Alberni. The Sierra Club and others wanted a park, and in 1970 they put pressure on the company. Vancouver newspapers were supportive and petitions attracted many names. For its part, MacMillan Bloedel resented the Sierra Club and challenged its campaign, arguing that jobs were more important. The company worked hard to enlist the support of working people and businesses in Port Alberni. J.V. Clyne, MacMillan Bloedel's combative chief executive officer, was spoiling for a fight, unwilling to give in on the Mt. Arrowsmith issue unless there was absolutely no alternative: "I think we should go on the offensive and do whatever we can to raise public opinion against the arguments of the Sierra Club. After all, the citizens of Alberni have or should have a vested interest in the continued economic operations of our company in the Valley."[61] The company called for meetings with targeted groups in the area and with government officials. Clyne promoted conservation forestry and prompt reforestation, and offered a blunt slogan: "Log Arrowsmith and Preserve Alberni Jobs." In 1972 MacMillan Bloedel was forced to capitulate, transferring 1,400 acres of timberland to the Regional District of Alberni-Clayoquot to be used as a park.[62]

The Sierra Club of BC was also instrumental in expanding Pacific Rim National Park by 13,400 acres to include three lakes in what is known as the Nitinat Triangle. The protected west coast trail hugged the coastline of Vancouver Island between Port Renfrew and Bamfield, near Port Alberni, and environmentalists wanted the protected area expanded. The land that they wanted preserved was part of Tree Farm Licence 27, which gave cutting rights to BC Forest Products. The company planned to log the area to feed its sawmill at Youbou, on Cowichan Lake. The debate involved the federal government, the provincial government, and the logging company, which had made heavy investments and needed the wood. BC Forest Products made its case against the Sierra Club proposal in a letter to employees in December 1971, arguing that if the company lost access to the timber, and was not compensated by the provincial government with timber elsewhere, there would be job losses. It countered the park proposal with an offer of greater public access to its timberland: "We do not believe that more wilderness in the Nitinat with its restricted use [recreation] is in the best interests of the most people. Our new multiple use plan for the area will provide much of what the majority of recreationists want without seriously infringing on productive harvesting of the renewable forest resource."[63]

Environmentalists were not impressed. The Sierra Club ran an effective campaign. Ric Careless, chairman of the Victoria Sierra Club, summarized three meetings with representatives of BC Forest Products, MacMillan Bloedel, and the Council of Forest Industries in the summer of 1972, and his comments exhibit the confidence and influence of the environmental movement. He told the companies that to this point the Sierra Club was moderate, willing to compromise on the size of the park – despite criticism from more radical environmental groups – and purposely avoiding "mudslinging and emotional tactics." He noted, however, that "we then stated that we would continue to conduct the issue along these lines but said that should Nitinat be lost, we intended to 'blow the whole thing out of proportion' and scream almost everytime a tree came down. In short, we made it quite clear that no matter how beautifully the forest industries logged the area, (under their Multi-use plans) they would lose in their public relation image and not gain."[64] In August the Sierra Club claimed victory. A deal to preserve the area was made; all that remained was for the provincial government to compensate the forest company with timber elsewhere.[65]

Forest companies responded to the new environmentalism in different ways. MacMillan Bloedel was hawkish. J.V. Clyne outlined the company position in early 1972: "We cannot afford to be casual about this and should come out with a hard hitting program and it would be well to devise some method of attacking the Sierra Club. It certainly has gained a poor reputation in the States as was evidenced by the series of articles in the New Yorker last year. I hate always being on the defence."[66] MacMillan Bloedel also established a new land-use policy, and expert staff members publicly rebutted Sierra Club positions whenever possible. All forest companies promoted a positive image. In the summer of 1973, COFI ran a set of four full-page advertisements in a number of BC newspapers to present the industry's perspective on modern forest management.[67]

Some companies were more conciliatory than MacMillan Bloedel. The Sierra Club was convinced that American-based corporations, especially Crown Zellerbach, treated environmentalists with less hostility. These companies knew the force of the movement because of their experiences south of the border. In early October 1972, American and BC Sierra Club members toured Crown Zellerbach and BC Forest Products timber and logging sites on Vancouver Island. Company officials as well as government officials from BC Fish and Wildlife participated, offering candid observations, showing areas where mistakes had been made and areas where things had gone right, and offering hope to the environmentalists. According to a Sierra Club member, Canadian Crown Zellerbach "is not as far along in its environmental forestry in Canada as it is in the U.S., but there is no reason it can't catch up."[68] The Forest Service was helpful too. In late October and early November, another international Sierra Club activist surveyed forestry and logging practices in the Okanagan with its support and help. Again, the American investigator noted that BC lagged behind the US in its environmental mentality: "The general situation in B.C. forestry is that of applying 20th century technology in a land where 19th century 'pioneer' attitude still prevails to a large degree. It is admittedly difficult to view B.C. as something other than a vast area with limitless resources, but the change is coming ever so slowly."[69]

Unionists and Environmentalists

Organized labour was less prominent than forest companies in the new environmental debates. The IWA had long made presentations to government forest management committees and commissions. In 1947 Harold Pritchett of the International Woodworkers of America (IWA) was on the executive of the new Chamber of Forests, an umbrella group representing existing societies and organizations for the purpose of doing research and education on the province's forests. The Chamber of Forests included representatives from the Canadian Legion and the BC Teachers' Federation,[70] but forestry issues were not at the forefront of union interests. Unions had neither the finances nor the expertise, although they were of course concerned about pollution to the extent that it affected the safety of workers on the job. For example, in 1957 IWA Local 1-85, Port Alberni, sent two ounces of lumber spray to chemists at the BC Research Council for testing. The spray, Permatox, was used on green lumber exported to the United Kingdom. Test results showed that the product was toxic and the union demanded better ventilation and rubber gloves for workers handling the product.[71]

In the early 1970s, some environmentalists, most notably members of SPEC, worked to forge closer links with the trade unions and employed the language of class. While the Sierra Club of BC successfully solicited donations from wealthy patrons, such as Lawrence Rockefeller of New York,[72] SPEC sought working-class alliances and was often skeptical of even middle-class support. A SPEC study opined that the "average man" intuitively knew that something was wrong with the system and that change was necessary, but educated middle-class people were too immersed in their careers and material culture to recognize social and environmental problems. All professions, though, were not equal: "When confronted, we find architects and engineers the most responsive, with lawyers, church representatives, politicians and business professionals being the least understanding and concerned, (in that order). All exhibit patterns of rationalization that make little sense, in terms of survival. The vested interest of business professionals offers some explanation, but the position of the medical profession (a specialty that cannot escape knowledge of the environment) is simply beyond understanding."[73] Still, the author hoped to win over middle-class support. Some SPEC activists were less optimistic: "Rather than worry about gaining the support of the middle-class lardasses ... we should be far more concerned with the gaining the support of the youngsters – at least those over 19. I feel that the middle class mess/mass are largely beyond reach and to try to reach them ... is to castrate SPEC entirely."[74]

The environmental movement and organized labour did find some common ground, although it was not straightforward. In 1969 the BC Federation of Labour set up a Natural Resources Committee and this committee produced a fourteen-page report.[75] A good portion of the committee's report demanded that the government recoup more revenue from the forest companies and called for greater protection of the commercial fishery, reflecting the financial interests of members. Comments on parks, wildlife, and healthy water were rather general, to say the least, and it is clear that the committee lacked the expertise and experience of those involved in SPEC or the Sierra Club. The report recommended that union members join SPEC or other environmental groups, and offered support to the new pollution committees established by the International Brotherhood of Pulp, Sulphite and Paper Mill Workers (IBPSPMW) locals in BC. Early supporters of the environmental movement included the Vancouver and District Labour Council and the Pulp and Paper Workers of Canada, which was notably enthusiastic, endorsing SPEC in 1970 and passing an anti-pollution resolution at the same convention.[76] The unions were only participants in SPEC and the broader environmental movement, however. They did not control it or set its agenda. The roots of the environmental movement were elsewhere.

There was tension between unionists and environmentalists early on. The *Western Canadian Lumber Worker,* the official newspaper of the IWA, heartily endorsed the report of the Natural Resources Committee of the BC Federation of Labour soon after it came out, recommending that members join SPEC and that locals become involved. Within months, however, the paper's editor was apoplectic over SPEC. Derrick Mallard had lambasted both industry and unions for environmental problems, linking higher worker wages with increased devastation of the resource, increased consumption, and rising levels of pollution. Mallard suggested that the union negotiate for an improved environment rather than higher wages. The IWA was stunned that the unions were portrayed as socially irresponsible and that an outsider had dared to comment on internal union matters regarding contract negotiations, "which we bluntly say are none of his business." The editorial concluded: "We suggest that Dr. Mallard [sic] get back to fighting the real source of pollution instead of attacking his friends. Both he and the Society he heads will need all the supporters they can get if they hope to succeed in their anti-pollution campaign."[77]

Many times, environmentalists did not distinguish between companies and workers, lumping them together as "the industry." A 1973 Sierra Club brief on stream bank logging stated that "in past years the economic strength of the forest industry has overshadowed other resource users to an unbelievable extent," arguing that the salmon fishery was better economically and environmentally than forestry and that BC had "sacrificed the high quality protein salmon to produce low grade cellulose which can readily be grown almost anywhere in the world that is not a desert, truly a short-sighted view."[78] Both workers and employers were alarmed at such views. Nor did environmentalists understand the union world, at times making demands that were impossible. In 1972 SPEC activists heatedly insisted that the BC Federation of Labour establish a 1 cent per capita tax on members to finance SPEC, without recognizing the ultimate authority of constituent unions in such matters: "We simply could not get it through their heads that the labour movement did not work that way."[79]

Politically, trade unionists and SPEC radicals lived in different discourses. Unionists had fought to build strong, centralized organizations with power to face the economic might of companies. Politically, they were tied to the social justice tradition of the Co-operative Commonwealth Federation/New Democratic Party and the Communist Party of Canada. SPEC political radicals, on the other hand, were part of the New Left, and as the name suggests, the New Left was opposed to the Old Left, the trade union and political structures developed in the 1930s and 1940s. The New Left sought to build a coalition of opposition, where unions were just one group among many, drawing on grassroots support from a broad spectrum of the population and creating decentralized, democratic institutions. A 1967 internal BC Communist Party report, seeking to find a way to lift the party's sagging fortunes, recognized the significance of the New Left, which had risen in North America in the context of the civil rights struggle, the peace movement, and the alienating character of modern capitalist society. The report offered a succinct analysis of the New Left in BC: "This ideology is essentially non-class, anti-organizational, existentialist, and bourgeois-objective in character, and has particular appeal to young people. It is significant in that it finds virtually no reflection in the industrial trade union movement."[80] Many environmentalists had no understanding of the political economy, merely desiring a pollution-free world with perpetual forests and large areas of wilderness. A great variety of people were attracted to environmentalism, and the politics of the movement did not fit comfortably into positions defined by labour and leftists in previous decades.[81] Unionists and traditional leftists chafed when called undemocratic and authoritarian by the environmentalists, rejecting analyses that marginalized class and work issues, and that at times even lumped workers and employers together as environmental abusers.

Culture was another divide, and it was evident even within the environmental movement. Drug use, age, musical taste, tactics, and notions of respectability were controversial. The Sierra Club was largely respectable and staid. They had a successful, established organizational structure and a tighter focus, and were more elitist. SPEC, on the other hand, was more rambunctious, committed to grassroots democracy, and geared towards a broad public, causing much internal turmoil. By late 1970, there were already notable splits in SPEC between a radical faction and a moderate faction over the democratic structure of the organization and tactics. The radicals, Dr. Robin Harger, Gary Culhane, and Jim Marunchak, left or were pushed from SPEC by the summer of 1972. They had wanted more confrontational, direct action against resource companies. For example, they planned to disrupt a meeting of the Council of Forest Industries at a Vancouver hotel by setting off a stink bomb in a hotel restaurant, but the plan was uncovered.[82] A more moderate group, led by Derrick Mallard, championed "responsible militancy."[83]

In 1972 Mallard resigned as the society's executive director and his wife, Gwen, resigned as project director. They were very unhappy with the direction of SPEC. Organizational laxness and the enthusiastic embrace of counterculture values did not sit well with them. In 1971 Derrick was fifty years old, a veteran of the Second World War and a trained engineer. SPEC's central office was in the heart of "Vancouver's drug/hip area," and, he noted, this did not help SPEC's image.[84] According to Gwen, files were disorganized, meetings lacked agendas and were much too informal, and office procedures were chaotic. Typing skill among the staff was abysmal and the standard of phone answering was atrocious: most of these "kids [volunteers] do not know the answers and they haven't bothered to pass on the requests to those who can answer them." She was also dismayed by the haphazard way in which SPEC had pursued legal action against the rock band Led Zeppelin, which had smashed SPEC sound equipment at one of its concerts; SPEC got the damaged equipment back only with the help of the police. Nor did deportment at SPEC headquarters meet Gwen's standards, as her notes reflect: "SPEC House untidy – a pigsty. Drinking of beer during office hours. Bottles on the desks, open to public view. The smell of pot often around the house. Smoking of pot may not always be due to some staff members but may be from 'freak' visitors of which there are many."[85] By 1973 the internal strife and the loose organizational structure was taking its toll. Membership was down and there were only twenty-five branches where there had once been forty-two.[86]

For unionists, the young, disrespectful environmentalists were suspect. Moreover, early environmentalists were often academics, professionals or university students, and young, living in urban areas. Loggers and mill workers, often without grade 12, toiled in plants and outlying camps, struggling to raise families and pay mortgages. A 1968 article by Clay Perry, an IWA employee who had done some teaching at Simon Fraser University, commented on the very public student activism at Simon Fraser. Perry was supportive of both trade unionism and the students, trying to persuade union officials and members to be more sympathetic to the student revolt. He noted the breakdown of the alliance between the organized worker and the intellectual, an alliance that "has given birth to virtually every important social change that has occurred in the world, and the absence of that alliance in North America must provide a lot of comfort for the seats of power. The two most militant groups in the society, instead of joining forces to effect change, are constantly at one another's throats." It was a simple fact, he noted, that trade unionists, office workers, and housewives hate students. Overwhelmingly, university students came from families that were not headed by industrial workers, and protesting students were seen as pampered, destined to be higher up the social scale than industrial workers, and ungrateful for the privilege of attending university.[87] The environmental movement came from this world. The forest unions retained links to the environmental movement but there was uneasiness, and although the new environmentalism was in many ways similar to the union crusade of the 1930s, attracting a diversity of progressive people in a struggle for large-scale social change, the established union movement and the exuberant environmental movement did not mesh neatly.[88]

IN 1966 THE *BRITISH COLUMBIA LUMBERMAN* identified the two most serious issues concerning the forest industry. One was the financial standing of the industry, but it was a problem that could be solved. As in the past, new technologies and techniques would enable the industry to harvest more timber and process it more rapidly. The second problem was also open to resolution. This was the conflict between fisheries conservationists and the logging companies over land and stream use. The editor was sure that the issue could be resolved in-house: government, scientists, and industry representatives would hold meetings and work together for the benefit of all.[89] The environmental movement challenged both these assumptions, offering a critical perspective on resource management, processing procedures, and the impact on the environment. The movement looked beyond the traditional nexus of capital, labour, and the state for its legitimacy, its values, and its experts, and in so doing challenged "the fundamental habits and assumptions of a society ... hooked on the exploitation of nature."[90]

For woods workers and forest companies, the world changed, but there was also continuity. Private companies still marshalled the machinery of production, organized the labour process, sold commodities in markets, and accumulated capital, while workers transformed the landscape and laboured in the mills in return for wages. The fundamentals of capitalism remained entrenched, and the environmental movement, with weak links to the labour movement, was not about to change this, in the short term at least.

Conclusion

In the decades after 1934, the BC forest industry delivered. Small companies harnessed productive forces to manufacture useful commodities, while more substantial corporations integrated diverse production facilities and operated in global markets. Economic achievements – measured by investment figures, production statistics, and profit levels – were remarkable. For their part, workers provided brawn and skills, manipulating heavy objects, operating machines, driving trucks, constructing facilities, and repairing expensive equipment. They organized their own institutions, unions, which won them dignity, higher wages, better working conditions, and a measure of fairness and democracy in the workplace. The forest industry also put its stamp on the landscape and social life of the province. It punched roads deep into the woods and levelled forests; located men in semi-permanent logging camps scattered throughout the hinterland; and built mill towns that housed families and attracted professionals and retailers. The wealth it generated provided wages and salaries for tens of thousands of British Columbians, government revenue for education and many other social initiatives, and profits for owners and shareholders.

Forest industry unions made singular contributions on a number of fronts. They confronted racism, despite mixed motives and the persistence of prejudice on the shop floor, establishing that all workers should have equal rights in unions. They also helped unify the province. As Jeremy Wilson argues, British Columbia came together as a political unit, overcoming regional divisions, at mid-century.[1] The International Woodworkers of America (IWA), by creating a province-wide organization, contributed to this process much earlier than coastal forest companies, which expanded into the Interior only after central Canadian and American companies had moved in.[2] Canadian nationalism, which surged in the 1960s and 1970s, was also anticipated by the forest unions. Informed by an anti-imperialist stance advocated by the Communist Party of Canada after the Second World War, a nationalist voice was loud in the provincial pulp workers' union in the 1950s, culminating in the creation of the Pulp and Paper Workers of Canada.[3]

Within the provincial forest sector, both division and unity were features of the Fordist era. The Interior and the coastal industries travelled distinct historical paths, and despite the importance of large forestry corporations, small operators retained an influential position and a particular perspective, stemming from their place in the political economy. Even among large operators, the competitive imperative

Logging camp at Mile 18, Chemainus River, Vancouver Island, 1946.
MacMillan Bloedel Collection (UBC), BC 1930/555/113

made unity fragile at times. Labour divided into a number of camps – industrial unions and craft unions, pulp unions and lumber unions, American unions and Canadian unions – and these positions did not blur as the decades passed. Internal union dissension was sometimes vicious. Still, in confrontations between employers and employees, solidarity usually prevailed, especially for company owners and officials, whose anti-unionism and anti-socialism trumped any internal disagreements. In 1972 the IWA struck two Vancouver shingle plants, trying to force a reduced workday on the companies involved. According to Forest Industrial Relations (FIR), the bargaining agent for many forest companies, there was no question "that if the IWA had been able to make a major breakthrough with these operations by reducing hours of work in 1972, we would have had immense difficulty in resisting the spread of the agreement through the industry." The FIR membership rallied, financially supporting the struck companies so that they could pay their fixed costs and "continue to hold out against the breaking of an Industry principle."[4] The job action dragged on for over three years, and the companies won.

Unions, once they were securely established in the early Fordist years, concentrated on workplace issues. In the 1930s and 1940s, union activists were part of the great progressive struggle for human rights and dignity, a movement that sought union and collective bargaining rights for industrial workers, as well as unemployment insurance, hospitalization insurance, better education for all, government housing initiatives, and richer old-age pensions, components of an emerging, if never wholly realized, welfare state. After the achievement of basic union rights, however, union officials, with limited resources and powerful corporate adversaries, focused on a narrow cluster of administrative interests: managing the contract, negotiating job classifications, winning wage and benefit increases, and dealing with workers' personal grievances. Political parties tended to the broader social and political agenda.[5]

Forest industry workers were restless in the late 1960s and early 1970s, as evidenced by the increase in the number of wildcat strikes. British Columbia had one of the highest rates of wildcats in Canada, and this rose noticeably in the late 1960s and early 1970s: in 1971 and 1973, peak years, about one-half of BC strikes were illegal, and of these over 70 percent occurred in the forest industry.[6] Wildcats are localized, short strikes that take place without the public authorization of union officials. As such, they were often protests against union leaders as well as companies, a challenge to the institutions of Fordism.[7] Technically illegal because they contravene provisions of collective agreements stipulating that there are to be no work stoppages, they tend to deal with very local issues such as the demotion of a colleague, the dismissal of a popular foreman, changes in scheduling or workplace assignments, or camp conditions. At times, wildcats pressure management and union negotiators during contract discussions. They are not necessarily bad; they can quickly force resolution of festering issues and clear the air, and often workers win their case. Despite the general disavowal of wildcats by union leaders and company officials, they can be used as tactics in negotiations: for unions, wildcats show the militancy and resolve of their members; for companies, they are examples of the lawlessness and irresponsibility of unions.

A number of factors contributed to the wildcat fever of the early 1970s. Workers had rising expectations and were more educated than previous generations. This was also a time, the Sixties, when young people sought personal satisfaction in their lives and their work. Union and company officials agreed that most mill jobs were boring, and saw routine and frustration as one cause for worker dissatisfaction and wildcats.[8] High employment levels gave workers confidence that they could find another job if necessary, so there was less fear of consequences for militant acts. The late 1960s and early 1970s saw high employment and turnover rates in both camps and mills. A Vanderhoof sawmill relied on high school students to operate because there was no other labour available, and the mill would have operated a second shift but for lack of workers. A similar situation existed on northern Vancouver Island in the fall of 1972, when the return of high school students for their fall semester led to a drastic reduction of labour in the mills and logging camps. Turnover was high: "Mill managers and contract loggers report that the men find the work 'too hard' and quit, sometimes after only a day!" Mill managers in Prince George and Pemberton had the same complaint.[9] Forest industry employers could offer comparatively good wages and steady work, but they could not offer satisfying occupations.

The richer social welfare programs of the era, especially unemployment insurance, improved by the Trudeau government in 1971, gave workers more freedom. This was not a new complaint by employers. One coastal operator in 1956 was blunt: "Advanced social legislation has hindered stabilizing of woods employment ... The 2½% holiday pay ceased to be useful when the three-month clause was altered to pay the amount direct into each pay-cheque: men no longer stayed to collect it. High wages, statutory holidays and a five-day week combine to create a further problem."[10]

The 1960s and early 1970s brought the welfare state to its greatest height, however. One logging foreman at Ootsa Lake, in the northwest of the province, opined: "I think the Government has made it too easy for people not to work." He elaborated: "The easy-going way of life is not hard to achieve in this province. Work for six months, then go on unemployment benefits for the rest of the year – 'why work yourself to death when you can get $400 a month on UIC?' How many times have you heard that statement?"[11] Another factor contributing to wildcats was the rising cost of living, which, from the perspective of workers, was rising more quickly than their take-home pay. The strength of unions also played a role. Wildcatters knew that despite the the public disapproval expressed by their union leadership, they would likely not lose their jobs.

Companies moved to increase the penalty for wildcat strikes in 1970. During the previous collective agreement, there had been over seventy wildcats in the coastal region, and the companies now demanded that the IWA take a hard line against them.[12] While the union considered wildcats a problem, leaders were not about to commit themselves to any punitive measures. Still, in the spring of 1970, the IWA and MacMillan Bloedel met informally to investigate ways of resolving grievances without the disruption of wildcats. It was hoped that any solutions would serve as a pattern for the rest of the industry.[13] The wildcats continued.[14] In December 1973, during contract negotiations, the coastal companies appealed to the IWA: "We are prepared to examine with you better approaches to solve our problems, such as the elimination of wildcat strikes, of which we have already experienced more than one hundred during the last eighteen months."[15]

Strike action fell off in 1974. Housing starts ebbed in the United States and the demand for lumber subsided. The Loggers' Agency, the hiring hall for coastal logging companies, reported its first drop in hiring since 1968. Sawmill and plywood workers suffered more. November statistics tabulated by the Council of Forest Industries showed some 6,000 Interior plywood workers out of work and 1,500 coastal workers laid off. In sawmills, about 3,080 coastal workers and 3,600 Interior workers were unemployed.[16] The IWA estimated that close to 10,000 provincial woodworkers were out of work in September.[17] In 1975 only two BC logging camps struck, and only for a few days; in 1976 only one struck, for one day, and in 1977, none. Sawmills also experienced relative labour peace, with only five strikes in 1975 and only one new strike in 1976. After the tumult of 1975, the pulp and paper industry was also more stable in 1976.[18]

Contradictions were evident at the twilight of the Fordist era. The Fordist regime generated more goods to satisfy consumers, but at the same time produced routine, mind-numbing workdays for employees. The wealth from the forest industry advanced educational levels in the province and led to richer social programs, but now people had higher expectations and a greater sense of security, both of which fuelled job action. In addition, growing global markets and increased productivity resulted in the harvest of more trees, the construction of a network of logging roads through the woods, and an expanding pulp and paper industry. The province's wealth and population increased, but these advances depleted great swathes of the provincial forest, facilitated an urban interest in nearby wilderness, and contributed to air and water pollution. BC's environmental movement emerged in this context.

For companies, the economic difficulties after 1974 encouraged attacks on collective agreements, provincial labour legislation, environmental proposals, and government social programs. Business was prepared: it had a long history fighting socialism, the state, and unions, as well as a coherent rhetorical package to further its goals. The new circumstances provided a stick with which to discipline workers in the production process. For unions there was little solace at the end of Fordism, even though worker frustration did not disappear. A 1978 MacMillan Bloedel report noted the negative attitudes of hourly employees towards the company and the industry. Workers did not trust the company, believing that MacMillan Bloedel was more interested in profits than in their concerns. They also felt that they had little control at the workplace.[19] Patricia Marchak shows that in the 1970s widespread hostility was directed against all decision makers, including corporate directors, managers, government bureaucrats, and politicians, as well as union leaders: "One could not properly identify this as 'class consciousness,' the more so since it sometimes takes the form of anger against other workers, such as 'the slackers' and the union."[20] No union or leftist discourse translated this frustration into a positive political program.

The critical voice had limits in the Fordist era. The way in which wealth was produced was rarely challenged, a testimony to the success of the dominant liberal capital discourse. Despite the establishment of unions, social welfare measures, and environmental groups, capitalists managed the production system, imposing control and employing technology to serve their ends. Full democracy and equality at work were not seriously considered. Socialism, which came to mean an expanded government role in social programs and economic management as well as support for basic union rights, was a fair-weather option, almost indistinguishable from welfare liberalism and dependent on the success of the capitalist economy. It was a socialism committed to the redistribution of wealth, not a socialism dedicated to rethinking power relations in the creation of wealth. Radical unionists participated in building a nationalist discourse in which local union democracy was an ideal, but did not construct an effective discourse critical of the relations of production. Nor was the notion that work should be a creative, meaningful experience, fundamental to human happiness and well-being, prominent in union or leftist discourse. Adequate wages were expected to compensate for tedium.

New movements will necessarily rework and rearticulate narratives, create fresh institutions and practices, construct new webs, and, in time, produce new human identities. There is much in the history of the BC forest industry that offers hope – the fight for social justice, the invention of new technologies, growing ecological understanding, the struggle for widening democracy, the achievement of some dignity for unskilled and semi-skilled workers, and examples of both individual initiative and collective solidarity – suggesting that despite the malaise of the Post-Fordist era, a positive future is possible. Of course, environmental devastation, class-based brutality, growing disparities between rich and poor, more intrusive market relations, and shrinking roles for reason and democracy are hardly out of the question.

Notes

Abbreviations

ABC	*The ABC British Columbia Lumber Trade Directory and Yearbook*
BCA	British Columbia Archives
BCFL	British Columbia Federation of Labour
BCL	*British Columbia Lumberman*
BCLW	*British Columbia Lumber Worker*
CLC	Canadian Labour Congress
CLR	Comox Logging and Railway
CDM	Courtenay and District Museum
COFI	Council of Forest Industries
IBPSPMW	International Brotherhood of Pulp, Sulphite and Paper Mill Workers
LAC	Library and Archives Canada
MB	MacMillan Bloedel
PPMC	*Pulp and Paper Magazine of Canada*
SCBC	Sierra Club of British Columbia
TL	*The Truck Logger*
TURB	Trade Union Research Bureau
UBC	University of British Columbia, The Library, Special Collections Division
UVic	University of Victoria, Archives and Special Collections

Introduction

1 This section is based on the experience of the author, who worked a few short stints in BC pulp mills in the 1970s.

2 F.L.C. Reed and Associates Ltd., *The British Columbia Forest Industry: Its Direct and Indirect Impact on the Economy* (Victoria: Department of Lands, Forests and Water Resources, 1973), 63.

3 Minister of Lands, Forests and Water Resources, Press Release, 9 June 1975, University of British Columbia, The Library, Special Collections Division, Angus Macphee Papers, vol. 4, file 8.

4 Price Waterhouse, *The Forest Industry in British Columbia* (Vancouver: Price Waterhouse, 1975-93); Michael James Garvin Dezell, "Grapple-Yarding with the Future: A New Mandate for COFI," MA thesis, University of Victoria, 1993, 12.

5 For perspectives on British Columbia in the tumultuous 1980s, see Warren Magnusson et al., eds., *The New Reality: The Politics of Restraint in British Columbia* (Vancouver: New Star Books, 1984); Allen Garr, *Tough Guy: Bill Bennett and the Taking of British Columbia* (Toronto: Key Porter Books, 1985); Trevor Barnes and Roger Hayter, "British Columbia's Private Sector in Recession, 1981-86: Employment Flexibility without Trade Diversification?" *BC Studies* 98 (Summer 1993): 20-42. For the 1986 IWA strike, see Jack Munro and Jane O'Hara, *Union Jack: Labour Leader Jack Munro* (Vancouver: Douglas and McIntyre, 1988), 153-88.

6 Richard Schwindt and Terry Heaps, *Chopping Up the Money Tree: Distributing the Wealth from British Columbia's Forests* (Vancouver: The David Suzuki Foundation, 1996), iv and 50.

7 Ken Drushka, *HR: A Biography of H.R. MacMillan* (Madeira Park, BC: Harbour Publishing, 1995); Munro and O'Hara, *Union Jack;* Andrew Neufeld and Andrew Parnaby, *The IWA in Canada: The Life and Times of an Industrial Union* (Vancouver: IWA Canada/New Star Books, 2000). See also Richard Mackie, *Island Timber: A Social History of the Comox Logging Company, Vancouver Island* (Victoria: Sono Nis Press, 2000).

8 Richard Rajala, "The Forest as Factory: Technological Change and Worker Control in the West Coast Logging Industry, 1880-1930," *Labour/Le Travail* 32 (Fall 1993): 73-104; Ken Drushka, *Working in the Woods: A History of Logging on the West Coast* (Madeira Park, BC: Harbour Publishing, 1992).

9 Ken Drushka, *Stumped: The Forest Industry in Transition* (Vancouver: Douglas and McIntyre, 1985); Richard Rajala, *Clearcutting the Pacific Rain Forest: Production, Science, and Regulation* (Vancouver: UBC Press, 1998); Rajala, *Up-Coast: Forests and Industry on British Columbia's North Coast, 1870-2005* (Victoria: Royal BC Museum, 2006); Jeremy Wilson, "Forest Conservation in British Columbia, 1935-1985: Reflections on a Barren Political Debate," *BC Studies* 76 (Winter 1987-88): 3-32.

10 Jerry Lembcke and William M. Tattam, *One Union in Wood* (Madeira Park, BC: Harbour Publishing, 1984). The many works of Ken Drushka provide the case for small operators.

11 For an introduction to the various positions within Post-Fordism, see Ash Amin, "Post-Fordism: Models, Fantasies and Phantoms of Transition," in *Post-Fordism: A Reader*, ed. Ash Amin (Oxford: Blackwell Publishers, 1994), 1-39; Paul Hirst and Jonathan Zeitlin, "Flexible Specialization versus Post-Fordism: Theory, Evidence and Policy Implications," *Economy and Society* 20 (February 1991): 1-56.

12 John Allen, "Post-Industrialism and Post-Fordism," in *Modernity and Its Futures*, ed. Stuart Hall, David Held, and Tony McGrew (London: Open University Press, 1992), 169-204; Alain Noël, "Accumulation, Regulation, and Social Change: An Essay on French Political Economy," *International Organization* 41 (Spring 1987): 303-33.

13 Roger Hayter, *Flexible Crossroads: The Restructuring of British Columbia's Forest Economy* (Vancouver: UBC Press, 2000), 36 and 65. See also Roger Hayter and Trevor J. Barnes, "Troubles in the Rainforest: British Columbia's Forest Economy in Transition," in *Troubles in the Rainforest: British Columbia's Forest Economy in Transition*, ed. Trevor J. Barnes and Roger Hayter, Canadian Western Geographical Series, vol. 33 (Victoria: Western Geographical Press, 1997), 1-11; Tanya Berhrisch, Roger Hayter, and Trevor Barnes, "'I Don't Really Like the Mill; In Fact I Hate the Mill,' Changing Youth Vocationalism under Fordism and Post-Fordism in Powell River, British Columbia," *BC Studies* 136 (Winter 2002-2003): 73-101.

14 Roger Hayter, "'The War in the Woods': Post-Fordist Restructuring, Globalization, and the Contested Remapping of British Columbia's Forest Economy," *Annals of the Association of American Geographers* 93 (September 2003): 709.

15 In Martin's analysis, wage workers responded by developing unions and organizing left-wing political parties, pushing class confrontation to centre stage, a feature that distinguished the province from other regions of the country: Martin Robin, *Pillars of Profit: The Company Province 1934-1972* (Toronto: McClelland and Stewart, 1973); Robin, *The Rush for Spoils: The Company Province 1871-1933* (Toronto: McClelland and Stewart, 1972); Robin, "The Social Basis of Party Politics in British Columbia," in *Party Politics in Canada*, 2nd ed., ed. Hugh Thorburn (Scarborough, ON: Prentice-Hall Canada, 1967), 200-11; Robin, "British Columbia: The Politics of Class Conflict," in *The Party Systems of the Ten Provinces*, ed. Martin Robin (Scarborough, ON: Prentice-Hall, 1972), 27-68. For an earlier version of this argument, see Thomas Michael Sanford, "The Politics of Protest: The Cooperative Commonwealth Federation and Social Credit League in British Columbia," PhD dissertation, University of California (Berkeley), 1961. Since Robin's time, studies by labour historians have undermined the notion that labour was notably more radical and militant in British Columbia than

elsewhere. See Robert A.J. McDonald, "Working-Class Vancouver, 1886-1914: Urbanism and Class in British Columbia," *BC Studies* 69-70 (Spring/Summer 1986): 33-69; John Douglas Belshaw, "The British Collier in British Columbia: Another Archetype Reconsidered," *Labour/ Le Travail* 34 (Fall 1994): 11-36; Gordon Hak, "The Socialist and Labourist Impulse in Small-Town British Columbia," *Canadian Historical Review* 70 (December 1989): 519-42; John Hinde, *When Coal Was King: Ladysmith and the Coal-Mining Industry on Vancouver Island* (Vancouver: UBC Press, 2003).

16　Kim Moody, *An Injury to All: The Decline of American Unionism* (London and New York: Verso, 1988), 45.

17　Nelson Lichtenstein, *State of the Union: A Century of American Labor* (Princeton, NJ: Princeton University Press, 2002), 98-99.

18　Peter S. McInnis, *Harnessing Labour Confrontation: Shaping the Postwar Settlement in Canada, 1943-1950* (Toronto: University of Toronto Press, 2002), 2, passim.

19　For IWA strikes on the Coast and in the Interior, see Neufeld and Parnaby, *The IWA in Canada.*

20　Lichtenstein, *State of the Union*, 99.

21　Peter S. McInnis puts forward this perspective forcefully in *Harnessing Labour Confrontation.* Regarding the postwar settlement, he argues that "in the long term, this development had deleterious consequences" (6); that "industrial legality stifled spontaneous worker self-activity, replacing it with complex, routinized collective-bargaining procedures which posed no serious threat to capital's essential property rights" (191); and that "the expulsion of left-wing unions in Canada left the role of leadership to the pragmatic, responsible men who never intended to challenge the system under which they operated" (179).

22　Ira Katznelson, "The 'Bourgeois' Dimension: A Provocation about Institutions, Politics and the Future of Labor History," *International Labor and Working-Class History* 46 (Fall 1994): 7-32.

23　Patricia Marchak, *Green Gold: The Forest Industry in British Columbia* (Vancouver: UBC Press, 1983). The staples approach has a long tradition in Canada, going back to the work of Harold Innis. The essay underpinning recent staples studies is M.H. Watkins, "A Staple Theory of Economic Growth," in *Approaches to Canadian Economic History*, ed. W.T. Easterbrook and M.H. Watkins (Toronto: McClelland and Stewart, 1967), 49-73. See too, Particia Marchak, "A Changing Global Context for British Columbia's Forest Industry," in *Troubles in the Rainforest*, ed. Barnes and Hayter, 149-64.

24　Within the environmental movement, too, there is increased skepticism about the power of the state. See Cheri Burda, Fred Gale, and Michael M'Gonigle, "Eco-Forestry Versus the State(us) Quo: Or Why Innovative Forestry Is Neither Contemplated nor Permitted within the State Structure of British Columbia," *BC Studies* 119 (Autumn 1998): 45-72; Michael M'Gonigle and Jessica Dempsey, "Ecological Innovation in an Age of Bureaucratic Closure: The Case of the Global Forest," *Studies in Political Economy* 70 (Spring 2003): 97-124. Roger Hayter argues that multinational corporations, the American protectionist lobby, environmentalists, and First Nations, in a tacit alliance, have "effectively disempowered the provincial government": Hayter, "'The War in the Woods,'" 716.

25　Marchak, *Green Gold*, 46.

26　Harry Braverman, *Labor and Monopoly Capital: The Degradation of Work in the Twentieth Century* (New York: Monthly Review Press, 1974).

27　Rajala, *Clearcutting the Pacific Rain Forest*, 5.

28　For an introduction to the Braverman debate, see David Stark, "Class Struggle and the Transformation of the Labor Process: A Relational Approach," *Theory and Society* 9 (January 1980): 89-130; Craig R. Littler and Graeme Salaman, "Bravermania and Beyond: Recent Theories of the Labour Process," *Sociology* 16 (May 1982): 251-69; Paul Attewell, "The Deskilling Controversy," *Work and Occupations* 14 (August 1987): 323-46; Sheila Cohen, "A Labour Process to

Nowhere," *New Left Review* 165 (September/October 1987): 34-50; John Storey, "The Means of Management Control," *Sociology* 19 (May 1985): 193-211; Paul S. Adler, "Marx, Machines, and Skill," *Technology and Culture* 31 (October 1990): 780-812; Andrew Zimbalist, ed., *Case Studies on the Labor Process* (New York: Monthly Review Press, 1979); Craig Heron and Robert Storey, eds., *On the Job: Confronting the Labour Process in Canada* (Montreal and Kingston, ON: McGill-Queen's University Press, 1986).

29 Bill Schwarz, "Re-assessing Braverman: Socialisation and Dispossession in the History of Technology," in *Science, Technology and the Labour Process*, Marxist Studies, vol. 2, ed. Les Levidow and Bob Young (London: Free Association Books, 1985), 202 (emphasis in original).

30 Rajala, *Clearcutting the Pacific Rain Forest*, 222.

31 This brief sketch of a position on discourse and the subject comes out of the line of thought that begins with the writings of Antonio Gramsci in the 1920s and 1930s. Key works are Antonio Gramsci, *Selections from the Prison Notebooks of Antonio Gramsci*, ed. Quintin Hoare and Geoffrey Nowell Smith (New York: International Publishers, 1971); Louis Althusser, "Ideology and Ideological State Apparatuses: Notes toward an Investigation," in *Lenin and Philosophy and Other Essays*, ed. Louis Althusser (New York and London: Monthly Review Press, 1971), 127-86; Ernesto Laclau and Chantal Mouffe, *Hegemony and Social Strategy: Towards a Radical Democratic Politics*, trans. Winston Moore and Paul Cammack (London: Verso, 1985); Ernesto Laclau, *Politics and Ideology in Marxist Theory* (London: Verso, 1979). For overviews connecting the dots that link the developing ideas in the Gramscian tradition, see Thomas Dunk, *It's a Working Man's Town: Male Working-Class Culture in Northwestern Ontario* (Montreal and Kingston, ON: McGill-Queen's University Press, 1991), 22-42; Dunk, "Talking about Trees: Environment and Society in Forest Workers' Culture," *Canadian Review of Sociology and Anthropology* 31 (February 1994): 14-34; Stuart Hall, "Introduction: Who Needs 'Identity'?" in *Questions of Cultural Identity*, ed. Stuart Hall and Paul Du Gay (London: Sage Publications, 1996), 1-17; Hall, "Introduction," in *Representation: Cultural Representations and Signifying Practices*, ed. Stuart Hall (London: Sage Publications, 1997), 1-11. For a short account of discourse by a political theorist, see Ernesto Laclau, "Discourse," in *A Companion to Contemporary Political Philosophy*, ed. Robert E. Goodin and Philip Pettit (London: Blackwell, 1995), 431-37.

32 This classic argument, which is empirically suspect, was developed by Clark Kerr and Abraham Siegel in "The Interindustry Propensity to Strike: An International Comparison," in *Industrial Conflict*, ed. Arthur Kornhauser, Robert Dubin, and Arthur M. Ross (New York: McGraw-Hill, 1954), 189-212. For a Canadian application, see Stuart M. Jamieson, *Times of Trouble: Labour Unrest and Industrial Conflict in Canada, 1900-66*, Task Force on Labour Relations, Study No. 22 (Ottawa: Queen's Printer, 1968).

33 Judith Butler, "Restaging the Universal: Hegemony and the Limits of Formalism," in *Contingency, Hegemony, Universality: Contemporary Dialogues on the Left*, ed. Judith Butler, Ernesto Laclau, and Slavoj Žižek (London: Verso, 2000), 13-14.

34 Ian McKay, "The Liberal Order Framework: A Prospectus for a Reconnaissance of Canadian History," *Canadian Historical Review* 81 (December 2000): 643.

35 James Procter, *Stuart Hall* (London: Routledge, 2004), 110.

36 McKay, "Liberal Order Framework," 623 (emphasis in the original).

37 The focus on political economy and the labour process from the perspective of the workplace gives short shrift to other discourses, such as colonialism, a key aspect in British Columbia history. First Nations people, although present as workers, were largely invisible as a group. First Nations claims to the provincial land base, and thus the forests, were reinvigorated by a decision by the Canadian Supreme Court in 1973. By suggesting that First Nations land claims just might have legal support, the decision in the *Calder* case forced change. First Nations now had to be considered by the forest industry. For the marginalization of First Nations in

the forest industrial economy, see Bruce Willems-Braun, "Colonial Vestiges: Representing Forest Landscapes on Canada's West Coast," *BC Studies* 112 (Winter 1996-97): 5-39.

Chapter 1: Companies, Markets, and Production Facilities

1 G.W. Taylor, *Timber: History of the Forest Industry in BC* (Vancouver: J.J. Douglas, 1975).
2 Ken Drushka, *Lignum: A History* (Vancouver: Lignum, 2002); Drushka, *HR: A Biography of H.R. MacMillan* (Madeira Park, BC: Harbour Publishing, 1995); Drushka, *Working in the Woods: A History of Logging on the West Coast* (Madeira Park, BC: Harbour Publishing, 1992); Donald MacKay, *Empire of Wood: The MacMillan Bloedel Story* (Vancouver: Douglas and McIntyre, 1982); E.G. Perrault, *Wood and Water: The Story of Seaboard Lumber and Shipping* (Vancouver: Douglas and McIntyre, 1985); Sue Baptie, ed., *First Growth: The Story of British Columbia Forest Products Limited* (Vancouver: British Columbia Forest Products, 1975).
3 Pacific Mills Ltd., *Annual Report for the Year Ended April 30, 1950*.
4 Minutes, Meeting of Directors, Pacific Mills, Vancouver, 9 August 1934, 26 July 1938, 13 March 1940, University of California (Berkeley), The Bancroft Library, Crown Zellerbach Corporation Records (hereinafter Crown Zellerbach Records), vols. 126 and 127.
5 Ken Drushka, *Tie Hackers to Timber Harvesters: The History of Logging in British Columbia's Interior* (Madeira Park, BC: Harbour Publishing, 1998); see also Ken Bernsohn, *Cutting Up the North: The History of the Forest Industry in the Northern Interior* (North Vancouver: Hancock House, 1982).
6 Patricia Marchak analyzes the structure of the industry in the early 1980s in *Green Gold: The Forest Industry in British Columbia* (Vancouver: UBC Press, 1983), 82-112.
7 See Walter G. Hardwick, *Geography of the Forest Industry of Coastal British Columbia* (Vancouver: Tantalus Research, 1963).
8 The relationship of Prince Rupert, 500 miles north of Vancouver on the mainland coast, to the coastal region is rather ambiguous due its distance from Vancouver. In many ways, it is more like an Interior centre. I follow past practices, however, and include Prince Rupert in the coastal region.
9 Except where otherwise noted, data in this chapter are drawn from the yearly reports of the department in the provincial government responsible for forests: British Columbia, Forest Service/Forest Branch, *Annual Reports*, 1928-80 (Victoria: King's/Queen's Printer, 1928-80). There were, of course, variations in forest cover within the coastal region. North of Rivers Inlet on the mainland, trees became smaller and Douglas-fir less prominent. Elevation also influenced forest cover.
10 In 1930 hemlock and balsam accounted for 16 percent of the coastal cut. In 1930 these two species accounted for 54 percent. By this time, too, the supply of fir, which had been harvested at a high rate for a long time, was seriously diminished.
11 Gordon Hak, *Turning Trees into Dollars: The British Columbia Coastal Lumber Industry, 1858-1913* (Toronto: University of Toronto Press, 2000).
12 The board foot measure is used to calculate quantities of lumber. It is also used to calculate the potential quantity of lumber in standing trees. One board foot is twelve inches by twelve inches by one inch. "MBM" refers to 1,000 board feet.
13 L.R. Andrews, Memorandum on Tariff Policies, Exhibit 220, Royal Commission on Forestry, 1944-5, Proceedings, British Columbia Archives (hereinafter BCA), GR-520, vol. 13, file 11.
14 L.R. Andrews to L.D. Wilgress, Director, Commercial Intelligence Service, Department of Trade and Commerce, 1 May 1936, University of British Columbia, The Library, Special Collections (hereinafter UBC), Council of Forest Industry (COFI) Papers, vol. 6, file 2; British Columbia Lumber and Shingle Manufacturers Association, "Annual Report 1937," 43-44, UBC, COFI Papers, vol. 71, file 9; *British Columbia Lumberman* (hereinafter BCL) 23 (July 1939): 22 and 24.

15 Ian M. Drummond, "Empire Trade and Russian Trade: Economic Diplomacy in the Nine-teen-Thirties," *Canadian Journal of Economics* 5 (February 1972): 35-47; H. Blair Neatby, *William Lyon Mackenzie King, 1932-1939: The Prism of Unity* (Toronto: University of Toronto Press, 1976), 17-27.

16 BC Lumber and Shingle Manufacturers Association, Report, 10 September 1937, BCA, GR-1222, vol. 139, file 6; Andrews, Memorandum on Tariff Policies.

17 BCA, GR-1441, vol. 313, file 11; BCA, GR-441, vol. 320, file 2.

18 L.R. Andrews, "Post War Export Markets for Canadian Lumber," Report, 1943, BCA, GR-1276, files 1-2.

19 H.R. MacMillan to Henry J. Fuller, 21 August 1936, UBC, H.R. MacMillan Papers, vol. 5, file 1.

20 H.R. MacMillan to George W. Allan, 24 June 1938, UBC, H.R. MacMillan Papers, vol. 6, file 2.

21 *Port Alberni News,* 12 October 1933.

22 Ibid., 5 October 1933.

23 *West Coast Advocate,* 24 March 1934, 27 September 1934, 28 February 1935; *BCL* 19 (March 1935): 63-70.

24 Testimony of Sydney G. Smith, Royal Commission on Forestry, 1944-5, Proceedings, vol. 14, 5,173-74, BCA, GR-520, vol. 5; *West Coast Advocate,* 7 January 1937.

25 "Details of Members' Shareholding and Their Participation in Commission Refund at December 31, 1936" (photocopy), UBC, Seaboard Lumber Company Papers, vol. 14, file 4.

26 MacKay, *Empire of Wood,* chs. 2 and 4.

27 H.R. MacMillan to J.D. McCormack, 30 March 1935, UBC, MacMillan Bloedel Papers (here-inafter MB Papers), vol. 405, file 26.

28 Manager, ASTEXCO [sic], to H.R. MacMillan Export Co., 1 February 1934, UBC, MB Papers, vol. 401, file 19.

29 HRM to ASUNACTRAD, 2 April 1935, telegram, UBC, MB Papers, vol. 401, file 19.

30 H.R. MacMillan to J.G. McConville, 27 December 1934, UBC, MB Papers, vol. 401, file 20.

31 M.A. Grainger to C.F. Denny, 11 December 1929, BCA, Add MS-0588; C.E. Denny to T.D. Pattullo, 15 November 1934, BCA, Add MS-0003, vol. 66, file 13.

32 *West Coast Advocate,* 17 September 1936.

33 *BCL* 20 (October 1936): 15. For a detailed account of the financing of the deals, see *British Columbia Lumber Worker,* 7 February 1939; H.R. MacMillan to M.A. Grainger, 5 March 1936, UBC, H.R. MacMillan Papers, vol. 4, file 4.

34 Minutes, Canadian Society of Forest Engineers, 18 December 1939, BCA, Add MS-0862, vol. 1, file 1.

35 *The Province,* 10 February 1976, found in BCA, Vertical Files, "H.R. MacMillan."

36 Perrault, *Wood and Water,* chs. 3-7; MacKay, *Empire of Wood,* chs. 5-7.

37 *BCL* 28 (May 1944): 25; 28 (June 1944): 26; E.P. Taylor to H.R. MacMillan, 11 March 1944 and 10 May 1946, UBC, MB Papers, vol. 416, file 44.

38 *BCL* 28 (May 1944): 25.

39 British Columbia, Royal Commission on Forestry, 1944-5, transcript, BCA, GR-520, vol. 3, file 3, 684-726; vol. 3, file 4, 1,181-1,227.

40 For the amount of timber held by forest companies, see British Columbia, Bureau of Eco-nomics and Statistics, Department of Trade and Industry, "A Submission to the Royal Com-mission on Forestry: A Statement Showing the Amount of Timber Held under All Types of Tenure, by Individuals and Firms in the Province of British Columbia during the Years 1938 and 1944," 3 vols., BCA, GR-181.

41 *BCL* 25 (December 1941): 32-34; 26 (May 1942): 24; *Pulp and Paper Magazine of Canada* (here-inafter *PPMC*) 42 (December 1941): 787 and 800.

42 Baptie, *First Growth,* 1.

43 MacKay, *Empire of Wood,* 174.

44 F.L.C. Reed and Associates Ltd., *Selected Forest Industry Statistics of British Columbia,* rev. ed. (Victoria: British Columbia Forest Service, 1975), 74.

45 British Columbia Lumber Manufacturers Association, *Annual Report, 1956,* 14, UBC, COFI Papers, vol. 72, file 10; Council of Forest Industries of British Columbia, *Annual Report, 1972,* 18.

46 Minutes, Board of Directors of BC Lumber Manufacturers Association, 31 December 1961, UBC, COFI Papers, vol. 7, file 3; "Managers Report" for Board of Directors, BC Lumber Manufacturers Association, 20 March 1962, 18 May 1962, 21 August 1962, 18 September 1962, 30 October 1962, 18 December 1962, UBC, COFI Papers, vol. 7, file 4; "Manager's Report," for Board of Directors, BC Lumber Manufacturers Association, 19 February 1963, UBC, COFI Papers, vol. 8, file 1.

47 "Manager's Report" for Board of Directors, BC Lumber Manufacturers Association, 28 May 1963, UBC, COFI Papers, vol. 8, file 1.

48 "Managers Report to the Board of Directors on BC Lumber Manufacturers Association Activities for the Period February 20th to April 23rd, 1964," UBC, COFI Papers, vol. 8, file 2. A discussion of the issues as perceived by both sides is found in *BCL* 46 (September 1962): 9, and 46 (October 1962): 68-69, 45-46, 9, and 71; *The Truck Logger* (hereinafter *TL*) 18 (August 1962): 6-7, and 18 (November 1962): 8; US Department of Agriculture, Forest Service, "Stumpage Prices and Pricing Policies in British Columbia," 1962, University of Victoria, Archives and Special Collections (hereinafter UVic), Ray Williston Fonds, 89-068, vol. 8, file 2.

49 "Manager's Report to the Board of Directors on Association Activities for the Period September 17th to October 15th, 1964," UBC, COFI Papers, vol. 8, file 2. At the same time as the American protectionist drive, BC lumbermen also lobbied to forestall tariff increases by the Australian government against lumber. Australia raised its tariffs, effective 13 January 1964: "Manager's Report," 19 June 1962, UBC, COFI Papers, vol. 7, file 4; "Manager's Report to the Board of Directors on Association Activities for the Period 18 December 1963 to 31 January 1964," UBC, COFI Papers, vol. 8, file 1.

50 *British Columbia Forest Industry Facts* 5 (July 1967): 1.

51 Council of Forest Industries of British Columbia, "BC Lumber Shipments 1978-1987," *Annual Report 1987* (April 1988). Other destinations in 1980 were Japan (9 percent), the European Economic Community (4.5 percent), Canada (26 percent), United Kingdom (4.1 percent), Australia (1.1 percent), and others (2.3 percent).

52 There were also two specialty paper operations that purchased logs on the open market or used rags and boxes: Westminster Paper Company in New Westminster, and Sidney Paper and Roofing in Victoria.

53 *PPMC* 48 (January 1947): 120.

54 Minutes, Directors of Pacific Mills, 24 January 1916, Vancouver, Crown Zellerbach Records, vol. 123.

55 *PPMC* 48 (September 1947): 66-77; 42 (December 1941): 804; 59 (December 1958): 98-105.

56 Minutes, Meeting of the Provisional Directors of the British Columbia Sulphite Fibre Co., 8 November 1909, BCA, Add MS-1996, vol. 1, file 1.

57 Minutes, Directors, Colonial Lumber and Paper Mills, 20 October 1911; Minutes, Extraordinary General Meeting of Shareholders, Colonial Lumber and Paper Mills, 4 October 1915 and 5 January 1916, BCA, Add MS-1996, vol. 1, file 3; Minutes, Meeting of First or Provisional Directors, Empire Pulp and Paper Mills, 10 August 1916, 9 November 1916, 25 November 1916, and 14 August 1917, BCA, Add MS-1996, vol. 1, file 2.

58 *PPMC* 19 (8 September 1921): 934.

59 Ibid., 19 (15 September 1921): 958.

60 Minutes, Whalen Pulp and Paper Mills, 7 May 1917 and October 1921, BCA, Add MS-1996, vol. 2, file 1.
61 Minutes, Directors, Whalen Pulp and Paper Mills, Toronto, 5 January 1920, 23 April 1923, and 6 September 1923, BCA, Add MS-1996, vol. 2, file 1; *PPMC* 19 (31 March 1921): 355.
62 *PPMC* 41 (May 1940): 420; 49 (July 1948): 70.
63 Ibid., 49 (July 1948): 77.
64 F.L.C. Reed, *Selected Forest Industry Statistics,* 81-84.
65 *PPMC* 36 (July 1935): 398.
66 Ibid., 39 (July 1938): 592.
67 Ibid., 38 (March 1937): 307; 41 (December 1940): 856.
68 Ibid., 40 (June 1939): 445; 40 (July 1939): 503.
69 Ibid., 45 (May 1944): 506(96).
70 Ibid., 40 (June 1939): 445; 41 (December 1940): 856; 42 (January 1941): 40; *BCL* 25 (September 1941): 26.
71 Minutes, Directors, Pacific Mills, 10 April 1941, 4 October 1941, 23 December 1942, 23 February 1943, and 18 December 1946, Crown Zellerbach Records, vols. 127 and 128.
72 Minutes, Special Meeting of Directors, Pacific Mills, 3 January 1947, Crown Zellerbach Records, vol. 128.
73 F.L.C. Reed, *Selected Forest Industry Statistics,* 81-84.
74 *PPMC* 49 (July 1948): 69-79; 49 (January 1948): 58-68.
75 Ibid., 49 (July 1948): 69 and 71.
76 *BCL* 34 (August 1950): 37.
77 *PPMC* 49 (May 1948): 164; 50 (August 1950): 168; 53 (September 1952): 114; *BCL* 34 (August 1950): 37.
78 Trade Union Research Bureau, "Report on Crown Zellerbach Limited Finances," March 1962, UBC, Trade Union Research Bureau Papers, vol. 44, file 18.
79 Crown Zellerbach Canada, *Management Journal,* Vancouver, 1 (December 20 1955): 3.
80 There was talk of a pulp mill in the years after the First World War: *PPMC* 18 (11 November 1920): 1,172; 19 (17 February 1921): 197.
81 *BCL* 35 (June 1951): 41.
82 Ibid., 34 (August 1950): 37; *PPMC* 52 (June 1951): 123-24.
83 *PPMC* 50 (July 1949): 166; 52 (January 1951): 126.
84 Ibid., 52 (June 1951): 202-4.
85 Ibid., 55 (February 1954): 100; 60 (September 1959): 233.
86 R.H. Fowler to Hon. Alvin Hamilton, 7 October 1959, UVic, Ray Williston Fonds, 89-068, vol. 8, file 15.
87 *PPMC* 49 (May 1948): 166; 55 (October 1954): 195.
88 Ibid., 59 (January 1958): 176; 59 (April 1958), whole issue.
89 Baptie, *First Growth,* 276-82.
90 British Columbia, Department of Industrial Development, Trade and Commerce, Economics and Statistics Branch, *The Pulp and Paper Industry of British Columbia* (Victoria: Queen's Printer, 1970).
91 The forest industry in the northeastern portion of the province – the Peace River and Fort Nelson regions – was small, isolated, and local in the period under study.
92 F.L.C. Reed, *Selected Forest Industry Statistics,* 66-67.
93 J.O. Wilson to G.S. Pearson, Minister of Labour, 21 August 1934, BCA, GR-1222, vol. 4, file 4. For a similar analysis, see W.N. Jaeck, President, Longworth Lumber Company, to H.G. Perry and T.D. Pattullo, 20 February 1934, BCA, GR-1222, vol. 3, file 5.
94 *BCL* 25 (April 1941): 19.

95 British Columbia, Department of Lands, *Report of the Forest Branch 1939* (Victoria: King's Printer, 1940), E32; *Report of the Forest Service 1945* (Victoria: King's Printer, 1946), 42.
96 Pacific Coast Labor Bureau, "Survey: Interior Woodworking and Logging Industry, July-October, 1945," UBC, Trade Union Research Bureau Papers, vol. 15, file 3.
97 *BCL* 42 (April 1958): 36-44; 29 (May 1945): 42.
98 Ibid., 45 (June 1961): 40-42. Another source cites 1945 as the year Federated Co-operatives purchased Shuswap Lumber. See *BCL* 35 (September 1951): 114.
99 Ibid., 32 (September 1948): 57 and 122; 34 (November 1950): 43-44. See also Drushka, *Lignum.*
100 Drushka, *Tie Hackers to Timber Harvesters,* 154.
101 *BCL* 35 (October 1951): 130.
102 Ibid., 25 (May 1941): 34; 29 (February 1945): 50; 29 (March 1945): 86.
103 Ibid., 35 (August 1951): 57.
104 *TL* (December 1954): 38 and 40.
105 *The ABC British Columbia Lumber Trade Directory and Yearbook* (hereinafter *ABC*), 1952, 76; 1960, 100.
106 Ibid., 1960, 86.
107 *TL* (June 1958): 11 and 18.
108 *BCL* 37 (March 1953): 44-45.
109 Ibid., 39 (December 1955): 18-40.
110 "Brief to the Royal Commission on Forestry by Eagle Lake Sawmills," May 1955, copy in author's possession; Drushka, *Tie Hackers to Timber Harvesters,* 124 and 181; *BCL* 28 (September 1944): 27; W.B. Milner to H. Cathcart, Deputy Minister of Lands, 1 September 1944, The Exploration Place, Prince George, Northwood Pulp and Timber Records, vol. 22, file A994.10.2.23.1.
111 *BCL* 44 (June 1960): 80; 44 (September 1960): 87; *PPMC* 61 (June 1960): 198; Drushka, *Tie Hackers to Timber Harvesters,* 173.
112 *BCL* 43 (September 1959): 82; 45 (February 1961): 32; 44 (June 1960): 80; 45 (September 1961): 21-25; 45 (November 1961): 38-41; *PPMC* 62 (June 1961), passim.
113 *BCL* 47 (September 1963): 18.
114 Ibid., 49 (February 1965): 20.
115 Ibid., 44 (January 1960): 48.
116 Much of this material on ownership in the Interior is based on British Columbia, *Pulp and Paper Industry;* Marchak, *Green Gold,* 82-112.
117 *PPMC* 54 (January 1953): 138; *TL* 22 (May 1966): 16.
118 British Columbia, *Pulp and Paper Industry,* 46.
119 Peter H. Pearse, *Timber Rights and Forest Policy in British Columbia,* Report of the Royal Commission on Forest Resources, vol. 2 (Victoria: Queen's Printer, 1976), B11-B16. Commissioner Pearse also calculated the degree of foreign ownership: "Companies with majority foreign ownership hold 29 percent of sawmilling capacity, 37 percent of pulp but only 18 per cent of paper capacity, and 43 per cent of veneer and plywood capacity" (B22).

Chapter 2: The State, Sustained Yield, and Small Operators

1 Richard Rajala, *Clearcutting the Pacific Rain Forest: Production, Science, and Regulation* (Vancouver: UBC Press, 1998), esp. 154-66.
2 Roger Hayter, *Flexible Crossroads: The Restructuring of British Columbia's Forest Economy* (Vancouver: UBC Press, 2000), 36; Patricia Marchak, *Green Gold: The Forest Industry in British Columbia* (Vancouver: UBC Press, 1983), 37. See also Keith Reid and Don Weaver, "Aspects of the Political Economy of the BC Forest Industry," in *Essays in BC Political Economy,* ed. Paul Knox and Philip Resnick (Vancouver: New Star Books, 1974), 13-24.

3 Ken Drushka, *HR: A Biography of H.R. MacMillan* (Madeira Park, BC: Harbour Publishing, 1995), esp. 317-20.
4 Richard Rajala, *Clearcutting the Pacific Rain Forest*.
5 See Peter G. Aylen, "Sustained Yield Forestry Policy in BC to 1956: A Deterministic Analysis of Development," MA thesis, University of Victoria, 1984.
6 Rajala, *Clearcutting the Pacific Rain Forest,* 84.
7 For business/state relations, see Gabriel Kolko, *The Triumph of Conservatism: A Reinterpretation of American History, 1900-1916* (New York: Free Press, 1963); James Weinstein, *The Corporate Ideal in the Liberal State: 1900-1918* (Boston: Beacon Press, 1968). Marxist perspectives are found in Leo Panitch, "The Role and Nature of the Canadian State," in *The Canadian State: Political Economy and Political Power,* ed. Leo Panitch (Toronto: University of Toronto Press, 1977), 3-27; Fred Block, "Beyond Relative Autonomy: State Managers as Historical Subjects," *Socialist Register* 16 (1980): 227-42; Block, "The Ruling Class Does Not Rule: Notes on the Marxist Theory of the State," *Socialist Revolution* 33 (May-June 1977): 6-28.
8 For BC forest policy and the conservation movement before 1930, see Gordon Hak, *Turning Trees into Dollars: The British Columbia Coastal Lumber Industry, 1858-1913* (Toronto: University of Toronto Press, 2000), 64-115; Peter R. Gillis and Thomas R. Roach, *Lost Initiatives: Canada's Forest Industries, Forest Policy and Forest Conservation* (Westport, CT: Greenwood, 1986), 31-105; Samuel P. Hays, *Conservation and the Gospel of Efficiency: The Progressive Conservation Movement, 1890-1920* (New York: Atheneum, 1969) [original 1959]; Andrew Denny Rodgers III, *Bernard Eduard Fernow: A Story of North American Forestry* (Princeton, NJ: Princeton University Press, 1951); Peter R. Gillis, "The Ottawa Lumber Barons and the Conservation Movement, 1880-1914," *Journal of Canadian Studies* 9 (February 1974): 14-31; Stephen Gray, "The Government's Timber Business: Forest Policy and Administration in British Columbia, 1912-1928," *BC Studies* 81 (Spring 1989): 24-49; Thomas R. Roach, "The Stewards of the People's Wealth: The Founding of British Columbia's Forest Branch," *Journal of Forest History* 28 (January 1984): 14-23.
9 F.D. Mulholland, *The Forest Resources of British Columbia* (Victoria: King's Printer, 1937), 53.
10 "C.D. Orchard," Transcript of Recorded Interview by C.D. Orchard, Interview No. 42, 1960, University of British Columbia, The Library, Special Collections (hereinafter UBC), C.D. Orchard Papers, vol. 4, p. 66.
11 P.Z. Caverhill, Memorandum, 1935, British Columbia Archives (hereinafter BCA), GR-1441, B4374, file 07709#5.
12 Address by the Chief Forester to the Forestry Committee of the British Columbia Legislature, 2 November 1937, BCA, GR-1242, vol. 1, file 1, p. 5.
13 Roderick Haig-Brown to Mr. Mitchell, 10 December 1937, UBC, Roderick Haig-Brown Collection, vol. 148, file 4.
14 Resolutions Submitted to the Annual Convention of the Associated Boards of Trade of Vancouver Island, 21-22 June 1939, UBC, Haig-Brown Collection, vol. 148, file 1. While Mulholland and Manning awakened public opinion about the necessity for forest management, they remained optimistic about the future of the forest industry. The chief forester reassured the worried Haig-Brown in late 1937: "While I believe at the present rate of cut our Douglas fir lumber industry will be definitely on the down grade within fifteen years, we must remember that there is approximately as much hemlock and cedar as there is fir and it is quite conceivable that if we go about our merchandizing properly we can continue large-scale operations in the old-growth timber considerably longer than fifteen years." In 60 to 100 hundred years, he added, second-growth Douglas-fir growing on cutover land would be ready to be logged: E.C. Manning to R.L. Haig-Brown, 28 December 1937, UBC, Haig-Brown Collection, vol. 148, file 4.

15 F. Malcolm Knapp (Acting Head, Department of Forestry, UBC), "Some Aspects of Forestry in British Columbia," *British Columbia Lumberman* (hereinafter *BCL*) 24 (April 1940): 26-27; F.W. Mulholland, "Forest Conservation: What Is It?" *BCL* 24 (January 1940): 22.

16 *BCL* 23 (December 1939): 22. The Mercer Report, describing forestry problems in East Kootenay, was also cited: William M. Mercer, "Growth of Ghost Towns: The Decline of Forest Activity in the East Kootenay District and the Effect on the Growth of Ghost Towns on the Distributing Centres of Cranbrook and Fernie," Report for the Royal Commission on Forestry, Victoria, February 1944.

17 R.V. Stuart (Secretary-Manager of the British Columbia Loggers' Association), "Forest Industries Will Be Permanent in BC: An Analysis of the Present Situation and a Prediction for the Future," *BCL* 25 (January 1941): 15-16; Sydney G. Smith (Manager, Logging Department, Bloedel, Stewart & Welch), "Views of a Western Timber Operator on Practical Sustained Yield," *BCL* 25 (April 1941): 38 and 40.

18 C.D. Orchard, "Forest Working Circles," Memorandum to the Honourable the Minister of Lands, 27 August 1942, UBC, MacMillan Bloedel Papers (hereinafter MB), vol. 46, file 40; C.D. Orchard to Hon. A. Wells Gray, August 1942, UBC, Orchard Papers, vol. 8, file 15.

19 *BCL* 25 (May 1941): 29.

20 Ibid., 25 (March 1941): 23.

21 M.C. Ironside, secretary of the ABTVI, to Hon. S.F. Tolmie, 15 July 1933, Ministry of Forests Records, Victoria, f.0103410; BCA, GR-441, vol. 303, file 1.

22 *The Commonwealth*, 11 September 1936; *The Federationist*, 16 June 1938.

23 Royal Commission on Forestry, 1944-5, Proceedings, BCA, GR-520, vol. 3, file 3, pp. 684-735; vol. 3, file 4, pp. 1,192-1,219.

24 Memorandum to the Honourable Minister of Lands, 22 June 1939, BCA, GR-1222, vol. 29, file 1; Royal Commission on Forestry, 1944-5, Proceedings, vol. 3, file 3, p. 1,125; T.D. Pattullo to W.L. Mackenzie King, 26 January 1938, BCA, Add MS-0003, vol. 70, file 2.

25 Memorandum to the Honourable Minister of Lands, 22 June 1939, BCA, GR-1222, vol. 29, file 1.

26 *The Commonwealth*, 22 February 1935, 1 March 1935, and 6 March 1936.

27 *The Federationist*, 29 October 1936.

28 Ibid., 12 November 1936.

29 C.D. Orchard, unpublished autobiography, 1960, UBC, Orchard Papers, vol. 4, file 20, pp. 85-86.

30 Minutes, Monthly Meeting of BC Loggers' Association, 20 July 1943, UBC, Council of Forest Industries Papers (hereinafter COFI Papers), 2/2; "Brief to be Presented to the Honorable Premier of British Columbia, and Members of the Executive Council by the British Columbia Natural Resources Conservation League," 1943; H.E. Harris, BC Natural Resources Conservation League, to Roderick L. Haig-Brown, 1 February 1943, UBC, Haig-Brown Collection, vol. 76, file 9.

31 *BCL* 27 (July 1943): 24.

32 Fort George Forest District, "Annual Management Report," 1944, BCA, GR-1441, B3401, f. 027391, p. 4.

33 *BCL* 32 (April 1948): 84.

34 Ibid., 30 (April 1946): 37.

35 John D. Gilmour, "A Discussion of the Sloan Report," 1946, UBC, MB Papers, vol. 419, file 42. For the industry's perspective on forest issues in the mid-1940s, see the synopsis of comments of Walter S. Owen, spokesman for the BC Loggers' Association, the Pulp and Paper Industry of BC, and the Truck Loggers Association, before the Sloan Commission. *BCL* 29 (August 1945): 32-34 and 52-56; 29 (September 1945): 50, 52, 55, 56, and 58. A core of professional foresters, both within the government and in the employ of private industry, also

stressed the benefits of private ownership. A 1950 policy statement from the Vancouver and Victoria Section of the Canadian Society of Forest Engineers argued that a "greater proportion of private ownership would result in a more responsible approach to forest management by a greater number of citizens," and that "those countries which have shown the greatest forestry development have a much larger percentage of private ownership than British Columbia": *BCL* 34 (April 1950): 38.

36 See the comment of H.R. MacMillan, *BCL* 40 (January 1956): 8.

37 Sue Baptie, ed., *First Growth: The Story of British Columbia Forest Products Limited* (Vancouver: British Columbia Forest Products, 1975), 35.

38 A.P. McBean to H.R. MacMillan, Inter-Office Memo, 4 November 1947, UBC, MB Papers, vol. 413, file 26.

39 *BCL* 27 (June 1943): 31.

40 *The Truck Logger* (hereinafter *TL*) (February 1956): 18.

41 *BCL* 25 (November 1941): 27.

42 Ibid., 26 (December 1942): 28; 29 (February 1945): 28.

43 Ibid., 29 (October 1945): 62.

44 Ibid., 31 (February 1947): 46.

45 Ibid., 34 (April 1950): 92.

46 Ibid., 29 (September 1945): 48; 29 (October 1945): 60.

47 *TL* (May 1948): 13; (August 1958): 14.

48 G.W. Taylor, "Early Days of Truck Logging," *BCL* 51 (January 1967): 60-61; 39 (January 1955): 12; *TL* (February 1949): 38; (November 1959): 15; 23 (September 1967): 46.

49 *BCL* 29 (October 1945): 62; *TL* (May 1949): 8; *West Coast Advocate,* 3 April 1952; *The ABC British Columbia Lumber Trade Directory and Yearbook* (hereinafter *ABC*), 1942, 69; 1950, 77; 1960, 111; *Campbell River Courier,* 28 May 1952.

50 *BCL* 29 (February 1945): 29; 34 (February 1950): 40.

51 *TL* 19 (January 1963): 33; (May 1960): 18-19; *BCL* 48 (January 1964): 1-12 and 14; *ABC,* 1950, 43; 1960, 52.

52 *BCL* 31 (May 1947): 48; *ABC,* 1942, 41.

53 *BCL* 40 (August 1956): 44.

54 Ibid., 28 (October 1944): 25.

55 Ibid., 32 (April 1948): 84.

56 H.R. MacMillan to Harry G. Perry, President, Prince George *Citizen,* 16 February 1946, BCA, C.D. Orchard Papers, Add. MS-0840, vol. 6, file 15.

57 *TL* (May 1948): 15.

58 *BCL* 34 (February 1950): 60.

59 T.T. Novis, Secretary-Manager, Truck Loggers Association, to Premier Bennett, 27 August 1952, BCA, GR-1222, vol. 90, file 1.

60 *BCL* 37 (February 1953): 42.

61 *TL* (July 1948): 22.

62 *BCL* 33 (November 1949): 62; *TL* (June 1953): 14 and 16.

63 *West Coast Advocate,* 7 February 1952, 3 April 1952, 1 May 1952; *BCL* 36 (September 1952): 30; *TL* (May 1952): 38.

64 *TL* (November 1948): 5.

65 *Cariboo Observer,* 31 January 1948, 20 September 1947.

66 Ibid., 14 February 1948, 21 February 1948, 15 May 1948, 31 July 1948.

67 *TL* (October 1950): 9.

68 *Nelson Daily News,* 18 February 1952, 11 March 1952, 15 March 1952, 23 April 1952; *Arrow Lake News,* 28 February 1952; Henry Murton to Prime Minister of British Columbia, 12 March 1952, BCA, GR-1222, vol. 90, file 2.

69 *Arrow Lake News,* 28 February 1952.
70 *BCL* 38 (November 1954): 30.
71 *TL* (May 1955): 28.
72 *BCL* 39 (June 1955): 30.
73 Ibid., 42 (August 1958): 50.
74 *The Coast News,* 28 February 1952; *West Coast Advocate,* 24 January 1952.
75 See, for example, *TL* (March 1955): 10 and 12; (June 1955): 38 and 40.
76 *TL* (November 1957): 7 and 12.
77 *BCL* 36 (September 1952); *TL* (April 1953): 14.
78 David J. Mitchell, *WAC: Bennett and the Rise of British Columbia* (Vancouver: Douglas and McIntyre, 1983), 216-58.
79 *BCL* 41 (September 1957): 84-85 and 93.
80 *TL* (March 1956): 50. During the Sloan hearings, H.R. MacMillan, at odds with other leading industrialists, argued in favour of a prominent place for small business in the forestry sector. See Ian Mahood and Ken Drushka, *Three Men and a Forester* (Madeira Park, BC: Harbour Publishing, 1990), 161-70; Drushka, *HR,* 307-25.
81 *BCL* 48 (February 1964): 9.
82 Ibid., 45 (April 1961): 70; Minutes, Special Meeting of BC Loggers' Association, 5 March 1962, UBC, COFI Papers, vol. 39, file 5, pp. 146-48.
83 *BCL* 45 (January 1961): 18-25.
84 British Columbia, Department of Industrial Development, Trade and Commerce, *The Sawmilling Industry of British Columbia* (Victoria: Queen's Printer, 1972), 16.
85 *BCL* 55 (August 1971): 7.
86 *TL* 19 (March 1963): 3.
87 Ibid., 9.
88 Ibid., 25 (April 1969): 12-13.
89 Ibid., (March 1949): 12-3.
90 Ibid., 22 (August 1966): 26-27. The fate of small loggers facing the subdivision of the production process is reminiscent of the fate of nineteenth- and twentieth-century skilled tradesmen who experienced the breakup of their crafts into smaller, more specialized segments.
91 *TL* 19 (May 1963): 3.
92 K.G. Boyd to J.O. Hemmingsen, 25 April 1963; J.O. Hemmingsen to H.R. Chisholm, 20 June 1963 [interoffice correspondence], UBC, MB Papers, vol. 704, file 7 [emphasis in original].
93 *BCL* 37 (March 1953): 100.
94 *TL* 22 (September 1966): 12-13.
95 *TL* 23 (April 1967): 26; 23 (June 1967): 22-23.
96 Not all government foresters, of course, agreed with the government's position, and many left the Forest Service to find their reward in the private sector. F.D. Mulholland, for example, author of the important 1937 report, was very much against government ownership of forestland and voiced his opinion regarding the weaknesses of government policy. In 1945, after twenty-two years with the government, he became chief forester for the Canadian Western Lumber Company: *BCL* 29 (August 1945): 38; Rajala, *Clearcutting the Pacific Rain Forest,* 189.
97 P.S. Bonney to P.Z. Caverhill, 29 October 1921, BCA, Add MS-0003, vol. 12, file 2.
98 *Hope Standard,* 2 April 1952; *Cariboo Observer,* 10 April 1952; *Nelson Daily News,* 13 May 1952.
99 "C.D. Orchard," Transcript of Recorded Interview by C.D. Orchard, Interview No. 42, 1960, UBC, Orchard Papers, vol. 4, 98-99.
100 W.H. Hildebrand to J.W. "Mac" McSwiney, 10 September 1964, The Exploration Place, Prince George, Northwood Pulp and Timber Records (hereinafter Northwood Pulp and Timber Records), vol. 56, file A994.10.2.40.1.

101 George G. Choban, Memo, 28 September 1964, Northwood Pulp and Timber Records, vol. 56, file A994.10.2.40.2 (P).
102 J.D. Little to H. Fichtner and D. Allan, 1 February 1965, Northwood Pulp and Timber Records, vol. 57, file A994.10.2.41.2.
103 A.H. Zimmerman to H. Fichtner, 27 October 1966, Northwood Pulp and Timber Records, vol. 57, file A994.10.2.41.4.
104 *BCL* 54 (January 1970): 31.
105 In 1994 logging contractors did 48 percent of the logging on the Coast and 100 percent in the Interior. Small companies also continued to get access to timber, aided by government initiatives such as the Small Business Forest Enterprise Program in the 1980s and 1990s. Smaller firms controlled 30 percent of harvesting rights in the province in 1995: Hayter, *Flexible Crossroads*, 72, 190. In 2003 the Small Business Forest Enterprise Program became BC Timber Sales.

Chapter 3: Establishing Unions

1 *Citizen*, 3 September 1953.
2 Myrtle Bergren, *Tough Timber: The Loggers of BC – Their Story* (Vancouver: Elgin Publications, 1979) [original 1966]; Andrew Neufeld and Andrew Parnaby, *The IWA in Canada: The Life and Times of an Industrial Union* (Vancouver: IWA Canada/New Star Books, 2000). For the Interior, see Ken Bernsohn, *Slabs, Scabs and Skidders: A History of the IWA in the Central Interior* (Prince George, BC: IWA Local 1-424, n.d.).
3 For accounts of labour in Canada in the 1940s, see Craig Heron, *The Canadian Labour Movement: A Short History*, 2nd ed. (Toronto: James Lorimer, 1996), 56-84; Laurel Sefton MacDowell, *"Remember Kirkland Lake": The Gold Miners' Strike of 1941-42* (Toronto: University of Toronto Press, 1983); Jeremy Webber, "The Malaise of Compulsory Conciliation: Strike Prevention in Canada During World War II," *Labour/Le Travail* 15 (Spring 1985): 57-88; Bryan D. Palmer, *Working-Class Experience: Rethinking the History of Canadian Labour, 1880-1991* (Toronto: McClelland and Stewart, 1992), 268-339.
4 Gordon Hak, "British Columbia Loggers and the Lumber Workers Industrial Union, 1919-1922," *Labour/Le Travail* 23 (Spring 1989): 67-90; Hak, "'Line Up or Roll Up': The Lumber Workers Industrial Union in the Prince George District," *BC Studies* 86 (Summer 1990): 57-74; Allen Seager and David Roth, "British Columbia and the Mining West: A Ghost of a Chance," in *The Workers' Revolt in Canada, 1917-1925*, ed. Craig Heron (Toronto: University of Toronto Press, 1998), 231-67.
5 Jeanne Meyers, "Class and Community in the Fraser Mills Strike, 1931," in *Workers, Capital, and the State in British Columbia: Selected Papers*, ed. Rennie Warburton and David Coburn (Vancouver: UBC Press, 1988), 141-57.
6 Vancouver Forest District, Management Reports, 1929, 1930, British Columbia Archives (hereinafter BCA), Lands Records, Rolls 1237-38, files 027636-1 and 027636-2.
7 Courtenay-area camps did not participate due to the tactics of the Comox Logging and Railway Company, which fired and intimidated union sympathizers: R.J. Filberg, Comox Logging and Railway, to H.J. Mackin, Canadian Western Lumber Co., 14 April 1934, Courtenay and District Museum (hereinafter CDM), Comox Logging and Railway Records (hereinafter CLR Records), vol. 7, file 17.
8 E.A. MacLennan, Secretary, BC Coast District Council, Lumber, Sawmill Workers' and Shingle Weavers' Union, 10 March 1938, to The Secretary, BC Loggers' Association; R.V. Stuart, Secretary-Manager, BC Loggers' Association, to G.S. Pearson, Minister of Labour, 11 March 1938, CDM, CLR Records, vol. 11, file 7.
9 *Labor Statesman*, March 1932.
10 *Port Alberni News*, 16 February 1928.

11   Gordon Hak, "Red Wages: Communists and the 1934 Vancouver Island Loggers Strike," *Pacific Northwest Quarterly* 80 (July 1989): 82-90.

12   *British Columbia Lumber Worker* (hereinafter *BCLW*), 5 June 1934.

13   Sara Diamond, "A Union Man's Wife: The Ladies' Auxiliary Movement in the IWA, The Cowichan Lake Experience," in *Not Just Pin Money: Selected Essays on the History of Women's Work in British Columbia*, ed. Barbara K. Latham and Roberta J. Pazdro (Victoria: Camosun College, 1984), 287-96; *BCLW*, 8 February 1936.

14   *BCLW*, 9 December 1936.

15   For an analytical overview of the strike, see Andrew Parnaby, "What's Law Got to Do with It? The IWA and the Politics of State Power in British Columbia, 1935-1939," *Labour/Le Travail* 44 (Fall 1999): 9-45. See also Judy Fudge and Eric Tucker, *Labour before the Law: The Regulation of Workers' Collective Action in Canada, 1900-1948* (Oxford: Oxford University Press, 2001), 221-25; British Columbia, Department of Labour, *Annual Report, 1938* (Victoria: King's Printer, 1939), P78 and P82-P84.

16   *BCLW*, 10 May 1938, 7 June 1938, 14 June 1938; *West Coast Advocate*, 9 June 1938; Library and Archives Canada (hereinafter LAC), RG27, T3005, vol. 397, file 92.

17   Memorandum, George S. Pearson to T.D. Pattullo, 30 September 1937, BCA, GR-1222, vol. 142, file 7.

18   P.J. Maw to BC Loggers' Association, 21 February 1938, CDM, CLR Records, vol. 11, file 7.

19   Stephen Gray, "Woodworkers and Legitimacy: The IWA in Canada, 1937-1957," PhD dissertation, Simon Fraser University, 1989, 36.

20   Robert H. Zeiger, *Rebuilding the Pulp and Paper Workers' Union, 1933-1941* (Knoxville: University of Tennessee Press, 1984), 46-51.

21   John Vincent et al. to John P. Burke, President-Secretary IBPSPMW, 11 May 1917; Vincent to Burke, 25 June 1917, Wisconsin Historical Society, Madison, International Brotherhood of Pulp, Sulphite and Paper Mill Workers Records, 1906-1957 (hereinafter IBPSPMW Records), Reel 1917 2P, file: Locals: Powell River; J. Bichard to John P. Burke, 2 October 1918, IBPSPMW Records, Reel 1918 2P, file: Locals: Powell River; C. Hill to Burke, 4 June 1919, IBPSPMW Records, Reel 1919 2P, file: Locals: Powell River; A. Lewthwaite to Burke, 29 July 1921, IBPSPMW Records, Reel 1921 4P, file: Locals: Powell River; Lewthwaite to Burke, 5 January 1922, IBPSPMW Records, Reel 1922 2P, file: Locals: Powell River; John P. Burke to H.L. Hansen, 21 June 1937, IBPSPMW Records, Reel 1937 5P, file: Locals: Powell River.

22   *Pulp and Paper Magazine of Canada* (hereinafter *PPMC*) 35 (February 1934): 186. Some union agitators were probably associated with the Communist Party of Canada.

23   *Powell River News*, 18 February 1937, 27 May 1937, 3 June 1937; Harvey J. White, International Representative, to John P. Burke, 15 May 1937, IBPSPMW Records, Reel 1937 3P, file: Organizers: White; James Killen, International Representative, to J.P. Burke, 18 June 1937, IBPSPMW Records, Reel 1937 2P, file: Organizers: Killen.

24   H.L. Hansen, Recording Secretary, Local 76, to J.P. Burke, 3 September 1937, IBPSPMW Records, Reel 1937 5P, file: Locals: Powell River.

25   H. Bamford to J.P. Burke, 4 July 1937, IBPSPMW Records, Reel 1937 5P, file: Locals: Ocean Falls; H.L. Hansen to J.P. Burke, 21 July 1937, IBPSPMW Records, Reel 1937 5P, Locals: Powell River; Harvey H. White to J.P. Burke, 24 August 1937, IBPSPMW Records, Reel 1937 3P, file: Organizers: White.

26   James S. Killen, International Representative, to J.P. Burke, 25 August 1937, IBPSPMW Records, Reel 1937 2P, file: Organizers: Killen; R. Williams, Recording Secretary and Treasurer, Local 297, to J.P. Burke, 31 August 1937, IBPSPMW Records, Reel 1937 5P, file: Locals: Port Mellon.

27   Harvey H. White to J.P. Burke, 11 August 1937, IBPSPMW Records, Reel 1937 3P, file: Organizers: White.

28 James Killen to J.P. Burke, 19 January 1938, IBPSPMW Records, Reel 1938 2P, file: Organizers: Killen.

29 Lawrence A. Hardy to J.P. Burke, 22 February 1939, IBPSPMW Records, Reel 1939 5P, file: Locals: Port Mellon.

30 J.F. Maguire to J.P. Burke, 10 December 1938, IBPSPMW Records, Reel 1938 6P, file: Locals: Powell River; H.L. Hansen to J.P. Burke, 19 May 1939, IBPSPMW Records, Reel 1939 5P, file: Locals: Powell River.

31 By 1940 the surviving unions at Powell River and Ocean Falls negotiated their agreements together: H.W. Sullivan, First Vice-President, IBPSPMW, to John H. Nihei, President, Japanese Section, Local 312, 26 May 1940, IBPSPMW Records, Reel 1940 5P, file: Locals: Ocean Falls.

32 Minutes, General Meeting of the BC Loggers' Association, 15 January 1941, University of British Columbia, The Library, Special Collections (hereinafter UBC), Council of Forest Industries Papers (hereinafter COFI Papers), vol. 2, file 2.

33 "A Labour Relations Plan for the British Columbia Forests Products Industries," 1941 or 1942, CDM, CLR Records, vol. 29, file 17.

34 Canada, Dominion Bureau of Statistics, *Censuses*, 1931-1961 [1951: vol. 4, table 20; 1931: vol.7, tables 49 and 60]; "Number of Orientals in Comparison with Other Nationalities Employed in British Columbia Lumber Industry Years 1929 to 1935 Inclusive," UBC, COFI Papers, vol. 66, file 9.

35 *PPMC* 43 (April 1942): 403.

36 The information in this section on Great Central Lake Sawmills is drawn from MacMillan Bloedel, Alberni Pacific Division, Schedule of Wages, 1930-1979, BCA, Add MS-1641, Reel 1237.

37 Minutes, Directors of the BC Loggers' Association, 13 June 1939, UBC, COFI Papers, vol. 1, file 2.

38 Ibid., 21 April 1942, UBC, COFI Papers, vol. 1, file 2.

39 *British Columbia Lumberman* (hereinafter *BCL*) 26 (May 1942): 23.

40 British Columbia Loggers' Association, Annual Report of the Chairman – Board of Directors 1944, UBC, COFI Papers, vol. 39, file 1, p. 5.

41 *BCL* 28 (November 1944): 25.

42 Ibid., 30 (September 1946): 47.

43 Minutes, Directors of BC Loggers' Association, 21 April 1942, UBC, COFI Papers, vol. 1, file 2; British Columbia Loggers' Association, Annual Report of the Chairman – Board of Directors 1944, UBC, COFI Papers, vol. 39, file 1; pp. 5-6; *BCL* 30 (October 1946): 45.

44 Ralph E. Smith, Special Representative, Powell River Company, to G.E. Raley, Assistant Chief (Administrative), Industrial Division, Wartime Prices and Trade Board, 14 October 1943; J.A. Young, Pacific Mills, to G. Harold Fisk, Special Assistant to the Newsprint Administrator, Wartime Prices and Trade Board, 27 October 1943, LAC, RG64, vol. 271, file 4-1-1.

45 Powell River Company to G. Harold Fisk, Special Assistant to the Newsprint Administrator, Wartime Prices and Trade Board, 20 November 1944 (telegram), LAC, RG64, vol. 273, file 4-2-1, vol. 1.

46 *PPMC* 45 (March 1944): 337; 44 (August 1943): 639-48; Minutes, Meeting of the Board of Directors, Pacific Mills, 17 November 1942, University of California (Berkeley), The Bancroft Library, Crown Zellerbach Corporation Records (hereinafter Crown Zellerbach Records), vol. 127; Minutes, Board of Directors, Pacific Mills, 18 December 1945, Crown Zellerbach Records, vol. 128. For a general perspective on women in the Second World War, see Ruth Roach Pierson, *"They're Still Women After All": The Second World War and Canadian Womanhood* (Toronto: McClelland and Stewart, 1986).

47 *PPMC* 44 (January 1943): 50.

48 Ibid., 44 (September 1943): 728.

49 There were exceptions. For example, women still worked as stencillers and tallymen at Alaska Pine Company's New Westminster sawmill in 1951: *BCL* 35 (May 1951): 55.

50 As Ruth Milkman notes: "The formative period is critical, because an industry's pattern of employment by sex, once established, quickly gains all the weight of tradition and becomes extraordinarily inflexible": *Gender at Work: The Dynamics of Job Segregation by Sex during World War II* (Urbana and Chicago: University of Illinois Press, 1987), 7-8.

51 *BCL* 26 (November 1942): 29-30; 26 (December 1942): 60-61; 33 (July 1949): 57, 120, 122; UBC, Trade Union Research Bureau Papers (hereinafter TURB Papers), vol. 13, file 13.

52 Susanne Klausen, "The Plywood Girls: Women and Gender Ideology at the Port Alberni Plywood Plant, 1942-1991," *Labour/Le* Travail 41 (Spring 1998): 199-235.

53 F.G. Compton, "Memorandum Re: Ladies' Quarters," 9 April 1942, UBC, MacMillan Bloedel Papers (hereinafter MB Papers), vol. 73, file 74.

54 L.H. Hansen to J.P. Burke, 3 January 1952, IBPSPMW Records, Reel 1952 3P, file: Organizers: Hansen.

55 C.M. Mouat, Secretary, Local 76, to J.P. Burke, 1 September 1942; Burke to Mouat, 17 October 1942, IBPSPMW Records, Reel 1946 6P, file: Locals: Powell River.

56 Hansen to Burke, 31 January 1952, IBPSPMW Records, Reel 1952 3P, file: Organizers: Hansen.

57 Burke to Hansen, 24 January 1952, ibid.

58 Hansen to Burke, 31 January 1952, ibid.

59 In the mid-1940s and early 1950s, Agnes Nickel was on the executive of Local 433, the Converters' Union in Vancouver, acting as secretary.

60 James Killen to J.P. Burke, 21 July 1937, IBPSPMW Records, Reel 1937 2P, file: Organizers: Killen; H.M. Bamford, President, Local 312, to John P. Burke, 26 April 1938; Burke to Bamford, 11 May 1938, IBPSPMW Records, Reel 1938 5P, file: Locals: Ocean Falls; J. Lawrence, Recording and Corresponding Secretary, Local 312, to J.P. Burke, 22 March 1941, IBPSPMW Records, Reel 1941 6P, file: Locals: Ocean Falls; C.M. Mouat, Secretary, Local 76, to J.P. Burke, 6 May 1942, IBPSPMW Records, Reel 1942 6P, file: Locals: Powell River.

61 H.L. Hansen to J.P. Burke, 5 December 1944; Leaflet in Chinese, 1944, IBPSPMW Records, Reel 1944 2P, file: Organizers: Hansen. At Woodfibre, recently hired "French-Canadians from New Brunswick" also posed a problem for organizers. While they seemed ready to join the union once it was established, they refused to help organize: H.L. Hansen, International Representative, "June Report," 4 July 1944; Hansen to J.P. Burke, 31 October 1944, IBPSPMW Records, Reel 1944 2P, file: Organizers: Hansen.

62 "Proceedings of the Emergency Conference Re: Lumber Production and Collective Bargaining," IWA, District Council No. 1, 1 November 1942, UBC, TURB Papers, vol. 70, file 9.

63 *BCLW,* 17 April 1944, 12 June 1944, 17 October 1944; Organizers' Conference, Minutes, 22 May 1944, UBC, Harold Pritchett – IWA District Council No. 1 Papers (hereinafter Pritchett – IWA Papers), vol. 5, file 4.

64 *BCLW,* 8 March 1943. In 1944 Nigel Morgan of the IWA publicly supported full citizenship right for BC First Nations people. In October 1946 the IWA presented a brief to the provincial government, demanding the vote for minorities that lacked the franchise: *BCLW,* 20 November 1944, 4 November 1946.

65 J. Lawrence to John P. Burke, 22 March 1941, IBPSPMW Records, Reel 1941 6P, file: Locals: Ocean Falls.

66 James Killen to J.P. Burke, 21 July 1937, IBPSPMW Records, Reel 1937 2P, file: Organizers: Killen.

67 Minutes, Conference of Representatives of Interior Locals of the IWA, Affiliated to BC District Council No. 1, 23 September 1945, UBC, Pritchett-IWA Papers, vol. 5, file 4, pp. 7 and 12;

Minutes, IWA Quarterly District Council Meeting, 7 October 1945, UBC, Pritchett-IWA Papers, vol. 4, file 25, pp. 9-11.

68 Gray, "Woodworkers and Legitimacy," 56-57.

69 Percy A. Tweedie, Secretary, Local 312, to J.P. Burke, 21 October 1943, IBPSPMW Records, Reel 1943 6P, file: Locals: Ocean Falls.

70 James Killen to John P. Burke, 31 July 1941, IBPSPMW Records, Reel 1941 6P, file: Locals: Port Mellon; Clarence Sharp, Financial Secretary, Local 297, to J.P. Burke, 26 May 1942, IBPSPMW Records, Reel 1942 6P, file: Locals: Port Mellon; J.P. Burke to C.M. Mouat, 27 July 1942, IBPSPMW Records, Reel 1942 6P, file: Locals: Powell River.

71 H.L. Hansen, "Report for Month of April," 1944, IBPSPMW Records, Reel 1944 2P, file: Organizers: Hansen.

72 H.L. Hansen to J.P. Burke, 5 January 1944, IBPSPMW Records, Reel 1944 2P, file: Organizers: Hansen; H.L. Hansen, "Report for Month of August," 1945, IBPSPMW Records, Reel 1945 3P, file: Organizers: Hansen; *PPMC* 45 (October 1944): 866.

73 At the end of 1945, the IBPSPMW had contracts with the following Vancouver converting operations: Pacific Mills Converting Plant, Bartram Paper Products, Canadian Bemis Bag Company, and Canadian Boxes: Agnes Nickel, Secretary, Local 433 to J.P. Burke, 24 January 1946, IBPSPMW Records, Reel 1946 9P, file: Locals: Vancouver Converters.

74 Strike Vote, 31 October and 2 November 1953, IBPSPMW Records, Reel 1953 3P, file: Organizers: Hansen. Of the total, about 530 workers in three mills belonged to the Paper Makers.

75 IWA-CIO District Council No. 1, Press Release, 16 July 1941; 2 August 1941, UBC, TURB Papers, vol. 12, file 25; *BCLW,* 25 October 1941.

76 *BCLW,* 31 January 1942, 14 March 1942.

77 Geo. S. Pearson, Minister of Labour, to A. Starks, Chair, Employees Conference Committee, MacMillan Industries, 2 June 1942, UBC, MB Papers, vol. 52, file 30. Note that of 725 eligible voters, 210 workers did not vote and 25 ballots were questionable.

78 H. Thornley to Mr. Harrison, 25 July 1939; Thornley to C.W. Bolton, 27 July 1939, LAC, RG27, Reel T3010, vol. 402, file 96.

79 "Proceedings of the Emergency Conference Re Lumber Production and Collective Bargaining," IWA, District Council No. 1, 1 November 1942, UBC, TURB Papers, vol. 70, file 9, p. 2.

80 Ibid., 10.

81 "IWA Submission to Federal Arbitration Board," 19 May 1943, UBC, John Stanton Papers, vol. 6, file 590; "Queen Charlotte Island Spruce Production," 1943, UBC, TURB Papers, vol. 12, file 17.

82 "Summary of Meeting Held with the Powell River Company Officials at Vancouver, on Saturday, March 20th, 1943," IBPSPMW Records, Reel 1943 6P, file: Locals: Powell River.

83 Gray, "Woodworkers and Legitimacy," ch. 4; "1943 Dispute," BCA, Add MS-1057, vol. 1, file 1; Richard Rajala, *Up-Coast: Forests and Industry on British Columbia's North Coast, 1870-2005* (Victoria: Royal BC Museum, 2006), 115-37.

84 Gray, "Woodworkers and Legitimacy," 135.

85 "Agreement between Bloedel, Stewart & Welch and IWA Local 1-217," 1 December 1943, UBC, TURB Papers, vol. 69, file 4; Reports, Organizers Conference, 26 March 1944, UBC, Pritchett-IWA Papers, vol. 5, file 1; Minutes, Organizers Conference, 24 April 1944, UBC, Pritchett-IWA Papers, vol. 5, file 7; Minutes, Organizers Conference, 22 May 1944, UBC, Pritchett-IWA Papers, vol. 5, file 4; *The Job Steward* (Local 1-85 newspaper), 3 October 1944.

86 Gray, "Woodworkers and Legitimacy," 178-255.

87 "Computation of Delegates for Convention and Voting Strength – Jan. 29 to Feb. 1st. 1952," UBC, International Woodworkers of America, Western Canadian Regional Council No. 1 Paper (hereinafter IWA Papers), Roll 13, file: District Convention, 1952.

88   Gordon McG. Sloan to J.M. Billings and J.S. Alsbury, 24 July 1952, BCA, Add MS-1057, vol. 2, file 3.
89   *BCL* 38 (March 1954): 112.
90   "Organizational Reports," UBC, IWA Papers, Roll 29, file: Organizational Reports, 1955.
91   See Gordon Hak, "The Communists and the Unemployed in the Prince George District, 1930-1935," *BC Studies* 68 (Winter 1985-86): 45-61.
92   Minutes, IWA Negotiations Conference, 12 March 1946, UBC, Pritchett-IWA Papers, vol. 5, file 6.
93   Herbert J. Paisley & Co., Chartered Accountants, Vancouver, "Northern Interior Lumbermen's Association, Prince George, B.C., Comparative Statements of Operating Results and Stump to Car Costs – Based on Actual Operations for the Fiscal Year 1945," and Union Insert, UBC, TURB Papers, vol. 13, file 33.
94   *BCLW,* December 1954 (1st issue), 9.
95   Minutes, Quarterly Council Meeting, IWA-CIO District No. 1, 13 October 1946, UBC, Pritchett-IWA Papers, vol. 4, file 26, p. 10.
96   John Huberman, Western Plywood (Cariboo) Ltd., to C.R. Margison, Board of Industrial Relations, Vancouver, 11 June 1952, UBC, IWA Papers, Roll 10, file: J. Stewart Alsbury – President – Locals – Correspondence.
97   J.C. Mueller, Weekly Report for the Week Ending August 13, 1949, UBC, IWA Papers, Roll 3, file: Organizers Reports, 1949.
98   J.C. Mueller, Weekly Report for Week Ending April 30, 1949, UBC, IWA Papers, Roll 3, file: Organizers Reports, 1949.
99   "Report of the Organization Committee," *BCLW,* 19 January 1950, 4.
100 M. Freylinger, Interior Representative Action Committee, to District Negotiating Committee, 20 March 1946, UBC, IWA Papers, Roll 2, file: Strike Local Report, 1946.
101 Mike Sekora, Organizer, to J.S. Alsbury, 10 February 1951, UBC, IWA Papers, Roll 17, file: J. Stewart Alsbury – Locals, 1951.
102 Mike Sekora, Representative's Weekly Report for the Week Ending October 11, 1952, UBC, IWA Papers, Roll 23, file: International Organizers' Reports – Mike Sekora, 1952.
103 Minutes, Conference of Representatives of Interior Locals of the IWA, Affiliated to BC District Council, No. 1, 23 September 1945, UBC, Pritchett-IWA Papers, vol. 5, file 4, p. 12; Minutes, IWA District Council No. 1, Executive Board Meeting, 3 January 1946, UBC, Pritchett-IWA Papers, vol. 4, file 7, p. 2.
104 Nelson Forest District, Annual Management Report, 1933, BCA, GR-1441, B3588, file: 059897.
105 Minutes, IWA Kamloops Negotiations Conference, 12 March 1946, UBC, Pritchett-IWA Papers, vol. 5, file 6, p. 8.
106 "Strike Bulletin Local 1-118 IWA-CIO," 12 June 1946, UBC, Pritchett-IWA Papers, vol. 6, file 10.
107 *BCL* 38 (March 1954): 22 and 25.
108 Pacific Coast Labor Bureau, "Survey: Interior Woodworking and Logging Industry, July-October, 1945," UBC, TURB Papers, vol. 15, file 3.
109 Bernsohn, *Slabs, Scabs and Skidders,* 12-13; Minutes, District Council Executive Meeting, 1 August 1945, UBC, Pritchett-IWA Papers, vol. 4, file 5, p. 5.
110 Minutes, IWA-CIO District Council, Executive Meeting, 13 September 1944, UBC, Pritchett-IWA Papers, vol. 4, file 3; Minutes, 28 November 1945, vol. 4, file. 6.
111 "Green Gold Radio Transcript," Radio CJOR, 12 February 1947, UBC, TURB Papers, vol. 13, file 28.
112 J. Stewart Alsbury to Bill Lynch, Secretary, Local 1-417, Kamloops, 7 June 1949, UBC, IWA Papers, Roll 5, file: Local 1-367, Haney, 1948-49.
113 E. Dalskog, International Board Member, to Hjalmer Bergren, 20 August 1947, UBC, IWA Papers, Roll 3, file: Hjalmer Bergren, 1947. The Terrace local was disbanded shortly thereafter: *BCLW,* 24 July 1944.

114 Certified Operations – Local 424, UBC, IWA Papers, Roll 3, file: Negotiations (Interior), 1949.
115 Mike Sekora to Geo. H. Mitchell, Secretary, BC District, IWA-CIO, 27 January 1951, UBC, IWA Papers, Roll 9, file: Mike Sekora – International Representative, 1951. For another account of a company, S.B. Trick Lumber Company at Aleza Lake, ignoring the contract, see C.H. Webb, Secretary, Local 1-424, to Geo. H. Mitchell, 30 January 1951, UBC, IWA Papers, Roll 17, file: Local 1-424 Prince George, Correspondence, 1951.
116 L.J.A. Rees, "Bulletin No. 115 to All Members," 20 October 1953, UBC, IWA Papers, Roll 26, file: Interior Situation, 1953-1954.
117 "Chronology of Interior Negotiations"; "1952-53 Negotiations between Interior Lumber Manufacturers Assn. and the Interior Locals of the IWA," UBC, IWA Papers, Roll 63, file: Research and Education Department, Southern Interior Negotiations, 1953; "Chronology of Interior Negotiations: 1953"; "1953 Strike at Prince George," UBC, IWA Papers, Roll 63, file: Research and Education Department, Northern Interior Negotiations, 1953.
118 Result of Government Supervised Strike Vote, 1953, UBC, IWA Papers, Roll 22, file: Local 1-424 Prince George – Interior Negotiations, 1953.
119 Cranbrook Report, UBC, IWA Papers, Roll 26, file: Interior Situation, 1953-54.
120 R. Ganzeveld to Mrs. _____, 13 October 1953; "Efforts by Operators (Members of the ILMA) to Obtain a 'No' Result in the Government Supervised Strike Vote of October 15th," UBC, IWA Papers, Roll 26, file: Interior Situation, 1953-54.
121 Minutes, Policy Committee Meeting, 14 November 1953, UBC, IWA Papers, Roll 24, file: Policy Committee Minutes, 1953.
122 L.J.A. Rees, Secretary-Manager, Interior Lumber Manufacturers' Association, "Bulletin No. 116 to All Members," 28 October 1953, UBC, IWA Papers, Roll 26, file: Interior Situation, 1953-1954.
123 *The Truck Logger* (January 1954): 24.
124 *BCLW,* January 1954 (1st issue), 1.
125 "Organizational Reports for the Period April 23rd to May 23rd, 1955," UBC, IWA Papers, Role 29, file: Organizational Reports, 1955.
126 *BCLW,* February 1959 (2nd issue).
127 R.M. Bibbs, Industrial Relations, to C.A. Specht, 4 May 1967, UBC, MB Papers, vol. 703, file 1.
128 Ibid.

Chapter 4: Union Politics

1 J.L. Granatstein, *The Politics of Survival: The Conservative Party of Canada, 1939-1945* (Toronto: University of Toronto Press, 1967), 130-34, 212.
2 C. Hill to J.P. Burke, 17 December 1919, Wisconsin Historical Society, Madison, International Brotherhood of Pulp, Sulphite and Paper Mill Workers Records, 1906-1957 (hereinafter IBPSPMW Records), Reel 1920 3P, file: Locals: Powell River.
3 H.L. Hansen to Mr. DeW. Lyons, Registrar, Labour Relations Board, Victoria, 9 October 1947, IBPSPMW Records, Reel 1947 3P, file: Organizers: Hansen.
4 H.L. Hansen to John P. Burke, 19 December 1949, IBPSPMW Records, Reel 1949 2P, file: Organizers: Hansen.
5 E. Dalskog to Pat Conroy, 15 June 1946, Library and Archives Canada (hereinafter LAC), Canadian Congress of Labour Papers, MG28-I 103, vol. 47, file 9; H.L. Hansen to G.S. Pearson, Minister of Labour, 12 May 1947; H.M. Lewis, General Manager, Sorg Pulp Company, to Chief Executive Officer, Wartime Labour Relations Board, Victoria, 6 May 1947, IBPSPMW Records, Reel 1947 3P, file: Organizers: Hansen; H.L. Hansen, "Report for Month of December 1947," IBPSPMW Records, Reel 1948 2P, file: Organizers: Hansen; Stanley G. Green, International Representative, to John P. Burke, 10 April 1951, IBPSPMW Records, Reel 1951 3P, file: Organizers: Green.

6 John Mathieson, Secretary, Local 312, to G.H. O'Neill, Labour Relations Board, Victoria, 25 May 1955, IBPSPMW Records, Reel 1955 8P, file: Locals: Ocean Falls. In the mid-1950s, the IBPSPMW also thwarted a raid by the Printing Pressmen's Union at the Vancouver Paper Box Company: S.G. Green to John P. Burke, 9 September 1954, IBPSPMW Records, Reel 1954 3P, file: Organizers: Green.

7 Correspondence and Clippings, LAC, RG27, Reel T4133, vol. 514, file 138.

8 H.L. Hansen to Pat Connolly, IBPSPMW, Cornwall, Ontario, 20 February 1953, IBPSPMW Records, Reel 1953 3P, file: Organizers: Hansen.

9 Rae Eddie, Recording Secretary, Local 1-357, to Donald MacDonald, Secretary Treasurer, CLC, 4 September 1964, LAC, MG28-I 103, Reel H124, file unclear.

10 Minutes, Special District Council Meeting, IWA, 16 June 1946, University of British Columbia, The Library, Special Collections Division (hereinafter UBC), Harold-Pritchett – IWA District Council No. 1 Papers (hereinafter Pritchett – IWA Papers), vol. 4, file 23. In 1946 the Lumber and Sawmill Workers Union, Local 2698, was certified at a number of Vancouver-area mills, and the Steam and Operating Engineers Union, Local 882, was certified to represent the engineers in four Port Alberni sawmills: *Labor Statesman* 565 (April 1946).

11 *Labor Statesman* 578 (February 1947), 8; 579 (March 1947), 6; 600 (December 1048), 11; Minutes, Executive Board Meeting, IWA District Council No. 1, 22 June 1947, UBC, Pritchett-IWA Papers, vol. 5, file 14.

12 J. Clayton Walls, "The Creston Raid ... The Story of a Brave Band of IWA Strikers," 1954, UBC, International Woodworkers of America, Western Canadian Regional Council No. 1 Papers (hereinafter IWA Papers), Roll 26, file: C. Walls – Interior Regional Director, 1954; *British Columbia Lumberman* (hereinafter BCL) 38 (June 1954): 22; St. Mary's Lake Report, UBC, IWA Papers, Roll 44, file: Correspondence Local 1-405, 1958.

13 D.L. Sherret, Recording Secretary, Local 2833, United Brotherhood of Carpenters and Joiners, Cranbrook, to Gordon G. Cushing, Executive Vice-President, CLC, 23 July 1957; Joe Morris, President, District Council No. 1, IWA, to Joe MacKenzie, Director of Organization, CLC, 28 October 1957, LAC, MG28-I 103, Reel H34, file: R-33; *BCL* 41 (October 1957): 96.

14 J.A. Moore, President, District Council No. 1, IWA, to Wm. Dodge, Executive Vice-President, CLC, 16 March 1964, LAC, MG28-I 103, Reel H38, file: R-122; *BCL* 57 (July 1973): 33.

15 H.L. Hansen, "Memorandum of General Policy Covering Mechanical Service Crews in the Pulp and Paper Industry in British Columbia," 8 December 1952; H.L. Hansen to John P. Burke, 4 December 1952, IBPSPMW Records, Reel 1952 3P, file: Organizers: Hansen.

16 "General policy for the guidance of the International Brotherhood of Pulp, Sulphite and Paper Mill Workers and the Buildings Trade Councils of the Province of British Columbia in defining demarcation between work to be performed by members of the International Brotherhood of Pulp, Sulphite and Paper Mill Workers and members of the respective Building Trades Councils in the Province of British Columbia," 1970(?), UBC, BC Federation of Labour Papers (hereinafter BCFL Papers), vol. 21, file 38.

17 H.L. Hansen to John P. Burke, 13 June 1952, IBPSPMW Records, Reel 1952 3P, file: Organizers: Hansen.

18 *BCL* 52 (January 1968): 23.

19 E.T. Staley to Richard Norris, President, Local No. 2318, Creston, 17 December 1953, UBC, IWA Papers, Roll 26, file: Interior Situation, 1953-54.

20 E.M. Golley, Recording Secretary, Local 76, to John P. Burke, 19 May 1955; Golley to Burke, 17 February 1955, IBPSPMW Records, Reel 1955 8P, file: Locals: Powell River.

21 John P. Burke to E.M. Golley, 25 February 1955, ibid.

22 John P. Burke to H.L. Hansen, 27 January 1947, IBPSPMW Records, Reel 1947 3P, file: Organizers: Hansen; H.L. Hansen to John P. Burke, 26 January 1954, IBPSPMW Records, Reel 1954 3P, file: Organizers: Hansen.

23 Harvey H. White to John P. Burke, 15 May 1937; Burke to White, 3 July 1937, IBPSPMW Records, Reel 1937 3P, file: Organizers: White.

24 Minutes, Executive Board Meeting, IWA-CIO District Council No. 1, 3 April 1946, UBC, Pritchett-IWA Papers, vol. 4, file 9; H.L. Hansen to John P. Burke, 28 July 1946, IBPSPMW Records, Reel 1946 3P, file: Organizers: Hansen.

25 Joe Morris to All Local Unions, 19 July 1956, UBC, IWA Papers, Roll 28, file: Correspondence to All Locals, 1956.

26 *Western Pulp and Paper Worker* 3 (September 1958): 15; 3 (November 1958): 5; "Unity Committee Meeting," Portland, Oregon, 21 February 1961, UBC, Angus Macphee Papers (hereinafter Macphee Papers), vol. 2, file 1; *The Barker* 11 (December 1971): 2.

27 H.L. Hansen, "Report for May," 1946, IBPSPMW Records, Reel 1946 3P, file: Organizers: Hansen.

28 Resolution from Local 76, April(?) 1947, IBPSPMW Records, Reel 1947 3P, file: Organizers: Hansen.

29 "Agreement between IBPSPMW and IWA," 21 May 1952, signed by H.L. Hansen, International Representative, IBPSPMW, and J. Stewart Alsbury, President, BC District Council No. 1, IWA, UBC, Macphee Papers, vol. 1, file 14.

30 H.L. Hansen to John P. Burke, 24 July 1952, IBPSPMW Records, Reel 1952 3P, file: Organizers: Hansen.

31 J. Morris, President, Regional Council No. 1, IWA, to H.L. Hansen, 8 July 1959; H.L. Hansen to All Locals, 9 July 1959, UBC, Macphee Papers, vol. 1, file 14.

32 *Western Pulp and Paper Worker* 4 (October 1959): 1. At times, IBPSPMW officials became involved in IWA strikes. According to H.L. Hansen, the IBPSPMW played a greater role than the government mediator, Gordon McGregor Sloan, in bringing the 1946 IWA strike to a conclusion. Conversations between the IBPSPMW vice president and the federal deputy minister of labour apparently were extremely salutary. Similarly, during the 1952 IWA strike, Hansen was asked by some IWA officials and a former CCF MLA to exert some influence on the negotiations. Hansen held a meeting with prominent lumbermen and, in his view, persuaded them to meet with the IWA, thus paving the way for a settlement: H.L. Hansen to John P. Burke, 14 July 1952, IBPSPMW Records, Reel 1952 3P, file: Organizers: Hansen; H.L. Hansen to Pat Connolly, 20 February 1953, IBPSPMW Records, Reel 1953 3P, file: Organizers: Hansen.

33 H.L. Hansen to Pat Connolly, 20 February 1953, IBPSPMW Records, Reel 1953 3P, file: Organizers: Hansen

34 Bryan M. Downie, *Relationships between Canadian-American Wage Settlements: An Empirical Study of Five Industries* (Kingston, ON: Industrial Relations Centre at Queen's University, 1970), 50-51. In making contract comparisons, BC pulp and paper workers were more concerned with BC IWA rates than pulp and paper rates in the United States.

35 Grant MacNeil, *The IWA in British Columbia* (Vancouver: Western Regional Council No. 1, International Woodworkers of America, AFL-CIO-CLC, 1971), offers the first case, while the latter argument is presented most forcefully by Jerry Lembcke and William M. Tattam, *One Union in Wood* (Madeira Park, BC: Harbour Publishing, 1984).

36 See Andrew Neufeld and Andrew Parnaby, *The IWA in Canada: The Life and Times of an Industrial Union* (Vancouver: IWA Canada/New Star Books, 2000), 110-21; Irving Abella, *Nationalism. Communism, and Canadian Labour: The CIO, the Communist Party, and the Canadian Congress of Labour, 1935-1956* (Toronto: University of Toronto Press, 1973), 86-138; Howard White, *A Hard Man to Beat: The Story of Bill White, Labour Leader, Historian, Shipyard Worker, Raconteur* (Vancouver: Pulp Press, 1983), 166-71.

37 Stephen Gray, "Woodworkers and Legitimacy: The IWA in Canada, 1937-1957," PhD dissertation, Simon Fraser University, 1989. Gray also sees the IWA as ensnared in the new

bureaucratic order over the course of the 1940s, arguing, less persuasively, that the creation of the WIUC was in part a last-ditch attempt by the communists to forestall the bureaucratization of the union and return to camp and shop-floor militancy.

38 Gordon Hak, "Red Wages: Communists and the 1934 Vancouver Island Loggers Strike," *Pacific Northwest Quarterly* 80 (July 1989): 82-90; Jeanne Meyers, "Class and Community in the Fraser Mills Strike, 1931," in *Workers, Capital, and the State in British Columbia: Selected Papers,* ed. Rennie Warburton and David Coburn (Vancouver: UBC Press, 1988), 141-60; Ian Radforth, *Bushworkers and Bosses: Logging in Northern Ontario, 1900-1980* (Toronto: University of Toronto Press, 1987), 110-25.

39 *Citizen,* 31 August 1933.

40 *British Columbia Lumber Worker* (hereinafter *BCLW*), 4 January 1936.

41 Ibid., 22 August 1936.

42 Ibid., 16 December 1936.

43 Ibid., 16 June 1937, 2 June 1937.

44 For a discussion of the Lumber and Sawmill Workers Union and the early years of the IWA, see Lembcke and Tattam, *One Union in Wood,* 30-74. For a broader perspective on the tumultuous history of North American labour in the mid-1930s, see Abella, *Nationalism, Communism, and Canadian Labour;* Irving Bernstein, *The Lean Years: A History of the American Worker, 1920-1933* (Baltimore: Penguin Books, 1966); Bernstein, *The Turbulent Years: A History of the American Worker* (Boston: Houghton Mifflin, 1969); Melvyn Dubofsky and Warren Van Tyne, *John L. Lewis: A Biography* (New York: Quadrangle Books, 1977).

45 Gray, "Woodworkers and Legitimacy," 315-37.

46 District Officer Election Results, Minutes, IWA District Council No. 1, Executive Board Meeting, 19 March 1946, UBC, Pritchett-IWA Papers, vol. 4, file 9; Gray, "Woodworkers and Legitimacy," 331.

47 "History of Local 1-357, IWA-CIO," UBC, IWA Papers, Roll 8, file: Misc. Locals, 1950.

48 Transcript, The Voice of the International Woodworkers of America, Radio Broadcast, 4 February 1948, UBC, Pritchett-IWA Papers, vol. 3, file 11.

49 Minutes, District Executive Board Meeting IWA, 17 May 1948, UBC, Pritchett-IWA Papers, vol. 4, file 18, pp. 18-21.

50 Harold Pritchett, District President, IWA-CIO, to George Brown, Director of Organization, IWA, 12 October 1945, UBC, Pritchett-IWA Papers, vol. 6, file 3.

51 A.R. Mosher, President, CCL, to Claude Ballard, President, IWA, 14 February 1945, LAC, MG28-I 103, vol. 103, file 1-13. For the media, see Transcript, "'Along the Skidroad': A Review of Labour Developments during the Past Week ... by Bob Morrison," 8 January 1948, UBC, Pritchett-IWA Papers, vol. 8, file 2, pp. 3-5.

52 Wm. Mahoney to Pat Conroy, 13 July 1948, LAC, MG28-I 103, vol. 315, file 1-31. For more on the CLC and the audit, see Wm Mahoney, Western Director of Organization, to Pat Conroy, Secretary-Treasurer, CCL, 24 June 1948, LAC, MG28-I 103, vol. 315, file 5-30; Mahoney to Conroy, 25 June 1948; Mahoney to Conroy, 2 July 1948; Eugene Forsey to Wm Mahoney, 16 July 1948, LAC, MG28-I 103, vol. 315, file 5-31.

53 By July 1948, the anti–Red Bloc forces saw the possibility of a secession move: Pat Conroy to Wm Mahoney, 2 July 1948, LAC, MG28-I 103, vol. 315, file 5-31; Wm Mahoney to Pat Conroy, 30 August 1948, LAC, MG28-I 103, vol. 103, file 1-22.

54 C.A. (Chuck) Thomas to Mike Sekora, 23 November 1948, UBC, IWA Papers, Roll 11, file: Chuck Thomas – Announcer Prince George.

55 Mike Sekora, Acting Secretary, BC District Council, to Peter Barkosha, IWA Organizer, Cranbrook, 6 December 1949, UBC, IWA Papers, Roll 5, file: Local 1-405 Cranbrook, 1940; "List of Certifications Granted to Local 405 WIUC," UBC, IWA Papers, Roll 5, file: Local 1-405 Cranbrook, 1948-49.

56 Local 1-363 Courtenay IWA, "The Facts about Iron River," December 1948(?), UBC, Pritchett-IWA Papers, vol. 11, file 9.
57 J. Stewart Alsbury, President, BC District Council No. 1, to D.E. McShane, Financial Secretary, Local 1-424, Prince George, 14 June 1949, UBC, IWA Papers, Roll 5, file: Local 1-424 Prince George, 1948-49. According to the WIUC, the IWA "imported a gang of 300 self-styled vigilantes, some of them from the U.S., and used violence against the pickets, some of them women": WIUC Bulletin, December 1948, UBC, Pritchett-IWA Papers, vol. 11, file 9; J. Creelman and G. Nichols, Iron River Strike Committee, 15 December 1948, UBC, IWA Papers, Roll 11, file: WIUC Propaganda, 1948.
58 Norman Penner, *Canadian Communism: The Stalin Years and Beyond* (Toronto: Methuen, 1988), 229-34.
59 William Beeching and Phyllis Clarke, eds., *Yours in the Struggle: Reminiscences of Tim Buck* (Toronto: NC Press, 1977), 366.
60 Local 1-80, Duncan, "Bulletin," UBC, IWA Papers, Roll 5, file: Local 1-80 Duncan, 1948-49.
61 P. Conroy to William Mahoney, 27 April 1949; Mahoney to Conroy, 19 April 1949, LAC, MG28-I 103, vol. 311, file 1-27.
62 Gad Horowitz, *Canadian Labour in Politics* (Toronto: University of Toronto Press, 1968), 159-61.
63 "To All Ontario CLC Staff Representatives," 10 March 1981, LAC, MG28-I 103, Reel H319, file L19.
64 Minutes, District Executive Board, Western Canadian Regional Council No. 1, 19 April 1951, UBC, IWA Papers, Roll 9, file: Safety Minutes: District Executive Board, 1951, p. 5; P.W. Berkosha, International Representative, IWA, to S. Alsbury, 1 September 1951, UBC, IWA Papers, Roll 17, file: J. Stewart Alsbury – Locals File 1951; J. Clayton Walls, Report for Week Ending 12/12/53, UBC, IWA Papers, Roll 26, file: Clayton Wells – International Organizer 1953; *BCL* 40 (May 1956): 100; 38 (October 1954): 24; 39 (August 1955): 14; 41 (January 1957): 36; Names all operations and certification of IWA and WIUC, 1955(?), UBC, IWA Papers, Roll 20, file: Local 1-405 1955.
65 Jean Elizabeth McIntosh, "Mark Mosher's Reconstruction of the Development of the Woodworkers Union in the Alberni Valley 1935-1950: A Participant's History," MA thesis, University of British Columbia, 1987, 86.
66 Fred Fieber to Arne Johnson, c/o Pioneer Timber Co., Port McNeil, 30 October 1950, UBC, Arne Johnson Fonds, vol. 1.
67 S.M. Hodgson, Financial Secretary, Local 1-217, to All Members of the IWA, 20 January 1955; Hodgson to Joe Morris, President, District Council No. 1, 31 January 1955; Gordon W. Elder to BC District Council No. 1, 14 February 1955, UBC, IWA Papers, Reel 37, file: Correspondence Local 1-217 1955.
68 S.M. Hodgson, Financial Secretary, Local 1-217, to George Mitchell, Secretary-Treasurer, District Council No. 1, 5 November 1957; Mitchell to Hodgson, 3 December 1957, UBC, IWA Papers, Roll 41, file: Correspondence Local 1-217 1957.
69 Edwin Linder, Financial Secretary, Local 1-80, to Fred Fieber, Acting Secretary-Treasurer, IWA Regional Council No. 1, 19 October 1960; Fieber to Linder, 21 October 1960; Linder to Fieber, 1 November 1960, UBC, IWA Papers, Roll 55, file: Local Correspondence 1-80 1960.
70 Gray, "Woodworkers and Legitimacy," 522n; *Western Canadian Lumber Worker*, September 1968 (2nd issue), 6.
71 Poster, "Ten Years of Poor Leadership 1948-1958 ... For President ... Elect Syd Thompson"; IWA Poster, "10 Years of Progress"; A.F. Hartung, International President, IWA, to Fellow Workers of Local 1-217, IWA, 3 December 1958; "Report of Committee Appointed by International President A.F. Hartung, to Investigate the Situation Relative to Local Election of Officers in IWA Local 1-217, Vancouver, BC," n.d., UBC, IWA Papers, Roll 44, file: Correspondence Local 1-217 1958.

72 *BCL* 43 (August 1959): 9.

73 *The Barker* 2 (May 1961): 1-3; 2 (June 1961): 6.

74 E.L. Freer, Secretary-Treasurer, Local 1-71, IWA, to All Camp Chairmen, Camp Secretaries, Staff and Board Members, Local 1-71 IWA, 19 October 1961; Freer to Joe Morris, 26 October 1961; "Resolution No. 33," submitted by Local 1-217, UBC, IWA Papers, Roll 55, file: Local Union Correspondence 1-71, 1961; *The Barker* 4 (August-September 1963): 1.

75 *Western Canadian Lumber Worker,* January 1962 (2nd issue), 1; August 1962 (1st issue), 6.

76 *The Barker* 5 (May 1964): 4.

77 *Western Pulp and Paper Worker* (September 1967): 6.

78 *The Barker* 9 (July 1968): 1.

79 *BCL* 51 (December 1967): 32-33.

80 *The Barker* 9 (September 1968): 1. For the election results by local, see *Western Canadian Lumber Worker,* October 1968 (2nd issue), 5.

81 Jack Munro and Jane O'Hara, *Union Jack: Labour Leader Jack Munro* (Vancouver: Douglas and McIntyre, 1988), 71.

82 Harold Pritchett, "A Critical Review of Our Party Work in Wood," September 1972, UBC, Harold Pritchett Papers, vol. 1, file 8; Jack Moore, cited in "Notes on Meeting with IWA Regional Officers," 30 May 1972, UBC, BC Federation of Labour Papers (hereinafter BCFL), vol. 32, file 13.

83 Communist Party of Canada (hereinafter CPC), BC Provincial Executive Meeting, 3 May 1973, LAC, CPC Fonds, MG28-IV4, Reel 1593, vol. 24, file 24-39. In 1973 the CPC changed its position on the issue of nationalism. Rather than fighting for Canadian autonomy in the IWA, the party advocated an independent union for Canadian woodworkers: CPC, BC Provincial Executive Meeting, 10 September 1973, ibid.

84 *The Barker* 13 (May 1971): 3.

85 H.L. Hansen to John Sherman, 19 September 1950, IBPSPMW Records, Reel 1950 3P, file: Organizers: Hansen.

86 John P. Burke to H.L. Hansen, 29 October 1952; Hansen to Burke, 15 July 1952; Hansen to Burke, 22 October 1952, IBPSPMW Records, Reel 1952 3P, file: Organizers Hansen.

87 "Membership of Pulp, Sulphite and Paper Mill Workers by Region Based on Per Capita Payments, 1953 and 1959," UBC, Macphee Papers, vol. 2, file 3.

88 John P. Burke to Cy Harding, Woodfibre, 2 June 1955; Cy Harding to John P. Burke, 28 May 1955, IBPSPMW Records, Reel 1955 9P, file: Locals: Woodfibre.

89 Stuart Jamieson, "West Coast Strikes: An Objective Study of Industrial Relations in British Columbia, with Particular Emphasis on the Background to Labour Problems within the Pulp and Paper Industry," *Pulp and Paper Magazine of Canada* 59 (July 1958): 105-8, 217-18, 221; "Strike Bulletin No. 1," 14 November 1957; "Bulletin," 4 February 1958, UBC, Macphee Papers, vol. 1, file 7.

90 Angus Macphee to H.L. Hansen, 3 January 1958, UBC, Macphee Papers, vol. 1, file 12. See also E.P. O'Neal, Corresponding Secretary, Local 708, to John P. Burke, 30 December 1957; Local 708 Strike Committee to International Executive Board, 3 January 1958, UBC, Macphee Papers, vol. 1, file 12.

91 John P. Burke to B.J. Fortune, Local 708, 16 September 1961, UBC, Macphee Papers, vol. 1, file 9.

92 Angus Macphee to H.L. Hansen, 11 December 1957, UBC, Macphee Papers, vol. 1, file 12.

93 Harry Edward Graham, *The Paper Rebellion: Development and Upheaval in Pulp and Paper Unionism* (Iowa City: University of Iowa Press, 1970). For a Canadian perspective, see Pulp and Paper Workers Union, "Brief to the Enquiry Commission," 1967(?), 1-15, UBC, Macphee Papers, vol. 3, file 37.

94 Graham, *Paper Rebellion,* 74-76; "A Program of Militant Industrial Unionism," UBC, Macphee Papers, vol. 1, file 28.

95 Graham, *Paper Rebellion,* 76.
96 Braaten to Macphee, 2 March 1961, UBC, Macphee Papers, vol. 1, file 27.
97 George Klan, Chairman, Committee of Inquiry and A. Macphee, Secretary, to Secretaries All Local Unions, 1 March 1961; R.B. McCormick, Secretary-Treasurer of Pulp and Paper Mill Unions, Ocean Falls, to Angus Macphee, 20 March 1961, UBC, Macphee Papers, vol. 1, file 25.
98 Graham, *Paper Rebellion,* 83.
99 "Locals Now Affiliated with the RFMDA, 29 June 1961," UBC, Macphee Papers, vol. 1, file 28.
100 Minutes, British Columbia Board of Inquiry and the Northwest Committee for Union Justice, 15 April 1961, UBC, Macphee Papers, vol. 1, file 25.
101 *The United Worker,* 7 July 1955.
102 Angus Macphee to Ken [Luckhardt], 30 October 1975, UBC, Macphee Papers, vol. 5, file 1; "Angus Macphee," Interviewed by Duncan Stacey, July 1981, transcript, UBC, MacMillan Bloedel Papers (hereinafter MB Papers), vol. 132, file 55.
103 Elections British Columbia and the Legislative Library, *An Electoral History of British Columbia 1871-1986* (Victoria: Queen's Printer, 1988), 221-40; Tom Langford and Chris Frazer, "The Cold War and Working-Class Politics in the Coal Mining Communities of the Crowsnest Pass, 1945-1958," *Labour/Le Travail* 49 (Spring 2002): 86, n. 56, and 69; *Vancouver Sun,* 8 March 1952, 9 April 1952.
104 O. Braaten to Burt Wells, 18 August 1961, Wisconsin Historical Society, Rank and File Movement for Democratic Action Papers, Micro 26, Reel 2, file 10.
105 Elections BC and the Legislative Library, *An Electoral History of British Columbia,* 275-82.
106 Angus Macphee, "A Visit to Cuba," photocopy, UBC, Macphee Papers, Vol. 5, file 11; Thomas K. Finch, "My Views on the Cuban Revolution," photocopy, UBC, Macphee Papers, vol. 2, file 32.
107 Macphee to Harold Michel, 2 June 1961, UBC, Macphee Papers, vol. 1, file 28 [emphasis in original].
108 Braaten to Henry Rogers, 24 August 1961, ibid.
109 Draft of Brief for the Sargent Commission, 1966, UBC, Macphee Papers, vol. 3, file 37, pp. 12-13.
110 Angus Macphee to Henry Rodgers [sic], 23 August 1961, UBC, Macphee Papers, vol. 1, file 28.
111 J.H. West to John P. Burke, 11 February 1963, UBC, Macphee Papers, vol. 1, file 9. Orville Braaten played an important role in the creation of the Columbia River for Canada Committee in 1962 and served as its chair.
112 Rick Salutin, *Kent Rowley, the Organizer: A Canadian Union Life* (Toronto: James Lorimer, 1980), 130.
113 Graham, *Paper Rebellion,* 154-55.
114 John P. Burke to J.H. West, Local 708, 2 April 1963, UBC, Macphee Papers, vol. 1, file 9.
115 H.L. Hansen to D.W. Coton, Registrar, Labour Relations Board, Victoria, 7 September 1960; John P. Burke to Al E. Brown, Vice-President and Regional Director, United Papermakers and Paperworkers, 10 October 1960; Paul L. Phillips, President, United Papermakers and Paperworkers, to Claude Jodoin, President, CCL, 12 February 1962; John P. Burke to Members of the Executive Board, 19 April 1962; R. Biasutti, Secretary, IBPSPMW Local 76, Powell River, to Claude Jodoin, President, CLC, 3 July 1962, LAC, MG28-I 103, Reel H-19, file J-124.
116 Submission of PPWC Executive, Local 9, to Leslie Petersen(?), Minister of Labour, 1967, UBC, Macphee Papers, vol. 4, file 6; Minutes, Executive Board, PPWC, 11-18 November 1967, UBC, Macphee Papers, vol. 3, file 15; Minutes, Executive Board, PPWC, 6 February 1968, UBC, Macphee Papers, vol. 3, file 16; *Citizen,* 17 November 1967.
117 The IBPSPMW went to court to recover the money that was transferred to the PPWC society. In May 1967, the courts ordered the PPWC to return the misappropriated $40,000 to Local 495.

118   On this date, the LRB also disallowed applications for the Port Mellon and Elk Falls mills because the PPWC did not have enough votes, as well as the Prince George mill.

119   Radio Transcript, 9 August 1966, UBC, Macphee Papers, vol. 2, file 12.

120   Thomas R. Berger to E. Rowntree, Registrar, Labour Relations Board, 26 August 1966; E. Rowntree to John N. Laxton, Solicitor, 17 October 1966, UBC, Macphee Papers, vol. 3, file 26.

121   J.V. Clyne to A.C. Kennedy, 29 August 1966, UBC, MB Papers, vol. 703, file 11.

122   Syd Thompson to Ray C. Haynes, BCFL, 17 April 1967, UBC, BCFL Papers, vol. 9, file 6.

123   Minutes, Executive Board, PPWC, 24 August 1966, UBC, Macphee Papers, vol. 3, file 12; E. Rowntree, Registrar, Labour Relations Board, to PPWC, 8 October 1969, Macphee Papers, vol. 3, file 23.

124   Prospective Northwood employees were screened to ensure that they were not associated with the PPWC. Henry G. Rhodes, Ass't Director of Organization, CLC, "Pulp Sulphite Situation in BC," 1967(?), LAC, MG28-I 103, Reel H-492, file 10.

125   William H. Burnell, Acting President-Secretary, IBPSPMW, to the Members of the International Executive Board et al., 21 November 1963, LAC, MG28-I 103, Reel H-124, file 3.

126   "Report of the Canadian Identity Committee," 1967(?), UBC, BCFL Papers, vol. 13, file 6.

127   *The Barker* 8 (January 1967): 1; *Western Canadian Lumber Worker,* March 1967 (2nd issue).

128   *The Barker* 7 (April 1967): 1; *Western Pulp and Paper Worker* (May 1967): 1; *Western Canadian Woodworker,* May 1967 (2nd issue), 1; O. Braaten, President, PPWC, to All Local Unions in BC, 31 August 1967, UBC, Trade Union Research Bureau Papers (hereinafter TURB Papers), vol. 48, file 8a.

129   *Western Canadian Lumber Worker* 38 (August 1970): 11.

130   Ibid., 39 (November 1971): 1; 38 (February 1971): 1; 39 (May 1971): 1.

131   IWA, "Report on the PPWC Raid at Somass, 26 June 1973" [emphasis in original], UBC, BCFL Papers, vol. 35, file 4. For disputes between the IWA and the IBPSPMW in the 1960s and early 1970s, see *Western Canadian Lumber Worker,* January 1964 (2nd issue), 11; 39 (November 1971); R.C. Haynes, Secretary-Treasurer, BCFL, to K.G. Wilson, Recording Secretary, IBPSPMW Local 592, Port Alberni, 17 January 1968, and 28 IBPSPMW and UPP BC executive members to Secretary-Treasurer, CLC, and Secretary-Treasurer, BCFL, 24 July 1968, UBC, BCFL Papers, vol. 13, file 6; *The Barker* 10 (June 1969): 2; "Organization Report 1972," IWA-Western Regional Council No. 1, UBC, BCFL Papers, vol. 32, file 12.

132   *The Barker* 17 (September 1975): 1.

133   R.C. Haynes, Secretary-Treasurer, BCFL, to Syd Thompson, President, IWA Local 1-217, 11 May 1967, UBC, BCFL Papers, vol. 7, file 36.

134   R.C. Haynes to Syd Thompson, 26 May 1967; D.G. Evans to R. Haynes, 24 May 1967, UBC, BCFL Papers, vol. 7, file 36.

135   Donald MacDonald, Secretary-Treasurer, CLC, to All CLC Locals in BC, 5 September 1967, ibid.

136   BCFL, Press Release, 8 September 1967, ibid.; *Western Canadian Lumber Worker* 36 (September 1967): 6-8.

137   Angus Macphee to Whom It May Concern, 17 November 1966, UBC, Macphee Papers, vol. 3, file 35.

138   R.A. Sargent, "Report of the Commission of Inquiry into Invasion of Privacy," 9 August 1967, 10, UBC, Macphee Papers, vol. 4, file 1. Bugging was not a new tactic. In 1939 leftists in the IWA used it to get evidence on collusion between American IWA union officials and business representatives: Lembcke and Tattam, *One Union in Wood,* 65.

139   John P. Burke to Angus Macphee, 10 March 1959, UBC, Macphee Papers, vol. 2, file 19.

Chapter 5: The Daily Grind

1 H.L. Hansen to John P. Burke, 27 November 1940, Wisconsin Historical Society, Madison, International Brotherhood of Pulp, Sulphite and Paper Mill Workers Records, 1906-1957 (hereinafter IBPSPMW Records), Reel 1940 5P, file: Locals: Powell River.

2 A. Lockwood, Financial-Secretary, Local 297, to John P. Burke, 11 April 1955; 15 October 1955, IBPSPMW Records, Reel 1955 5P, file: Locals: Port Mellon.

3 John P. Burke to A.W. McCandlish, Local 695, 24 February 1956, IBPSPMW Records, Reel 1956 7P, file: Locals: Harmac.

4 John P. Burke to J.W. Terry, International Representative, Vancouver, 6 June 1955, IBPSPMW Records, Reel 1955 3P, file: Organizers: Green.

5 *British Columbia Lumberman* (hereinafter *BCL*) 39 (March 1954): 112-13.

6 H.L. Hansen, Recording Secretary Local 76, to John P. Burke, 8 July 1937; Hansen to Burke, 3 September 1937, IBPSPMW Records, Reel 1937 5P, file: Locals: Powell River.

7 H.L. Hansen to John P. Burke, 31 January 1952, IBPSPMW Records, Reel 1952 3P, file: Organizers: Hansen.

8 *The Truck Logger* (hereinafter *TL*) (September 1948): 12.

9 Minutes, Monthly Meeting of BC Loggers' Association, 23 June 1959, University of British Columbia, The Library, Special Collections (hereinafter UBC), Council of Forest Industries Papers (hereinafter COFI Papers), vol. 39, file 5; *TL* (August 1957): 21.

10 *Western Canadian Lumber Worker* 40 (October 1972): 10.

11 John P. Burke to H.L. Hansen, 10 February 1953, IBPSPMW Records, Reel 1953 3P, file: Organizers: Hansen. For an IWA statement against overtime, see J. Stewart Alsbury to C.H. Webb, Financial Secretary, Local 1-424, 26 June 1952, UBC, International Woodworkers of America, Western Canadian Regional Council No. 1 Papers (hereinafter IWA Papers), Roll 10, file: J. Stewart Alsbury – President – Locals – Correspondence, 1952.

12 *Pulp and Paper Magazine* 62 (March 1961): 176.

13 E.M. Golley, Recording Secretary, Local 76, to R.M. Cooper, Resident Manager, Powell River Company, 15 February 1954, IBPSPMW Records, Reel 1954 3P, file: Organizers: Hansen.

14 "Strike Vote," 31 October and 1 November 1953, IBPSPMW Records, Reel 1953 3P, file: Organizers: Hansen.

15 "Summary of IWA Strike Vote, 1967," UBC, BC Federation of Labour Papers (hereinafter BCFL Papers), vol. 7, file 35.

16 H.L. Hansen, "Report for the Month of April," 1944, IBPSPMW Records, Reel 1944 2P, file: Organizers: Hansen.

17 *BCL* 38 (August 1954): 36.

18 S.G. Green to John P. Burke, 21 September 1953, IBPSPMW Records, Reel 1953 3P, file: Organizers: Green.

19 S.M. Hodgson, Financial Secretary, IWA Local 1-217, to George Mitchell, Secretary-Treasurer, IWA District Council No. 1, 27 February 1958, UBC, IWA Papers, Roll 44, file: Correspondence: Local 1-217, 1958.

20 Angus Macphee, Local 708, to J.P. Burke, 10 January 1957, IBPSPMW Records, Reel 1957 9P, file: Locals: Watson Island.

21 Minutes, British Columbia Plywoods Ltd., First Meeting of Employees Co-operative Committee, 16 August 1937, UBC, MacMillan Bloedel Papers (hereinafter MB Papers), vol. 73, file 68.

22 IWA, District Council No. 1, "Proceedings of the Emergency Conference Re Lumber Production and Collective Bargaining," 1 November 1942, UBC, Trade Union Research Bureau Papers (hereinafter TURB Papers), vol. 70, file 9.

23 John P. Burke to C.M. Mouat, 16 November 1942, IBPSPMW Records, Reel 1942 6P, file: Locals: Powell River.

24 Treasurer, Sorg Pulp Company and Local 297, Port Mellon, to Regional War Labour Board, 17 May 1943, IBPSPMW Records, Reel 1943 6P, file: Locals: Port Mellon; Summary of Meeting between Union and Powell River Company Officials, 20 March 1943, IBPSPMW Records, Reel 1943 6P, file: Local Unions: Powell River.

25 For a national perspective, see Peter S. McInnis, *Harnessing Labour Confrontation: Shaping the Postwar Settlement in Canada, 1943-1950* (Toronto: University of Toronto Press, 2002).

26 Richard Edwards, in a study of the workplace in the twentieth century, outlines three methods of control in industrial capitalism: simple control, where personal relationships such as loyalty and bullying by foremen and owners obtain "proper" worker behaviour; technical control, where control is embedded into the design of machines and the physical features of the operations; and bureaucratic control, where "control is embedded in the social and organizational structure of the firm and is built into job categories, work rules, promotion procedures, discipline, wage scales, definitions of responsibilities, and the like." Job evaluation fits into the last category: Richard Edwards, *Contested Terrain: The Transformation of the Workplace in the Twentieth Century* (New York: Basic Books, 1979), 131.

27 For a national perspective, see Tim Krywulak, "Inventing Labour Problems and Solutions: The Emergence of Human Resource Management in Canada, 1900-1945," *Journal of the Canadian Historical Association,* New Series, 15 (2004): 71-95.

28 Stevenson and Kellog, Ltd., Consulting Managing Engineering, Vancouver, "Job Evaluation Manual for Operational Hourly Paid Jobs in the Plywood Industry of British Columbia," September 1955, UBC, IWA Papers, Roll 29, file: Plywood, 1955.

29 See also Edwards, *Contested Terrain*, 138.

30 Minutes, Special Local Plywood Conference, 2 May 1959, UBC, IWA Papers, Roll 54, file: Local Union Correspondence, 1-217, 1959; Progress Reports on Job Evaluation, Plywood Industry of British Columbia, October to December 1955, UBC, IWA Papers, Roll 29, file: Plywood, 1955; Plywood Evaluation Breakdown for Lower Mainland Mills, April 1959, UBC, IWA Papers, Roll 55, file: General Plywoods, 1959.

31 *Western Pulp and Paper Worker* 1 (August 1956): 1; 1 (April 1957): 8; 3 (November 1958): 2; 9 (July 1964): 4.

32 *The Barker* 8 (October 1967): 8; 13 (March 1971): 5; *British Columbia Lumber Worker* (hereinafter *BCLW*), June 1959 (1st issue), 11; August 1959 (4th strike issue); *Western Canadian Lumber Worker,* April 1963 (2nd issue), 2.

33 Brother Fieber, "Eleventh Annual Convention Proceedings of Local 1-71, IWA, December 21 and 22, 1960," UBC, IWA Papers, vol. 3, file 2, p. 52.

34 *BCL* 54 (October 1970): 38.

35 Howell John Harris, *The Right to Manage: Industrial Relations Policies of American Business in the 1940s* (Madison: University of Wisconsin Press, 1982), 10.

36 For strike preparation, see C.A. Specht to J.V. Clyne, 24 November 1967; G.J. Towill to R.M. Bibbs, Inter-Office Memo, 19 March 1968, UBC, MB Papers, vol. 703, file 7; R.M. Bibbs to D.W. Timmis, 9 June 1971, UBC, MB Papers, vol. 807, file 23; R.W. Bonner to J.V. Clyne, Inter-Office Memo, 21 March 1972, UBC, MB Papers, vol. 349, file 18.

37 Gordon Hak, "Red Wages: Communists and the 1934 Vancouver Island Loggers Strike," *Pacific Northwest Quarterly* 80 (July 1989): 86.

38 R.V. Stuart, Secretary-Manager, BC Loggers' Association, to R.J. Filberg, Comox Logging and Railway Company, 10 April 1935, Courtenay and District Museum (hereinafter CDM), Comox Logging and Railway Records (hereinafter CLR Records), vol. 8, file 8, pt. 2; British Columbia Loggers' Association, Annual Report of the Chairman – Board of Directors, 1936,

UBC, COFI Papers, vol. 39, file 1; BC Loggers' Association, "Report of the Publicity Committee for 1938," CDM, CLR Records, vol. 11, file 7.

39 "Comments by Paul E. Cooper," President of Pacific Mills, 18 July 1944, in Minutes, Directors Meeting, Pacific Mills, 25 July 1944, University of California (Berkeley), The Bancroft Library, Crown Zellerbach Corporation Records, (hereinafter Crown Zellerbach Records), vol. 128.

40 British Columbia Lumber Manufacturers Association, "Annual Report 1950," 7, UBC, COFI Papers, vol. 72, file 10.

41 Minutes, Executive Committee, Canadian Pulp and Paper Association, Western Division, 11 July 1956, UBC, COFI Papers, vol. 87, file 5.

42 *BCL* 37 (February 1953): 39.

43 Minutes, Monthly Meeting of BC Loggers Association, 27 August 1963; 24 September 1963, UBC, COFI Papers, vol. 40, file 1.

44 See, for example, Ben W. Crow and Associates, "Public Attitudes toward, and Images of, the Forest Industry in British Columbia: 1968 and Changes since 1965," conducted for the Council of Forest Industries, November 1968, UBC, MB Papers, vol. 115, file 4.

45 *TL* 26 (March 1970): 6; F.H. Moonen, Vice-President, Communications, COFI, to COFI Members, 12 September 1974, Campbell River Museum and Archives, Elk River Timber Company Records, 88-10, vol. 1, file 3.

46 Ken Drushka, *HR: A Biography of H.R. MacMillan* (Madeira Park, BC: Harbour Publishing, 1995), 11, 228-29, 235.

47 Ibid., 249.

48 *TL* (February 1949): 5.

49 H.R. MacMillan to George W. Allan, 30 May 1935, UBC, H.R. MacMillan Papers, vol. 3, file 5.

50 H.R. MacMillan to Henry J. Fuller, 22 June 1935, ibid.

51 *TL* (February 1949): 6.

52 H.R. MacMillan to George W. Allan, 6 March 1936, UBC, H.R. MacMillan Papers, vol. 4, file 4.

53 British Columbia Lumber and Shingle Manufacturers Association Annual Report, 1937, 34, UBC, COFI Papers, vol. 71, file 9.

54 British Columbia Loggers' Association, "Annual Report of the Chairman – Board of Directors, 1951," UBC, COFI Papers, vol. 39, file 2.

55 H.R. MacMillan to A.D. Purvis, President, Canadian Industries Limited, 4 May 1938, UBC, MB Papers, vol. 405, file 22; Ross Pendleton, Manager, Alberni Pacific Lumber Company, to H.R. MacMillan, 15 February 1947, UBC, MB Papers, vol. 412, file 22.

56 British Columbia Plywoods to Our Employees, 20 October 1936, UBC, MB Papers, vol. 73, file 75; British Columbia Plywoods, "Ballot for Mutual Benefit Fund – March 17, 1938," UBC, MB Papers, vol. 74, file 4; *BCL* 25 (March 1941): 32; 28 (November 1944): 29.

57 *BCL* 39 (May 1955): 10.

58 H. Thornley to Mr. Harrison, 25 July 1939; Hugh Thornley to C.W. Bolton, 27 July 1939, Library and Archives Canada (hereinafter LAC), RG27, Reel T3010, vol. 402, file 96.

59 Clippings, LAC, RG27, Reel T3022, vol. 416, file 78.

60 H.R. MacMillan to Justice Manson, 26 October 1939, UBC, H.R. MacMillan Papers, vol. 6, file 6.

61 "Proceedings of the Emergency Conference re Lumber Production and Collective Bargaining," IWA, District Council No. 1, 1 November 1942, UBC, Trade Union Research Bureau Papers (hereinafter TURB Papers), vol. 70, file 9.

62 "Local 1-80 Bulletin," 14 December 1949, UBC, IWA Papers, Roll 5, file: Local 1-80 Duncan 1948-49.

63 Ibid.
64 H.M. Lewis to H.L. Hansen, 25 November 1946, IBPSPMW Records, Reel 1946 3P, file: Organizers: Hansen.
65 Bert Hoffmeister, General Manager, MacMillan Industries Ltd. (Plywood Division), to Our Employees, 11 May 1946, UBC, MB Papers, vol. 415, file 28.
66 Exhibit 17, 1946 Negotiations, British Columbia Archives (hereinafter BCA), Add MS-1057, vol. 1, file 7.
67 John P. Burke to H.L. Hansen, 27 November 1943, IBPSPMW Records, Reel 1943 2P, file: Organizers: Hansen.
68 John P. Burke to H.L. Hansen, 3 November 1943, ibid. Burke's democratic vision for unions included distaste for business agents: "I do not like to see so many locals engaging business agents or talking about business agents. In a democratic labor union the work of running the union should be done by the elected officers of the local. Our union will lose its distinctive democratic character if members just content themselves with having their dues checked-off in order to keep good standing, and then place in the hands of some paid business agent the job of running the local union": John P. Burke to H.L. Hansen, 25 January 1952, IBPSPMW Records, Reel 1952 3P, file: Organizers: Hansen.
69 W.J. Van Dusen to Gladstone Murray, 11 March 1946, UBC, H.R. MacMillan Papers, vol. 9, file 5; Arthur Meighen to H.R. McMillan [sic], 18 August 1943, UBC, H.R. MacMillan Papers, vol. 8, file 3; Gladstone Murray to H.R. MacMillan, 1 March 1946; Samuel Rogers to H.R. MacMillan, 25 February 1946, UBC, H.R. MacMillan Papers, vol. 9, file 5. By 1952, Gladstone Murray was addressing MacMillan as "My dear H.R": G.M to H.R., 29 August 1952, UBC, MB Papers, vol. 417, file 18.
70 Drushka, *HR*, 303-4.
71 Fraser Institute, *Challenging Perceptions: Twenty-five Years of Influential Ideas, 1974-1999: A Retrospective* (Vancouver: The Institute, 1999), 5-6.
72 *BCL* 29 (January 1944): 26.
73 *TL* 20 (January 1964): 40.
74 Ibid., 20 (November 1964): 18-19.
75 Ibid., 20 (January 1964): 12 [emphasis in original].
76 Ibid., (December 1954): 38.
77 "Proceedings of the Fourteenth Annual Convention of the Truck Loggers' Association," Vancouver, 16, 17, 19 January 1957 (Vancouver: Truck Loggers' Association, April 1957), 16, Campbell River Museum and Archives, Wallace Baikie Collection, vol. 2, no file number.
78 F.R.S. Whiskin, Secretary-Manager, Truck Loggers' Association, to R.G. Williston, Minister of Lands, Forest, and Water Resources, 26 June 1962, Campbell River Museum and Archives, Wallace Baikie Collection, 89-1, vol. 2, file 3.
79 Campbell River and District Chamber of Commerce, Minutes, 30 April 1974, Campbell River Museum and Archives, Elk River Timber Company Records, 88-10, vol. 1, file 1.
80 *BCL* 42 (April 1958): 86.
81 For a taste of employer attitudes as expressed in the business journals, see *BCL* 38 (March 1954): 35; 42 (May 1958): 13; 43 (July 1959): 9; 45 (January 1961): 9; 50 (May 1966): 8; 54 (August 1970): 6-7; 54 (May 1970): 12; *TL* 24 (May 1968): 16-17; 28 (May 1972): 16 and 18.
82 Statement by P.J.G. Bentley, Executive Vice President, Canadian Forest Products Ltd., 11 January 1973, UBC, MB Papers, vol. 807, file 16.
83 *TL* 25 (June 1969): 8.
84 Ben W. Crow and Associates, Public Attitudes toward, and Images of, the Forest Industry in British Columbia: 1968 and Changes since 1965," conducted for the Council of Forest Industries, November 1968, UBC, MB Papers, vol. 115, file 4.

85 Colin Cameron, *Forestry: BC's Devastated Industry and Its Rehabilitation* (Vancouver: CCF [BC Section], n.d.), UBC, Colin Cameron Papers, vol. 1, file 4; Max Paulik, *Reforestation Policy of British Columbia: A Critical Analysis* (Vancouver: Foresta Publishers, 1948), UBC, TURB Papers, vol. 73, file 10c.

86 D. Gretchen Steeves to Colin Cameron, 16 April 1956, UBC, Colin Cameron Papers, vol. 1, file 1.

87 D. Gretchen Steeves to People [Colin Cameron], 1 February 1956, UBC, Cameron Papers, vol. 1, file 1.

88 Gordon Hak, "Populism and the 1952 Social Credit Breakthrough in British Columbia," *Canadian Historical Review* 85 (June 2004): 277-96.

89 Jeremy Wilson, *Talk and Log: Wilderness Politics in British Columbia, 1965-96* (Vancouver: UBC Press, 1998), 112-48.

90 Newspaper Clippings, LAC, RG27, Reel T3468, vol. 3639, file 75-611.

Chapter 6: Technology

1 See, for example, "The Search for Efficiency: Survey of New Techniques in Forestry, Logging and Milling," in *The British Columbia Forest Industries 1965-66 Yearbook* (Vancouver: Mitchell Press, 1965), C20-C25. In 1957 a union official commented on the comparatively stagnant nature of the shingle industry: "Down through the years we have seen many new pieces of machinery and equipment introduced in the forest products industry. There have been plenty of changes in the logging camps, new machinery in the sawmills and plywood plants, but very little, if any, in the shingle mills. Actually in shingle, with the exception of the deck and the introduction of the grooving machine and staining plants, the actual sawing and packing of shingles hasn't changed in 50 years": S.M. Hodgson, Financial Secretary, Local 1-217, to All Local Unions, 5 November 1957, University of British Columbia, The Library, Special Collections (hereinafter UBC), IWA Papers, Roll 40, file: Correspondence, Local 1-217, 1957.

2 For a fine history of coastal logging, see Ken Drushka, *Working in the Woods: A History of Logging on the West Coast* (Madeira Park, BC: Harbour Publishing, 1992).

3 Richard Rajala, *Clearcutting the Pacific Rain Forest: Production, Science, and Regulation* (Vancouver: UBC Press, 1998), 49; Harry Braverman, *Labor and Monopoly Capital: The Degradation of Work in the Twentieth Century* (New York: Monthly Review Press, 1974).

4 Ken Drushka and Hannu Konttinen, *Tracks in the Forest: The Evolution of Logging Machinery* (Helsinki: Timberjack Group, 1997), 168.

5 *British Columbia Lumberman* (hereinafter *BCL*) 51 (January 1967): 8 and 10.

6 *BCL* 54 (January 1970): 29.

7 *The Truck Logger* (hereinafter *TL*) 19 (October 1963): 3.

8 *Citizen,* 28 October 1926.

9 *TL* (February 1949): 38; (November 1959): 15; 24 (January 1968): 8; 23 (September 1967): 46; *BCL* 39 (January 1955): 12; 51 (January 1967): 60-61.

10 *BCL* 26 (March 1942): 19.

11 Ibid., 37 (December 1953): 30.

12 *TL* (November 1950): 21.

13 Ibid., (June 1957): 11.

14 Ibid., (November 1959): 16.

15 *Western Canadian Lumber Worker* 38 (February 1970): 11.

16 *TL* 20 (May 1964): 24.

17 Ibid., 24 (January 1968): 48.

18 Fort George Forest District, "Annual Report," 1926, British Columbia Archives (hereinafter BCA), GR-1441, B33401, file 027391, no. 1-3.

19 *BCL* 34 (October 1950): 42.

20 Ibid., 30 (February 1946): 86.
21 Minutes, Directors of BC Loggers' Association, 16 February 1937, UBC, Council of Forest Industries Papers (hereinafter COFI Papers), vol. 1, file 2. The BC Loggers' Association, it should be noted, had been considering power saw tests as early as 1933: R.V. Stuart, BC Loggers' Association, to R.J. Filberg, Comox Logging, 12 January 1933, Courtenay District Museum (hereinafter CDM), Comox Logging and Railway Records (hereinafter CLR Records), vol. 7, file 16.
22 *BCL* 30 (February 1946): 90. This article is also in *Pulp and Paper Magazine of Canada* (hereinafter *PPMC*) 47 (February 1946): 65-67.
23 *BC Lumber Worker* (hereinafter *BCLW*), 8 May 1939, 3.
24 *BCL* 30 (February 1946): 92.
25 Ibid., 30 (February 1946): 92.
26 *TL* (June 1948): 12.
27 Ibid., (June 1948): 13. A 1956 article noted similar positive features of the power saws. The author also commented that "relative production per man on power saws was almost double at the early stages. Today it has averaged out at more than four times the production of 'hand sets'": *BCL* 40 (August 1956): 20-21.
28 *TL* 24 (July 1968): 28-29; (June 1948): 13; *BCL* 46 (May 1962): 12-14.
29 *BCLW*, 31 December 1945, 2.
30 Minutes, Executive Board Meeting, IWA-CIO District Council No. 1, 19 February 1947, UBC, Harold-Pritchett – IWA District Council No. 1 Papers (hereinafter Pritchett-IWA Papers), vol. 4, file 13, pp. 2 and 3.
31 T. Poje, President, IWA Local 1-80, to George H. Mitchell, Secretary-Treasurer, IWA District Council No. 1, 1 August 1953, UBC, International Woodworkders of America, Western Canadian Regional Council No. 1 Papers (hereinafter IWA Papers), Roll 18, file: Fallers and Buckers, 1953.
32 J. Holst, Financial Secretary, Local 1-363, to G. Mitchell, Secretary-Treasurer, IWA District Council No. 1, 3 August 1953, UBC, IWA Papers, Roll 18, file: Fallers and Buckers, 1953.
33 *TL* 25 (January 1969): 60.
34 *BCL* 40 (February 1956): 28; 47 (January 1963): 56, 58 and 60.
35 H.W. Townsend, "How They Harvest the Big Wood in BC," *PPMC* 72 (November 1971): 26.
36 *TL* (June 1951): 12; *BCL* 40 (August 1956): 54-6; 49 (December 1965): 20-22 and 24.
37 *Western Canadian Lumber Worker*, June 1967 (1st issue), 5.
38 *BCL* 53 (October 1969): 34.
39 Drushka and Konttinen, *Tracks in the Forest*, 93-192. In 1972 operators in the Prince George District were experimenting with seven different machines, "aimed at stabilizing costs and offsetting a shortage of trained manpower": Prince George Forest District, "Management Annual Report, 1972," 7-8, The Exploration Place, Prince George, Northwood Pulp and Timber Records, vol. 17, file A994.10.2.18.4.2.
40 *TL* 25 (December 1969): 12-13.
41 "C.D. Orchard," Transcript of Recorded Interview by C.D. Orchard, Interview No. 42, 1960, UBC, Orchard Papers, 80.
42 British Columbia, Department of Lands, *Report of the Forest Branch, 1943* (Victoria: King's Printer, 1944), BB15; *Report of the Forest Branch, 1944* (Victoria: King's Printer, 1945), DD20; *PPMC* 45 (August 1944): 669-70.
43 *TL* 20 (December 1964): 30.
44 Ibid., 21 (August 1965): 26.
45 Prince George Forest District, "Management Annual Report, 1971," 7, The Exploration Place, Prince George, Northwood Pulp and Timber Records, vol. 17, file A994.10.2.18.4.3.

46 A.R.M. Stewart, "The Powell River Hydraulic Barkers and the New Wood Preparing Plant," *PPMC* 47 (November 1946): 95-102; *PPMC* 47 (October 1946): 171; 47 (August 1946): 124; 45 (August 1944): 704.

47 *Daily Colonist,* 3 February 1952.

48 K.G. Fensom, "Sawdust for Pulp Big Breakthrough for Sawmills," *BCL* 48 (September 1964): 52-53.

49 Ken Bernsohn, *Cutting Up the North: The History of the Forest Industry in the Northern Interior* (North Vancouver: Hancock House, 1982), 96-113.

50 *BCL* 40 (August 1956): 75.

51 Ibid., 46 (July 1962): 61.

52 Ibid., 54 (June 1970): 25-27. For more on technological change in sawmills, see British Columbia, Department of Industrial Development, Trade and Commerce, *The Sawmilling Industry of British Columbia* (Victoria: Queen's Printer, 1972), 15-16.

53 F.H. Fullerton, "Modernization at Woodfibre and Port Alice," *PPMC* 49 (January 1948): 74-75; Donald W. Emmerson, "Port Alberni's New Kraft Pulp Mill," *PPMC* 49 (February 1948): 39-51; "Five Years of Modernization and Restoration at Ocean Falls, BC," *PPMC* 51 (July 1950): 62-64.

54 *PPMC* 66 (July 1965): 99-102.

55 G.D. Eccott, "Computer Applications in MacMillan, Bloedel and Powell River Limited," 8 October 1965, UBC, MacMillan Bloedel Papers (hereinafter MB Papers), vol. 707, file 19, p. 1.

56 *BCL* 51 (December 1967): 27.

57 *The Barker* 5 (August 1964): 1.

58 *BCL* 28 (June 1944): 28-29; Transcript of Sessions of Royal Commission on Forestry, 1944-45, vol. 2, BCA, GR-520, vol. 3, exhibit 62, pp. 661-62.

59 *BCL* 53 (October 1969): 34-36. The study is by D.W. Ross, Research Branch, BC Department of Labour.

60 Comments by Paul E. Cooper, President of Pacific Mills, 18 July 1944, in Minutes, Directors Meeting, 25 July 1944, University of California (Berkeley), The Bancroft Library, Crown Zellerbach Corporate Records (hereinafter Crown Zellerbach Records), vol. 128.

61 "Data for 1966 Negotiations," 9 March 1966, IBPSPMW Local 695, UBC, Trade Union Research Bureau Papers (hereinafter TURB Papers), vol. 42, file 22.

62 R.M. Strachan, "Report of the Provincial Leader to the New Democratic Party Provincial Convention," 22 May 1965, Library and Archives Canada (hereinafter LAC), MG28-IV1, Reel H1594, vol. 25, file 07.

63 Joe Miyazawa to All Locals in BC, 18 January 1955, and inserts, UBC, IWA Papers, Roll 29, file: Plywood 1955.

64 Ibid.

65 *CCF Policy for British Columbia* (Vancouver: CCF BC-Yukon Section, 15 July 1955), LAC, MG28-IV1, vol. 317, file BC1956.

66 *BCLW,* March 1956 (1st issue), 4; March 1956 (2nd issue), 1-2.

67 Joe Morris, "Address on Automation," 1956, UBC, IWA Papers, Roll 39, file: Morris, Joe – Personal – 1956; *BCLW,* September 1956 (2nd issue), 2 and 10.

68 *BCLW,* July 1957 (2nd issue), 9.

69 "Officers' Report to Annual Meeting Local 1-424, IWA," 10 January 1960, UBC, IWA Papers, Roll 55, file: Local Correspondence, 1-424, 1960, p. 7.

70 "Officers' Report," Eleventh Annual Convention Proceedings of Local 1-71, IWA, 21 and 22 December 1960, UBC, IWA Papers, vol. 3, file 2, p. 5.

71 Andre LaMarche, Corresponding Secretary, Local 592, to John Sherman, Vice-President, IBPSPMW, 24 July 1956, Wisconsin Historical Society, Madison, International Brotherhood

of Pulp, Sulphite and Paper Mill Workers Records, 1906-1957 (hereinafter IBPSPMW Records), Reel 1956 8P, file: Locals: Port Alberni.

72 "Interim Report of the CLC Education Institute Seminar Held at Harrison Hot Springs Hotel – Nov. 9, 10, 11 – 1960," UBC, Angus Macphee Papers, vol. 2, file 31.

73 Orville Braaten to Angus Macphee, 14 November 1960, ibid.

74 *BCL* 46 (June 1962): 59.

75 *Western Canadian Lumber Worker* 29 (August 1962): 6.

76 Ibid., 3.

77 Ibid., November 1966 (1st issue), 7.

78 *The Barker*, 7/10 (November 1966), 3.

79 *Western Canadian Lumber Worker,* October 1962 (2nd issue), 4.

80 *BCL* 39 (April 1955): 84.

81 *TL* 18 (October 1962): 6.

82 J.O. Hemmingsen to C.A. Specht, Inter-Office Correspondence, 15 December 1964, UBC, MB Papers, vol. 703, file 1.

83 A.C. Kennedy to C.A. Specht, 10 December 1964, UBC, MB Papers, vol. 703, file 1. The IWA monitored what was going on in other sectors of the economy. In 1963 the BC Section of the Longshoremen and Warehousemen's Union signed an agreement with automation safeguards, and the next year the Oil, Chemical and Atomic Workers also negotiated an enviable contract with job security in the face of automation: *The Barker* 4 (August-September 1963): 3; *Western Canadian Lumber Worker,* November 1965 (2nd issue), 1.

84 H.V. Townsend to C.A. Specht, 21 December 1964, Inter-Office Correspondence, UBC, MB Papers, vol. 703, file 1.

85 Joe Miyazawa to All Locals in BC, 18 January 1955, and inserts, UBC, IWA Papers, Roll 29, file: Plywood 1955.

86 Ibid.

87 Joe Morris, "Address on Automation," 1956, UBC, IWA Papers, Roll 39, file: Morris, Joe – Personal – 1956; *BC Lumber Worker,* September 1956 (2nd issue), 2 and 10.

88 *Western Pulp and Paper Worker* 1 (May 1956): 11. For the perspective of the IBPSPMW, see John P. Burke and John J. McNiff, *Automation: Economic Implications and Impact upon Collective Bargaining* (n.p.: International Brotherhood of Pulp, Sulphite and Paper Mill Workers, 1964).

89 *CCF Policy for British Columbia* (Vancouver: CCF BC-Yukon Section, 15 July 1955), LAC, MG28-IV1, vol. 317, file BC1956.

90 *Western Canadian Lumber Worker,* October 1964 (1st issue), 12.

91 "Remarks of T.C. Douglas to IWA Convention, Portland, Oregon, September 1967," UBC, Vancouver and District Trades and Labour Council Papers, vol. 6, file 2.

92 Colin Cameron, "Notes on a New Policy for the New Democratic Party," 1964, LAC, MG28-IV1, vol. 428, file: C. Cameron.

93 "The 30 Hour Week: A Program for the General Strike," LAC, MG28-IV4, Reel H1594, vol. 25, file 25-08.

94 *Western Canadian Lumber Worker* 32 (July 1965): 1-12.

95 The IWA was hardly unique. See Pam Roper, "The Limits of *Laissez-innover:* Canada's Automation Controversy, 1955-1969," *Journal of Canadian Studies* 34 (Autumn 1999): 87-105.

96 *BCL* 49 (November 1965): 12. See also 50 (March 1966): 8.

97 *Western Canadian Lumber Worker,* September 1964 (1st issue), 8.

98 Leslie Ehrlich and Bob Russell, "Employment Security and Job Loss: Lessons from Canada's National Railways, 1956-1995," *Labour/Le Travail* 51 (Spring 2003): 115-52.

99 John L. Fryer, "Collective Bargaining and Automation," Address to BC Federation of Labour Conference on Automation, 18 June 1966, LAC, MG28-IV1, vol. 578, file 29.

Chapter 7: Companies and Unions Meet the Environmental Movement

1 For a discussion of the interaction of industry representatives, government officials, and scientists in the politics of BC fisheries science in the 1950s, see Matthew D. Evenden, *Fish versus Power: An Environmental History of the Fraser River* (Cambridge: Cambridge University Press, 2004), 231-66.

2 H.R. MacMillan to Dick [Orchard], 13 January 1955, British Columbia Archives (hereinafter BCA), Add. MS-0840, vol. 6, file 115.

3 Dennis Guest, *The Emergence of Social Security in Canada* (Vancouver: UBC Press, 1980), 101-201.

4 Jeremy Wilson, *Talk and Log: Wilderness Politics in British Columbia, 1965-96* (Vancouver: UBC Press, 1998).

5 See "The Decline and Rise of Working-Class Identity," in Stanley Aronowitz, *The Politics of Identity: Class, Culture, Social Movements* (New York and London: Routledge, 1992), 10-75.

6 For a general historical introduction to the North American environmental movement, see Samuel P. Hays, *A History of Environmental Politics since 1945* (Pittsburgh: University of Pittsburgh Press, 2000); Hays, "From Conservation to Environment: Environmental Politics in the United States since World War II," *Environmental Review* 6 (1982): 14-41.

7 For the social and ideological context for 1960s environmentalism in Vancouver, see Rex Weyler, *Greenpeace: How a Group of Ecologists, Journalists and Visionaries Changed the World* (Vancouver: Raincoast Books, 2004); Frank Zelko, "Making Greenpeace: The Development of Direct Action Environmentalism in British Columbia," *BC Studies* 142/143 (Summer/Autumn 2004): 197-239. SPEC members were not consistent in rendering the name of their organization, sometimes referring to it as the Scientific Pollution and Environmental Control Society and Society Promoting Environmental Conservation, as well as in other ways: Wilson, *Talk and Log,* 415.

8 Robin Harger and Derrick Mallard, "Origin of the Society for Pollution & Environmental Control," January 1970, University of Victoria, Archives and Special Collections (hereinafter UVic), Derrick Mallard Papers (hereinafter Mallard Papers), vol. 5, file 54.

9 "SPEC ... A Year and Six Months to Where?" UVic, Mallard Papers, vol. 5, file 31, p. 2.

10 "SPEC Constitutional Convention, November 7-8, 1970," University of British Columbia, The Library, Special Collections Division (hereinafter UBC), Roderick Haig-Brown Collection, vol. 112, file 7.

11 Michael P. Cohen, *The History of the Sierra Club, 1892-1970* (San Francisco: Sierra Club Books, 1988).

12 Sierra Club, Pacific Northwest Chapter, Membership Report, 20 November 1971, UVic, Katy Madsen Fonds, vol. 2, file 21; *The Sierra Report* 13 (Winter 1994-95): 4-5; Constitution of Sierra Club of British Columbia, 6 November 1969, UVic, Sierra Club of BC Fonds (hereinafter SCBC Fonds), 95-036, vol. 2, file 1.

13 Minutes, Sierra Club, Victoria, Executive, 10 March [1971?], UVic, Sierra Club of Western Canada Fonds, 95-036, vol. 7, file 1/1.

14 Dave Corkran, Leader, Tweedsmuir Wilderness Survey, to Jim Bohlen, 25 May 1971; Dave Corkran to Ken Farquharson, 18 March 1971, UVic, SCBC Fonds, vol. 2, file 13.

15 Ken Farquharson to Lawrence Rockefeller, New York, 19 September 1972, UVic, SCBC Fonds, vol. 2, file 11.

16 Derrick Mallard to Robert Allan, Cornwall, England, 6 July 1973, UVic, Mallard Papers, vol. 2, file 2.

17 BCA, Add MS-0862, vol. 4, file 6.

18 Lois Boyce, Executive Director, British Columbia Environmental Council, to Ray Haynes, BC Federation of Labour, 3 April 1973, UBC, BC Federation of Labour Papers (hereinafter BCFL Papers), vol. 38, file 14.

19 J.P. Kimmins, "Forest Ecology: The Biological Basis for the Management of Renewable Forest Resources," *Forestry Chronicle* 49 (February 1973): 25.

20 Ibid.

21 A.H. Vyes, Chairman, Vancouver Island Section, Canadian Institute of Forestry, to Dr. J.P. Kimmins, 15 August 1972; Vyse to Kimmins, 21 August 1972, BCA, Add MS-0862, vol. 6, file 6; Course Outline, "The Ecology of Forestry," by Dr. J.P. Kimmins, 1973, BCA, Add MS-0862, vol. 5, file 1.

22 J.P. Kimmins, "The Ecology of Forestry: The Ecological Role of Man, the Forester, in Forest Ecosystems," *Forestry Chronicle* 48 (December 1972): 301-7; Kimmins, "The Renewability of Natural Resources: Implications for Forest Management," *Journal of Forestry* 71 (May 1973): 290-92; Kimmins, "Sustained Yield, Timber Mining, and the Concept of Ecological Rotation: A British Columbian View," *Forestry Chronicle* 50 (February 1974): 27-31.

23 *The Truck Logger* (hereinafter *TL*) 26 (September-October 1970): 19.

24 In the mid-1960s, a group at the University of Victoria called Enqual met to discuss and critique resource issues and policies. A biologist was the main organizer. Proceedings, Enqual (BC Resources Discussion Group), 1 February 1965, UBC, Haig-Brown Collection, vol. 79, file 7; M.A.M. Bell to Mr. Haig-Brown, 19 December 1966, UBC, Haig-Brown Collection, vol. 79, file 2.

25 *TL* 26 (September-October 1970): 19.

26 Zelko, "Making Greenpeace," 220.

27 "Personal Resumes," UVic, Katy Madsen Fonds, vol. 1, file 1.

28 UVic, Emlen Littell Fonds, vol. 1.

29 Gordon Hak, *Turning Trees into Dollars: The British Columbia Coastal Lumber Industry, 1858-1913* (Toronto: University of Toronto Press, 2000), 80-94.

30 Associated Boards of Trade of Vancouver Island to Premier Tolmie, 15 July 1933, BCA, GR-441, vol. 303, file 1.

31 Roderick Haig-Brown, Reforestation Committee, Associated Boards of Trade of Vancouver Island, to Mr. Mitchell, 10 December 1937, UBC, Haig-Brown Collection, vol. 148, file 4.

32 Minutes, Steering Committee, Chemical Barking Project, Canadian Pulp and Paper Association, 23 February 1954; 19 November 1953, UBC, Council of Forest Industry Papers (hereinafter COFI Papers), vol. 87, file 4; Minutes, Canadian Pulp and Paper Association, Western Canada Branch, 6 June 1951; 8 May 1952; 5 September 1952, UBC, COFI Papers, vol. 87, file 3.

33 BC Loggers' Association, "Annual Report of the Chairman – Board of Directors, 1957," 7, UBC, COFI Papers, vol. 39, file 2.

34 Richard A. Rajala, "The Vernon Laboratory and Federal Entomology in British Columbia," *Journal of the Entomological Society of British Columbia* 98 (December 2001): 186.

35 BC Loggers' Association, "Annual Report of the Chairman – Board of Directors, 1959," 7, UBC, COFI Papers, vol. 39, file 3.

36 BC Loggers' Association, "Annual Report, 1965," 12, ibid.

37 Prentice Bloedel to Dr. R.E. Foerster, Director, Pacific Marine Biological Laboratory, Nanaimo, BC, 16 October 1942, UBC, MacMillan Bloedel Papers (hereinafter MB Papers), vol. 852, file 9.

38 Bloedel, Stewart & Welch, "Statement to the Public," 6 June 1949, UBC, MB Papers, vol. 852, file 9 [emphasis in original]; John P. Tully, *Oceanography and Prediction of Pulp Mill Pollution in Alberni Inlet*, Fisheries Research Board of Canada, Bulletin No. 83 (Ottawa: King's Printer, 1949), UBC, MB Papers, vol. 852, file 8.

39 Minutes, Executive Committee, Canadian Pulp and Paper Association, 19 March 1956; 11 April 1956; 29 May 1956, UBC, COFI Papers, vol. 87, file 4.

40 Alberni Valley Citizens' Committee on Pollution, "Submission ... to Honourable W.A.C. Bennett, Premier of the Province of British Columbia," February 1966, UVic, Port Alberni Pollution Campaign Collection, 1966-1970, file 19/20.
41 Colin S. Wilson, Chairman, Alberni Valley Citizens' Committee on Pollution, to Hon. Ray Williston, Minister of Resources, 21 May 1966; George A. McKnight, Chairman, Public Relations Committee, Alberni Valley Citizens' Committee on Pollution, to All Groups and Individuals in BC Who Are Interested in the Elimination of Control of All Forms of Pollution, 10 June 1966, UBC, Haig-Brown Collection, vol. 78, file 2.
42 Nigel Morgan to Nelson Clarke, Executive Secretary, CPC, 14 March 1966, Library and Archives Canada, MG28-IV4, Reel H1594, vol. 25, file 25-09.
43 *Pulp and Paper Magazine of Canada* (hereinafter *PPMC*) 68 (October 1967): 101.
44 *British Columbia Forest Industry Facts* 3 (December 1965): 2.
45 Minutes, General Meeting of the BC Loggers' Association, 29 November 1966, UBC, COFI Papers, vol. 40, file 2.
46 "Report to the Members' Council on Division Activities for the Period August 16th to September 19th, 1968, BC Lumber Manufacturers Association," UBC, COFI Papers, vol. 10, file 5.
47 *British Columbia Lumberman* (hereinafter *BCL*) 54 (September 1970): 11.
48 SPEC, "Brief Regarding the Status of the Forest Industry in the Province of British Columbia Canada," 24 July 1970, UVic, Mallard Papers, vol. 5, file 27.
49 Ibid., 4-5.
50 Ibid., 11-12.
51 *British Columbia Forest Industry Facts* 8 (August 1970): 2.
52 *TL* 26 (September-October 1970): 38; 26 (July-August 1970): 28-30, 40-41.
53 Robin Harger, Executive Vice President, SPEC, "The Development of SPEC: Position Paper," 1970(?), UVic, Mallard Papers, vol. 5, file 54.
54 SPEC, "Pulp Mill Pollution," 1972, UVic, Mallard Papers, vol. 5, file 29.
55 Minutes, Monthly Meeting of the BC Loggers' Association, 25 June 1957, UBC, COFI Papers, vol. 39, file 4.
56 Minutes, Monthly Meeting of the BC Loggers' Association, 22 December 1959, UBC, COFI Papers, vol. 39, file 5.
57 Minutes, Monthly Meeting of the BC Loggers' Association, 26 January 1960, ibid.
58 Roderick Haig-Brown, "The Crisis in Outdoor Recreation," speech given at seminar on parks and nature reserves in Toronto, 21 September 1960, UBC, Haig-Brown Collection, vol. 67, file 15.
59 F.S. McKinnon, Speech, Resources for Tomorrow Conference, 24 October 1961, UBC, International Woodworkers of America, Western Canadian Regional Council No. 1 Papers (hereinafter IWA Papers), Roll 66, file: Reports and Statistical Summary, 10-13.
60 *PPMC* 66 (September 1965): WR-395.
61 J.V. Clyne to J.O. Hemmingsen, 30 October 1970, UBC, MB Papers, vol. 718, file 11.
62 Minutes, Meeting re Mt. Arrowsmith Logging, MacMillan Bloedel Head Office, 29 April 1970; J.O. Hemminsen to A.P. McBean, 27 October 1970; J.V. Clyne to J.O. Hemmingsen, Inter-Office Memo, 12 November 1970; Hemmingsen to Clyne, 13 November 1970, UBC, MB Papers, vol. 18, file 11; G.L. Ainscough to F.H. Britton, Inter-Office Memo, 28 June 1972; "Agreement," October 1972, UBC, MB Papers, vol. 718, file 12; K.G. Farquharson, President, Sierra Club of BC, to John Hemmingsen, Executive Vice-President, Natural Resources, MacMillan Bloedel, 15 April 1971, UVic, SCBC Fonds, vol. 2, file 2/6.
63 Ian A. Barclay, President, BCFP, to Fellow Employees, 17 December 1971, UVic, SCBC Fonds, vol. 8, file 4/1.

64 Ric Careless to Jean Chretien, Ron Malis(?), John Nichols, and Dave Street, 3 July 1972, UVic, SCBC Fonds, vol. 8, file 4/2.
65 Sierra Club of BC, Press Release, 26 August 1972, ibid. This account of Nitinat draws on *British Columbia Forest Industry Facts* 9 (February 1971): 2-3; 9 (May 1971): 1-4; Ray Williston to Ric Careless, 15 April 1971; Lloyd Brooks, Acting Deputy Minister, Department of Recreation and Tourism, to Professor V.C. Brink, UBC, 1 October 1971, UVic, SCBC Fonds, vol. 8, file 4/1.
66 J.V. Clyne to P.M. Downes, Inter-Office Memo, 28 February 1972; G.L. Ainscough to W.E. Ryan, Inter-Office Memo (Subject: Sierra Club Position of Clear-Cutting & Forest Management), 19 April 1971, UBC, MB Papers, vol. 718, file 10; E.F. Campbell to P.M. Downes, Inter-Office Memo, 21 April 1971, "Introduction to MacMillan Bloedel Land Use Policy," 1971(?), UBC, MB Papers, vol. 718, file 8.
67 *BC Forest Industry Facts* 10 (July 1973).
68 "An Initial Survey of Forestry and Logging Practices on Vancouver Island, British Columbia, Canada," UVic, SCBC Fonds, vol. 2, f. Forest Old Growth, file 6.
69 Bill Conway to Brock Evans, 9 November 1972, UVic, SCBC Fonds, 95-029, vol. 2, f. Forest Old Growth, file 6.
70 Minutes, Executive Committee of the Chamber of Forests, 25 June 1947; "Document of Foundation," 7 May 1947, UBC, Trade Union Research Bureau Papers (hereinafter TURB Papers), vol. 73, file 10c.
71 W.F. Allen, President, Local 1-85, to Joe Morris, President, District Council No. 1, 9 January 1957 (1958?); British Columbia Research Council to District Council No. 1, IWA, 9 December 1957, UBC, IWA Papers, Roll 44, file: Correspondence – Local 1-85, 1958.
72 Ken Farquharson to Lawrence Rockefeller, 19 September 1972, SCBC Fonds, UVic, 95-036, vol. 2, file 11. For a class-analysis perspective on Greenpeace, see John-Henry Harter, "Environmental Justice for Whom? Class, New Social Movements, and the Environment: A Case Study of Greenpeace Canada, 1971-2000," *Labour/Le Travail* 54 (Fall 2004): 83-119.
73 "SPEC ... A Year and Six Months to Where?" 1970, UVic, Mallard Papers, vol. 5, file 31.
74 Jim [Currie?] to Emlen Littell, 12 August 1970(?), UVic, Emlen Littell Fonds, vol. 1, file 16.
75 The Natural Resources Committee, BC Federation of Labour, "Destination Devastation? A Report on Pollution and the Destruction of British Columbia's Natural Environment," 1969, UBC, Vancouver and District Trades and Labour Council Papers, vol. 13, file 36.
76 Derrick Mallard , Executive Director, SPEC, to C.P. Neale, Vancouver and District Labour Council, 6 August 1971, SPEC, "Labour Project, 1973-74," UBC, Vancouver and District Trades and Labour Council Papers, vol. 14, file 15; "Policy Statements," PPWC, 8th Annual Convention, 1970, UBC, Angus Macphee Papers, vol. 3, file 18.
77 *Western Canadian Lumber Worker* 38 (February 1970): 12; 37 (November 1969): 9.
78 Sierra Club of Canada, "Brief on Streambank Logging," 17 April 1973, UVic, Sierra Club of Western Canada Fonds, vol. 2, file 2/11.
79 Phyllis (Boyce?) to Ray Haynes, 30 June 1972, UBC, BCFL Papers, vol. 38, file 14.
80 Osmo Lahti, Rosaleen Ross, and Bruce Yorke, "Report of Special Commission to BC Provincial Committee February 24, 1967," LAC, MG28-IV4, H1543, vol. 24, file 24-43.
81 A study of BC environmental activists in the 1990s concludes that while environmentalists were not totally independent of conventional left/right politics, they were motivated by notions of radical democracy, giving more prominence to communities and individuals in policy making rather than wealth redistribution or egalitarianism: Debra J. Salazar and Donald K. Alper, "Beyond the Politics of Left and Right: Beliefs and Values of Environmental Activists in British Columbia," *BC Studies* 121 (Spring 1999): 5-34; Salazar and Alper, "Reconciling Environmentalism and the Left: Perspectives on Democracy and Social Justice in British Columbia's Environmental Movement," *Canadian Journal of Political Science* 35

(September 2002): 527-66. For the argument that environmentalism is a coherent, self-standing ideology in the same way as conservatism, liberalism, and socialism, neither left nor right on the political spectrum, see Robert C. Paehlke, *Environmentalism and the Future of Progressive Politics* (New Haven, CT: Yale University Press, 1989).

82 "SPEC Constitutional Convention, November 7-8, 1970," UBC, Haig-Brown Collection, vol. 112, file 7, p. 2; CHQM Editorial, 19 April 1971, transcript, UVic, Mallard Papers, vol. 5, file 54; Phyllis Boyce (?) to Ray Haynes, 30 June 1972, UBC, BCFL Papers, vol. 38, file 14.

83 "Newspaper Clipping," n.d., UVic, Emlen Littell Fonds, vol. 1, file 16.

84 Derrick Mallard to Robert Allan, 6 July 1973, UVic, Mallard Papers, vol. 2, file 2.

85 Gwen Mallard, "Notes," 1972; Gwen Mallard, "Gwen's Report," 1972, UVic, Mallard Papers, vol. 5, file 54.

86 Derrick Mallard to Robert Allan, 6 July 1973, UVic, Mallard Papers, vol. 2, file 2.

87 *Western Canadian Lumber Worker* 36 (December 1968): 7.

88 For a good discussion of environmentalists and workers in northern Ontario, see Thomas Dunk, "Talking about Trees: Environment and Society in Forest Workers' Culture," *Canadian Review of Sociology and Anthropology* 31 (February 1994): 14-34.

89 *British Columbia Lumberman* 50 (July 1968): 8.

90 Wilson, *Talk and Log*, xvii.

Conclusion

1 R. Jeremy Wilson, "The Impact of Communications Developments on British Columbia Electoral Patterns, 1903-1975," *Canadian Journal of Political Science* 13 (September 1980): 509-35.

2 The economic, social, and political unity imposed on the province at mid-century may have been only temporary. Studies argue that the differences between the Coast and the Interior are growing. See H. Craig Davis, "Is the Metropolitan Vancouver Economy Uncoupling from the Rest of the Province?" *BC Studies* 98 (Summer 1993): 3-19; H. Craig Davis and Thomas A. Hutton, "The Two Economies of British Columbia," *BC Studies* 82 (Summer 1989): 3-15; Thomas A. Hutton, "The Innisian Core-Periphery Revisited: Vancouver's Changing Relationship with British Columbia's Staple Economy," *BC Studies* 113 (Spring 1997): 69-100.

3 In the late 1960s and 1970s, when nationalism across Canada was at its height, the BC pulp and paper locals that had remained loyal to the international, in concert with members in other parts of Canada, peacefully seceded from their American parent, establishing the Canadian Paperworkers Union in 1974. The Canadian IWA became an independent Canadian union in 1986, but returned to the international fold in 2004, when it became a division within the United Steelworkers of America. For the first part of this story, see Jack Munro and Jane O'Hara, *Union Jack: Labour Leader Jack Munro* (Vancouver: Douglas and McIntyre, 1988), 176-82; Marcus R. Widenor, "International Unionism in Retreat: The Dissolution of the International Woodworkers of America," in *Labour Gains, Labour Pains: Fifty Years of PC 1003*, ed. Cy Gonick, Paul Phillips, and Jesse Vorst (Winnipeg/Halifax: Society for Socialist Studies/Fernwood Publishing, 1995), 285-305. By the 1970s, the reach of nationalist sentiment was wide. In 1971 Vancouver members of the Sierra Club complained that their dues were going to San Francisco and a special committee was struck to consider the relations between the BC organization and its parent: Executive Minutes, Sierra Club, Victoria, 10 March 1971(?), University of Victoria, Archives and Special Collections (hereinafter UVic), Sierra Club of Western Canada Fonds, vol. 7, file 1/1; Sierra Club of British Columbia, "Newsletter," September 1971, UVic, Sierra Club of Western Canada Fonds, vol. 3; David W. Harris to John Myers and John R. Laing, 22 January 1974; Paul Swatek to Dick Searle, Dues Allocation Study Committee, 30 September 1973, UVic, Sierra Club of British Columbia Fonds, vol. 1, file JB11; Joe Fontaine to Jim Bonfanti et al., 23 December 1981; "Agreement between

the Sierra Club, the Sierra Club of Alberta, the Sierra Club of British Columbia, the Sierra Club of Ontario, the Sierra Club of Western Canada, and the Sierra Club of Ontario Foundation," Fifth Draft, August 1982, University of California (Berkeley), The Bancroft Library, Sierra Club International Program Records, Add. Mss. 71/290c, vol. 12, file 13 and vols. 12 to 15.

4 K.J. Bennett, Vice-President, FIR, to Wm. L.B. Chambers, Elk River Timber Company, 15 March 1976, Campbell River Museum and Archives, Elk River Timber Company Records, vol. 2, file 13.

5 Unions, of course, did not completely abandon social activism in the postwar era. See Alvin Finkel, "Trade Unions and the Welfare State in Canada, 1945-90," in *Labour Gains, Labour Pains*, 59-77.

6 E.G. Fisher, "Strike Activity and Wildcat Strikes in British Columbia: 1945-1975," *Relations industrielles/Industrial Relations* 37 (1982): 284 and 290.

7 Wildcats made union leaders uncomfortable. In 1952, H.L. Hansen, a representative of the International Brotherhood of Pulp, Sulphite and Paper Mill Workers, voiced his disapproval regarding a prospective wildcat at Powell River: "It is my humble opinion that this would serve no useful purpose. It certainly would destroy any semblance of cooperation we have created with the Company in our Local and have a far-reaching effect that would make it difficult to determine the damage that would be created by a stoppage of work." Four years later, Hansen took a similar position during a wildcat that shut down the Prince Rupert pulp and paper mill: "Were it not for the gravity of the situation," he wrote, "I feel the company would be well advised to let the plant close down for a while and let our members sweat it out": H.L. Hansen to John P. Burke, 24 July 1952, Wisconsin Historical Society, Madison, International Brotherhood of Pulp, Sulphite and Paper Mill Workers Records, 1906-1957 (hereinafter IBPSMW Records), Reel 1952 3P, file: Organizers: Hansen; H.L. Hansen to John P. Burke, 30 July 1956, IBPSMW Records, Reel 1956 3P, file: Organizers: Hansen.

8 *British Columbia Lumberman* (hereinafter *BCL*) 55 (March 1971): 23-24.

9 Ibid., 56 (September 1972): 12.

10 Ibid., 40 (February 1956): 31.

11 Ibid., 56 (September 1972): 12.

12 Ibid., 54 (April 1970): 32-33; *The Truck Logger* (hereinafter *TL*) 36 (May-June 1970): 14.

13 *TL* 27 (January 1971): 14 and 17.

14 C.J. Towill, Labour Relations, to D.W. Timmis, Inter-Office Memo, 15 May 1973, MacMillan Bloedel, University of British Columbia, The Library, Special Collections Division (hereinafter UBC), MacMillan Bloedel Papers (hereinafter MB Papers), vol. 807, file 16; G.J. Towill to D.W. Timmis, Inter-Office Memo, 4 July 1973, UBC, MB Papers, vol. 807, file 20.

15 R.J. Whittle, Chairman, Executive Advisory Committee, FIR, to J.J. Munro, IWA, 7 December 1973, UBC, MB Papers, vol. 803, file 16.

16 *BCL* 59 (January 1975): 52.

17 *The Barker* 16 (September 1974): 1.

18 Canada, Department of Labour, *Strikes and Lockouts in Canada*, 1970-1979 (Ottawa: Queen's Printer, 1970-80).

19 Salaried employees and consumers also had a negative attitude towards MacMillan Bloedel according to the study: Goldfarb Consultants, "MacMillan Bloedel: The Hourly Employees' View," November 1978, UBC, MB Papers, vol. 114, file 11. For a study that offers a more positive view of worker attitudes, based on interviews carried out in 1971 with seventy-eight woods workers in the Northern Interior of BC, workers who had been with an employer for at least six months, see Philip L. Cottell, "Why Work in the Woods?" *PPMC* 75 (October 1974): 27-32.

20 Patricia Marchak, *Green Gold: The Forest Industry in British Columbia* (Vancouver: UBC Press, 1983), 264.

Bibliography

Primary Sources

BRITISH COLUMBIA ARCHIVES
British Columbia. Bureau of Economics and Statistics, Department of Trade and Industry.
    A Submission to the Royal Commission on Forestry, 1945. GR-181.
C.D. Orchard Papers. Add. MS-0840.
Canadian Institute of Forestry. Vancouver Island Section. Papers. Add. MS-0862.
Crown Lands. Correspondence Files. GR-1441.
Forest Branch. Report on Export Lumber Markets for Canadian Lumber compiled by L.R.
    Andrew. GR-1276.
Forest Branch. Reports Presented to the Forest Committee of the Legislative Committee of
    the Legislative Assembly by the Chief Forester, 1936-1943. GR-1242.
Gordon McGregor Sloan Papers. Add. MS-1057
IWA Local 1-367 Papers. Add. MS-0352
MacMillan Bloedel. Alberni Pacific Division. Schedule of Wages, 1930-1979. Add. MS-1641
Martin Allerdale Grainger Papers. Add. MS-0588
Pattullo Papers. Add. MS-0003
Premiers' Papers, 1917-1952. GR-1222.
Premiers' Records, 1883-1933. GR-441.
Royal Commission on Forestry, 1944-5, Proceedings. GR-520.
Western Forest Products Papers. Add. MS-1996

CAMPBELL RIVER MUSEUM AND ARCHIVES
Elk River Timber Company Records
Wallace Baikie Collection

COURTENAY AND DISTRICT MUSEUM
Comox Logging and Railway Company Records

THE EXPLORATION PLACE, PRINCE GEORGE
Northwood Pulp and Timber Records

LIBRARY AND ARCHIVES CANADA
Canadian Congress of Labour Papers. MG28-I 103.
Communist Party of Canada Fonds. MG28-IV4.
Co-operative Commonwealth Federation and New Democratic Party Fonds. MG28-IV1.
Strikes and Lockouts Files. RG27.
Wartime Prices and Trade Board sous-fonds. RG64.

MINISTRY OF FORESTS ARCHIVES, VICTORIA
Ministry of Forests Records, Land Files

UNIVERSITY OF BRITISH COLUMBIA, THE LIBRARY, SPECIAL COLLECTIONS DIVISION
Angus Macphee Papers
Arne Johnson Fonds
BC Federation of Labour Papers
Colin Cameron Papers
Council of Forest Industries Papers
Harold Pritchett-IWA District Council No. 1 Papers
H.R. MacMillan Papers
International Woodworkers of America, Western Regional Council No. 1 Papers
John Stanton Papers
MacMillan Bloedel Papers
Orchard Papers
Roderick Haig-Brown Collection
Seaboard Lumber Company Papers
Trade Union Research Bureau Papers
Vancouver and District Trades and Labour Council Papers

UNIVERSITY OF CALIFORNIA, BERKELEY, THE BANCROFT LIBRARY
Crown Zellerbach Corporation Records. BANC MSS 88/215 cp.
Sierra Club International Program Records. Add. Mss. 71/290c.
Sierra Club Papers.

UNIVERSITY OF VICTORIA, ARCHIVES AND SPECIAL COLLECTIONS
Derrick Mallard Fonds. 2001-034.
Emlen Littell Fonds. 95-033.
Katy Madsen Fonds. 97-044.
Port Alberni Pollution Campaign Collection, 1966-1970.
Ray Williston Fonds. 89-068.
Sierra Club of British Columbia Fonds, Jim Bonfonti Files. 96-090.
Sierra Club of British Columbia/Sierra Club of Western Canada Fonds. 95-029; 95-036; 95-046.

WISCONSIN HISTORICAL SOCIETY, MADISON
International Brotherhood of Pulp, Sulphite and Paper Mill Workers Records
Rank and File Movement for Democratic Action Papers

GOVERNMENT PUBLICATIONS
British Columbia. Department of Industrial Development, Trade, and Commerce. *The Sawmilling Industry of British Columbia.* Victoria: Queen's Printer, 1972.
–. Department of Industrial Development, Trade, and Commerce, Economics and Statistics Branch. *The Pulp and Paper Industry in British Columbia.* Victoria: Queen's Printer, 1970.
–. Department of Labour. *Annual Reports,* 1930-80.
–. Forest Branch/Service. *Annual Reports,* 1928-81.
Canada. Department of Labour. *Strikes and Lockouts in Canada,* 1956-79. Ottawa: Queen's Printer, 1957-80.
–. Dominion Bureau of Statistics. *Census,* 1931-81. Ottawa: King's/Queen's Printer, 1931-82.
Elections British Columbia and the Legislative Library. *An Electoral History of British Columbia 1871-1986.* Victoria: Queen's Printer, 1988.
Mulholland, F.D. *The Forest Resources of British Columbia.* Victoria: King's Printer, 1937.

Pearse, Peter H. *Timber Rights and Forest Policy.* Report of the Royal Commission on Forest Resources, 2 vols. Victoria: Queen's Printer, 1976.

Sloan, Gordon McGregor. *Report of the Commissioner Relating to the Forest Resources of British Columbia, 1945.* Victoria: King's Printer, 1945.

–. *Report of the Commissioner Relating to the Forest Resources of British Columbia, 1956.* Victoria: Queen's Printer, 1957.

Tully, John P. *Oceanography and Prediction of Pulp Mill Pollution in Alberni Inlet.* Fisheries Research Board of Canada, Bulletin No. 83. Ottawa: King's Printer, 1949.

TRADE PUBLICATIONS

BC Lumber Manufacturers Association. *Annual Reports,* 1966.

Council of Forest Industries of British Columbia. *Annual Reports,* 1970-87.

Emmerson, Donald W. "Port Alberni's New Kraft Pulp Mill." *Pulp and Paper Magazine of Canada* 49 (February 1948): 39-51.

Fensom, K.G. "Sawdust for Pulp Big Breakthrough for Sawmills." *British Columbia Lumberman* 48 (September 1964): 52-53.

Fullerton, F.H. "Modernization at Woodfibre and Port Alice." *Pulp and Paper Magazine of Canada* 49 (January 1948): 74-75.

Knapp, F. Malcolm. "Some Aspects of Forestry in British Columbia." *British Columbia Lumberman* 24 (April 1940): 26-27.

Mulholland, F.W. "Forest Conservation: What Is It?" *British Columbia Lumberman* 24 (January 1940): 22.

Pacific Mills Ltd. *Annual Report for the Year Ended April 30, 1950.*

Price Waterhouse. *The Forest Industry in British Columbia.* Vancouver: Price Waterhouse, 1975-93.

"The Search for Efficiency: Survey of New Techniques in Forestry, Logging and Milling." In *The British Columbia Forest Industries 1965-66 Yearbook.* Vancouver: Mitchell Press, 1965.

Smith, Sydney G. (Manager, Logging Department, Bloedel, Stewart & Welch). "Views of a Western Timber Operator on Practical Sustained Yield." *British Columbia Lumberman* 25 (April 1941): 38, 40.

Stewart, A.R.M. "The Powell River Hydraulic Barkers and the New Wood Preparing Plant." *Pulp and Paper Magazine of Canada* 47 (November 1946): 95-102.

Stuart, R.V. (Secretary-Manager of the British Columbia Loggers' Association). "Forest Industries Will Be Permanent in BC: An Analysis of the Present Situation and a Prediction for the Future." *British Columbia Lumberman* 25 (January 1941): 15-16.

NEWSPAPERS AND TRADE JOURNALS

The ABC British Columbia Lumber Trade Directory and Yearbook, Vancouver

Arrow Lake News, Nakusp

The Barker, Vancouver

Bloedel Bulletin, Bloedel and Menzies Bay

British Columbia Lumber Worker, Vancouver

British Columbia Forest Industry Facts, Vancouver

British Columbia Lumberman, Vancouver

Campbell River Courier

Cariboo Observer, Quesnel

Citizen, Prince George

The Commonwealth, Vancouver

Daily Colonist, Victoria

The Coast News, Gibsons
The Federationist, Vancouver
The Job Steward, Port Alberni
Labor Statesman, Vancouver
Nelson Daily News
Port Alberni News
Pulp and Paper Magazine of Canada
The Province, Vancouver
The Sierra Report
The Truck Logger, Vancouver
Vancouver Sun
The United Worker, Ocean Falls
West Coast Advocate, Port Alberni
Western Canadian Lumber Worker, Vancouver
Western Pulp and Paper Worker, Vancouver

Secondary Sources

Books

Abella, Irving. *Nationalism, Communism and Canadian Labour: The CIO, the Communist Party, and the Canadian Congress of Labour, 1935-1956.* Toronto: University of Toronto Press, 1973.

Aglietta, Michel. *A Theory of Capitalist Regulation: The US Experience.* Translated by David Fernbach. London: NLB, 1979.

Amin, Ash, ed. *Post-Fordism: A Reader.* Oxford: Blackwell Publishers, 1994.

Aronowitz, Stanley. *False Promises: The Shaping of American Working Class Consciousness.* New York: McGraw-Hill, 1973.

–. *The Politics of Identity: Class, Culture, Social Movements.* New York and London: Routledge, 1992.

Azzi, Stephen. *Walter Gordon and the Rise of Canadian Nationalism.* Montreal and Kingston, ON: McGill-Queen's University Press, 1999.

Baikie, Wallace, with Rosemary Phillips. *From Gypo to B.T.O.: The First Twenty Five Years of the Truck Loggers' Association of British Columbia.* Campbell River, BC: Ptarmigan Press, 1986.

Baptie, Sue, ed. *First Growth: The Story of British Columbia Forest Products Limited.* Vancouver: British Columbia Forest Products, 1975.

Barnes, Trevor J., and Roger Hayter, eds. *Troubles in the Rainforest: British Columbia's Forest Economy in Transition.* Canadian Western Geographical Series, vol. 33. Victoria: Western Geographical Press, 1997.

Beeching, William, and Phyllis Clarke, eds. *Yours in the Struggle: Reminiscences of Tim Buck.* Toronto: NC Press, 1977.

Bergren, Myrtle. *Tough Timber: The Loggers of BC – Their Story.* Vancouver: Elgin Publications, 1979 [original 1966].

Bernsohn, Ken. *Cutting Up the North: The History of the Forest Industry in the Northern Interior.* North Vancouver: Hancock House, 1982.

–. *Slabs, Scabs and Skidders: A History of the IWA in the Central Interior.* Prince George, BC: IWA Local 1-424, n.d.

Bernstein, Irving. *The Lean Years: A History of the American Worker, 1920-1933.* Baltimore: Penguin Books, 1966.

–. *The Turbulent Years: A History of the American Worker.* Boston: Houghton Mifflin, 1969.

Braverman, Harry. *Labor and Monopoly Capital: The Degradation of Work in the Twentieth Century.* New York: Monthly Review Press, 1974.

Breisach, Ernst. *On the Future of History: The Postmodernist Challenge and Its Aftermath.* Chicago: University of Chicago Press, 2003.

Burke, John P., and John J. McNiff. *Automation: Economic Implications and Impact upon Collective Bargaining.* N.p.: International Brotherhood of Pulp, Sulphite and Paper Mill Workers, 1964.

Butler, Judith, Ernesto Laclau, and Slavoj Žižek. *Contingency, Hegemony, Universality: Contemporary Dialogues on the Left.* London: Verso, 2000.

Clyne, J.V. *"What's Past Is Prologue": The History of MacMillan, Bloedel and Powell River Limited.* New York: The Newcomen Society in North America, 1965.

Cohen, Michael P. *The History of the Sierra Club, 1892-1970.* San Francisco: Sierra Club Books, 1988.

Crispo, John. *International Unionism: A Study in Canadian-American Relations.* Toronto: McGraw-Hill Canada, 1967.

Downie, Bryan M. *Relationships between Canadian-American Wage Settlements: An Empirical Study of Five Industries.* Kingston, ON: Industrial Relations Centre at Queen's University, 1970.

Drache, Daniel, ed. *Staples, Markets, and Cultural Change: Selected Essays/Harold A. Innis.* Montreal and Kingston, ON: McGill-Queen's University Press, 1995.

Drushka, Ken. *HR: A Biography of H.R. MacMillan.* Madeira Park, BC: Harbour Publishing, 1995.

–. *Lignum: A History.* Vancouver: Lignum, 2002.

–. *Stumped: The Forest Industry in Transition.* Vancouver: Douglas and McIntyre, 1985.

–. *Tie Hackers to Timber Harvesters: The History of Logging in British Columbia's Interior.* Madeira Park, BC: Harbour Publishing, 1998.

–. *Working in the Woods: A History of Logging on the West Coast.* Madeira Park, BC: Harbour Publishing, 1992.

Drushka, Ken, and Hannu Konttinen. *Tracks in the Forest: The Evolution of Logging Machinery.* Helsinki: Timberjack Group, 1997.

Dubofsky, Melvyn, and Warren Van Tyne. *John L. Lewis: A Biography.* New York: Quadrangle Books, 1977.

Dunk, Thomas W. *It's a Working Man's Town: Male Working-Class Culture in Northwestern Ontario.* Montreal and Kingston, ON: McGill-Queen's University Press, 1991.

Edwards, Richard. *Contested Terrain: The Transformation of the Workplace in the Twentieth Century.* New York: Basic Books, 1979.

Evenden, Matthew. *Fish versus Power: An Environmental History of the Fraser River.* Cambridge: Cambridge University Press, 2004.

F.L.C. Reed and Associates Ltd. *Selected Forest Industry Statistics of British Columbia,* rev. ed. Victoria: British Columbia Forest Service, 1975.

–. *The British Columbia Forest Industry: Its Direct and Indirect Impact on the Economy.* Victoria: Department of Lands, Forests and Water Resources, 1973.

Fones-Wolf, Elizabeth A. *Selling Free Enterprise: The Business Assault on Labor and Liberalism, 1945-1960.* Urbana and Chicago: University of Illinois Press, 1994.

Fraser Institute. *Challenging Perceptions: Twenty-five Years of Influential Ideas, 1974-1999: A Retrospective.* Vancouver: The Institute, 1999.

Freeman, Bill. *1005: Political Life in a Union Local.* Toronto: James Lorimer, 1982.

Fudge, Judy, and Eric Tucker. *Labour before the Law: The Regulation of Workers' Collective Action in Canada, 1900-1948.* Oxford: Oxford University Press, 2001.

Furniss, Elizabeth. *The Burden of History: Colonialism and the Frontier Myth in a Rural Canadian Community.* Vancouver: UBC Press, 1999.

Garner, Joe. *Never Under the Table: A Story of British Columbia's Forests and Government Mismanagement.* Nanaimo, BC: Cinnabar Press, 1991.

Garr, Allen. *Tough Guy: Bill Bennett and the Taking of British Columbia.* Toronto: Key Porter Books, 1985.

Gibson, Gordon, with Carol Renison. *Bull of the Woods: The Gordon Gibson Story.* Vancouver: Douglas and McIntyre, 1980.

Gillis, Peter R., and Thomas R. Roach. *Lost Initiatives: Canada's Forest Industries, Forest Policy and Forest Conservation.* Westport, CT: Greenwood, 1986.

Gonick, Cy, Paul Phillips, and Jesse Vorst, eds. *Labour Gains, Labour Pains: Fifty Years of PC 1003.* Winnipeg/Halifax: Society for Socialist Studies/Fernwood Publishing, 1995.

Gordon, David M., Richard Edwards, and Michael Reich. *Segmented Work, Divided Workers: The Historical Transformation of Labor in the United States.* Cambridge: Cambridge University Press, 1982.

Gorz, André. *Capitalism, Socialism, Ecology.* Translated by Chris Turner. London: Verso, 1994.

–. *Reclaiming Work: Beyond the Wage-Based Society.* Translated by Chris Turner. Cambridge: Polity Press, 1999.

Graham, Harry Edward. *The Paper Rebellion: Development and Upheaval in Pulp and Paper Unionism.* Iowa City: University of Iowa Press, 1977.

Gramsci, Antonio. *Selections from the Prison Notebooks of Antonio Gramsci.* Edited by Quintin Hoare and Geoffrey Nowell Smith. New York: International Publishers, 1971.

Granatstein, J.L. *The Politics of Survival: The Conservative Party of Canada, 1939-1945.* Toronto: University of Toronto Press, 1967.

–. *Yankee Go Home? Canadians and Anti-Americanism.* Toronto: HarperCollins, 1996.

Greening, W.E. *Paper Makers in Canada: A History of the Paper Makers Union in Canada.* Cornwall, ON: International Brotherhood of Paper Makers, 1952.

Guest, Dennis. *The Emergence of Social Security in Canada.* Vancouver: UBC Press, 1980.

Haig-Brown, Roderick. *Timber.* Corvallis: Oregon State University Press, 1993 [original 1942].

Hak, Gordon. *Turning Trees into Dollars: The British Columbia Coastal Lumber Industry, 1858-1913.* Toronto: University of Toronto Press, 2000.

Hardwick, Walter G. *Geography of the Forest Industry of Coastal British Columbia.* Vancouver: Tantalus Research, 1963.

Harris, John Howell. *The Right to Manage: Industrial Relations Policies of American Business in the 1940s.* Madison: University of Wisconsin Press, 1982.

Harvey, David. *Justice, Nature and the Geography of Difference.* Cambridge, MA: Blackwell, 1996.

–. *Spaces of Capital: Towards a Critical Geography.* New York: Routledge, 2001.

Hays, Samuel P. *Beauty, Health, and Permanence: Environmental Politics in the United States, 1955-1985.* Cambridge: Cambridge University Press, 1987.

–. *Conservation and the Gospel of Efficiency: The Progressive Conservation Movement, 1890-1920.* New York: Atheneum, 1969 [original 1959].

–. *A History of Environmental Politics since 1945.* Pittsburgh: University of Pittsburgh Press, 2000.

Hayter, Roger. *Flexible Crossroads: The Restructuring of British Columbia's Forest Economy.* Vancouver: UBC Press, 2000.

Heron, Craig. *The Canadian Labour Movement: A Brief History.* 2nd ed. Toronto: James Lorimer, 1996.

Heron, Craig, and Robert Storey, eds. *On the Job: Confronting the Labour Process in Canada.* Montreal, and Kingston, ON: McGill-Queen's University Press, 1986.

Hinde, John. *When Coal Was King: Ladysmith and the Coal-Mining Industry on Vancouver Island.* Vancouver: UBC Press, 2003.

Horowitz, Gad. *Canadian Labour in Politics.* Toronto: University of Toronto Press, 1968.

Jamieson, Stuart Marshall. *Times of Trouble: Labour Unrest and Industrial Conflict in Canada, 1900-66.* Task Force on Labour Relations, Study No. 22. Ottawa: Queen's Printer, 1968.

Kimmins, Hamish. *Balancing Act: Environmental Issues in Forestry.* 2nd ed. Vancouver: UBC Press, 1997.

Knox, Paul, and Philip Resnick, eds. *Essays in BC Political Economy.* Vancouver: New Star Books, 1974.

Kolko, Gabriel. *The Triumph of Conservatism: A Reinterpretation of American History, 1900-1916.* New York: Free Press, 1963.

Kovel, Joel. *The Enemy of Nature: The End of Capitalism or the End of the World?* Halifax and London, UK: Fernwood Publishing and Zed Books, 2002.

Krahn, Harvey J., and Graham S. Lowe. *Work, Industry, and Canadian Society.* 3rd ed. Toronto: International Thomson Publishing, 1998.

Laclau, Ernesto. *Politics and Ideology in Marxist Theory.* London: Verso, 1979.

Laclau, Ernesto, and Chantal Mouffe. *Hegemony and Socialist Strategy: Towards a Radical Democratic Politics.* Translated by Winston Moore and Paul Cammack. London: Verso, 1985.

Leier, Mark. *Red Flags and Red Tape: The Making of a Labour Bureaucracy.* Toronto: University of Toronto Press, 1995.

–. *Where the Fraser River Flows: The Industrial Workers of the World in British Columbia.* Vancouver: New Star Books, 1990.

Lembcke, Jerry, and William M. Tattam. *One Union in Wood.* Madeira Park, BC: Harbour Publishing, 1984.

Levitt, Kari. *Silent Surrender: The Multinational Corporation in Canada.* Toronto: Macmillan, 1970.

Lichtenstein, Nelson. *Labor's War at Home: The CIO in World War II.* Cambridge: Cambridge University Press, 1982.

–. *State of the Union: A Century of American Labor.* Princeton, NJ: Princeton University Press, 2002.

Littler, Craig R., and Graeme Salaman. *Class at Work: The Design, Allocation and Control of Jobs.* London: Batsford Academic and Educational, 1984.

Mackie, Richard. *Island Timber: A Social History of the Comox Logging Company, Vancouver Island.* Victoria: Sono Nis Press, 2000.

Magnusson, Warren, et al., eds. *The New Reality: The Politics of Restraint in British Columbia.* Vancouver: New Star Books, 1984.

Mahood, Ian, and Ken Drushka. *Three Men and a Forester.* Madeira Park, BC: Harbour Publishing, 1990.

Marchak, Patricia. *Green Gold: The Forest Industry in British Columbia.* Vancouver: UBC Press, 1983.

MacKay, Donald. *Empire of Wood: The MacMillan Bloedel Story.* Vancouver: Douglas and McIntyre, 1982.

McInnis, Peter S. *Harnessing Labour Confrontation: Shaping the Postwar Settlement in Canada, 1943-1950.* Toronto: University of Toronto Press, 2002.

MacNeil, Grant. *The IWA in British Columbia.* Vancouver: Western Regional Council No. 1, International Woodworkers of America, AFL-CIO-CLC, 1971.

Milkman, Ruth. *Gender at Work: The Dynamics of Job Segregation by Sex During World War II.* Urbana and Chicago: University of Illinois Press, 1987.

Mitchell, David. *WAC: Bennett and the Rise of British Columbia.* Vancouver: Douglas and McIntyre, 1983.

Moody, Kim. *An Injury to All: The Decline of American Unionism.* London and New York: Verso, 1988.

Morton, Desmond, with Terry Copp. *Working People.* Ottawa: Deneau Publishers, 1980.

Munro, Jack, and Jane O'Hara. *Union Jack: Labour Leader Jack Munro.* Vancouver: Douglas and McIntyre, 1988.

Neatby, H. Blair. *William Lyon Mackenzie King, 1932-1939: The Prism of Unity.* Toronto: University of Toronto Press, 1976.

Neufeld, Andrew, and Andrew Parnaby. *The IWA in Canada: The Life and Times of an Industrial Union.* Vancouver: IWA Canada/New Star Books, 2000.

Noble, David F. *Progress without People: New Technology, Unemployment, and the Message of Resistance.* Toronto: Between the Lines, 1995.

Norrie, Kenneth, and Douglas Owram. *A History of the Canadian Economy.* Toronto: Harcourt Brace Jovanovich Canada, 1991.

Paehlke, Robert C. *Environmentalism and the Future of Progressive Politics.* New Haven: Yale University Press, 1989.

Palmer, Bryan D. *Working-Class Experience: Rethinking the History of Canadian Labour, 1800-1991.* 2nd ed. Toronto: McClelland and Stewart, 1992.

–. *Solidarity: The Rise and Fall of an Opposition in British Columbia.* Vancouver: New Star Books, 1987.

Penner, Norman. *Canadian Communism: The Stalin Years and Beyond.* Toronto: Methuen, 1988.

Pennier, Henry. *Chiefly Indian: The Warm and Witty Story of a British Columbia Half Breed Logger.* West Vancouver: Graydonald Graphics, 1972.

Perrault, E.G. *Wood and Water: The Story of Seaboard Lumber and Shipping.* Vancouver: Douglas and McIntyre, 1985.

Phillips, Paul. *No Power Greater: A Century of Labour in British Columbia.* Vancouver: BC Federation of Labour, 1967.

Procter, James. *Stuart Hall.* London: Routledge, 2004.

Prouty, Andrew Mason. *More Deadly than War! Pacific Coast Logging, 1827-1981.* New York: Garland, 1985.

Radforth, Ian. *Bushworkers and Bosses: Logging in Northern Ontario, 1900-1980.* Toronto: University of Toronto Press, 1987.

Rajala, Richard. *Clearcutting the Pacific Rain Forest: Production, Science, and Regulation.* Vancouver: UBC Press, 1998.

–. *The Legacy and the Challenge: A Century of the Forest Industry at Cowichan Lake.* Lake Cowichan, BC: Lake Cowichan Heritage Advisory Committee, 1993.

–. *Up-Coast: Forests and Industry on British Columbia's North Coast, 1870-2005* (Victoria: Royal BC Museum, 2006).

Rezler, Julius. *Automation and Industrial Labor.* New York: Random House, 1969.

Rifkin, Jeremy. *The End of Work: The Decline of the Global Labor Force and the Dawn of the Post-Market Era.* New York: G.P. Putnam's Sons, 1995.

Roach Pierson, Ruth. *"They're Still Women After All": The Second World War and Canadian Womanhood.* Toronto: McClelland and Stewart, 1986.

Robin, Martin. *Pillars of Profit: The Company Province 1934-1972.* Toronto: McClelland and Stewart, 1973.

–. *The Rush for Spoils: The Company Province 1871-1933.* Toronto: McClelland and Stewart, 1972.

Rodgers, Andrew Denny III. *Bernard Eduard Fernow: A Story of North American Forestry.* Princeton, NJ: Princeton University Press, 1951.

Roy, Patricia E. *The Oriental Question: Consolidating a White Man's Province, 1914-41*. Vancouver: UBC Press, 2003.

Salutin, Rick. *Kent Rowley, the Organizer: A Canadian Union Life*. Toronto: James Lorimer, 1980.

Schor, Juliet B. *The Overworked American: The Unexpected Decline of Leisure*. New York: Basic Books, 1991.

Schwindt, Richard. *The Existence and Exercise of Corporate Power: A Case Study of MacMillan Bloedel Ltd*. Royal Commission on Corporate Concentration, Study No. 15. Ottawa: Minister of Supply and Services, 1977.

Schwindt, Richard, and Terry Heaps. *Chopping Up the Money Tree: Distributing the Wealth from British Columbia's Forests*. Vancouver: The David Suzuki Foundation, 1996.

Sefton MacDowell, Laurel. *"Remember Kirkland Lake": The Gold Miners' Strike of 1941-42*. Toronto: University of Toronto Press, 1983.

Shils, Edward B. *Automation and Industrial Relations*. New York: Holt, Rinehart and Winston, 1963.

Stanton, John. *Never Say Die! The Life and Times of a Pioneer Labour Lawyer*. Ottawa: Steel Rail Publishing, 1987.

Taylor, G.W. *Timber: History of the Forest Industry in BC* Vancouver: J.J. Douglas, 1975.

Weinstein, James. *The Corporate Ideal in the Liberal State: 1900-1918*. Boston: Beacon Press, 1968.

Wejr, Patricia, and Howie Smith, eds. *Fighting for Labour: Four Decades of Work in British Columbia 1910-1950*. Sound Heritage, vol. 7, no. 4. Victoria: Aural History Program, Province of British Columbia, 1978.

Weyler, Rex. *Greenpeace: How a Group of Ecologists, Journalists and Visionaries Changed the World*. Vancouver: Raincoast Books, 2004.

White, Howard. *A Hard Man to Beat: The Story of Bill White, Labour Leader, Historian, Shipyard Worker, Raconteur*. Vancouver: Pulp Press, 1983.

Williston, Eileen, and Betty Keller. *Forest, Power and Policy: The Legacy of Ray Williston*. Prince George, BC: Caitlin Press, 1997.

Wilson, Jeremy. *Talk and Log: Wilderness Politics in British Columbia, 1965-96*. Vancouver: UBC Press, 1998.

Zeiger, Robert H. *Rebuilding the Pulp and Paper Workers' Union, 1933-1941*. Knoxville: University of Tennessee Press, 1984.

Zimbalist, Andrew, ed. *Case Studies on the Labor Process*. New York: Monthly Review Press, 1979.

ARTICLES, THESES, UNPUBLISHED PAPERS

Adler, Paul S. "Marx, Machines, and Skill." *Technology and Culture* 31 (October 1990): 780-812.

Allen, John. "Post-Industrialism and Post-Fordism." In *Modernity and Its Futures*, edited by Stuart Hall, David Held, and Tony McGrew, 169-204. London: Open University Press, 1992.

Althusser, Louis. "Ideology and Ideological State Apparatuses: Notes toward an Investigation." In *Lenin and Philosophy and Other Essays*, edited by Louis Althusser, 127-86. New York and London: Monthly Review Press, 1971.

Attewell, Paul. "The Deskilling Controversy." *Work and Occupations* 14 (August 1987): 323-46.

Aylen, Peter G. "Sustained Yield Forestry Policy in BC to 1956: A Deterministic Analysis of Development." MA thesis, University of Victoria, 1984.

Barnes, Trevor, and Roger Hayter. "British Columbia's Private Sector in Recession, 1981-86: Employment Flexibility without Trade Diversification?" *BC Studies* 98 (Summer 1993): 20-42.

Belshaw, John Douglas. "The British Collier in British Columbia: Another Archetype Reconsidered." *Labour/Le Travail* 34 (Fall 1994): 11-36.

Berhrisch Tanya, Roger Hayter, and Trevor Barnes. "'I Don't Really Like the Mill; In Fact I Hate the Mill,' Changing Youth Vocationalism under Fordism and Post-Fordism in Powell River, British Columbia." *BC Studies* 136 (Winter 2002-2003): 73-101.

Bernsohn, Ken. "How Wobbly Are BC's Forest Unions?" *ForesTalk* (Summer 1982): 26-31.

Block, Fred. "Beyond Relative Autonomy: State Managers as Historical Subjects." *Socialist Register* 16 (1980): 227-42.

–. "The Ruling Class Does Not Rule: Notes on the Marxist Theory of the State." *Socialist Revolution* 33 (May-June 1977): 6-28.

Burda, Cheri, Fred Gale, and Michael M'Gonigle. "Eco-Forestry Versus the State(us) Quo: Or Why Innovative Forestry Is Neither Contemplated nor Permitted within the State Structure of British Columbia." *BC Studies* 119 (Autumn 1998): 45-72.

Butler, Judith. "Restaging the Universal: Hegemony and the Limits of Formalism." In *Contingency, Hegemony, Universality: Contemporary Dialogues on the Left,* edited by Judith Butler, Ernesto Laclau, and Slavoj Žižek, 11-43. London: Verso, 2000.

Cohen, Shiela. "A Labour Process to Nowhere." *New Left Review* 165 (September/October 1987): 34-50.

Cohn, Werner. "The Persecution of Japanese Canadians and the Political Left in British Columbia, December 1941 – March 1942." *BC Studies* 68 (Winter 1985-86): 2-22.

Copithorne, Lawrence. "Natural Resources and Regional Disparities: A Skeptical View." *Canadian Public Policy* (Spring 1979): 181-94.

Cottell, Philip L. "Why Work in the Woods?" *Pulp and Paper Magazine of Canada* 75 (October 1974): 27-32.

Davis, H. Craig. "Is the Metropolitan Vancouver Economy Uncoupling from the Rest of the Province?" *BC Studies* 98 (Summer 1993): 3-19.

Davis, H. Craig, and Thomas A. Hutton. "The Two Economies of British Columbia." *BC Studies* 82 (Summer 1989): 3-15.

Deutsch, J.J., et al. "Economics of Primary Production in British Columbia," vols. 1 and 4. Typescript, Vancouver, 1959.

Dezell, Michael James Garvin. "Grapple-Yarding with the Future: A New Mandate for COFI." MA thesis, University of Victoria, 1993.

Diamond, Sara. "A Union Man's Wife: The Ladies' Auxiliary Movement in the IWA, the Lake Cowichan Experience." In *Not Just Pin Money: Selected Essays on the History of Women's Work in British Columbia,* edited by Barbara K. Latham and Roberta J. Pazdro, 287-96. Victoria: Camosun College, 1984.

Drummond, Ian. "Empire Trade and Russian Trade: Economic Diplomacy in the Nineteen-Thirties." *Canadian Journal of Economics* 5 (February 1972): 35-47.

Dunk, Thomas. "Talking about Trees: Environment and Society in Forest Workers' Culture." *Canadian Review of Sociology and Anthropology* 31 (February 1994): 14-34.

"Eggheads are Leaving Unions." *Nation's Business* 51 (September 1963): 34, 36, 42, 46, 48, 50.

Ehrlich, Leslie, and Bob Russell. "Employment Security and Job Loss: Lessons from Canada's National Railways, 1956-1995." *Labour/Le Travail* 51 (Spring 2003): 115-52.

Elkins, David J. "British Columbia as a State of Mind." In *Two Political Worlds: Parties and Voting in British Columbia,* edited by Donald E. Blake, 49-63. Vancouver: UBC Press, 1985.

Finkel, Alvin. "Trade Unions and the Welfare State in Canada, 1945-90." In *Labour Gains, Labour Pains: Fifty Years of PC 1003,* edited by Cy Gonick, Paul Phillips, and Jesse Vorst, 59-77. Winnipeg/Halifax: Society for Socialist Studies/Fernwood Publishing, 1995.

Fisher, E.G. "Strike Activity and Wildcat Strikes in British Columbia: 1945-1975." *Relations Industrielles/Industrial Relations* 37 (1982): 284-312.

Fisher, Robin. "Matter for Reflection: *BC Studies* and British Columbia History." *BC Studies* 100 (Winter 1993-94): 59-77.

Foster, John Bellamy. "The Fetishism of Fordism." *Monthly Review* 39 (March 1988): 14-33.

–. "The Limits of Environmentalism without Class." *Capitalism, Nature, Socialism* 13 (March 1993): 11-41.

Friedman, Andrew L. "The Means of Management Control and Labour Process Theory: A Critical Note on Storey." *Sociology* 21 (May 1987): 287-94.

Gillis, Peter R. "The Ottawa Lumber Barons and the Conservation Movement, 1880-1914." *Journal of Canadian Studies* 9 (February 1974): 14-31.

Gray, Stephen. "The Government's Timber Business: Forest Policy and Administration in British Columbia, 1912-1928." *BC Studies* 81 (Spring 1989): 24-49.

Gray, Stephen. "Woodworkers and Legitimacy: The IWA in Canada, 1937-1957." PhD dissertation, Simon Fraser University, 1989.

Griffin, Robert. "Success and Failure in British Columbia's Softwood Plywood Industry, 1913 to 1999." PhD dissertation, University of Victoria, 1999.

Gross, James A. "The Making and Shaping of Unionism in the Pulp and Paper Industry." *Labor History* 5 (Spring 1964): 183-208.

Hak, Gordon. "British Columbia Loggers and the Lumber Workers Industrial Union, 1919-1922." *Labour/Le Travail* 23 (Spring 1989): 67-90.

–. "The Communists and the Unemployed in the Prince George District, 1930-1935." *BC Studies* 68 (Winter 1985-86): 45-61.

–. "'Line Up or Roll Up': The Lumber Workers Industrial Union in the Prince George District." *BC Studies* 86 (Summer 1990): 57-74.

–. "Populism and the 1952 Social Credit Breakthrough in British Columbia." *Canadian Historical Review* 85 (June 2004): 277-96.

–. "Red Wages: Communists and the 1934 Vancouver Island Loggers Strike." *Pacific Northwest Quarterly* 80 (July 1989): 82-90.

–. "The Socialist and Labourist Impulse in Small-Town British Columbia." *Canadian Historical Review* 70 (December 1989): 519-42.

Hall, Stuart. "Encoding/Decoding." In *Culture, Media, Language,* edited by Stuart Hall, 128-38. London: Hutchinson, 1980.

–. "Introduction." In *Representation: Cultural Representations and Signifying Practices,* edited by Stuart Hall, 1-11. London: Sage Publications, 1997.

–. "Introduction: Who Needs 'Identity'?" In *Questions of Cultural Identity,* edited by Stuart Hall and Paul Du Gay, 1-17. London: Sage Publications, 1996.

Harter, John-Henry. "Environmental Justice for Whom? Class, New Social Movements, and the Environment: A Case Study of Greenpeace Canada, 1971-2000." *Labour/Le Travail* 54 (Fall 2004): 83-119.

Hays, Samuel P. "From Conservation to Environment: Environmental Politics in the United States since World War II." *Environmental Review* 6 (1982): 14-41.

Hayter, Roger. "'The War in the Woods': Post-Fordist Restructuring, Globalization, and the Contested Remapping of British Columbia's Forest Economy." *Annals of the Association of American Geographers* 93 (September 2003): 706-29.

Hayter, Roger, and Trevor Barnes. "The Restructuring of British Columbia's Coastal Forest Sector: Flexibility Perspectives." *BC Studies* 113 (Spring 1997): 7-34.

High, Steven. "'I'll Wrap the F*#@ Canadian Flag Around Me': A Nationalist Response to Plant Shutdowns, 1969-1984." *Journal of the Canadian Historical Association,* New Series, 12 (2001): 199-225.

Hirst, Paul, and Jonathan Zeitlin. "Flexible Specialization versus Post-Fordism: Theory, Evidence and Policy Implications." *Economy and Society* 20 (February 1991): 1-56.

Hollingsworth, J. Rogers, and Robert Boyer. "Coordination of Economic Actors and Social Systems of Production." In *Contemporary Capitalism: The Embeddedness of Institutions,* edited by J. Roger Hollingsworth and Robert Boyer, 1-47. Cambridge: Cambridge University Press, 1997.

Howell, Chris. "The End of the Relationship between Social Democratic Parties and Trade Unions?" *Studies in Political Economy* 65 (Summer 2001): 7-37.

Hutton, Thomas A. "The Innisian Core-Periphery Revisited: Vancouver's Changing Relationship with British Columbia's Staple Economy." *BC Studies* 113 (Spring 1997): 69-100.

Jacoby, Sanford M. "Union-Management Cooperation in the United States during the Second World War." In *Technological Change and Workers' Movements,* edited by Melvyn Dubofsky, 100-29. Beverly Hills, CA: SAGE Publications, 1985.

Jamieson, Stuart. "West Coast Strikes: An Objective Study of Industrial Relations in British Columbia, with Particular Emphasis on the Background to Labour Problems within the Pulp and Paper Industry." *Pulp and Paper Magazine of Canada* 59 (July 1958): 105-8, 217-18, 221.

Katznelson, Ira. "The 'Bourgeois' Dimension: A Provocation about Institutions, Politics, and the Future of Labor History." *International Labor and Working-Class History* 46 (Fall 1994): 7-32.

–. "Working-Class Formation: Constructing Cases and Comparisons." In *Working-Class Formation: Nineteenth-Century Patterns in Western Europe and the United States,* edited by Ira Katznelson and Artistide R. Zolberg, 3-41. Princeton, NJ: Princeton University Press, 1986.

Kerr, Clark, and Abraham Siegel. "The Interindustry Propensity to Strike: An International Comparison." In *Industrial Conflict,* edited by Arthur Kornhauser, Robert Dubin, and Arthur M. Ross, 189-212. New York: McGraw-Hill, 1954.

Kimmins, J.P. "The Ecology of Forestry: The Ecological Role of Man, the Forester, in Forest Ecosystems." *Forestry Chronicle* 48 (December 1972): 301-7.

–. "Forest Ecology: The Biological Basis for the Management of Renewable Forest Resources." *Forestry Chronicle* 49 (February 1973): 25-30.

–. "The Renewability of Natural Resources: Implications for Forest Management." *Journal of Forestry* 71 (May 1973): 290-92.

–. "Sustained Yield, Timber Mining and the Concept of Ecological Rotation: A British Columbian View." *Forestry Chronicle* 50 (February 1974): 27-31.

Klausen, Susanne. "The Plywood Girls: Women and Gender Ideology at the Port Alberni Plywood Plant, 1942-1991." *Labour/Le Travail* 41 (Spring 1998): 199-235.

Krywulak, Tim. "Inventing Labour Problems and Solutions: The Emergence of Human Resource Management in Canada, 1900-1945." *Journal of the Canadian Historical Association,* New Series, 15 (2004): 71-95.

Laclau, Ernesto. "Discourse." In *A Companion to Contemporary Political Philosophy,* edited by Robert E. Goodin and Philip Pettit, 431-37. London: Blackwell, 1995.

–. "Post-Marxism without Apologies." *New Left Review* 166 (November/December 1987): 79-106.

Langford, Tom, and Chris Frazer. "The Cold War and Working-Class Politics in the Coal Mining Communities of the Crowsnest Pass, 1945-1958." *Labour/Le Travail* 49 (Spring 2002): 43-81.

Lawrence, Joseph Collins. "Markets and Capital: A History of the Lumber Industry of British Columbia (1778-1952)." MA thesis, University of British Columbia, 1957.

Lipton, Charles. "Canadian Unionism." In *Capitalism and the National Question in Canada,* edited by Gary Teeple, 101-19. Toronto: University of Toronto Press, 1972.

Littler, Craig R., and Graeme Salaman. "Bravermania and Beyond: Recent Theories of the Labour Process." *Sociology* 16 (May 1982): 251-69.

Macdonald, Robert M. "Pulp and Paper." In *The Evolution of Wage Structure*, edited by Lloyd G. Reynolds and Cynthia Taft, 99-166. New Haven, CT: Yale University Press, 1956.

Marchak, Patricia. "A Changing Global Context for British Columbia's Forest Industry." In *Troubles in the Rainforest: British Columbia's Forest Economy in Transition*, edited by Trevor J. Barnes and Roger Hayter, 149-64. Canadian Western Geographical Series, vol. 33. Victoria: Western Geographical Press, 1997.

Marcuse, Gary. "Labour's Cold War: The Story of a Union that Was Not Purged." *Labour/Le Travail* 22 (Fall 1988): 199-210.

McDonald, Robert A.J. "Victoria, Vancouver, and the Economic Development of British Columbia, 1886-1914." In *British Columbia: Historical Readings*, edited by W. Peter Ward and Robert A.J. McDonald, 369-95. Vancouver: Douglas and McIntyre, 1981.

–. "Working-Class Vancouver, 1886-1914: Urbanism and Class in British Columbia." *BC Studies* 69-70 (Spring/Summer 1986): 33-69.

M'Gonigle, Michael, and Jessica Dempsey. "Ecological Innovation in an Age of Bureaucratic Closure: The Case of the Global Forest." *Studies in Political Economy* 70 (Spring 2003): 97-124.

McIntosh, Jean Elizabeth. "Mark Mosher's Reconstruction of the Development of the Woodworkers Union in the Alberni Valley 1935-1950: A Participant's History." MA thesis, University of British Columbia, 1987.

McKay, Ian. "The Liberal Order Framework: A Prospectus for a Reconnaissance of Canadian History." *Canadian Historical Review* 81 (December 2000): 617-45.

McRoberts, Mary L. "When Good Intentions Fail: A Case of Forest Policy in the British Columbia Interior, 1945-56." *Journal of Forest History* 32 (July 1988): 138-49.

Mercer, William M. "Growth of Ghost Towns: The Decline of Forest Activity in the East Kootenay District and the Effect of the Growth of Ghost Towns on the Distributing Centres of Cranbrook and Fernie." Report for the Royal Commission on Forestry, Victoria, February 1944, unpublished.

Meyers, Jeanne. "Class and Community in the Fraser Mills Strike, 1931." In *Workers, Capital, and the State in British Columbia: Selected Papers*, edited by Rennie Warburton and David Coburn, 141-60. Vancouver: UBC Press, 1988.

Moulton, David. "Ford Windsor 1945." In *On Strike: Six Key Pabour Struggles in Canada 1919-1949*, edited by Irving Abella, 129-61. Toronto: James Lewis and Samuel, 1974.

Noël, Alain. "Accumulation, Regulation, and Social Change: An Essay on French Political Economy." *International Organization* 41 (Spring 1987): 303-33.

Panitch, Leo. "The Role and Nature of the Canadian State." In *The Canadian State: Political Economy and Political Power*, edited by Leo Panitch, 3-27. Toronto: University of Toronto Press, 1977.

Parnaby, Andrew. "What's Law Got to Do with It? The IWA and the Politics of State Power in British Columbia, 1935-1939." *Labour/Le Travail* 44 (Fall 1999): 9-45.

Rajala, Richard. "The Forest as Factory: Technological Change and Worker Control in the West Coast Logging Industry, 1880-1930." *Labour/Le Travail* 32 (Fall 1993): 73-104.

–. "The Vernon Laboratory and Federal Entomology in British Columbia." *Journal of the Entomological Society of British Columbia* 98 (December 2001): 177-88.

Read, Jennifer. "'Let Us Heed the Voice of Youth': Laundry Detergents, Phosphates and the Emergence of the Environmental Movement in Ontario." *Journal of the Canadian Historical Association* 7 (1996): 227-50.

Reid, Keith, and Don Weaver. "Aspects of the Political Economy of the BC Forest Industry." In *Essays in BC Political Economy*, edited by Paul Knox and Philip Resnick, 13-24. Vancouver: New Star Books, 1974.

Roach, Thomas R. "The Stewards of the People's Wealth: The Founding of British Columbia's Forest Branch." *Journal of Forest History* 28 (January 1984): 14-23.

Robin, Martin. "British Columbia: The Politics of Class Conflict." In *The Party Systems of the Ten Provinces*, edited by Martin Robin, 27-68. Scarborough, ON: Prentice-Hall, 1972.

–. "The Social Bias of Party Politics in British Columbia." In *Party Politics in Canada*, 2nd ed., edited by Hugh Thorburn, 200-11. Scarborough, ON: Prentice-Hall Canada, 1967.

Roper, Pam. "The Limits of *Laissez-innover:* Canada's Automation Controversy, 1955-1969." *Journal of Canadian Studies* 34 (Autumn 1999): 87-105.

Sabel, Charles, and Jonathan Zeitlin. "Historical Alternatives to Mass Production: Politics, Markets and Technology in Nineteenth-Century Industrialization." *Past and Present* 108 (August 1985): 133-76.

Salazar, Debra J., and Donald K. Alper. "Beyond the Politics of Left and Right: Beliefs and Values of Environmental Activists in British Columbia." *BC Studies* 121 (Spring 1999): 5-34.

–. "Reconciling Environmentalism and the Left: Perspectives on Democracy and Social Justice in British Columbia's Environmental Movement." *Canadian Journal of Political Science* 35 (September 2002): 527-66.

Sanford, Thomas Michael. "The Politics of Protest: The Cooperative Commonwealth Federation and Social Credit League in British Columbia." PhD dissertation, University of California (Berkeley), 1961.

Schwarz, Bill. "Re-assessing Braverman: Socialisation and Dispossession in the History of Technology." In *Science, Technology and the Labour Process*, Marxist Studies, vol. 2, edited by Les Levidow and Bob Young, 189-205. London: Free Association Books, 1985.

Schwindt, R. "The Pearse Commission and the Industrial Organization of the British Columbia Forest Industry." *BC Studies* 41 (Spring 1979): 3-35.

Seager, Allen, and David Roth. "British Columbia and the Mining West." In *The Workers' Revolt in Canada, 1917-1925*, edited by Craig Heron, 231-67. Toronto: University of Toronto Press, 1998.

Simon, Alexander Thomas. "Common Ground and Conflict in the Struggle over the Use of Forests and Labour in British Columbia: The Case of Greenpeace and the Pulp, Paper, and Woodworkers of Canada." PhD dissertation, Simon Fraser University, 2000.

Stark, David. "Class Struggle and the Transformation of the Labor Process: A Relational Approach." *Theory and Society* 9 (January 1980): 89-130.

Storey, John. "The Means of Management Control." *Sociology* 19 (May 1985): 193-211.

Taylor, G.W. "Early Days of Truck Logging." *British Columbia Lumberman* 51 (January 1967): 60-61.

Watkins, M.H. "A Staple Theory of Economic Growth." In *Approaches to Canadian Economic History*, edited by W.T. Easterbrook and M.H. Watkins, 49-73. Toronto: McClelland and Stewart, 1967.

Webber, Jeremy. "The Malaise of Compulsory Conciliation: Strike Prevention in Canada during World War II." *Labour/Le Travail* 15 (Spring 1985): 57-88.

Wedley, John R. "Laying the Golden Egg: The Coalition Government's Role in Post-War Northern Development." *BC Studies* 88 (Winter 1990-91): 58-92.

White, Julie. "Workers' Attitudes to Shorter Hours of Work." In *Reshaping Work 2: Labour, the Workplace and Technological Change*, edited by Christopher Schenk and John Anderson, 157-71. Ottawa/Aurora, ON: Canadian Centre for Policy Alternatives/Garamond, 1999.

White, Richard. "'Are You an Environmentalist or Do You Work for a Living?': Work and Nature." In *Uncommon Ground: Toward Reinventing Nature*, edited by William Cronon, 171-85. New York: W.W. Norton, 1995.

Widenor, Marcus R. "International Unionism in Retreat: The Dissolution of the International Woodworkers of America." In *Labour Gains, Labour Pains: Fifty Years of PC 1003*, edited by Cy Gonick, Paul Phillips, and Jesse Vorst, 285-305. Winnipeg/Halifax: Society for Socialist Studies/Fernwood Publishing, 1995.

Willems-Braun, Bruce. "Colonial Vestiges: Representing Forest Landscapes on Canada's West Coast." *BC Studies* 112 (Winter 1996-97): 5-39.

Wilson, Jeremy. "Forest Conservation in British Columbia, 1935-1985: Reflections on a Barren Political Debate." *BC Studies* 76 (Winter 1987-88): 3-32.

–. "The Impact of Communications Developments on British Columbia Electoral Patterns, 1903-1975." *Canadian Journal of Political Science* 13 (September 1980): 509-35.

Yarmie, Andrew. "The State and Employers' Associations in British Columbia: 1900-1932." *Labour/Le Travail* 45 (Spring 2000): 53-101.

Zelko, Frank. "Making Greenpeace: The Development of Direct Action Environmentalism in British Columbia." *BC Studies* 142/143 (Summer/Autumn 2004): 197-239.

Index